Distributed Database Architecture

Distributed Database Architecture

Editor:

Dr. Jovan Pehcevski, Ph.D.

ArclerPress

www.arclerpress.com

Distributed Database Architecture

Editor: Dr. Jovan Pehcevski, Ph.D.

© 2017 Arcler Press LLC
708 3rd Avenue, 6th Floor
New York
NY 10017
United States of America
www.arclerpress.com

ISBN: 978-1-68094-458-7

Library of Congress Control Number: 2016951152

About the Editor

Dr. Jovan Pehcevski, Ph.D.

Jovan obtained his PhD in Computer Science from RMIT University in Melbourne, Australia in 2007. His research interests include big data, business intelligence and predictive analytics, data and information science, information retrieval, XML, web services and service-oriented architectures, and relational and NoSQL database systems. He has published over 30 journal and conference papers and he also serves as a journal and conference reviewer. He is currently working as a Dean and Associate Professor at European University in Skopje, Macedonia.

Contents

Section 2 - Queries and Transactions in a Distributed Environment

List of Contributors

Rizik M. H. Al-Sayyed
King Abdullah II School for Information Technology, The University of Jordan, Amman, Jordan

Fawaz A. Al Zaghoul
King Abdullah II School for Information Technology, The University of Jordan, Amman, Jordan

Dima Suleiman
King Abdullah II School for Information Technology, The University of Jordan, Amman, Jordan

Mariam Itriq
King Abdullah II School for Information Technology, The University of Jordan, Amman, Jordan

Ismail Hababeh
Faculty of Computer Engineering and Information Technology, German Jordanian University, Amman, Jordan

Ashraf Ahmed
Department of Computer, University of Khartoum, Khartoum, Sudan

P.D.D.Dominic
Department of Computer and Information Sciences, Universiti Teknologi PETRONAS, Perak, Malaysia

Azween Abdullah
Department of Computer and Information Sciences, Universiti Teknologi PETRONAS, Perak, Malaysia

Hamidah Ibrahim
Faculty of Computer Science and Information Technology, Universiti Putra Malaysia, Selangor, Malaysia

Yousef J. Al-Houmaily
Department of Computer and Information Programs, Institute of Public Administration, Riyadh, Saudi Arabia
Salman Abdul Moiz
Research Scientist, Centre for Development of Advanced Computing, Bangalore

Supriya N.Pal
Associate Director, Centre for Development of Advanced Computing, Bangalore

Jitendra Kumar
Senior Staff Scientist, Centre for Development of Advanced Computing, Bangalore

Lavanya P
Staff Scientist, Centre for Development of Advanced Computing, Bangalore

Deepak Chandra Joshi
Staff Scientist, Centre for Development of Advanced Computing, Bangalore

Venkataswamy G
Staff Scientist, Centre for Development of Advanced Computing, Bangalore

Dr. Sunita M. Mahajan
Mumbai Education Trust, Reclaimation,Bandra, Mumbai ,India

Ms.Vaishali P. Jadhav
NMIMS University, Mumbai, India

Y. Jayanta Singh
Faculty of Information Technology, 7 th October University, Misurata, Libya

Yumnam Somananda Singh
Faculty of Computer Application Institute of Management Studies & I. T (IMSIT), India

Ashok Gaikwad
Faculty of Computer Application Institute of Management Studies & I. T (IMSIT), India

S.C. Mehrotra
Dept of Information Technology and Computer Science Dr. B. A. Marathwada University, Aurangabad, India

Abhijeet R Raipurkar
M.E. Final Year, Department of Computer Science & Engineering, PRMIT&R, Badnera, India

G.R.Bamnote
Head & Professor, Department Of Computer Science & Engineering, PRMIT&R, Badnera, India

Salman Abdul Moiz
Centre for Development of Advanced Computing, Bangalore, India

Dr. Lakshmi Rajamani
University College of Engineering, Osmania University, Hyderabad, India

Supriya N.Pal
Centre for Development of Advanced Computing, Bangalore, India

Raghvendra Kumar
Dept of Computer Engineering LNCT Group of College Jabalpur, M.P., India

Ashish Jaiswal
Dept of Computer Engineering LNCT Group of College Jabalpur, M.P., India

Divyarth Rai
Dept of Computer Engineering LNCT Group of College Jabalpur, M.P., India

Jyotirmayee Rautaray
School of Computer Engineering, KIIT University, Odisha, India

Raghvendra Kumar
School of Computer Engineering, KIIT University, Odisha, India

Ilung Pranata
Faculty of Science and IT, University of Newcastle, Callaghan, Australia

Geoff Skinner
Faculty of Science and IT, University of Newcastle, Callaghan, Australia

Rukshan Athauda
Faculty of Science and IT, University of Newcastle, Callaghan, Australia

Ahmed Tallat
Applied Information Engineering, Tokyo Denki University, Tokyo, Japan

Hiroshi Yasuda
Applied Information Engineering, Tokyo Denki University, Tokyo, Japan

Kilho Shin
Applied Information Engineering, Tokyo Denki University, Tokyo, Japan

Elias P. Duarte Jr
Department of Informatics, Federal University of Parana (UFPR), Curitiba, Brazil

Ana Flavia B. Godoi
Department of Informatics, Federal University of Parana (UFPR), Curitiba, Brazil

Xiaoguang Wang
Computer School, Communication University of China, Beijing, China

Hui Wang
Information Engineering School, Communication University of China, Beijing, China

Yongbin Wang
Computer School, Communication University of China, Beijing, China

Ping Zhang
Department of Mathematics and Computer Science, Alcorn State University, Lorman, USA;

Xi Guo
Department of Mathematics and Computer Science, Alcorn State University, Lorman, USA;

Jyotirmay Gadedadikar
Department of Advanced Technologies, Alcorn State University, Lorman, USA.

Arif Sari
Department of Management Information Systems, Girne American University, Kyrenia, Cyprus

Murat Akkaya
Department of Management Information Systems, Girne American University, Kyrenia, Cyprus

Grzegorz Chmaj
Department of Electrical and Computer Engineering, University of Nevada Las Vegas, Las Vegas, USA

Shahram Latifi
Department of Electrical and Computer Engineering, University of Nevada Las Vegas, Las Vegas, USA

Fenggui Wang
Institute of Automation, Shandong Academy of Sciences, Jinan, China

Lin Zhang
Institute of Automation, Shandong Academy of Sciences, Jinan, China

Zhongmin Wang
Institute of Automation, Shandong Academy of Sciences, Jinan, China

Yanbo Zhang
Institute of Automation, Shandong Academy of Sciences, Jinan, China

Preface

In distributed systems, clients access data that is stored in multiple server locations. The computers in a distributed system are called points (sites, nodes) and they can have different purposes and/or roles. Computers communicate with each other via permanent or temporarily links. In distributed database architectures there is a distinction between local and global transactions: the former are transactions made on one computer, while the latter are transactions that access data on different computers.

Several issues emerge when dealing with distributed data, which require different data management approaches. Some of these approaches deal with fragmentation, replication of data, data consistency by the ACID principle (atomicity, consistency, isolation, durability) and other issues. Transactions in a distributed data environment can be in one of the following states: begin transaction, read or write operation, commit or abort transaction, end transaction. The data must keep its consistency during and after the transaction execution, which means if a transaction is aborted, the rollback operation has to apply on the database to bring back the database to the last consistent state. Security of distributed database systems is of huge importance, since the threats to the data privacy and integrity, which are present in a regular environment (single database server), are now omnipresent when dealing with several different locations. Basic and extended security mechanisms are used by the distributed database systems to deal with these security threats. Many modern web applications are built on top of distributed database architectures. These include large banking databases, problem-solving architectures, and middleware components, among others. This edition consists of four sections and covers the following aspects of distributed database architectures: management of the distributed database, transactions and queries in a distributed database, security of a distributed database system and possible applications of distributed databases. Section 1 focuses on distributed database management, describing database fragmentation and allocation to improve the distributed database management, replication strategy for large-scale mobile distributed database systems, deferred constraints in distributed database systems, and concurrency control in mobile environments. Section 2 focuses on queries and transactions in a distributed environment, describing framework for optimization of distributed queries, dynamic management of transactions in distributed real-time processing systems, fuzzy logic based query optimization in a distributed database, commit protocols in mobile environments, as well as FP tree algorithm with and without trusted party for environmentally distributed databases. Section 3 focuses on distributed system security, describing privacy preserving in distributed database using the DES algorithm, distributed secure mechanisms for resource protection in a digital ecosystem, secure file archiving in a uniformly random distributed archive, and reliable content distribution in P2P networks. Section 4 focuses on distributed databases applications, describing unified monitoring framework for distributed environment, online fingerprint verification algorithm and distributed system, fault tolerance mechanisms in distributed systems, decentralization of a multi data source distributed processing system using a distributed hash table, and a wireless distributed monitoring terminal used for on-line application.

Editor
Dr. Jovan Pehcevski, Ph.D.

SECTION I
DISTRIBUTED DATABASE MANAGEMENT

CHAPTER 1

A NEW APPROACH FOR DATABASE FRAGMENTATION AND ALLOCATION TO IMPROVE THE DISTRIBUTED DATABASE MANAGEMENT SYSTEM PERFORMANCE

Rizik M. H. Al-Sayyed[1], Fawaz A. Al Zaghoul[1], Dima Suleiman[1], Mariam Itriq[1], Ismail Hababeh[2]

[1] King Abdullah II School for Information Technology, The University of Jordan, Amman, Jordan

[2] Faculty of Computer Engineering and Information Technology, German Jordanian University, Amman, Jordan

ABSTRACT

The efficiency and performance of Distributed Database Management Systems (DDBMS) is mainly measured by its proper design and by network communication cost between sites. Fragmentation and distribution of data are the major design issues of the DDBMS. In this paper, we propose new approach that integrates both fragmentation and data allocation in one strategy based on high performance clustering technique and transaction processing cost functions. This new approach achieves efficiently and effectively the objectives of data fragmentation, data allocation and network sites clustering. The approach splits the data relations into pair-wise disjoint fragments and determine whether each fragment has to be allocated or not in the network sites, where allocation benefit outweighs the cost depending on high performance clustering technique. To show the performance of the proposed approach, we performed experimental studies on real database application at different networks connectivity. The obtained results proved to achieve minimum total data transaction costs between different sites, reduced the amount of redundant data to be accessed between these sites and improved the overall DDBMS performance.

INTRODUCTION

Many researches have been done in the last few years in order to improve the performance of distributed database management systems (DDBMS). DDBMS is a collection of logically interrelated data that are physically allocated at different locations over a computer network [1]. Most of recent researches are concerned about keeping the performance of DDBMS high so that they focused on how to design the database such that the overall cost is kept minimal. Keeping the cost minimal is not an easy task as there are huge amount of transactions processing that increase the complexity of distributed databases. Several techniques have been proposed in order to improve database performance which can be achieved by improving at least one of the following database management issues: database fragmentation, data allocation and replication, and the network sites clustering. The fragmentation process divides the database into portions each of which is called a fragment. Fragmentation can be horizontal,

Citation: Al-Sayyed, R.M.H., Al Zaghoul, F.A., Suleiman, D., Itriq, M. and Hababeh, I. (2014) A New Approach for Database Fragmentation and Allocation to Improve the Distributed Database Management System Performance. Journal of Software Engineering and Applications, 7, 891-905. http://dx.doi.org/10.4236/jsea.2014.711080

vertical or mixed. The main advantage of fragmentation is to improve the performance of distributed database design by increasing the efficiency since data is stored only where it is needed. Fragments can be allocated at different network sites in a process called data allocation. The fragments allocation is an NP-complete problem so that the complexity is high. In order to reduce the complexity, some heuristic algorithms have been proposed to solve the problem. In the allocation process, each fragment is assigned to a network node and sometimes to more than one node to achieve the data availability, system reliability and performance. The clustering technique is used for grouping distributed database network sites into logical clusters. In order to reduce the communication time for data allocation, there are many algorithms that are use to find the optimal solution for grouping distributed database network sites into a disjoint clusters and making a better data distribution among them. The clustering technique aims at eliminating the extra communication costs between the network sites and then enhancing the DDBMS performance. Many existing algorithms of data fragmentation and allocation in DDBMS assume some restrictions on the number of network sites so that the results of such algorithms are impractical, and reflected on the efficiency and validity of their outcomes. Moreover, some constraints on network connectivity and transactions processing time will limit the applicability of the proposed solutions to a small number of DDBMS cases [1]. One of the drawbacks of fragmentation and allocation solutions is the high computational complexity of their associated algorithms. In fact, when distributing a database over a network with a big number of sites and then finding an efficient, reliable and optimal solution for fragmentation and allocation are considered difficult tasks. This paper proposed a new technique that splits the database relations into disjoint fragments. In addition, it introduces a high speed clustering technique that groups the distributed network sites into a set of clusters according to their communication cost. Also, it proposes a new intelligent technique for data allocation and redistribution based on transactions processing cost functions. Moreover, it implements a user-friendly simulation tool that performs fragmentation, clustering, allocation and replication of a database, in addition to assisting database administrators in measuring DDBMS performance. The rest of this paper is organized as follows. Section 2 summarizes related work. A method for partitioning the database is presented in Section 3. A description of network site clustering is covered in Section 4. In Section 5, fragments allocation to the clusters and then to their sites is discussed. Performance evaluation is presented in Section 6. Finally, the conclusions and the future work are presented in Section 7.

RELATED WORK

Many studies have been published on attempts of improving the performance of DDBMS. These researches have mostly investigated fragmentation, allocation and sometimes clustering problems. In this section, we present the main contributions related to these problems, discuss them and highlight novelties of our proposed solutions with respect to fragmentation, allocation and clustering. There are many types of fragmentation [2] vertical, horizontal and mixed. In vertical fragmentation each schema is divided into small fragments and all fragments must contain a common candidate key. A new algorithm; as proposed by [3]; has employed vertical fragmentation for object relational database system; this fragmentation method depends on user input at different sites. In [4], the authors provide a solution for initial fragmentation problem of relational database for DDBMS. It partitioned the relational database properly at the initial stage when no data statistics and query execution frequencies are available.

In order to minimize communication time required for data allocation and query processing, many researches have been done to group large number of network sites into a small number of logical clusters which improve the performance of a DDBMS by increasing transactions response time [5]. The authors of [6] present a new formulation for the problem of fragmentation and allocating those fragments with minimum cost for both structured and unstructured data, by grouping sites which are nearer to each other into one cluster, hence they have low cost. Also, a dynamic clustering method is adopted for both structured and unstructured database to reduce the movement of data between sites. In a DDBMS, the cost of communication is high so that many researches tried to minimize the cost and load sharing by making load balancing which can be achieved by making analysis of sharing resources, allocation of fragments and transaction in DDBMS [7]. The complexity of a distributed database algorithm depends on the allocation method used. Some enhancements have been done in reallocation algorithms. The authors of [8] proposed an algorithm that reallocates fragments based on calculating the cost for each fragment individually. The reallocation depends on finding the maximum update cost value for each fragment. This technique takes into account the network topology and set of queries frequency values employed over the network. Data allocation of a DDBMS can be done by means of mobile agents and many algorithms implemented to make optimization and solve allocation problems [9]. The authors of [10] present a biogeography-based optimization technique for no-replicated static allocation of data fragments during database design that minimize total data transmission cost during the execution of a set of queries.

DATABASE PARTITIONING

Various methods already exist describe data fragmentation in distributed DDBMS. Naturally, there are benefits and drawbacks to all schemes. Some methods need to incorporate performance evaluation ways, may not minimize the transactions response time and cannot guarantee the ability to process a given portion of a given transaction in all sites [2] [3] and [4]. In our proposed approach, the database will be partitioned into pair-wise disjoint fragments by using a horizontal partitioning technique, in which the records of a relation split into disjoint fragments; this strategy guarantees the ability to processing all portions of a given transaction and distributes it precisely over the DDBMS sites. Generating data fragments accomplished by performing the following processes respectively: defining transactions, creating segments and extracting disjoint fragments. Figure 1 below describes the architecture of the fragmentation method that supports the use of knowledge extraction and helps to achieve the effective use of small data packets.

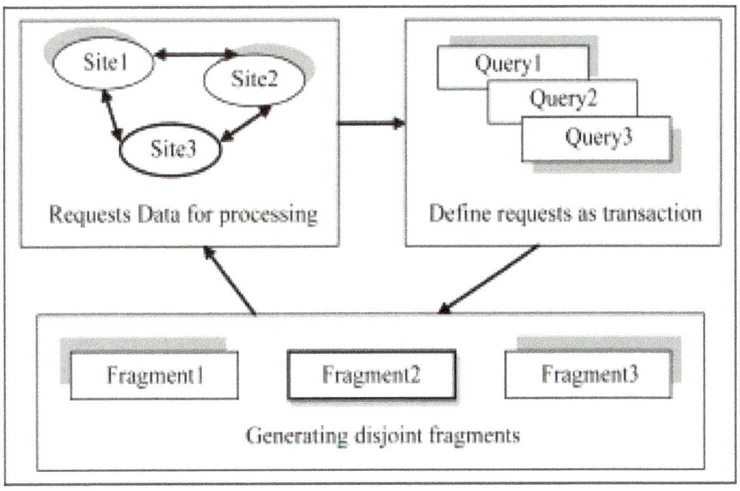

Figure 1. Generating disjoint fragments

As shown in Figure 1, the data request is initiated from the DDBMS sites (Site1, Site2, and Site3) and defines transactions as queries (Query1, Query2, and Query3) and then these transactions (queries) are processed into disjoint fragments (Fragment1, Fragment2, and Fragment3). The database transaction could be associated with more than one relation, in this case, the transaction should be divided into a number of sub-transactions equal to the number of relations used that transaction. The process of generating fragments is described as follows: 1) Database fragmentation starts with any two fragments having intersection records between them. If there is an intersection, then three disjoint fragments will be generated as follows:

- The common records in the two intersected fragments,
- The records in the first fragment but not in the second segment, and
- The records in the second fragment but not in the first segment. 2)

The intersecting fragments are then removed from the fragments list. This process continues until removing all the intersecting fragments. 3) The new derived fragments and the non-overlapped ones that do not intersect with any other fragments from the new list of totally disjoint fragments. We developed the fragmentation algorithm described in Listing 1 to generate database disjoint fragments. In the partitioning method, all transactions are processed, redundant transactions are eliminated, and the application speed and efficiency are improved by getting the minimum number of fragments to be accessed.

NETWORK SITES CLUSTERING

The benefit of generating database disjoint fragments can't be completed unless it enhances the performance of the distributed database system. As the number of database sites becomes too large, a problem of supporting high system performance with consistency and availability constraints becomes crucial. Different techniques could be developed for this purpose; one of them consists of clustering distributed networking sites. Clustering database sites is a technique in which the sites that have similar physical property (e.g., having comparable communication costs) are logically grouped together in order to increase the performance of the distributed database system. However, grouping sites into clusters is still an open problem and it is proven that the optimal solution to this problem is NP-Complete since it is transformed to a cheapest path problem. Therefore, near-optimal solution for grouping database sites into clusters helps to eliminate the extra communication costs between the sites during the process of data allocation and improves the system performance. Performing sites grouping after database fragmentation, will speed up the process of data allocation by distributing the fragments over clusters of sites rather than site by site. Thus, the communication costs are minimized and the distributed database system performance is improved. A high speed clustering technique based on the least average communication cost between sites will be introduced. This is suitable for distributed databases where the communication costs between two sites are equal or near-equal, and similar computers on the network are used. The clustering parameters that will be used to control the input/output computations for generating clusters and determining the set of site(s) in each cluster are described and computed as follows:

- The Clustering Decision Value (cdv) that determines whether or not a site can be grouped in a specific cluster.

$$cdv(S_i, S_j) = \begin{cases} 1: \text{IF} \quad CC(S_i, S_j) <= CCR \wedge i \neq j \\ 0: \text{IF} \quad CC(S_i, S_j) > CCR \vee i = j \end{cases} \quad (1)$$

Accordingly, if cdv(S_i, S_j) is equal to 1, then the sites Si and S_j are assigned to one cluster, otherwise they are assigned to different clusters. Each site should be included in only one cluster, and the final distribution of the network sites will be represented by the cluster that satisfies the least average communication cost between the sites.

- The Communication Cost between the sites CC(S_i, S_j). This is the cost of loading and processing database fragment(s) in ms/byte between any two sites in the distributed database system. CC(S_i, S_j) = cost of creation the data packet + cost of transmitting the data packet between S_i, S_j
- The Communication Cost Range CCR (ms/byte) that the site should match to be grouped in a specific cluster.

This value is determined by the network administrators and depends on how much time is allowed for the sites to transmit or receive their data to be considered in the same cluster.

Based on the parameters, assumptions, and computations described above, we developed the following clustering algorithm illustrated in Listing 2 to classify the networks clusters and their respective sites.

Listing 1. Fragmentation algorithm

```
Input: K: Number of the last fragment
Rmax: Number of database relations
Nmax: Number of fragments in each relation
Step 1: Set 0 to K
Step 2: Set 1 to R
Step 3: Do steps (4 - 21) until R > Rmax
Step 4: Set 1 to I
Step 5: Do steps (6 - 20) until I > Nmax
Step 6: Set 1 to J
Step 7: Do steps (8-18) until J > Nmax
Step 8: If I ≠ J and ∃ S_i ,S_j ∈ S_R go to step (9)
Else Add 1 to J, go to step (18)
Step 9: If S_i ∩ S_j ≠ Ø do steps (10)-(17)
        Else, Add 1 to J and go to step (19)
Step 10: Add 1 to K
Step 11: Create new fragment F_k = S_i ∩ S_j and add it to F
Step 12: Create new fragment F_k+1 = S_i - F_k and add it to F
Step 13: Create new fragment F_k+2 = S_j - F_k and add it to F
Step 14: Delete S_i
Step 15: Delete S_j
Step 16: Set Nmax + 1 to J
Step 17: End IF
Step 18: End IF
Step 19: Loop
Step 20: Add 1 to I
Step 21: Loop
Step 22: Set 1 to I
Step 23 Do steps (24 - 35) until I > Nmax
Step 24: Set 1 to J
Step 25: Do steps (26 - 33) until J > Nmax
Step 26: If I ≠ J and ∃ S_i, S_j ∈ S_R go to step (27)
         Else Add 1 to J, go to step (33)
Step 27: If S_i ∩ S_j = Ø do steps (28)-(33)
Step 28: Add 1 to K
Step 29: Create new fragment F_k = R_j - UF
Step 30: End IF
Step 31: If F_k ≠ Ø Add F_k to the set of F
Step 32: End IF
Step 33: Loop
Step 34: Add 1 to I
Step 35: Loop
Step 36: Set 1 to I
Step 37: Do steps (38 - 53) until I > F
Step 38: Set 1 to J
Step 39: Do steps (40 - 51) until J > F
Step 40: If I ≠ J and ∃ F_i, F_j ∈ F_R go to step (41)
         Else, Add 1 to J and go to step (50)
Step 41: If F_i ∩ F_j ≠ Ø do steps (42)-(49)
         Else, Add 1 to J and go to step (49)
Step 42: Add 1 to K
Step 43: Create new fragment F_k = F_i ∩ F_j and add it to F
Step 44: Create new fragment F_k+1 = F_i - F_k and add it to F
Step 45: Create new fragment F_k+2 = F_j - F_k and add it to F
Step 46: Delete F_i
Step 47: Delete F_j
Step 48: Set F + 1 to J
Step 49: End IF
Step 50: End IF
Step 51: Loop
Step 52: Add 1 to I
Step 53: Loop
Step 54: Add 1 to R
Step 55: Loop
```

Listing 2. Clustering algorithm.

```
Input: CC(S_i, S_j): Matrix of communication cost between sites
CR: Clustering Range
NS: Number of sites in the distributed database system network
Output: CSM: Clusters Set Matrix
Step 1: Set 1 to i
Step 2: Do steps (3 - 12) until i > NS
Step 3: Set 1 to j
        Set 0 to k
        Set 0 to Sum
        Set 0 to Average
        Set 0 to clusters matrix CM
Step 4: Do steps (5 - 10) until j > NS
Step 5: If i ≠ j AND CC(S_i, S_j) <= CR, go to step (6)
        Else, go to step (7)
Step 6: Set 1 to the CM(S_i, S_j) and CM(S_j, S_i) in the clusters matrix
        Add CC(S_i, S_j) to sum
        Add 1 to k
        Go to step 8
Step 7: Set 0 to the CM(S_i, S_j) and CM(S_j, S_i) in the clusters matrix
Step 8: End IF
Step 9: Add 1 to j
Step 10: Loop
Step 11: Average = Sum/k
         Average(i) = Average
         Add 1 to i
Step 12: Loop
Step 13: Set 1 to m
Step 14: Do steps (15 - 36) until m > NS
Step 15: Set 1 to q
         Set 0 to Minaverage
         Set 0 to Minrow

Step 16: Do steps (17 - 20) until q > NS or Minaverage > 0
Step 17: If Average(q) > 0 Then
           Minaverage = Average(q)
         Else
           Go to Step 18
Step 18: End If
Step 19: Add 1 to q
Step 20: Loop
Step 21: If Minaverage = 0 Then
           Set site number to a new cluster
         Else
           Go to Step 22
Step 22: End If
Step 23: Set 1 to p
Step 24: Do steps (25 - 28) until p > NS
Step 25: If Average(p) > 0 AND Average(p) < Minaverage Then
           Minaverage = Average(p)
           Minrow = p
Step 26: End IF
Step 27: Add 1 to p
Step 28: Loop
Step 29: Set 1 to a
Step 30: Do steps (31 - 34) until a > NS
Step 31: If CM(S_minrow, S_a) = 1 Then
           Set 1 to CSM(S_minrow, S_a)
           CM(S_minrow, S_a) = 0
Step 32: End IF
Step 33: Add 1 to a
Step 34: Loop
Step 35: Add 1 to m
Step 36: Loop
Step 37: Stop
```

Clustering Example

To demonstrate the applicability of clustering, a simulation of the clustering algorithm on the given communication cost between 12 sites will take place at clustering range CR equals to 5 (CR could be any communication cost as multiples of 0.125 ms/byte). The cluster set matrix resulted as shown in Table 1. From the cluster set matrix, it is clear that only S1 can be grouped in the first cluster because the other sites can't match the cluster range along with S1. The sites S2, S5, S6, S7, and S8 are also grouped in the second cluster because their communication costs match the cluster range between them. Since the cluster range match the communication costs between S3, S9, S10 and the other sites are far from them, then these three sites can be only grouped in the third cluster. In the same way, the fourth cluster is constructed only from sites S4, S11, and S12. Table 2 displays the generated clusters and their respective sites. The communication costs within and between clusters have to be taken into consideration in the computation of the fragment allocation. The optimal way to find the communication cost between clusters and between sites within each cluster is to find the shortest path between the clusters/sites and compute the communication cost between them. However, this way is considered to be NP complete, therefore, the cluster average communication cost with symmetric communication cost between clusters is suitable for the computations of fragments allocation in many distributed database environments where similar computers with similar communication costs between sites are used.

Table 1. Cluster set matrix

Site #	S1	S2	S3	S4	S5	S6	S7	S8	S9	S10	S11	S12
S1	1	0	0	0	0	0	0	0	0	0	0	0
S2	0	1	0	0	1	1	1	1	0	0	0	0
S3	0	0	1	0	0	0	0	0	1	1	0	0
S4	0	0	0	1	0	0	0	0	0	0	1	1
S5	0	1	0	0	1	1	1	1	0	0	0	0
S6	0	1	0	0	1	1	1	1	0	0	0	0
S7	0	1	0	0	1	1	1	1	0	0	0	0
S8	0	1	0	0	1	1	1	1	0	0	0	0
S9	0	0	1	0	0	0	0	0	1	1	0	0
S10	0	0	1	0	0	0	0	0	1	1	0	0
S11	0	0	0	1	0	0	0	0	0	0	1	1
S12	0	0	0	1	0	0	0	0	0	0	1	1

Table 2. The generated clusters and their sites.

Cluster #	Cluster Sites											
	S1	S2	S3	S4	S5	S6	S7	S8	S9	S10	S11	S12
C1	✓	-	-	-	-	-	-	-	-	-	-	-
C2	-	✓	-	-	✓	✓	✓	✓	-	-	-	-
C3	-	-	✓	-	-	-	-	-	✓	✓	-	-
C4	-	-	-	✓	-	-	-	-	-	-	✓	✓

FRAGMENTS ALLOCATION

Data allocation and replication technique places and distributes the database fragments on the clusters and their respective sites. Initially fragments are allocated to the clusters that have transactions using that fragments. Allocating fragments to a small number of clusters instead of large number of sites will reduce the number of communications and therefore enhance the system performance. Figure 2 illustrates the structure of data allocation and replication technique. A heuristic fragment allocation and replication technique will be introduced to perform the processes of fragments allocation in the distributed database system. Initially, all fragments are subject for allocating to all clusters having transactions using these fragments at their sites. If the fragment shows positive allocation decision value (i.e. allocation benefit greater than or equal to zero) for a specific cluster, then the fragment is subject for allocating at each site in this cluster, otherwise the fragment is not allocated (cancelled) from this cluster. This step is repeated for each cluster in the distributed database system. As a result of the previous step, the fragment that shows positive allocation decision value at any cluster is a candidate for allocating at all sites of this cluster. If the fragment shows positive allocation decision value at a site of cluster that already shows positive allocation decision value, then the fragment is allocated at this site, otherwise, the fragment is not allocated to this site. This step is repeated for each site at this cluster. To ensure data availability in the distributed database system, each fragment should be allocated to at least one cluster and one site. In case a fragment shows negative allocation decision value at all clusters, the fragment is allocated to the cluster that holds the least average communication cost and then to the site that has the least communication cost in this cluster.

Allocation Cost Functions

The allocation cost functions identifies the allocation status which is computed as a logical value for the comparison between the cost of remote access the fragment to the cluster/site and the cost of allocating the fragment to the cluster/site. If the cost of remote access the fragment to the cluster/site is greater than or equals to the cost of allocating the fragment to the cluster/site, then the allocation status is positive and the fragment is allocated to the cluster/site. On the other hand, if the cost of remote access is less than the cost of allocating, then the allocation status is negative and the fragment is cancelled from the cluster/site.

Cost of Allocating Fragments

The cost of allocating the fragment Fi issued by the transaction T_k to the cluster C_j, identified as $CA(T_k, F_i, C_j)$, is defined in terms of the following costs:

- Cost of Local Retrievals issued by the transaction T_k to the fragment Fi at cluster C_j. It is computed as the multiplication of the average cost of local retrievals for all sites (m) at cluster C_j times the average number of frequency of local retrievals issued by the transaction T_k to the fragment Fi for all sites at cluster C_j.

$$CLR(T_k,F_i,C_j)=\left(\frac{\sum_{q=1}^{m} CLR(T_k,F_i,C_j,S_q)}{m}\right)*\left(\frac{\sum_{q=1}^{m} FREQLR(T_k,F_i,C_j,S_q)}{m}\right) \tag{2}$$

Cost of Local Updates issued by the transaction T_k to the fragment F_i at cluster C_j. This cost is computed as the result of the product of the average cost of local updates for all sites (m) at cluster C_j times the average frequency of local updates.

$$CLU(T_k,F_i,C_j)=\left(\frac{\sum_{q=1}^{m} CLU(T_k,F_i,C_j,S_q)}{m}\right)*\left(\frac{\sum_{q=1}^{m} FREQLU(T_k,F_i,C_j,S_q)}{m}\right) \tag{3}$$

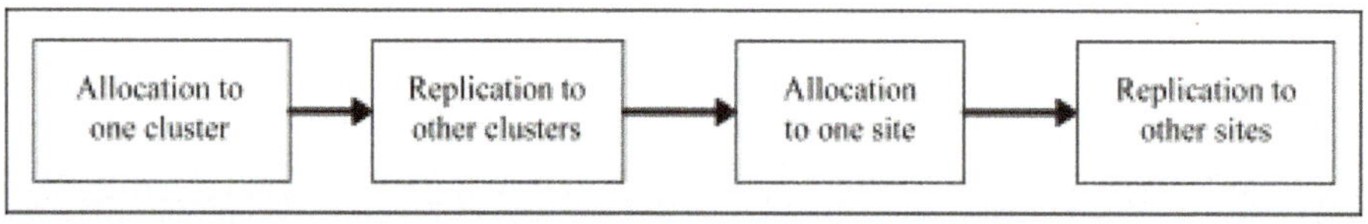

Figure 2. Data allocation and replication technique.

Cost of Space occupied by the fragment F_i in the cluster C_j. The space is computed as a result of multiplication of the average space cost for all sites (m) at cluster C_j occupied by the fragment F_i times the fragment size.

$$SCP(T_k,F_i,C_j)=\left(\frac{\sum_{q=1}^{m} SCP(T_k,F_i,C_j,S_q)}{m}\right)*F_{size}(T_k,F_i) \tag{4}$$

Cost of Remote Updates issued by the transaction T_k to the fragment F_i sent from all clusters (n) in the distributed database system except the current cluster C_j. This remote cost is computed as the result of the product of cost of local updates (Equation (3)) times the average frequency of remote update.

$$CRU(T_k,F_i,C_j)=\left(\sum_{q=1,q\neq j}^{m} CLU(T_k,F_i,C_q)\right)*\left(\sum_{q=1,q\neq j}^{m}\left(\sum_{\alpha=1}^{m} FREQRU(T_k,F_i,C_j,S_q)/m\right)\right) \tag{5}$$

Update ratio which determines the percentage of update transactions

$$U_{ratio}=\left(\frac{\sum_{q=1}^{m} FREQLU(T_k,F_i,C_j,S_q)}{\sum_{q=1}^{m} FREQLR(T_k,F_i,C_j,S_q)+\sum_{q=1}^{m} FREQLU(T_k,F_i,C_j,S_q)}\right) \tag{6}$$

Cost of Remote Communications issued for the transaction T_k to the fragment F_i sent from all clusters (n) in the distributed database system except the current cluster C_j. This cost is computed as the result of multiplication of the average cost of remote communication times the average frequency of local update times update ratio.

$$CRC(T_k,F_i,C_j)=\sum_{q=1,q\neq j}^{n}\left(\sum_{\alpha=1,\beta=1,\alpha\neq\beta}^{m} CRC(T_k,F_i,C_j,(S_\alpha,S_\beta))/m\right) *\left(\frac{\sum_{q=1}^{m} FREQLU(T_k,F_i,C_j,S_q)}{m}\right)*U_{ratio} \tag{7}$$

According to the computations in the previous cost Equations (2)-(7), the Cost of Allocating a fragment to a cluster is computed as the sum of costs of local retrievals, local updates, space, remote update, and remote communication.

$$CA(T_k, F_i, C_j) = CLR(T_k, F_i, C_j) + CLU(T_k, F_i, C_j) + SCP(T_k, F_i, C_j)$$
$$+ CRU(T_k, F_i, C_j) + CRC(T_k, F_i, C_j)$$

(8)

Cost of Not Allocating Fragments The cost of not allocating the fragment Fi issued by the transaction T_k to the cluster C_j, identified as CN(T_k, Fi, C_j), is defined in terms of the following costs:

- Cost of local retrievals issued by the transaction T_k to the fragment F_i at cluster C_j as computed in Equation (2).
- Retrieval ratio which determines the percentage of retrieval transactions

$$R_{ratio} = \left(\frac{\sum_{q=1}^{m} FREQLR(T_k, F_i, C_j, S_q)}{\sum_{q=1}^{m} FREQLR(T_k, F_i, C_j, S_q) + \sum_{q=1}^{m} FREQLU(T_k, F_i, C_j, S_q)} \right)$$

(9)

Cost of Remote Retrievals issued by the transaction T_k to the fragment Fi sent from all clusters (n) in the distributed database system except the current cluster C_j. This cost is computed as the product of the cost of communications between all clusters times the frequency of remote retrieval times the retrieval ratio

$$CRR(T_k, F_i, C_j) = \sum_{q=1}^{n} \left(\sum_{\alpha=1,\beta=1,\alpha\neq\beta}^{m} CCC(T_k, F_i, C_j, (S_\alpha, S_\beta)) / m \right)$$
$$* \left(\sum_{q=1,q\neq l}^{n} \left(\sum_{\alpha=1}^{m} FREQRR(T_k, F_i, C_j, S_q) / m \right) \right) * U_{ratio}$$

(10)

According to the computations in the previous cost equations (2,9,10), the Cost of Not allocating a fragment to a cluster is computed as follows:

$$CN(T_k, F_i, C_j) = CLR(T_k, F_i, C_j) + CRR(T_k, F_i, C_j)$$

(11)

Cost of Allocation Decision Value

The Allocation Decision Value ADV determines the allocation status of the fragment at the cluster and its respective sites. ADV is computed as a logical value resulted from the comparison between the cost of not allocating the fragment to the cluster CN(T_k, Fi, C_j) and the cost of allocating the fragment to the cluster CA(T_k, Fi, C_j).

$$ADV(T_k, F_i, C_j) = \begin{cases} 1; & CN(T_k, F_i, C_j) >= CA(T_k, F_i, C_j) \\ 0; & CN(T_k, F_i, C_j) > CA(T_k, F_i, C_j) \end{cases}$$

(12)

Accordingly, if CN(T_k, Fi, C_j) is greater than or equal to CA(T_k, Fi, C_j), then the allocation status ADV(T_k, Fi, C_j) shows positive allocation benefit and the fragment is allocated to the cluster. On the other hand, if CN(T_k, Fi, C_j) is less than CA(T_k, Fi, C_j), then the allocation status ADV(T_k, Fi, C_j) shows negative allocation benefit and the fragment is cancelled (not allocated) from the cluster. Based on the fragment allocation procedures and the generated equations described above, we developed the fragment allocation algorithm described in Listing 3 to allocate database fragments in the network clusters and their respective sites. Once the fragments are allocated and replicated at the clusters of distributed database systems, then studying the benefit of allocating the fragments at all sites of each cluster becomes crucial. To get better system performance, fragments should be distributed over the sites of clusters where a clear allocation benefit is accomplished. The same allocation and replication algorithm will be applied in this case, taking to consideration the costs for/ between sites in each cluster.

PERFORMANCE EVALUATION

We believe that the performance of allocation and network load are the major performance issues; hence, we will focused our performance evaluation on these two issues as they will maximize the overall system throughput at each network site in the distributed database environment, and minimize the cost of data that has been transferred and processed.

Fragment Allocation Performance Evaluation

The technique of fragment allocation and replication at clusters is evaluated according to the performance generated by reducing the size of fragments that allocated finally at the clusters. The closest methods in the literature to the proposed technique of fragment allocation and replication are those proposed in [7]-[10]. The main differences between these two methods are described as follows. Compared to the allocation techniques in the literature, our allocation and replication technique considers different communication costs, namely, the cost of the real network communication between cluster sites, the update and retrieval costs (i.e., it mostly represents the cost of writing operation that takes place during the execution time). Moreover, with our clustering technique, database sites are grouped according to a clustering range and not only to a specific communication cost. Our clusters can communicate with each other instead of preferring to have all fragments in their sites. This communication is cheaper than allocating fragments in all sites. In addition to the gain in term of communication cost, the independency of our clusters makes our DDBMS more reliable and more functional. Figure 3 illustrates the effectiveness of the proposed fragment allocation and replication technique in terms of average computation time over the other two fragment allocation methods. This figure shows that the proposed fragment allocation and replication technique results in the least average computation time required for fragment allocation. This is because the clustering technique produces groups (clusters) of small number of sites, and then the fragments will be reduced to the related fragments at each cluster. From Figure 3, it can be inferred that the average computation time for fragment allocation increases as the number of sites in the cluster increases and vice versa. Besides, this figure depicts the fact that our fragment allocation and replication technique outperform the other two methods

Listing 3. Allocation algorithm.

Input: *Tmax*: number of transactions issued in the database
Fmax: number of the disjoint fragments used for allocation
Cmax: number of clusters in the distributed database system
Step 1: Set 1 to k
Step 2: Do steps (3 - 32) until k > *Tmax*
Step 3: Set 1 to i
Step 4: Do steps (5 - 30) until i > *Fmax*
Step 5: Set False to allocation flag
Step 6: Set 1 to j
Step 7: Do steps (8 - 26) until j > *Cmax*
Step 8: initialize Cost of Remote Update (0) to 0
    initialize Cost of Remote Communication (0) to 0
    initialize Cost of Remote Retrieval (0) to 0
Step 9: Set 1 to y
Step 10:Do steps (11 - 17) until y > *Cmax*
Step 11: If y ≠ j Then
    Do steps (12-15)
    Else
    Go to step (15)
Step 12: Cost of Remote Update(y) = Cost of Remote Update(y -1)
    + (Cost of Local Update * Average Frequency of Remote Update)
Step 13: Cost of Remote Communication(y) = Cost of Remote Communication(y -1)
    + (Average Cost of Remote Communication * Average Frequency of Local Update * U_{ratio})
Step 14: Cost of Remote Retrieval(y) = Cost of Remote Retrieval(y -1)
    + (Cost of Communication between Clusters * Frequency of Remote Retrieval * R_{ratio})
Step 15: End If
Step 16: Add 1 to y
Step 17: Loop
Step 18: Cost of Allocation = Cost of Local Retrieval + Cost of Local Update + Cost of Storage
    + Cost of Remote Update + Cost of Remote Communication
Step 19: Cost of Not allocating = Cost of Local Retrieval + Cost of Remote Retrieval
Step 20: Allocation Decision Value = (Cost of Not allocating >= Cost of Allocation)
    # Comments: Allocation Decision Value is a Boolean value #
Step 21: If Allocation Decision Value = *True* Then
    Go to step (22)
    Else
    Go to step (23)
Step 22: Allocate the fragment to the current cluster
    Set True to allocation flag
    Go to step (24)
Step 23: Cancel the fragment from the current cluster
Step 24: End If
Step 25: Add 1 to j
Step 26: Loop
Step 27: If allocation flag = False Then

    Allocate the fragment to the cluster who has the least communication cost
Step 28: End If
Step 29: Add 1 to i
Step 30: Loop
Step 31: Add 1 to k
Step 32: Loop

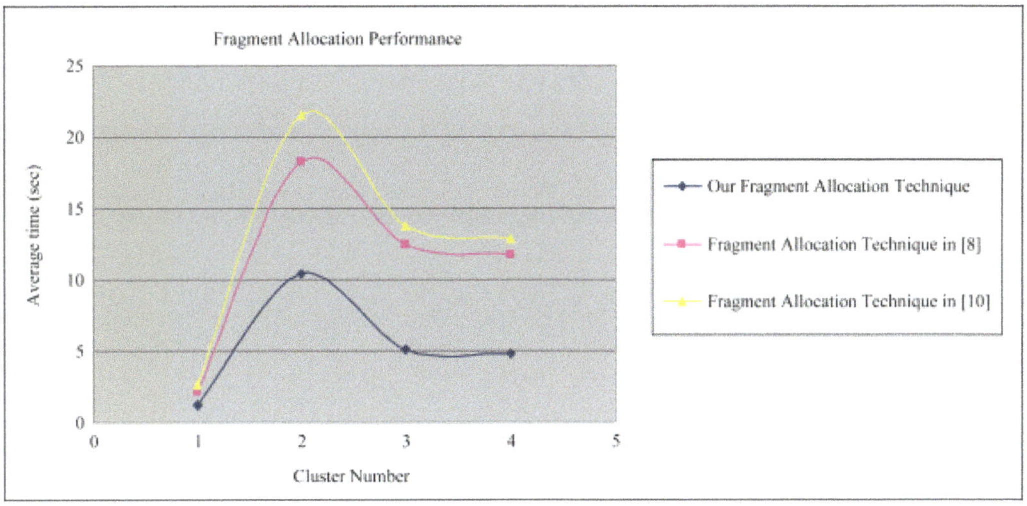

Figure 3. Fragments allocation after clustering.

Network Performance Evaluation

The DDBMS network workload involves the queries from a number of database users who access the same database simultaneously. The amount of data needed per second and the time in which the queries should be processed depend on performance of the database applications running under DDBMS network. The DDBMS network system performance evaluation will be simulated by using the OPNET IT Guru Academic Edition 9.1 software [11]. Figure 4 shows the distribution of disjoint fragments over 4 clusters: C1 (node_12), C2 (node_5), C3 (node_7) and C4 (node_17). The first cluster (C1), combines node_18 and represents Site 1. The second cluster (C2) combines node_0, node_1, node_2, node_3 and node_4 and represents Sites 2, 5, 6, 7 and 8 respectively. The third cluster (C3) combines node_8, node_9 and node_10 and represents Sites 3, 9 and 10 respectively. The fourth cluster (C4) combines node_13, node_14 and node 15 and represents Sites 4, 11 and 12 respectively. Figure 4 depicts the network topology for the proposed DDBMS should be evaluated. The figure depicts a simulation of building DDBMS and consists of 12 sites which are represented by nodes (0, 1, 2, 3, 4, 9, 10, 11, 16, 17, 18, and 20).

Server Load

The server load determines how much the speed of the server in terms of bits per seconds. The following figures depict the network server loads in the proposed DDBMS. The loads (bits/sec) on the DDBMS servers (C1, C2, C3, C4) are compared and illustrated in Figure 5. This figure shows that at its peak, the load on server 2 (node 6) is well below 1300 bits/second, on server 3 (node 13) the load is well below 750 bits/second. The load on server 4 (node 14) is also well below 750 bits/second, and the load on server 1 (node 22) is well below 500 bits/second. The results of comparison states that the network is almost balanced throughout processing sites clustering.

Network Delay

The network delay is the delay caused by the transactions traffic on the server of the distributed database system. The maximum time required for the network system to reach the steady state is defined as network delay, it's measured in millisecond. Figure 6 shows the network delay caused by each server (C1, C2, C3, C4). The distributed database system reaches the steady state after 0.065 milliseconds and less network delay time

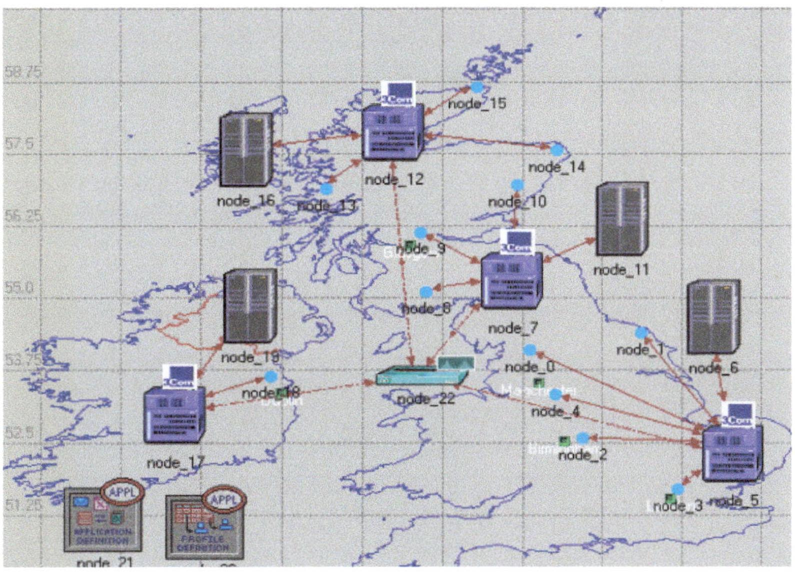

Figure 4. DDBMS network topology.

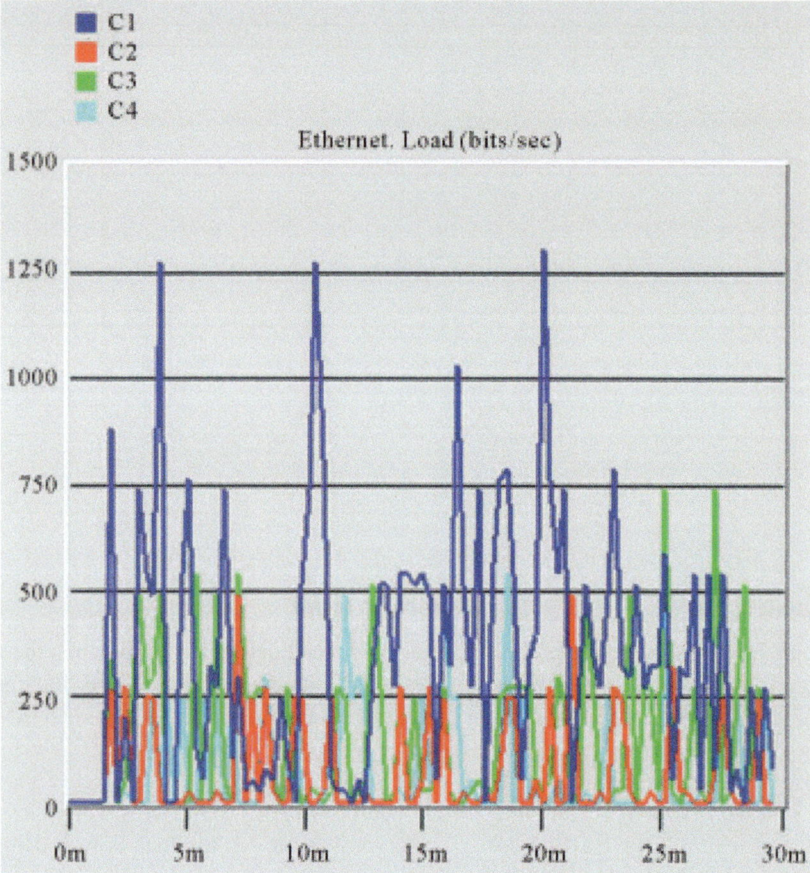

Figure 5. DDBMS network servers load.

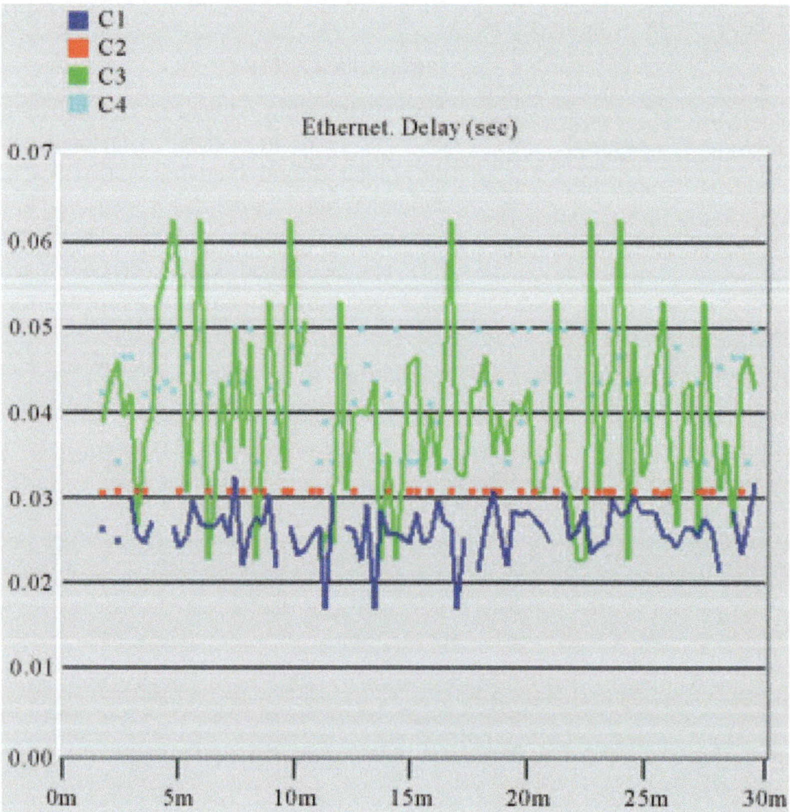

Figure 6. DDBMS network delay.

is consumed in case of distributing the sites over 4 servers compares to the delay time consumed in case of having all sites connected to 1 or 2 servers.

CONCLUSION AND FUTURE

Work In this work we proposed a new approach to improve DDBMS performance. This approach is integrating three enhanced techniques namely; database fragmentation, network sites clustering and fragments allocation. These techniques are developed to avoid drawbacks of database fragmentation and data allocation like data redundancy and complexity of data redistribution problem. In addition, a novelty of our approach is to satisfy a certain level of data availability and consistency. The results obtained in our evaluation showed that our approach significantly improved performance requirement satisfaction in distributed systems. This conclusion requires more investigation and experiments. Therefore, as future work we plan to investigate our approach on larger scale networks involving great number of database sites. Also, we will apply different types of clustering and use strong database sites grouping criteria. Finally, we plan to introduce search based technique to perform more intelligent data redistribution.

REFERENCES

1. Özsu, M.T. and Valduriez, P. (2011) Principles of Distributed Database Systems. Springer, Berlin.
2. Huang, Y.F. and Chen, J.H. (2001) Fragment Allocation in Distributed Database Design. Journal of Information Science and Engineering, 17, 491-506.
3. Gupta, S. and Panda, S. (2012) Vertical Fragmentation, Allocation and Re-Fragmentation in Distributed Object Relational Database Systems-(Update Queries Included). International Journal of Engineering Research and Development, 4, 45-52.
4. Khan, S.I. and Hoque, A.S.M.L. (2010) A New Technique for Database Fragmentation in Distributed Systems. International Journal of Computer Applications, 5, 20-24. http://dx.doi.org/10.5120/940-1318
5. Hababeh, I. (2012) Improving Network Systems Performance by Clustering Distributed Database Sites. The Journal of Supercomputing, 59, 249-267. http://dx.doi.org/10.1007/s11227-010-0436-9
6. Suganya, A. and Kalaiselvi, R. (2013) Efficient Fragmentation and Allocation in Distributed Database. International Journal of Engineering Research & Technology (IJERT), 2, 1-7.
7. Jagannatha, S., Geetha, D.E., Kumar, T.S. and Kanth, K.R. (2013) Load Balancing in Distributed Database System Using Resource Allocation Approach. International Journal of Advanced Research in Computer and Communication Engineering, 2, 2529-2535.
8. Abdalla, H.I. (2012) A New Data Re-Allocation Model for Distributed Database Systems. International Journal of Database Theory and Application, 5, 45-60.
9. Grebla, H., Moldovan, G., Darabant, S.A. and Câmpan, A. (2004) Data Allocation in Distributed Database Systems Performed by Mobile Intelligent Agents. Proceedings of the International Conference on Theory and Applications of Mathematics and Informatics-ICTAMI, Greece, 164-173.
10. Singh, A., Kahlon, K.S. and Virk, R.S. (2014) Nonreplicated Static Data Allocation in Distributed Databases Using Biogeography-Based Optimization. Chinese Journal of Engineering, 1-9.
11. OPNET Technologies, Inc. (2014) OPNET IT Guru Academic Edition 9.1. http://www.opnet.com/university_program/itguru_academic_edition

CHAPTER 2

A NEW OPTIMISTIC REPLICATION STRATEGY FOR LARGE-SCALE MOBILE DISTRIBUTED DATABASE SYSTEMS

Ashraf Ahmed[1] , P.D.D.Dominic [2], Azween Abdullah [2] and Hamidah Ibrahim [3]

[1]Department of Computer, University of Khartoum, Khartoum, Sudan

[2]Department of Computer and Information Sciences, Universiti Teknologi PETRONAS, Perak, Malaysia

[3] Faculty of Computer Science and Information Technology, Universiti Putra Malaysia, Selangor, Malaysia

ABSTRACT

This paper proposes a new optimistic replication strategy for maintaining the eventual consistency in large-scale mobile distributed database systems. The proposed strategy consists of three components in order to support the characteristics of such systems. These components are: replication architecture, updates propagation protocol, and replication method. The purpose of the replication architecture is to provide a comprehensive infrastructure for distributing replicas among wide areas. The purpose of the propagation protocol is to transfer data updates between the components of the replication architecture in a manner that achieves the eventual consistency of data and improves the availability of recent updates to all replicas. The replication method provides a mechanism for implementing the propagation protocol, and automating the propagation of updates among the different replicas. The effectiveness of the proposed strategy is compared with two baseline replication strategies and shown that it achieves updates propagation delay reduction. Also, the results showed that the horizontal extension provided by the proposed strategy is more suitable than the vertical extension for large scale mobile distributed database systems.

INTRODUCTION

Rapid advancements in wireless technologies and portable devices have given mobile computing considerable attention in the past few years as a new dimension in data communication and processing, and a fertile area of work for researchers in the areas of database and data management [3,5]. As mobile computing devices (e.g. laptop, PDA, and cell phones) become more and more common, mobile databases are becoming popular [2,20]. According to [13] and [22], the mobile database can be defined as a database that is portable and physically separate from a centralized database server but is capable of communicating with server from remote sites allowing the sharing of data. Mobility of users and portability of devices pose new problems in the management of data [10,19,24], including transaction management, query processing, and data replication. Therefore, mobile computing environments require data management approaches that are able to provide complete and highly available access to shared data at any time

Citation: Ahmed A., P. D. D. Dominic, A. Abdullah and H. Ibrahim, "A New Optimistic Replication Strategy for Large-scale Mobile Distributed Database Systems", International Journal of Database Management Systems (IJDMS), Vol.2, No.4, November 2010, DOI: 10.5121/ijdms.2010.2408.

from any where. One way to achieve such goal is through data replication techniques. The importance of such techniques is increasing as collaboration through widearea and mobile networks becomes popular [30]. However, maintaining the consistency of replicated data among all replicas represents a challenge in mobile computing environments when updates are allowed at any replica.

This paper addresses the problem of maintaining consistency of replicated data in Large Scale Mobile Distributed Database Systems (LMDDBSs). This type of systems is characterized by a large number of replicas (i.e. thousands of replicas) and a large number of updates (i.e. tens of updates may be performed on each replica at any period of time) that are performed on these replicas. The replicas are distributed over both mobile and fixed environments. Examples of such systems include mobile health care, mobile data warehousing, news gathering, and traffic control management systems. The characteristics of LMDDBSs, and the ability of the mobile users to issue a large number of concurrent update operations, which may occur during the disconnection periods extremely aggravate this problem than in the ordinary replicated database systems, which they have a small number of replicas. The concurrent updates during disconnection periods influence consistency of the replicated data by leading to a divergence in the database states (i.e. the data that are stored in the database at a particular moment in time) within replicas that are hosted in mobile environments, and between these replicas and the replicas that are hosted in fixed environments. To cope with the problem of maintaining consistency of the replicated data, several replication strategies are proposed. These strategies are divided into optimistic and pessimistic approaches [15,30]. Pessimistic strategies operate under a pessimistic assumption that if an inconsistency can occur, it will occur. Therefore, these strategies restrict updates to a single replica or a group of replicas by locking access to these replicas during the processing of update requests. Then, updates are applied to all other replicas. Accordingly, the pessimistic strategies provide the strong consistency guarantee that is called one-copy equivalence [26]. This consistency guarantee requires that all replicas be mutually consistent (i.e. have identical values for all shared data items) at the end of each update operation. Examples of such strategies include ROWA [1,18], and primary copy approaches [16,29]. According to the description of the pessimistic strategies, it can generally be said that these strategies rely on two factors as follows. The first factor is a reliable and constant communication between replicas. The second factor is the coordination between the replicas that are involved in the performing of operations, which may require the blocking of access to these replicas during performing the operations. However, these factors are not feasible in mobile environments where frequent disconnections is common, which makes these pessimistic strategies are not suitable for maintaining consistency of replicated data in such environments, especially when some of mobile nodes hold updatable replicas. In contrast with pessimistic strategies, optimistic strategies operate under the optimistic assumption that inconsistencies, even if possible, rarely occur [30]. Operations (read and write) may be executed on any replica. At the reconnection time, the system must first detect inconsistencies and then resolve them. Accordingly, optimistic replication allows replicas to access and update data independent from one another by delaying consistency checks. Then, replicas exchange updates with one another in a process called reconciliation, which occurred periodically [8,23]. During the reconciliation process, two replicas exchange all updates that occurred since the last reconciliation. Optimistic replication is often used to increase database availability in systems where communication is unreliable or nodes require access to data while disconnected from the network (e.g. mobile environments) [15]. However, optimistic replication strategies face the challenge of keeping replicas consistent. This challenge is complicated, because these strategies let updates to be issued at multiple replicas at the same time. Accordingly, optimistic replication strategies cannot guarantee strong consistency through achieving one-copy equivalence. Instead of that, they provide a weak type of replica consistency guarantee called eventual consistency [11,30]. Eventual consistency guarantees that the contents of all the replicas become identical eventually. Eventual consistency is important because it is the minimal requisite of a replication strategy; without this guarantee, the replica contents may remain corrupted forever, making the system practically useless. To achieve eventual consistency, optimistic replication algorithms should provide mechanisms for rapid propagation (dissemination) of updates among replicas in order to minimize the divergence between them. Optimistic replication is used in several solutions for handling data replication issues in mobile environments. This is because it meets the goal of providing higher availability. However, these strategies have not explicitly addressed the issues of consistency and availability of data in large scale mobile distributed database systems that contain large number of both fixed and mobile hosts. Therefore, this paper comes to a conclusion that additional research toward a dedicated replication strategy for LMDDBSs is needed to investigate and address data consistency issue in such systems.

Accordingly, the paper proposes a new replication strategy that acts in accordance with the characteristics of these systems (i.e. large number of updatable replicas). This paper is organized as follows. The next section provides the related work. Section 3 outlines the proposed replication strategy, and presents the system model that is used in this paper. Section 4 describes the replication architecture. Section 5 gives the details of the updates propagation protocol and its performance evaluation. Section 6 describes the replication method. Section 7 concludes the paper.

RELATED WORK

Using optimistic replication in mobile environments has been studied in several research efforts. Roam [7,8] is an optimistic replication system that provides a scalable replication solution for the mobile user. ROAM is based on the Ward Model [6]. Replicas are grouped into wards (wide area replication domains). All ward members are peers, allowing any pair of ward members to directly synchronize and communicate. Each ward has a ward master that maintains consistency with the other wards. Updates are exchanged within each ward (i.e. between ward members) and among wards (i.e. between ward masters) using ring topology. Accordingly, Roam employs optimistic replica control mechanism that ensures an eventual convergence for replica updates to maintain the consistency within each ward and among wards. ROAM tries to provide high scalability without discussing a mechanism of ensuring rapid propagation of large numbers of updates that can be performed on both fixed and mobile replicas, which are distributed over wide geographic areas. An n-ary tree based updates propagation strategy [25,27,28] assumed an environment where update information is immediately sent to all peers holding replicas when an update occurs. The proposed strategy creates an n-ary tree, whose root is the owner of the original data while the other nodes are peers holding its replicas, and propagates the update information according to the tree. Each peer in the tree records its parent and children, and by using this information, the location of a newly participating peer in the tree is autonomously determined. However, in this strategy, the updated data must be propagated to all replica holders and this causes heavy traffic for update propagation when the number of replicas becomes large. Also, there is an overhead originated from the need of each peer to manage information about the parent and children peers. A multi-master scheme is used in [14], that is, read-any/write-any. To reach an eventual consistency in which the servers converge to an identical copy, an adaptation in the primary commit scheme is used. In this adaptation, a server chosen as a primary has the responsibility to synchronize and commit the updates. The committed updates are propagated to the other servers. This strategy inherits the drawbacks of primary-copy approach, since it relies on a selected server that is responsible for synchronizing all updates between the different replicas. A hybrid replication strategy is presented in [12] that has different ways of replicating and managing data on fixed and mobile networks. In the fixed network, the data object is replicated synchronously to all sites in a manner of logical three dimensional grid structure, while in the mobile network, the data object is replicated asynchronously at only one site based on the most frequently visited site. In this strategy, the synchronous replication hinders the fixed network to be scale to wide areas. Cedar [17] is a replication strategy focuses on preserving eventual consistency through using a simple Client/Server design in which a central server holds the master copy of the database. At infrequent intervals when a client has connectivity to the server (which may occur hours or days apart), its replica is refreshed from the master copy. The using of a central server to hold the master copy in this strategy, limits its implementation in large scale environments. A mobile database replication strategy called Transaction-Level Result-Set Propagation is proposed in [9]. Each fixed and mobile nodes store a replica of the data. The mobile node is allowed to update its local replica. However, updates locally committed at the mobile nodes need to be verified at the fixed node before they can be globally committed. In summary, we argue that existing replication strategies are not coping well with the characteristics of large-scale mobile systems containing large number of geographically distant replicas that experience large number of updates. Accordingly, such systems demand new solutions for addressing data consistency through ensuring fast propagation of recent updates among replicas as well as supporting scalability for encompassing new replicas, especially when the replication system covers new geographic areas.

THE PROPOSED REPLICATION STRATEGY

The proposed replication strategy encompasses three components: replication architecture, updates propagation protocol, and replication method. The purpose of the replication architecture is to provide a comprehensive infrastructure for distributing replicas among wide areas, improving data availability, and supporting large number of replicas in mobile environments by determining the required components that are involved in the replication process. The purpose of the propagation protocol is to transfer data updates between the components of the replication architecture in a manner that achieves the consistency of data and improves the availability of recent updates to all replicas. The replication method provides a mechanism for implementing the propagation protocol, and automating the propagation of updates among the different levels of the replication architecture.

System Model

This paper considers a large-scale environment that consists of Fixed Hosts (FH), Mobile Hosts (MH), a replica manager on each host, and a replicated database on each host. A part of fixed hosts represent servers with more storage and processing capabilities than the rest. The replica manger is a software that manages and facilitates the application's accesses (read and update operations) to the replicated database. A replicated database is called mobile database when it is stored on a mobile host. The replicated database contains a set of objects stored on the set of hosts. The database is fully replicated on the servers, while it is partially replicated on both fixed and mobile hosts. Update can take place at any host. Update information is sent to the other hosts in a form of message. A replica is in consistent state if and only if all updates that are performed on the other replicas are received by this replica. Each host has a unique address, called Host- ID. The information of hosts and their replicated data are stored on objects called Hosts-Obj and Host-Replicated-Objects-Obj, respectively, which are replicated on each server. When a failure occurs in any host, the affected host is considered as disconnected. In this paper, the terms replica and host will be used interchangeably because each host has a replica.

REPLICATION ARCHITECTURE

The proposed replication architecture (see Figure 1) considers a total geographic area called the master area that has a server called Master Server (MS) and a set of fixed hosts. The master area is divided into a set $Z = \{z_1, \ldots, z_n\}$ of zones. Each zone has a server called Zone Server (ZS) and a set of fixed hosts and it consists of a set $C = \{c_1, \ldots, c_m\}$ of smaller areas called cells. Each cell represents an area, where the mobile users can perform their duties at a particular period of time before moving to another cell. Each cell has a server called Cell Server (CS). In this architecture, the network is divided into fixed network and mobile network. The fixed network consists of fixed hosts and wired local area network to connect them in the master area. Also, it includes wide area network to connect the master server with zone servers, and to connect zone server with underlying cell servers. The cell server is augmented with a wireless interface and acts as a mobile support station for connecting mobile hosts to the fixed network. On the other hand, the mobile network consists of wireless network and mobile hosts in the cell area. To provide more flexibility and application areas for this architecture, replicas are divided into three levels: Master Level: In this level, the replica that is stored on the master server must be synchronized with replicas from the zone level. The master server is responsible for synchronizing all changes that have been performed on both infrequently changed data and frequently changed data with the lower level. Zone Level: In this level, each replica must be synchronized with replicas from the lower level. The zone server is responsible for synchronizing all intra-level changes with the master server. Cell Level: Each replica in this level is updated frequently, and then synchronized with the cell server's replica and in turn the cell server synchronizes all intra-level data with the zone server. In this architecture, initially, the database is stored on the master server. When dividing the master area into multiple zones, a replica of that database is distributed to zone servers. Similarly, new replicas are created when dividing the zone area into multiple cells to represent the cell servers and when registering new mobile hosts and fixed hosts in the replication system. The information of each new replica is stored on the hosts object in the server of the area where the replica is created and then it is replicated to other servers. This information includes the Host ID, Host Type (FH, MH, CS, ZS, and MS), and Region where it is registered. The details of the replicated objects on that host are stored on the object of host's replicated data.

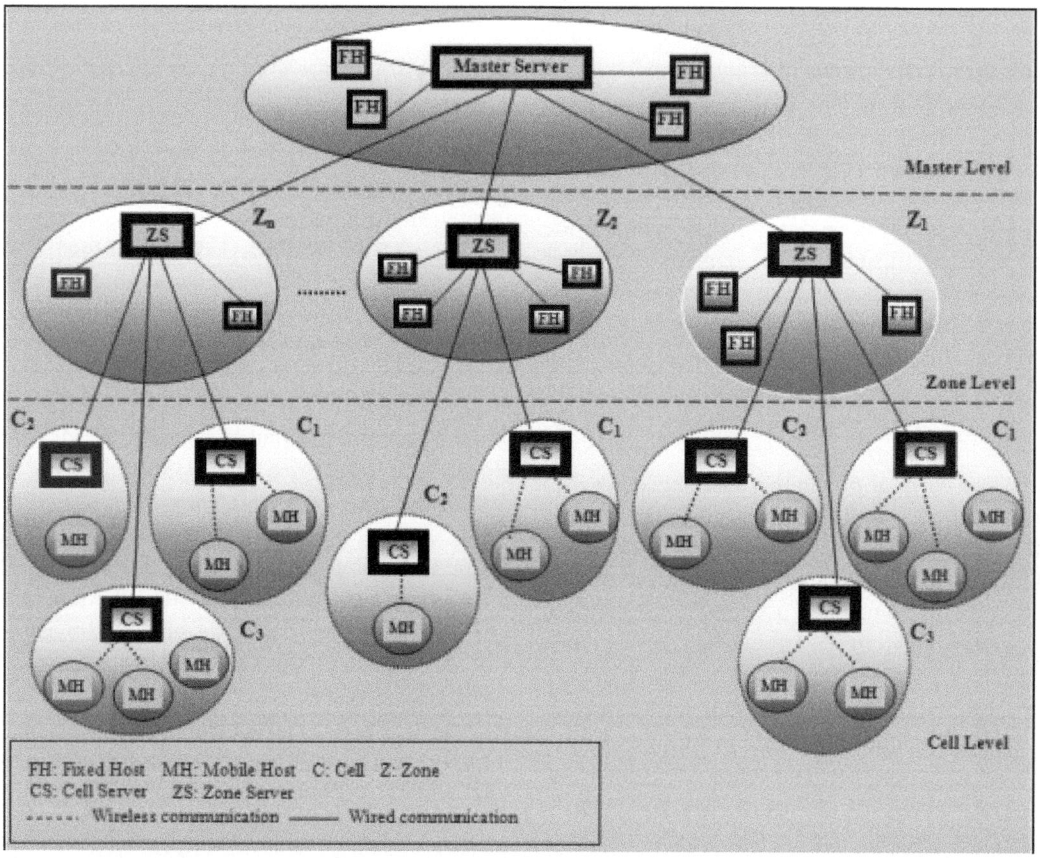

Figure 1. The replication architecture for large-scale mobile environments

WHEEL-BASED UPDATES PROPAGATION PROTOCOL

This section provides the details of the proposed protocol for updates propagation through the components of replication architecture. The protocol consists of a logical structure for arranging replicas and propagation mechanisms for exchanging updates among these replicas. The logical structure is a wheel-like structure that organizes replicas according to their types, areas where they inhabit (cell, zone, and master areas), and responsibility with regard to updates propagation. The propagation mechanisms act as interaction mechanisms between the replicas for propagating recent updates from their sources to other replicas that are distributed over the wheel. Accordingly, the resulting protocol is called Wheel-Based updates propagation protocol.

Updates Propagation Wheel

The logical structure that is involved in the updates propagation is a water wheel inspired structure called updates propagation wheel, which represents a logical structure for exchanging recent updates between the hosts that are distributed over the replication architecture. The application of the water wheel structure here is arising from its general design and functionality. The water wheel structure [21] links an axle (i.e. acts as a central point) with multiple buckets (act as points) that are located in different directions on a circular rim through spokes. The functionality of the water wheel depends on the rotation of the buckets that are located on the rim after they are filled by the water. This rotation leads to the revolution of the whole wheel including the center point. To apply this idea, updates propagation wheel is structured in a manner that includes the basic components of the water wheel with different explanations and functionalities. Given N replicas of the database, the propagation protocol organizes them logically into the wheel structure based on their areas and types as shown in Figure 2. The following definition will formally define the propagation wheel (PW).

Definition 1. PW is 9-tuple < F, H, S, L, R, P, U, M, T >, where:

F= $\{FH_1,\ldots, FH_n\}$ is a finite set of fixed hosts that act as fixed points (i.e. buckets), which are distributed over the wheel.

H= $\{MH_1,\ldots, MH_h\}$ is a finite set of mobile hosts that act as mobile buckets over the wheel.

S= $\{s_1 ,\ldots, s_s\}$ is a finite set of servers that act as fixed center points where a sub set of F, H, or S can be connected to each center point.

L = $\{l_1,\ldots, l_l\}$ is a finite set of communication links that act as spokes for linking the different points distributed over the wheel.

R = $\{r_1 , r_2, r_3\}$ is a finite set of virtual circular rims that act as a collection of points that have same area.

P= $\{p_1, \ldots, p_p\}$ is a finite set of parts that constitute each rim. Each part is called a sector.

U: $F \cup H \cup S \rightarrow \{1, 2, 3,\ldots, k\}$ is a function for assigning a unique identifier serially for each host in the wheel according to its type.

M = $\{m_1, m_2, m_3\}$ is a finite set of mechanisms for exchanging updates between the different points in the wheel.

T= $\{t_1,\ldots, t_{n+h+s}\}$ is a finite set of total number of updates that are currently stored in each host

Center points. As depicted in Figure 2, the different types of hosts are represented by circles in the propagation wheel. Some hosts act as center points where multiple spokes are collected on them. These points represent the servers of the different areas. Accordingly, these points can be classified into master server, zone servers, and cell servers according to their areas. The master server acts as the main center point, while both zone servers and cell servers act as secondary center points. The center points are linked through spokes to a set of either other center points or ordinary points (i.e. points act as either fixed or mobile hosts) in the next outer rim. In this wheel, both center and ordinary points represent the different types of hosts of the replicated system, while the spokes between them represent the network connections (channels).

Rims. They are formed by the hosts that have same area regardless of their directions. Accordingly, we have three rims as follows.

(i) Master Rim: It contains all zone servers as well as fixed hosts on the master area. The master server is responsible for all hosts exist in this rim in that it receives their updates and sends their missed updates to them.

(ii) Zone Rim: It contains all cell servers as well as fixed hosts on the zone area. The zone server is responsible for a part of this rim called a sector, which represents the cell servers and fixed hosts that are located in its area.

(iii) Cell Rim: It contains all mobile hosts and fixed hosts in the cell area. The cell server is responsible for a part of the cell rim which represents the fixed hosts and mobile hosts that are located in its cell.

The rotation of the MHs in both clockwise and anticlockwise directions in the cell rim can be envisioned as a motivation for the revolution of the wheel since the MHs are located here on the most outer rim (i.e. cell rim). Sectors. Both the zone and cell rims have multiple sectors (i.e. they are divided into multiple parts). Each sector consists of a set of hosts that have same area (either zone or cell) and are connected to the same center point in the next inner rim (i.e. their area's server). For example, the fixed hosts and cell servers that belong to specific zone form a sector on the zone rim and they connect to the server of this zone in the master rim. The sector is named using the name of the responsible secondary point in the next inner rim. For example, the sector S_{Z2}-Sec= $\{CS_{21},\ldots, CS_{2c}\}$ $\cup$ $\{FH_{21},\ldots, FH_{2v}\}$ represents a part of the zone rim under the responsibility of the zone server number 2.

Spokes. The hosts in a given rim are linked to their related hosts in another rim or nearby hosts in the same rim through spokes. Two categories of spokes exist in the propagation wheel as follows.

a. Fixed spokes. This category links the servers in a given rim with their related servers and fixed hosts in the next outer rim.

b. Temporary spokes. They link the cell server with mobile hosts that are currently roaming in its cell (i.e. its sector). Also, this category links two nearby hosts from the same type in same level. For example, it links two nearby cell serves in the same zone or two mobile hosts in the same cell.

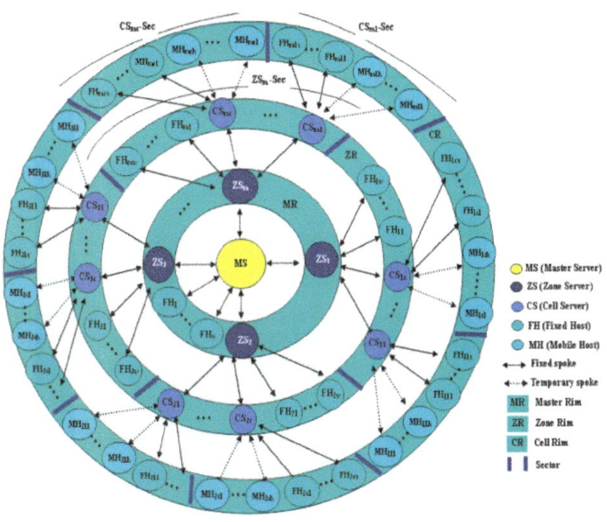

Figure 2. Updates propagation wheel.

Naming schema. The hosts are named using the schema: Host-Type$_{\text{Zone-No Cell-NO Host-Serial}}$ (e.g. FH_{212} is the name of the fixed host number 2 in cell number 1, which belongs to zone number 2). MHs are named by considering the zone and cell areas where they have been registered at the first time. The cell servers are named using the following schema $CS_{\text{Zone-No Cell-Serial}}$ (e.g. CS_{41} is the name of the cell server number 1 in zone number 4). The zone servers are identified serially.

Propagation mechanisms. Three basic mechanisms are identified for propagating updates from their sources to a set of other hosts in the propagation wheel as follows.

1. **Outer-to-Inner Propagation.** In this mechanism, updates flow through the rims in the direction of the wheel center from their sources in an outer rim into an inner rim until they pour into the master center point. Each intermediate rim keeps the poured updates for a certain period for the purpose of accumulating them before pouring them into the next inner rim. Accordingly, the steps that are carried out for this type of propagation are as follows.

- Updates on the hosts (i.e. MHs and FHs) that populate the cell rim flow into their responsible secondary center points (i.e. CSs) in the zone rim.
- The secondary center points in the zone rim accumulate the poured updates from the cell rim for further processing that implies the ordering of these updates.
- Processed updates on the CSs of zone rim flow into their responsible secondary center points (i.e. ZSs) that populate the master rim.
- The secondary center points in the master rim accumulate the poured updates from the zone rim for processing them in a total manner.
- All accumulated and processed updates on the zone rim flow to the master center point.

This type models the propagation of updates from the lowest level in the replication architecture to the highest level. The lowest level represents the cell level, which is modeled by the cell rim, while the highest level represents the master server and it is modeled by the main center point. Accordingly, this mechanism can be called Bottom-Up propagation (BUP).

2. **Inner-to-Outer Propagation.** In this mechanism, totally ordered updates by the main center point are pumped from an inner rim into an outer rim in the direction of the most outer rim. Each intermediate rim contributes the pumping by pushing those updates to reach the most outer rim. Accordingly, the steps that are carried out for this type of propagation are as follows.

- Totally processed updates on the main center point are pumped into the secondary center points that populate the master rim.
- Each secondary center point in the master rim pushes those updates to its underlying secondary center points that populate the zone rim.
- Each center point in the zone rim pushes those updates to underlying points that populate the cell rim.

This type models the propagation of updates from the highest level (i.e. master level) in the replication architecture to the lowest level (i.e. cell level). Thus, this mechanism can be called TopDown propagation (TDP).

3. **Inside-Sector propagation.** In this propagation, updates are exchanged inside the rim between the hosts that have same type and sector (i.e. they populate same area), and have a possibility to communicate with each other. Accordingly, this mechanism is also called P2P propagation. Each peer pumps its received updates (either from other rim or generated on it) into a subset of the other peers that can communicate directly with them in the same sector. The pumping process continues from the other peers to ensure that updates are pushed to all peers in the sector. In the case of existing of more than one master area, this implies exchanging of updates between the master servers of the wheels that represent these master areas in a peer-to-peer manner. This is because there is no higher level than the master server.

The three basic propagation mechanisms represent the possible alternatives for exchanging recent updates between the different types of hosts that are included in the propagation wheel. Outer-to-Inner propagation is necessary to ensure that all recent updates, which occurred in the lower level hosts reach the servers that are located in the higher levels. This is because these servers cover different areas, and are required to provide their underlying hosts with the recent updates that occurred in the other areas. Inner-to-Outer propagation is required for each server to disseminate the received updates from other areas to the hosts that are located in its area. Inside-Sector propagation mechanism is provided to enable the hosts, which exist in the same area to exchange their updates directly without needing to send these updates to the server of area where they are located. For example, some hosts may be involved in performing duties that are associated with their area. Accordingly, they can share their updates using this mechanism without needing to send these updates to the other areas.

Hybrid Propagation Mechanisms

The following mechanisms act as a hybrid of two or all basic mechanisms for propagating updates from their sources to all hosts:

1. **Hierarchical-Concentrate propagation.** It represents a hybrid of both Outer-to-Inner and Inner-toOuter propagation mechanisms. In this mechanism, updates are propagated to all hosts by delegating the responsibility of the propagation to the center points, which have a stable connectivity with their both underlying center points in the next outer rim and the responsible center point in the next inner rim. For instance, the main center point, which represents the server that exists in the highest level (i.e. master server) in the replication architecture, has a stable connectivity with the servers that cover all areas in the replication system (i.e. zone servers). The resolution of updates conflicts through updates ordering process is carried out at the server in the higher level. The steps are as follows.

- The hosts in the lower levels propagate their updates using BUP mechanism to the server in the higher level till they reach the server in the highest level.
- The collected updates are propagated from the highest level to the lower levels using TDP mechanism.

2. **P2P-Concentrate propagation.** It represents a hybrid of the three basic mechanisms for exchanging updates in the same area (i.e. same cell, same zone, or same master area). In this hybrid, the role of the server of the area where peers inhabit (i.e. the center point in the next inner rim) is eliminated to allow the peers to exchange their updates without needing to send them to the higher level. However, peers need to propagate their updates to this server when these updates should be propagated to the other areas of the replication architecture. The steps are as follows.

- The lower level hosts propagates their updates to the servers in the higher level of their region using BUP propagation.
- Each server propagates those updates to the peers that can communicate with them until updates reach all peers in the same region (i.e. same sector) using P2P propagation.
- Each server propagates these updates to the lower level hosts using TDP Propagation. In this technique, each peer has the responsibility of the resolution of update conflicts before propagating these updates to the other peers. As an example, in the zone area, this mechanism is applied as follows.
  - The hosts in each cell propagate their updates to the cell server using BUP propagation.
  - The cell servers exchange those updates using P2P propagation.
  - Each cell server propagates these updates to its underlying hosts using TDP propagation.

Performance Evaluation

The two proposed propagation techniques, which are Hierarchical-Concentrate and P2P-Concentrate are evaluated and compared with Roam propagation technique with regard to achieving propagation delay reduction. The required equations that characterize the updates propagation are developed analytically in this section for computing the update propagation delay. In the analysis, a single update operation is tracked. The description of the update propagation delay as a performance metric and the required equations for analyzing it as well as the evaluation are as follows.

Update Propagation Delay (UPD). It is measured based on the number of hops that are required for propagating an update from a replica to another replica. This is because measuring the exact time that is consumed in updates propagation depends on many complicated factors such as connectivity (bandwidth and network delays) and availability of hosts. Moreover, mobile environments suffer from the inherited frequent disconnections, accordingly, we cannot rely on the actual propagation times and delays from a host to another.

Definition 2. UPD is the total number of hops from the host that represents the source of update to another host that is either in the same area or in different area.

Measuring UPD. To measure the propagation delay, we analytically developed the required equations that are based on the following assumptions:

- Two replicas: a replica on MH_i, which generates an update that must be propagated to all other hosts. The other replica is MH_j, which acts on behalf of all other hosts in that the same results are applied as they have been examined.
- Two cases for the location of the destination, which are as follows.
  - Worst case: The purpose of this case is to determine the maximum number of hops that are required to propagate an update to all hosts. Therefore, the location of MH_j (i.e. the destination) is assumed in the last cell, which exists in the last zone, or last master area, or it represents the last mobile host in the same cell of the MH_i.
  - Average case: In this case, UPD is calculated on average regardless of the location of the MHj.

The required equations are developed by considering both worst and average cases for each propagation technique in a separate manner as follows.

(a) Measuring UPD for Hierarchical-Concentrate propagation In Hierarchical-Concentrate propagation, the following equation is applied for both worst case and average cases.

$$UPD = \begin{cases} 1, m = 0, z = 0, c = 1 \\ 3, m = 0, z = 1, c \geq 2 \\ 5, m = 1, z \geq 2 \\ m + 4, m \geq 2 \end{cases} \quad (1)$$

Where: -

m is the number of master servers. –

z is the number of zone servers. –

c is the number of cell servers.

Proof. As provided at the appendix

Same values of UPD are hold in despite of the number of the cell where the update occurs (MH_i exists) or the number of the other cell where MH_j exists. This means that values do not change for different number of cells in the zone and different number of zones in the master area. This is in contrast with Roam.

(b) **Measuring UPD for P2P-Concentrate propagation.** In this technique, different equations are used for the worst case and the average case by considering that in each sector of the wheel rims, the peer can communicate only with the next nearby peer in the direction of the destination.

(i) Worst case

$$\text{UPD} = \begin{cases} n-2, \text{MHi and MHj in same cell, n} \geq 2 \\ c, \text{MHi and MHj in different cells in same zone, c} \geq 2 \\ z+2, \text{MHi and MHj in different zones in same master area, z} \geq 2 \\ m+4, \text{MHi and MHj in different master areas, m} \geq 2 \end{cases}$$

Where:

- n is the number of MHs in the cell.
- c is the number of CSs in the zone.
- z is the number of ZSs in the master area.
- m is the number of MSs.

Proof. As provided at the appendix

(2)

(ii) Average case

$$\text{UPD} = \begin{cases} \frac{1}{2}(n-2), \text{MHi and MHj in same cell, n} \geq 2 \\ \frac{c}{2}, \text{MHi and MHj in different cells in same zone, c} \geq 2 \\ \frac{1}{2}(z+2), \text{MHi and MHj in different zones in same master area, z} \geq 2 \\ \frac{1}{2}(m+4), \text{MHi and MHj in different master areas, m} \geq 2 \end{cases}$$

(3)

(c) Measuring UPD for Roam's propagation. In Roam, propagating an update from a replica MH_i to MH_j requires first sending it from MH_i to MH_i's ward master, then sending it from MH_i's ward master to MH_j's ward master, and then finally to MH_j. Accordingly, UPD is calculated as follows.

(i) Worst case

$$\text{UPD} = \begin{cases} n-2, \text{MHi and MHj in same ward} \\ w, \text{MHi and MHj in different wards} \end{cases}$$

(4)

(ii) Average case

$$\text{UPD} = \begin{cases} \frac{1}{2}(n-2), \text{MHi and MHj in same ward} \\ \frac{w}{2}, \text{MHi and MHj in different wards} \end{cases}$$

Where:

- n is the number of mobile hosts in the ward
- w is the number of wards

(5)

Comparative Study using ANOVA and Duncan's Test based on UPD In this section, a comparative study for the three updates propagation techniques (i.e. HierarchicalConcentrate, P2P-Concentrate, and Roam) is performed based on UPD as a performance metric. The purpose of the study is to determine the best technique among the three that can be used to propagate updates in large scale mobile distributed database systems. The techniques are compared by varying the number of cells (i.e. equivalent to wards in Roam) and computing UPD based on the developed equations. We assume that the number of cells in each zone is 5 and similarly, the number of zones in each master area is 5 (same conclusions are drawn when the number of cells or zones is greater than or equal 5 as already examined for different values). This means that in this comparison, varying the number of cells leads to the variation of the number of both zones and master servers in our strategy. In this comparison, if MHi and MHj in the same cell, we consider that there are no any MHs between them. This because the number of MHs that act as hops between them cannot be estimated, since this depends on the number of MHs roaming at that cell on that time instant. Therefore, we consider UPD = 0 in this case as the best case for Roam. Two replications for each cell number are taken into consideration for the calculation of UPD using the different techniques. Accordingly, for this comparison, the following factors are considered:

- Different techniques for updates propagation (Factor A)
- Number of cells (Factor B)

A summary of the factors and their levels in the experimentation is presented in Table 1.

Table 1. Levels of the two factors A and B

Serial No.	Factors	Values	Number of Levels
1	Propagation techniques	---	3
2	Number of cells	1,2,3,...,100	100

Based on these factors, the experimental combination contains the number of the cell and the corresponding UPD values for the three techniques. Since two replications for each cell number (factor B) are taken into consideration for the calculation of UPD using the different levels of techniques (factor A), this means that the total number of experimental combinations is equal to 200. The UPD values are analyzed in two stages using ANOVA and Duncan's multiple range tests [4]. The summary of these analyses is as follows.

Stage 1. ANOVA

The problem (i.e. comparing three techniques) is treated as two ANOVA.

- **Factor A:** Techniques

Levels: 3

- **Factor B:** Number of cells Levels: 100
- **Response Variable:** Performance metric (measure or value) namely UPD.
- **Number of observations** (n): 600 (3*100*2)
- **Model:**

The model of 2-factor experiment is as follows.

$$Y_{ijk} = \mu + \alpha_i + \beta j + \alpha\beta_{ij} + \varepsilon_{ijk} \quad (i=1, 2, 3; j=1, 2, 3, \ldots, 100; k=1,2) \tag{6}$$

Where:

- Y_{ijk} is the performance measure namely UPD of the k th replicate under the i th and j th treatments of the factors A and B respectively
- μ is the overall mean effect.
- αi is the effect of the performance measure namely UPD due to the i th treatment of Factor A.
- β_j is the effect of the performance measure namely UPD due to the j th treatment of Factor B.
- $\alpha_\beta j$ is the effect of the performance measure namely UPD due to the i th treatment of Factor A and j th treatment of Factor B.
- ε_{ijk} is the random error (the effect of random experimental error)

Null hypotheses:

$H_0{}^1 : \alpha_1 = \alpha_2 = \alpha_3 = 0$ Three techniques (Factor A) do not have significant effect on UPD.

$H_0{}^2 : \beta_1 = \beta_2 = \ldots = \beta_{100} = 0$ Number of cells (Factor B) does not have significant effect on UPD.

$H_0{}^3 : (\alpha\ \beta)_{ij} = 0$ for all i, j Interaction between techniques (Factor A) and number of cells (Factor B) does not have significant effect on UPD.

Alternative hypotheses:

$H_1{}^1$: at least one $\alpha_i \neq 0$

$H_1{}^2$: at least one $\beta_i \neq 0$

$H_1{}^3$: at least one $(\alpha\ \beta)_{ij} \neq 0$

Level of Significance: It is assumed as 0.05.

ANOVA Table: It is as shown in Table 2. From this table, if the calculated value of F of a particular source of variation is greater than the corresponding tabulated value of F (FT), then it can be concluded that the above source of variation is having significant effect on the performance measure namely UPD (i.e. the null hypothesis corresponding to the source of variation is rejected). Otherwise, it can be concluded that the source of variation is not having any significant effect on the performance measure namely UPD (i.e. the null hypothesis corresponding to the source of variation is accepted).

Results: From the ANOVA statistics shown in Table 2, the following conclusions can be arrived at:

a. Techniques (Factor A) are having significant effect on the performance measure namely UPD (i.e. $H_0^{\,1}$ is rejected).

b. Number of cells (Factor B) is having significant effect on the performance measure namely UPD (i.e. $H_0^{\,2}$ is rejected).

c. Interaction between Factor A and Factor B is having significant effect on the performance measure namely UPD (i.e. $H_0^{\,3}$ is rejected).

In accordance with ANOVA results, the model components A, B, and AB are statistically significant.

Table 2. Two way ANOVA table

Source of Variation	Sum Of Squares (SS)	Degrees Of Freedom (v)	Mean Sum Of Squares (MS)	F (Calculated)	F_T	$F > F_T$ Yes or No
A	139479.29	2	69739.65	496.1322	3.025846	YES
B	37930.74	99	383.14	2.725673	1.296908	YES
AB	56554.04	198	285.63	2.031964	1.234578	YES
E	42170	300	140.57			
Total	276134.1	599				

Stage 2. Test of means using Duncan's multiple range test. The first stage of the analysis concludes that the factor "Techniques" (Factor A) is having significant effect on UPD resulted into rejecting the null hypothesis. Accordingly, the next stage is the test of means to check whether the difference between any pair of treatment means is significant at a given confidence level. This stage is performed using Duncan's multiple range test.

Now, the steps that are carried out for this test are as follows.

1. Arranging the means in the ascending order of their respective values as shown in Table 3.
2. Calculation of the standard error of each average:

$$S = (^{MSE}/n)^{1/2}$$

Where:
- MSE is mean sum of square error from ANOVA (i.e. MSE= 210.85)
- n is the sample size (i.e. n= 200)

Thus S= $(210.85/200)^{1/2}$ = 1.027

3. Finding the critical value $q_\alpha(k, v)$ from the table of significant ranges [4]

Where:
- α is the significance level
- k the number of means being compared, and all means in-between (k=2,3)
- v is the degrees of freedom for error from the ANOVA table.

Accordingly, the critical values are: $q_{0.05}(2,200) = 3.687$ and $q_{0.05}(3,200) = 3.843$

4. Calculating the value of the least significant range (R_k):

$$R_k = q_\alpha(k, v) * S \tag{7}$$

Accordingly, the least significant ranges are:

$R_2 = q_{0.05}(2,200) * S = 3.787$

$R_3 = q_{0.05}(3,200) * S = 3.947$

(8)

Calculating the actual differences between the different pairs of means and comparing them with the corresponding least significant ranges. the actual differences between the different pairs of means are:

$A_3 - A_2 = 33.03 > R_3$

$A_3 - A_1 = 31.61 > R_2$

$A_1 - A_2 = 1.42 < R_2$

Table 3. Ordering of mean values

Technique	Mean Symbol	Mean Value	Order
Hierarchical-Concentrate	A1	6.38	2
P2P- Concentrate	A2	4.96	1
Roam	A3	37.99	3

Duncan's test results. According to the previous analysis it can be concluded that there are significant differences between two pairs of means. The remaining pair is not significantly different. Accordingly, one can come to the following conclusions:

- The Roam propagation technique (corresponding to the mean value: A3 = 37.99) performs most badly than the other two techniques, which are Hierarchical-Concentrate (corresponding to the mean value: A1 = 6.38) and P2P-Concentrate (corresponding to the mean value: A2 = 4.96).
- There is no significant difference between Hierarchical-Concentrate and P2P-Concentrate techniques.
- P2P-Concentrate technique (corresponding to the mean value: A2 = 4.96) performs better than Hierarchical-Concentrate (corresponding to the mean value: A1 = 6.38), but this in the case that the ordering process can be performed at any peer and then delegated from a peer to another peer.

Since there is no significant difference between Hierarchical-Concentrate and P2P-Concentrate, we conclude that the Hierarchical-Concentrate technique can be used mainly for propagating updates within the same master area in order to perform the ordering process in a hierarchical manner. This achieves fair conflict resolution for all updates that are generated on the lower levels by delegating the responsibility of the resolution to the server in the higher level, while we use the P2P-Concentrate technique for propagating updates between the master areas, since there is no higher level than the master area. In this case, the ordering process is performed in a peer-to-peer manner in that each peer orders the merged updates (i.e. the received updates in addition to its generated updates), and then delegates the responsibility of ordering to the other peers.

Comparison with N-ary Tree Based Updates Propagation Protocol

The purpose of this comparison is to determine which mode of extension (that characterizes the propagation protocol) is suitable for LMDDBSs in that it achieves lower values of UPD. The extension here refers to the method that the propagation protocol follows for accommodating new replicas and servicing them through providing them with recent updates in the case of the replication system scales up in terms of its size and the number of replicas. Two modes of extensions are compared, which are: vertical extension that characterizes N-ary Tree Based Propagation Protocol (NTPP) and horizontal extension that characterizes Wheel-Based Propagation Protocol (WPP). The vertical extension requires adding new replicas to the last level of the N-ary tree or placing them in new levels in the case of the last level is full (i.e. there are no empty places for accommodating new replicas). The horizontal extension implies creating new propagation wheels when the replication system covers new distant areas. The vertical extension also characterizes the other tree based protocols. However, here we concern on comparing with NTPP because it is the most recent. Moreover, same conclusions are applied for the other tree based protocols. In this comparison, the worst case is assumed for both protocols. For NTPP, this case implies that MHj (the host that receives updates occurred in MHi) exists in the last level, while MHi (where update occurred) exists in the root of the tree as this protocol implies. For WPP, the worst case implies that both MHi and MHj exist in the last level of the propagation wheel (most outer rim) and the location of MHj is assumed in the last cell. Hierarchical-Concentrate propagation technique is considered for propagation updates between the different propagation wheels, since it is equivalent to P2P-Concenterate in the case of the number of propagation wheels is greater than 1. We assume the propagation technique that is used in NTPP is Top-Down propagation according to its characteristics. Based on the worst case, the number of hops that is imposed by NTPP for propagating an update from the root of the tree to a host in the last level is L -2, where L is the number of levels of N-ary tree. In contrast, in WPP, the number of hops that are required for propagating an update from MHi to MHj in another cell is fixed (as proved above), which equals 5 in the case of the number of master servers is 1 and the number of zones is greater than or equals 2. For the sake of equivalent conditions for both NTPP and WPP, we assume that the number of propagation wheels increases as the levels of N-ary tree increase. This means that each propagation wheel is equivalent to a certain number of levels of N-ary tree. Accordingly, the number of propagation wheels is varied by considering the following cases:

- 1 propagation wheel is equivalent to 4 levels of N-ary tree.
- 1 propagation wheel is equivalent to 5 levels of N-ary tree.
- 1 propagation wheel is equivalent to 6 levels of N-ary tree.
- 1 propagation wheel is equivalent to 7 levels of N-ary tree.

This variation is based on the aforementioned characteristic of the WPP that it extends in a horizontal manner as the replication system covers new areas, while NTPP extends in a vertical manner to encompass new hosts. By considering this variation, UPD values for each case of the above four cases are calculated based on the following equations:

- For NTPP:

$UDP = L-2$

Where L is the number of levels (9)

- For WPP:

$$UDP= 4+m \quad (10)$$

Where m is the number of propagation wheels as in equation 1 and 2 for measuring UPD for both Hierarchical-Concentrate and P2P-Concentrate (Note that one propagation wheel means one master server).

Based on the calculated values of UPD for both protocols, the following conclusions can be reached which are shown in Figure 3.

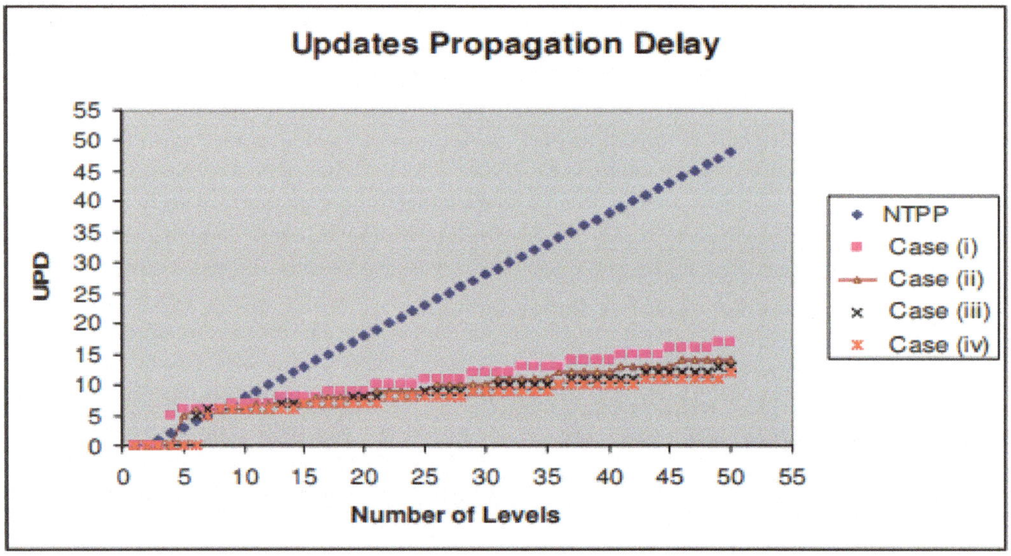

Figure 3. Comparison of the NTPP and the four cases of WPP based on the Updates Propagation Delay for the worst case.

In Figure 3, NTPP has higher values for UPD than WPP for any case of the four cases when the number of levels gets higher. The value of this metric is slightly higher in case (i) than the other three cases when the number of levels gets higher. Also, it is slightly higher in case (ii) than the other two cases (i.e. case (iii) and case (iv)), and it is slightly higher in case (iii) than case (iv). This means that when the number of levels that are represented by one propagation wheel increases, the values of UPD get lower. Accordingly, the horizontal extension of WPP affects the value of UPD with a small amount of increasing (i.e. equals to 1) when a new wheel is constructed, while the vertical extension of NTPP increases the value of UPD with amount that is proportional to the number of new levels. Thus, the horizontal exertion is more suitable for LMDDBSs, since these systems extend by covering new areas. Moreover, placing new hosts of those areas in the last level of the N-ary tree is not reasonable due to the large values of UPD that are resulted by sending updates to these new hosts.

REPLICATION METHOD

The replication method is based on a new type of software agent called Instance-Immigration-Removed Agent (IIRA) that is introduced in this research. The research chose this name according to IIRA working nature, since it creates an instance of itself, and this instance migrates to another host and performs its task before removing itself. The purpose of the instance is to propagate recent updates that occurred or are collected in one level to another level in the replication architecture.

The following definition formally defines IIRA. Definition 3. IIRA is a 5-tuple < I, D, T, S, U>, where:

$I = \{i_1, \ldots, i_n\}$ is a finite set of instructions that are required to perform IIRA tasks.

$D = \{d_1, d_2, d_3, d_4\}$ is a finite set of data structures that are involved in propagating recent updates between the components of the replication architecture, and collecting recent updates from underlying levels.

$T= \{t1, t_2, t_3, t_4\}$ is a finite set of IIRA types. A type ti maps each IIRA to a certain level (i.e. the type determines the location of IIRA).

$S = \{s_1, s_2, s_3, s_4, s_5, s_6\}$ is a finite set of IIRA states. Each state represents the current activity that is carried out by IIRA.

$U: T \rightarrow \{1, 2, 3, \ldots, k\}$ is a function for assigning a unique identifier for IIRA in the system.

According to this definition, the IIRA consists of code and database and it has type, state, and unique identifier.

IIRA Types. The paper divides IIRA into four types according to the level in which the IIRA carries out its activities. The four types share common structure and behavior, but they inhabit different levels. These types are as follows

- MH-Resident IIRA (MHR-IIRA). Every MH has IIRA, and it is responsible for propagating recent updates that are performed on MH to the other hosts in the mobile network or to the cell server that covers the cell where the MH is located at the time of connection.
- Cell Server-Resident IIRA (CSR-IIRA). This type acts as a broker for propagating recent updates between the fixed network and the mobile network. It propagates all updates that are received from MHR-IIRA to the zone server and vice versa. It is responsible for providing a unified ordering for all updates that occurred in its cell and maintaining total ordering of messages that are received from the higher level.
- Zone Server-Resident IIRA (ZSR-IIRA). This type receives all updates that are performed in the fixed

network and the mobile network, which are associated with specific zone level, and provides a unified ordering for these updates on this level. Then, it propagates these updates directly to the master server. Also, this type provides underlying cell servers with a set of totally ordered updates that is received from the master server.

- Master Server-Resident IIRA (MSR-IIRA). This type receives all updates that are performed in the zone level and provides a total unified ordering for all updates occurred in the replication system. Then, it propagates these ordered updates directly to each zone server, which in turn propagates these updates to underlying levels.

IIRA states. The possible states for IIRA are monitoring the connection with the other hosts, retrieving the set of recent updates, creating the instance, migration of the instance to the host that the connection is realized with it, execution of the instance on the other host, and removing the instance after completion of its task.

IIRA-based Propagation System

The purpose of this system is to implement the proposed propagation protocol through automating the propagation of updates between the components of the replication architecture in a manner that ensures bounding unavailability of recent updates and inconsistency of replicated data. The IIRA-Based propagation system (see Figure 4) is composed of the four types of IIRA. Each type interacts with the other types through a synchronization process in which two types exchange their recent updates via their created instances of IIRA. In this system, each type can exchange updates directly with the same type or a different type in the server of the level where it inhabits or in a server from underlying level. For example, MHR-IIRA can exchange updates directly with CSR-IIRA or another MHR-IIRA, while MHR-IIRA cannot directly interact with either ZSR-IIRA or MSR-IRRA.

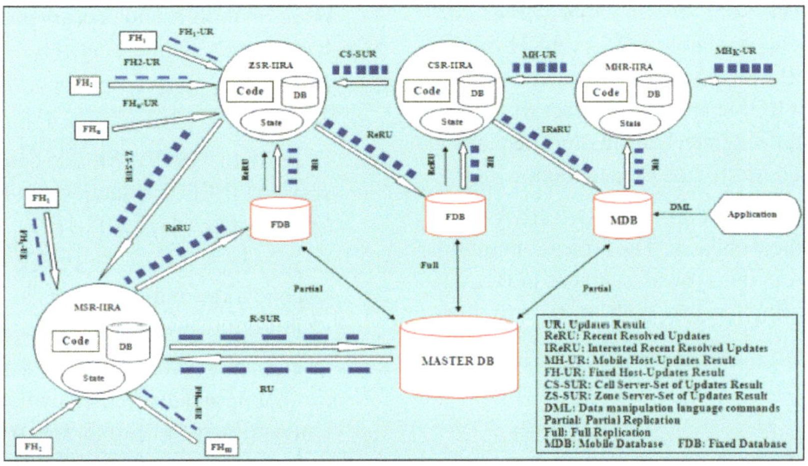

Figure 4. IIRA-Based propagation system.

When the connection takes place between any two IIRA types, an instance of IIRA type that inhabits the lower level will propagate a set of recent updates called Updates-Result (UR), which is produced by an application, in addition to updates that may have been collected from the underlying level to the database of IIRA type that inhabits the higher level. Then, an instance of the type that inhabits the higher level propagates a set of updates called Recent-Resolved-Updates (ReRU) that is received from the higher level to the replicated database in the lower level. Accordingly, IIRA has different responsibilities for updates propagation with respect to implementing the three basic mechanisms of updates propagation (Bottom-Up Propagation, Top-Down Propagation, and Peer-to-Peer Propagation). These responsibilities are identified in the following subsection.

IIRA Responsibilities for Updates Propagation The responsibilities of IIRA can be identified according to the mechanism of the propagation as follows. Bottom-Up Propagation: In this type, each MHR-IIRA propagates the set of recent updates (MH-UR) that occurred in its host to the database of the type that inhabits a cell server. Also, each server's IIRA collects the received recent updates from underlying level in addition to its server's updates-result in a set called Set of Updates Result (SUR), and resolves updates conflict through ordering updates in this set, and then propagates this set to the database of IIRA in the higher level.

The typical operations that are involved in this propagation, which are performed by IIRA are:

- Resolving updates conflict through ordering the collected updates, which are stored on the database of the IIRA type that inhabits the host in the current level.
- Creating the instance and filling it with the ordered updates.
- Migration of the instance to the host that exists in the higher level.
- Execution of the instance in the destination host through insertion of recent updates in its IIRA type's database.

Thus, this propagation takes place in the servers that exist in the fixed network when IIRA orders the collected updates. Then, the ordered updates are shipped via the created instance to the host in the higher level. This means that updates are pushed from a level to the higher level in a unicasting manner where each host pushes them to a single host in the higher level. Updates occurred on mobile hosts are pushed to cell servers when the connection occurs.

Top-Down Propagation: In this type, each server's IIRA propagates the set of recent resolved updates (ReRU) that is received from the higher level to the lower level. For example, each ZSR-IIRA propagates the ReRU that is received from the master server to underlying cell servers and in turn each cell server propagates a subset of this set called Interested-Recent Resolved-Updates (IReRU) to underlying mobile hosts. IReRU represents the set of updates that are performed on the data items that are replicated on mobile hosts. The typical operations that are performed by IIRA for carrying out this propagation are:

- Creating the instance and storing the set of recent resolved updates on it. |
- Migration of the instance to the host that exists in the lower level.
- Execution of the instance on the destination host.

Thus, for a given set of updates, this propagation takes place when these updates are totally ordered (i.e. resolved) by MSR-IIRA. The ordered updates (i.e. ReRU) are then propagated through the instance to the underlying level. The MS pushes ReRU to all available zone servers through sending the same instance to each zone server. Similarly, the zone server does same pushing to its underlying available cell servers. However, the cell servers push ReRU only to connected MHs, while disconnected MHs pull ReRU when they connect to the cell servers. According to this pushing mechanism, this mechanism of propagation can be called Multi-cast Propagation.

Peer-to-Peer Propagation: In this type, two IIRA of the same type may exchange their updates. The typical operations that are performed by IIRA in this type are same as in Bottom-Up propagation with a distinction that both hosts, which are involved in the synchronization process inhabit the same level and have same type.

CONCLUSIONS

This paper presented a data replication strategy for maintaining the eventual consistency of replicated data in large scale mobile distributed database systems with large number of updates. The strategy encompassed three-level replication architecture, wheel-based updates propagation protocol, and the replication method as a ternary combination that is needed to act in accordance with the characteristics of such systems. The strategy supports frequent disconnections and mobility of hosts by enabling the users to perform their updates in a disconnected mode and then synchronizing their updates with the higher levels. The effectiveness of the proposed strategy with respect to updates propagation is verified through the comparative study with Roam replication system, which represents one of the fewer replication systems that are devoted to large scale mobile environments. The results revealed that the proposed strategy achieves better propagation delay than Roam replication system. The better propagation delay represents an essential feature that characterizes scalable replication strategies with regard to updates propagation to all replicas. Also, the proposed updates propagation protocol is compared with N-ary tree based propagation protocol, which represents one of the most recent tree based propagation protocols. The results showed that the horizontal extension provided by the proposed protocol is more suitable than the vertical extension for LMDDBSs, since such type of systems is extended to cover new geographic areas. Moreover, placing new hosts of those areas in a tree structure with a variable number of levels as in N-ary tree based propagation protocol is not reasonable due to the large values of updates propagation delay that are resulted by sending updates to the new hosts, especially when they are placed in either the last level of the tree or a new established level. As a part of our future research, a plan will be provided to develop the required specifications, tools, and interfaces to implement the proposed strategy in large-scale mobile healthcare environments to provide healthcare practitioners with an efficient access to updates that are performed on healthcare data.

REFERENCES

1. Helal, A. Heddaya and B. Bhargava, (1996) "Replication techniques in distributed systems", Kluwer Academic Publishers.
2. Waluyo, B. Srinivasan and D. Taniar, (2005) "Research in mobile database query optimization and processing", Mobile Information Systems, 1(4), 225–252.
3. B. Nishio and M. Tsukamoto, (2002) "Data management issues in mobile and peer-to-peer environments", Data & Knowledge Engineering, 41(2–3), 183–204.
4. D.C. Montgomery, (1991) "Design and analysis of experiments", 3rd edition, John wiley & Sons.
5. D. Barbara, (1999) "Mobile computing and databases – a survey", IEEE Transactions on Knowledge and Database Engineering, 11(1), 108-117.
6. D. Ratner, P. Reiher, G. Popek and G. Kuenning, (2001) "Replication requirements in mobile environments", Mobile Networks and Applications 6(6), 525–533.
7. D. Ratner, (1998) "Roam: a scalable replication system for mobile and distributed computing", PhD Dissertation, University of California, Los Anglos.
8. D. Ratner, P. Reiher and G. Popek, (2004), "Roam: a scalable replication system for mobility", Mobile Network and Applications, 9(5), 537-544.
9. D. Zhiming, M. Xiaofeng and W. Shan, (2002) "A transactional asynchronous replication scheme for mobile database systems", Journal of Computer Science and Technology, 17(4), 389 – 396.
10. G. Sushant, and R. Buyya, (2006). "Data replication strategies in wide-area distributed systems", Chapter IX of Enterprise Service Computing: From Concept to Deployment, IGI Global, pp. 211-241.
11. H. Yu and A. Vahdat, (2000) "Design and evaluation of a continuous consistency model for replicated services", In proceedings of the 4th Symposium on Operating Systems Design and Implementation (OSDI), San Diego, CA, USA, pp. 305–318.
12. J.Abawajy, M. Deris and M. Omer, (2006) "A novel data replication and management protocol for mobile computing systems", Mobile Information Systems, 2(1), pp. 3-19.
13. J. Holliday, D. Agrawal and A. Abbadi, (2002) "Disconnection modes for mobile databases", Wireless Networks 8(4), pp. 391-402.
14. J. Monteiro, A. Brayner and S. Lifschitz, (2007) "A Mechanism for replicated data consistency in mobile computing environments", In Proceedings of the ACM

symposium on Applied computing, Seoul, Korea, 914 – 919.

15. J.P. Barreto, (2003) "Information sharing in mobile networks: a survey on replication strategies", Technical Report RT/015/03, Instituto Superior T´ecnico, Lisboa.
16. M. Stonebraker, (1979) "Concurrency control and consistency of multiple copies of data in distributed INGRES", IEEE Transactions on Software Engineering, SE-5, pp. 188–194.
17. N. Tolia, M. Satyanarayanan and A. Wolbach, (2007) "Improving mobile database access over wide-area networks without degrading consistency", In Proceedings of the 5th international conference on Mobile systems, applications and services, San Juan, Puerto Rico, pp. 71 – 84.
18. P.A. Bernstein, V. Hadzilacos and N. Goodman, (1987) "Concurrency control and recovery in database systems", Addison-Wesley.
19. S. Madria and S. Bhowdrick, (2001) "Mobile data management", Potentials, IEEE, 20(4), pp. 11 – 15.
20. S. Phatak and B. Nath, (2004) "Transaction-Centric reconciliation in disconnected Client-Server databases", Journal of Mobile Networks and Applications, 9(5), pp. 459–471.
21. S.R. Terry, (1983) "Stronger than a hundred men: a history of the vertical water wheel", Johns Hopkins University Press.
22. T. Connolly and C.E. Begg, (2004) "Database systems: a practical approach to design, implementation and management", 4th edition, Addison-Wesley.
23. T. Ekenstam, C. Matheny, P. Reiher and G. Popek, (2001) "The bengal database replication system", Distributed and Parallel Databases, 9(3), 187-210.
24. T. Imielinksi and B. Badrinath, (1994) "Wireless mobile computing: challenges in data management", Communications of ACM, 37(10), 18-28.
25. T. Hara, M. Nakadori, W. Uchida, K. Maeda, and S. Nishio, (2005) "Update propagation based on tree structure in peer-to-peer networks", In proceedings of AICCSA, pp. 40–48.
26. T. Ozsu and P. Valduriez, (1999) "Principles of distributed database systems", 2nd Edition, Prentice-Hall.
27. T. Watanabe, T. Hara, Y. Kido and S. Nishio, (2007) "An update propagation strategy for delay reduction and node failure tolerance in peer-to-peer networks", In Proceedings of the 21st IEEE International Conference on Advanced Information Networking and Applications Workshops (AINAW'07), pp. 103-108.
28. T. Watanabe, K. Akimitsu, T. Hara and S. Nishio, (2008) "An update propagation strategy considering access frequency in peer-to-peer networks", DASFAA 2008, LNCS 4947, Springer-Verlag Berlin Heidelberg, pp. 661– 669.
29. Y. Breitbart and H. Korth, (1997) "Replication and consistency: being lazy helps sometimes", In Proceedings of 16 ACM Sigact/Sigmod Symposium on the Principles of Database Systems, Tucson, Arizona, 173 – 184.
30. Y. Saito and M. Shapiro, (2005) "Optimistic replication", ACM Computing Surveys, 73(1), pp. 42 - 81.

APPENDIX

1. Proof for equation of Measuring UPD for Hierarchical-Concentrate

Assume that h is the number of hops. The following cases are considered:

a. If $c=1 \rightarrow h=1$

b. If $c=2 \rightarrow h=3$

This is because if $c = 2$, this implies existing of one zone server according to our assumption that two or more cell servers need a zone server for resolving their conflicts.

Thus, $c = 2 \leftrightarrow z = 1$

c. If $z = 2 \rightarrow h=5$

Also, if $z= 2$, this implies existing of one master server for resolving their conflicts.

Thus, $z = 2 \leftrightarrow m=1$

d. For $m \geq 2$, we use mathematical induction as follows:

If $m=2 \rightarrow h=6$

This is because updates should be propagated in P2P manner in case of existing more than one master server since there is no higher level than the master level in our strategy. Update conflicts are resolved by delegating the responsibility of resolving to the next peer.

Accordingly, the If $m = k \rightarrow h=k+4$

Thus, if $m = k + 1 \rightarrow h=(k+1)+4$

2. Proof for equation of measuring UPD for P2P-CONCENTRATE

By using mathematical induction and assuming h is the number of hops, we consider the following cases.

a. MHi and MHj in the same cell

If $n=2 \rightarrow h=0$ (There are no hops between MHi and MHj)

If $n=3 \rightarrow h=1$

Accordingly, If $n=k \rightarrow h=k-2$

Since the equation holds for $n=k$, this implies that:

If $n=k+1 \rightarrow h= (k- 2) +1= (k+1)-2$

b. MH_i and MH_j in different cells in the same zone

If $c=2 \rightarrow h=2$

If $c=k \rightarrow h=k$

Thus, if $c= k+1 \rightarrow h=k+1$

c. MH_i and MH_j in different zones in the same master area

If $z=2 \rightarrow h=4$

If $z=k \rightarrow h=k+2$

Thus, if $z= k+1 \rightarrow h= (k+1) +2$

d. MH_i and MH_j in different master areas

The proof is performed in same manner as above.

CHAPTER 3

ON DEFERRED CONSTRAINTS IN DISTRIBUTED DATABASE SYSTEMS

Yousef J. Al-Houmaily

Department of Computer and Information Programs, Institute of Public Administration, Riyadh, Saudi Arabia

ABSTRACT

An atomic commit protocol (ACP) is a distributed algorithm used to ensure the atomicity property of transactions in distributed database systems. Although ACPs are designed to guarantee atomicity, they add a significant extra cost to each transaction execution time. This added cost is due to the overhead of the required coordination messages and log writes at each involved database site to achieve atomicity. For this reason, the continuing research efforts led to a number of optimizations that reduce the aforementioned cost. The most commonly adopted optimizations in the database standards and commercial database management systems are those designed around the early release of read locks of transactions. In this type of optimizations, certain participating sites may start releasing the read locks held by transactions before they are fully terminated across all participants. Hence, greatly enhancing concurrency among executing transactions and, consequently, the overall system performance. However, this type of optimizations introduces possible "execution infections" in the presence of deferred consistency constraints; a devastating complication that may lead to non-serializable executions of transactions. Thus, this type of optimizations could be considered useless, given the importance of preserving the consistency of the database in presence of deferred constraints, unless this complication is resolved in a practical and efficient manner. This is the essence of the "unsolicited deferred consistency constraints validation" mechanism presented in this paper.

INTRODUCTION

Preserving the atomicity property of transactions at the local level of individual database sites is not sufficient in a distributed database system. This is because a distributed transaction might end up committing at some participating sites and aborting at others due to a site or a communication failure. This jeopardizes global atomicity and, consequently, the consistency of the entire database. For this reason, an atomic commit protocol (ACP) has to be used in any distributed database system.

An ACP is essentially a distributed synchronization algorithm that guarantees a unanimous and deterministic

Citation: Al-Houmaily Y. (2013), "On Deferred Constraints in Distributed Database Systems", International Journal of Database Management Systems (IJDMS) Vol.5, No.6, December 2013, DOI: 10.5121/ijdms.2013.5601

final outcome for each distributed transaction. This outcome represents either the execution of a transaction as a whole, across all participating sites, or none at all. ACPs, such as the basic two-phase commit (2PC) [1, 2] or one of its widely known variants (see [3, 4] for surveys of the most common 2PC variants and optimizations), ensure atomicity but with a significant extra cost added to each transaction execution time. This added cost is due to the overhead of the required coordination messages and log writes at each involved database site to achieve atomicity. To minimize the adverse effects of this overhead on the overall system performance, there is a continuing interest in developing more efficient ACPs and optimizations, albeit for different distributed database system environments with inherently different characteristics. These include main memory databases (e.g., [5]), mobile and ad hoc networks (e.g., [6, 7, 8]), real-time databases (e.g., [9, 10, 11]) and component-based architectures (e.g., [12]); besides traditional distributed database systems (e.g., [3, 13]). One of the most notable results of these continuing efforts is a type of optimizations in which transactions are allowed to release their read locks at certain participants before they have fully terminated across all participants. An example to this type of optimizations is the (traditional) read-only optimization [14]. This optimization is considered one of the most pronounced optimizations and is currently part of the distributed database standards [15]. In this optimization, an exclusively read-only participant in a transaction execution terminates the transaction and releases the read locks held on behalf of the transaction before the transaction has fully terminated at the update participants. Hence, this early release of read locks at readonly participants significantly enhances concurrency among executing transactions and, consequently, the overall system performance. This is especially important considering that read-only transactions (i.e., retrieval transactions that do not contain any update operations) are the majority of executing transactions in any general database management system. The performance enhancement of the read-only optimization on the overall system performance has been addressed in a number of simulation studies (e.g., [4, 16]) although basic analytical evaluations can still reveal the fact of enhanced performance using this optimization (e.g., [14]). In spite of the significance of the above type of optimizations on the overall performance of distributed database systems, its applicability is curtailed due to the fact that it may lead to nonserializable executions of transactions. This is a devastating possibility which could occur whenever transactions are allowed to continue to execute at some participants, acquiring further locks, after they have already terminated at others [15, 17]. These possible infected executions of transactions at individual participating sites cannot be captured by any (local) concurrency control mechanism without a sort of an additional global synchronization mechanism among all involved participating sites. Furthermore, these infected executions could occur not only in the context of the more general non-request/response processing paradigm, but also in the context of the simpler, widely accepted and standardized request/response paradigm where each operation processing request is acknowledged [15]. In the context of the latter paradigm, infected executions of transactions arise when the ACP used in the system incorporates an optimization that is designed around the early release of read locks and, at the same time, consistency constraints are allowed to be evaluated in deferred mode. This mode for evaluating consistency constraints is currently part of the SQL (Structured Query Language) standards [18] and is defined to enhance performance, in certain situations, and to resolve some applicability limitations of consistency constraints, in others. When this mode is used, a transaction may need to acquire further locks at its commit time/point (i.e., the time/point at which the transaction issues its final commit DCL (Data Control Language) statement). While the transaction is still executing at some participants to evaluate deferred constraints, it may terminate and start releasing its read locks at others, using the above type of optimizations, providing an opportunity for possible execution infections. Thus, to benefit from any optimization that is designed around the early release of read locks in the presence of deferred consistency constraints, the above possible infections have to be eliminated in a practical and efficient manner. This is the essence of the "unsolicited deferred consistency constraints validation" (UDCCV) mechanism presented in this paper. UDCCV is designed to detect the above possible execution infections during the execution of individual transactions and, once detected, UDCCV prohibit each susceptible transaction from being infected by disallowing it from using any early read lock release optimization at commit time. Thus, UDCCV allows for the use of both deferred constraints as well as early read lock release optimizations in the system without penalizing those transactions that are not susceptible to execution infections. In UDCCV, this is accomplished through the use of an inexpensive piggybacking of control information in the messages exchanged among involved sites during the course of the execution of each transaction (before the transaction reaches its final commit point). The rest of this paper is structured as follows. First, Section 2 discusses consistency constraints and highlights their impotence on performance and applicability. Section 2 also explains, through an example, the two operating modes of consistency constraints: immediate and deferred, and explains the differences between them. Then, Section 3 thoroughly explains execution infections in the presence of deferred consistency constraints. After that, Section 4 presents the UDCCV mechanism. Lastly, Section 5 summaries this paper and provides some concluding remarks.

HIGHLIGHTS OF CONSISTENCY CONSTRAINTS

In any organization, data is governed by predefined set of rules called consistency constraint (data integrity) rules. These rules are extracted by data administrators or application developers from the business rules of the organization and used to ensure the quality of data. Consistency constraints could be managed (i.e., both checked and enforced) at the application level or at the database management system level. One of the most important advantages of managing consistency constraints at the database management system level is that it relieves application programmers from performing this tedious, slow and error-prone task at their application level once defined within the database management system. Relational database management systems allow for the definition of certain types of consistency constraints in a declarative manner using SQL. Once defined, the database management system is responsible about their management. In the SQL standards, a consistency constraint can be defined in an immediate or deferred mode. The immediate mode for the management of consistency constraints is the default mode and the most commonly used in practice. In this mode, a consistency constraint is evaluated at the level of each individual SQL DML (Data Manipulation Language) statement that manipulates the data governed by the consistency constraint. If a DML statement of a transaction violates a consistency constraint, the transaction is immediately aborted (i.e., rolled-back).

Deferred Constraints

Unlike the immediate mode, when a consistency constraint is defined in deferred mode, it is evaluated at the commit time of the transaction. Thus, the consistency constraint is evaluated at the transaction level instead of each individual DML statement. At commit time of a transaction, all deferred constraints that governs the data manipulated by the transaction are evaluated. If any of the constraints is violated, the transaction is aborted. Otherwise, the transaction is allowed to commit. The SQL standards incorporate the deferred mode for evaluating consistency constraints for two essential reasons:

- erformance: deferred constraints enhance system performance when transactions tend to abort because of users' requests to abort or because of congestion over the system resources (other than the locks on data). Thus, in such systems, by using deferred constraints, the system can avoid wasting computing resources on evaluating consistency constraints at the level of individual DML statements for transactions that will most probably end up aborting before reaching their final commit points. Similarly, system performance is enhanced when inserting (or loading) large amounts of data associated with consistency constraints into the database.
- Applicability: deferred constraints solve the problem of "cyclic consistency constraints" [19]. This problem arises whenever there is a circular chain of referential consistency constraints between two or more relations (i.e., tables). Once exist, it is impossible to insert any tuple (i.e., row or record) into any of the relations unless a method is used to temporarily breaks the chain.

Next, the above two reasons are discussed in further details.

Performance of Deferred Constraints

In deferred mode, any locks that are exclusively needed for the evaluation of a deferred consistency constraint are acquired at commit time of transactions. This is in contrast with immediate constraints where all the locks needed for the execution of a DML statement are acquired during the execution of the DML statement. This includes any exclusively needed locks for the evaluation of the consistency constraint. Thus, there is a clear trade-off between the two modes of consistency constraints. Deferred constraints hold the locks that are exclusively needed to evaluate the constraints for shorter periods of time compared with immediate constraints, allowing for more concurrency in the system. This is besides not wasting any time on evaluating the constraints during the execution of a transaction until the transaction issues its final commit statement. On the other hand, deferred constraints introduce the risk of conflicts among concurrently executing transactions at commit time. This is due to the contention over the locks that are exclusively needed to evaluate the deferred constraints compared with immediate constraints where all needed locks are acquired during execution time (before reaching the final commit point). This increases the possibility of transactions that are associated with deferred constraints to abort at commit time after they have already consumed all the required computing resources for their execution.

Based on the above trade-off, it can concluded that deferred constraints significantly enhance the system performance when transactions tend to abort because of users' requests to abort or because of congestion over the system resources (other than the locks on data). Similarly, system performance is enhanced when loading large amounts of data into the database, delaying the validation of constraints until the loading of the data is completed. Otherwise, immediate constraints are best to use.

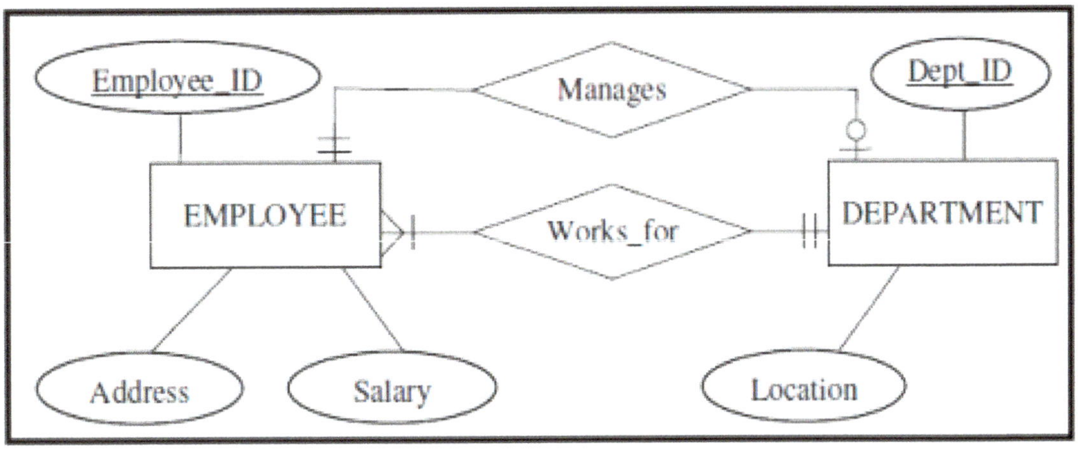

Figure 1. A cyclic consistency constraints example.

Applicability of Deferred Constraints

Consider the ER (Entity-Relationship) diagram shown in Figure 1. The diagram consists of two entities: "Employee" and "Department"; and two relationships between them: "Works_for" and "Manages". The "Works_for" relationship states that "each employee works for one and only one department; and each department is worked for by one or more employees". The "Manages" relationship states that "each employee manages zero or one department; and each department is managed by one and only one (managing) employee". Usually, when transforming the conceptual ER diagram shown in Figure 1 to the relational model, two relations are created: one that corresponds to the "Employee" entity and one that corresponds to the "Department" entity. We also need to observe the cardinality constraints when transforming the two relationships in the ER diagram to the relational model. That is, each employee has to be assigned to an exactly one department and each department has to be assigned to an exactly one (managing) employee. This can be accomplished by placing a "NOT NULL" constraint in the "Dept_ID" field that corresponds to the department for which an employee works, and placing another "NOT NULL" constraint in the "Mgr_ID" field that corresponds to the employee who manages the department, respectively. This is, of course, besides defining two referential consistency constraints: one that ties each employee to a valid department, and one that ties each department to a valid (managing) employee. This leads to the SQL DDL (Data Definition Language) statements shown in Figure 2. Notice that the two referential consistency constraints are added after the two relations are defined. This is because of the presence of a cyclic referential consistency constraints that prohibits the definition of one referential consistency constraint within the definition of one relation before the creation of the second relation, and vice versa.

```
CREATE TABLE Employee(
Emp_ID        INTEGER     PRIMARY KEY,
...
...
Dept_ID       INTEGER     NOT NULL
);

CREATE TABLE Department(
Dept_ID       INTEGER     PRIMARY KEY,
...
...
Mgr_ID        INTEGER     NOT NULL
);

ALTER TABLE Employee ADD CONSTRAINT Emp_FK FOREIGN KEY (Dept_ID)
  REFERENCES Department(Dept_ID) DEFERRABLE INITIALLY IMMEDIATE;

ALTER TABLE Department ADD CONSTRAINT Dept_FK FOREIGN KEY (Mgr_ID)
  REFERENCES Employee(Emp_ID) DEFERRABLE INITIALLY IMMEDIATE;
```

Figure 2. SQL DDL statements for the two relations.

Based on the SQL definitions shown in Figure 2, consider a transaction T that attempts to insert two tuples: one into the EMPLOYEE relation and one into the DEPARTMENT relation, as shown in Figure 3. Such a transaction will be aborted by the system during the execution of its first DML statement (regardless of the order of the two INSERT statements within the transaction). This is because both of the Dept_ID in the EMPLOYEE relation and the Mgr_ID in the DEPARTMENT relation cannot be "NULL", and a tuple in one of the two relations requires the existence of a valid tuple in the other one (according to the rules of referential consistency constraints), and vice versa. That is, if an employee tuple is to be inserted, it has to reference a pre-existing department tuple and, if a department tuple is to be inserted, it has to reference a preexisting (managing) employee tuple. In fact, no transaction can insert any tuples in either of the two relations at all. This dilemma is called "cyclic consistency constraints" and could span any number of relations, and not just two, in its general case.

```
INSERT INTO Employee values(100,..,1);
INSERT INTO Department values(1,..,100);
COMMIT;
```

Figure 3. The two DML statements of transaction T.

The only way to resolve the above dilemma is by breaking the cycle in the consistency constraints such that one of them is delayed (i.e., violated temporarily) until the end of T. This represents the other reason for using deferred consistency constraints. That is, deferred constraints solve the above dilemma by allowing a transaction to delay the validation of some or all the consistency constraints until its commit time. This is, of course, so long as the validation of each constraint that is to be delayed is defined "deferrable" (as shown in the definition of the two referential consistency constraints (i.e., foreign keys) in Figure 2). To defer the validation of a constraint until commit time or to set it back to the immediate mode, the SQL standards provide the statement shown in Figure 4 which can be invoked from within a transaction.

```
SET CONSTRAINTS ConstName DEFERRED | IMMEDIATE
```

Figure 4. SQL statement to set the constraint mode.

Once one of the consistency constraints is set to deferred, the cycle in the consistency constraints is broken. Hence, T can insert an employee tuple and a department tuple, as shown in Figure 5. At commit time of the transaction, all deferred constraints are validated and the transaction is allowed to commit if it does not violate any of them. Otherwise, the transaction is aborted. In our example, only the Dept_ID in the EMPLOYEE relation is validated at commit time and the transaction is allowed to commit. This is because T has already inserted a department tuple that satisfies the foreign key referential consistency constraint in the DEPARTMENT relation before reaching its commit point and this constraint was evaluated in immediate mode (during the INSERT DML statement of the department tuple).

```
SET CONSTRAINTS Emp_FK DEFERRED;
INSERT INTO Employee values(100,..,1);
INSERT INTO Department values(1,..,100);
COMMIT;
```

Figure 5. Breaking the cyclic consistency constraints.

CONSTRAINTS IN DISTRIBUTED DATABASES

The need for deferred constraints in distributed database systems is similar to their need in centralized database systems. However, their use in distributed database systems introduces a significant complication. This complication stems from the fact that any release of locks prior to the full termination of transactions across all participants may introduce non-serializable executions, jeopardizing the consistency of the entire database. This scenario arises when the ACP used incorporates optimizations that are designed around the early release of read locks, which is the case of the majority of current implementations of commercial database management systems. This scenario is thoroughly explained in the next section.

2PC and Early Release of Read Locks

In distributed database systems, once a transaction finishes its execution and issues its final "commit" request, the transaction manager at the site where the transaction was first initiated acts as the coordinator for the termination of the transaction across all participating sites. This is achieved by initiating an ACP such as 2PC. As the name implies, 2PC consists of two phases. These two phases are the voting phase and the decision phase. During the voting phase, the coordinator of a transaction requests all the participants in the execution of the transaction to prepare-to-commit, whereas, during the decision phase, the coordinator either decides to commit the transaction if all the participants are prepared to commit (voted "yes"), or to abort if any participant has decided to abort (voted "no"). On a commit decision, the coordinator sends out commit messages to all participants whereas, on an abort decision, it sends out abort messages to only those (required) participants that are prepared to commit (voted "yes"). When a participant receives a decision, it enforces the decision and sends back an acknowledgment. When a participant receives a prepare-to-commit message for a transaction, it validates the transaction with respect to data consistency. If the transaction can be committed, the participant responds with a "yes" vote. Otherwise, the participant responds with a "no" vote and aborts the transaction, releasing all the resources held by the transaction including the locks held on behalf of the transaction. When the coordinator receives acknowledgments from all the participants that had voted "yes", it forgets the transaction by discarding all information pertaining to the transaction from its protocol table that is kept in main memory. The resilience of 2PC to system and communication failures is achieved by recording the progress of the protocol in the logs of the coordinator and the participants. Specifically, the coordinator of a transaction force-writes a decision record for the transaction prior to sending out its final decision to the participants. Since a forced write of a log record causes a flush of the log onto a stable storage that survives system failures, the final decision is not lost if the coordinator fails. Similarly, each participant force-writes a prepared record before sending its "yes" vote and a decision (i.e., either commit or abort) record before acknowledging a final decision. When the coordinator completes the protocol, it writes a non-forced end record in the volatile portion of its log that is kept in main memory. This record indicates that all (required) participants have received the final decision and none of them will inquire about the transaction's status in the future. Hence, allowing the coordinator to (permanently) forget the transaction, with respect to the 2PC protocol, and to garbage collect the log records of the transaction when necessary.

The Read-Only Optimization

The read-only optimization significantly reduces the cost of 2PC for read-only transactions. This is because any exclusively read-only participant, a participant that has not performed any updates to data at its site on behalf of a transaction, can be completely excluded from the decision phase of the transaction. Specifically, in this optimization, when a read-only participant in the execution of a transaction receives a prepare-to-commit message, it simply releases all the locks held by the transaction and responds with a "read-only" vote (instead of a "yes" vote). This vote means that the transaction has read consistent data and the participant does not need to be involved in the second phase of the protocol because it does not matter whether the transaction is finally committed or aborted. Consequently, this optimization allows each read-only participant to terminate and to release all the resources held by the transaction, including the read-locks, earlier than its update counterparts and without having to write any log records. This represents the essence of the traditional readonly optimization [14].

```
T1: r(x) w(y) commit
T2: w(x) w(c) commit
```

Figure 6. Two representative executing transactions.

Dangers of Early Release of Locks

The significance of the read-only optimization on the overall system performance is faced with the possibility of execution infections in the presence of deferred constraints. This possibility arises even if each participant deploys strict two-phase locking (S2PL) for concurrency control, the one that guarantees serializability in distributed database systems and the de facto concurrency control mechanism in the industry. In fact, any optimization that terminates a transaction at some participants while the transaction is still executing at others, acquiring further locks, may lead to execution infections. This represents a major complication that may jeopardize the consistency of the entire database if not resolved in a practical manner. To illustrate execution infections and their possible consequences, consider two transactions: T_1 and T_2 that contain read (r) and write (w) operations. Each transaction also contains a final commit request, as shown in Figure 6. Assume that the data items (y) and (c) are located at one participant (P_1) and data item (x) is located at another participant (P_2). Furthermore, assume that (y) is associated with a deferred consistency constraint that has to examine the value of (c) for consistency before any transaction that modifies (y) can commit. One possible execution scenario for the two transactions is shown in Figure 7. In the figure, each operation (Op) of a transaction (T) submitted to a participant (P) is represented as (OpP_ID, T_ID (data_item)) and when an operation pertaining to a transaction is executed successfully at a participant, it is acknowledged (AckP_ID, T_ID) by the participant. In this transaction execution scenario, T_1 executes its first operation at P2 and then its second operation at P_1. Once the two operations of T_1 are executed and acknowledged, the coordinator initiates 2PC for T_1. Participant P_2 of T_1 is read-only and releases the read lock that it holds on behalf of T_1 when it receives the prepare (PrepP_ID, T_ID) message. It also sends a "read-only" vote (ROP_ID, T_ID) to the coordinator in response to the prepare message. Participant P1 does not receive the prepare message of T1 until some latter time (possibly due to queuing or communication delays). Meanwhile, T_2 starts executing and changes the released data (x) of T_1 at P_2. Thus, T_2 is "serialized after" T_1 at P_2 ($T_1 \rightarrow T_2$). T_2 also changes (c) prior to T_1 had the chance to examining it at P1 (according to the consistency constraint that is placed on (y)). After the commitment of T_2 at both participants, P1 receives the delayed prepare message of T_1 and acquires a read lock on (c) to evaluate the deferred constraint associated with (y) that T_1 has modified during the course of its execution. Then, P_1 proceeds with the commit processing of T_1. Thus, T_2 is "serialized before" T_1 at P1 ($T_2 \rightarrow T_1$). By merging the two local schedules, this scenario results in a global schedule that is not serializable ($T_1 \rightarrow T_2 \rightarrow T_1$), although local serializability is preserved at each participant.

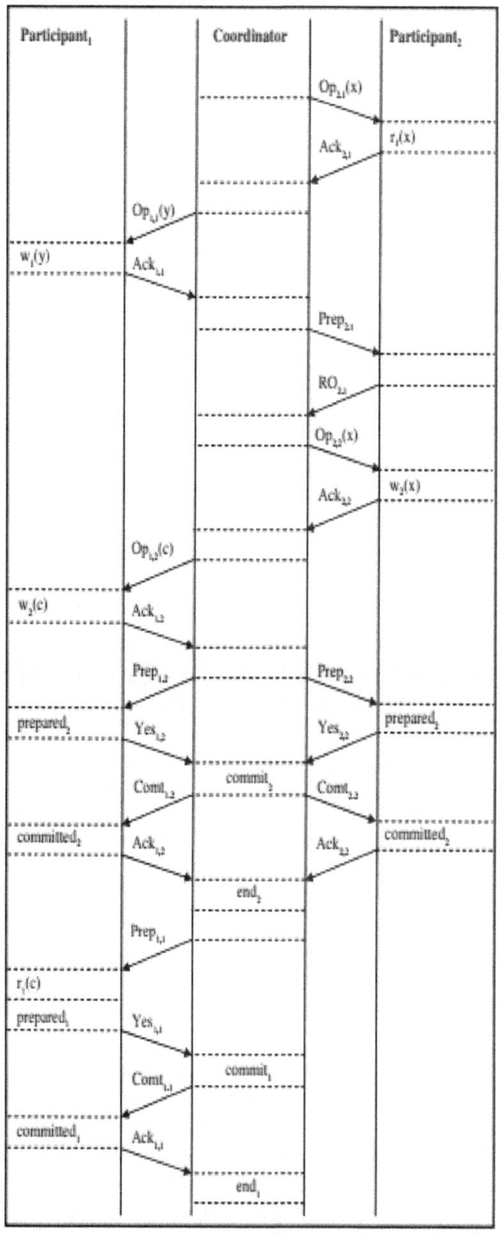

Figure 7. An example to an infected execution.

The above possible execution infection could happen not only with the read-only optimization but with any optimization designed around the early release of read locks before a transaction is fully terminated across all participants. Consequently, as this type of optimizations has been shown to significantly enhance system performance and so widely popular in the implementation of commercial database management systems, there is an absolute necessity for a mechanism that is able to detect and to prohibit scenarios similar to the one above from occurring. This is the essence of the unsolicited deferred consistency constraint validation mechanism.

THE UDCCV MECHANISM

As explained in the previous section, when deferred constraints are used in conjunction with optimizations designed around the early release of read locks, there are possibilities for execution infections. These infections may occur because the time at which a transaction terminates and starts releasing its read locks at some participants is not the same as the time it terminates at the other participants. This creates a different termination time/point for the same transaction at different participants, providing an opportunity for execution infections. Consequently, this difference in termination time is called infection prone time period and is formally stated as follows:

Definition: The infection prone time period is the time period between the earliest terminating time of a transaction at one participant and the latest terminating time of the same transaction at another participant. To exclude the possibility of execution infections, the infection prone time period has to be eliminated, disallowing any further locking between the earliest terminating time at one participant and the latest terminating time at another participant. This can be accomplished by prohibiting the use of either any optimization that is designed around the early release of read locks, or deferred consistency constraints. The first approach makes the earliest terminating time of a transaction at any participant to be the same as the latest terminating time for the same transaction at any other participant; whereas, the second approach makes the latest terminating time of a transaction at any participant to be the same as the earliest terminating time for the same transaction at any other participant. In other words, regardless of which approach is used, the termination time of each transaction will be the same across all participants. However, neither of these two approaches are acceptable from performance point of view. This is because both of them deprive the system of the anticipated performance enhancement gain. Not only that, but the second approach also deprives the system of a solution to a consistency constraint applicability limitation, as explained in Section 2.1.2. A third approach that also eliminates the infection prone time period is also visible. In this approach, all exclusively needed locks for the evaluation of deferred constraints are acquired during the execution of individual DML statements and postponing the (actual) validation process of deferred constraints until commit time of transactions. This approach enhances system performance by not performing the actual validation of deferred constraints until the end of transactions but reduces the level of concurrency among executing transactions. This is because it leads to the holding of the locks exclusively needed for the evaluation of deferred constraints, unnecessarily, from the time that a DML statement is executed until the termination time of the transaction. Thus, all the three approaches above fall short of providing the full anticipated benefits of deferred constraints and, at the same time, the optimizations designed around the early release of read locks, motivating the design of the UDCCV mechanism. Unlike the first two approaches above, UDCCV eliminates the infection prone time period on a per transaction basis and not on the system design level. That is, UDCCV allows for optimizations that are designed around the early release of read locks to co-exist with deferred constraints and resolves any possible execution infections on a per transaction basis. More specifically, in UDCCV, when a participant executes an operation pertaining to a transaction and the operation is associated with a deferred consistency constraint that needs to be validated at commit time of the transaction, the participant sends an UDCCV flag as part of the operation acknowledgment message. When the coordinator of the transaction receives such a message from a participant, it means that the transaction may need to acquire further locks at the participant at commit processing time. In this way, the coordinator, with the help of the participant, can detect possible execution infections at the participant and it has to prohibit it from occurring at commit processing time of the transaction. At the commit time of a transaction (i.e., when the transaction issues its final commit statement), the coordinator knows which participants have executed operations associated with deferred consistency constraints. If any participant has executed such an operation, the coordinator needs to prohibit the possibility of execution infections. This is accomplished by sending an UDCCV flag as part of each prepare message that the coordinator sends to each participant not aware of the possible execution infections. Notice that more than participant may have already sent UDCCV flags during the execution of the transaction as they have deferred constraints to be validated at their sites at commit time of the transaction. Thus, these participants are already aware of possible execution infections and do not need to be informed about this possibility. When a participant receives a prepare message with an UDCCV flag for a transaction, the participant becomes aware of possible execution infections. Based on that, the participant continues to hold all the locks, including the read-only ones, until the final decision is received. That is, the participant does not apply any of its implemented early read lock release optimizations with this specific transaction. This means that the participant will follow 2PC until the completion of both of its phases and not just the first phase as though it does not implement any early read lock release optimization. Thus, when a potential case of execution infection is encountered, all participants continue to hold all locks until the final decision is made, eliminating the possibility of execution infections. If none of the participants had executed any operation that is associated with deferred constraints, the received prepare message by a read-only participant will not contain an UDCCV flag. Hence, the participant can utilize the read-only optimization and releases the read locks earlier than its update counterparts. Thus, the UDCCV delays the early release of read locks only when there is a possibility of execution infections, eliminating the infection prone time period on a per transaction basis. Returning to the previous example with the UDCCV in mind, when P1 executes the second operation of T_1, it will send an UDCCV flag as part of its acknowledgment (Ack1,1 in Figure 7). Based on that, the coordinator will send an UDCCV flag as part of the prepare message to P2 ($Prep_{2,1}$). Hence, P2 will be aware of the possibility of the execution infection and, instead of releasing the read lock held on behalf of T_1 and sending a "read-only" message ($RO_{2,1}$), P_2 will continue to hold the read lock and sends a "yes" vote, awaiting the final decision from the coordinator. Based on that, T_2 will not be able to execute its operation at P_1 as the lock needed on (x) at P_2 is still held on behalf of T_1, preventing the execution progress of T_2. This eliminates the possibility for the two transactions to engage in a non-serializable execution due to an execution infection. This result can be generalized with the following theorem.

Theorem: In any distributed database system that is based on a request/reply paradigm and implements deferred consistency constraints, the UDCCV mechanism guarantees infection-free executions of transactions when combined with S2PL and an ACP that incorporates an optimization designed around the early release of read locks. **Proof:** The proof proceeds by contradiction and consists of two parts.

For an execution infection to occur, there has to be a lock on a data item (d) that is released by a transaction Ti before its commit point at some participant P and (d) is locked and modified by another transaction T_j which commits before Ti in the global serialization schedule as follows: $lock_i(d) < lockj(d)$ and $T_j \rightarrow Ti$ I. If $lock_i$ is a "write" lock then it is impossible for T_j to acquire a lock on (d) and reaches its commit point before Ti reaches its commit point first because, in S2PL with an ACP, the write locks are released after transactions are terminated across all participants. II. If $lock_i$ is a "read" lock then it is possible for T_j to acquire a lock on (d) and reaches its commit point before Ti terminates across all participants according to any early read lock release optimization incorporated in the ACP used and not S2PL. But, as UDCCV is used, $lock_i$ cannot be released until Ti terminates across all participants. Thus, it is impossible for T_j to precede Ti in the serialization order.

The UDCCV Mechanism and Other Optimizations

The UDCCV can be used with other optimizations designed around early release of read locks such as early release of read locks (ERRL) [17] and the unsolicited update vote (UUV) [20, 21]. In ERRL, a participant in a transaction execution does not have to be an exclusively read-only participant for it to release the read locks held on behalf of the transaction at prepare time of the transaction. That is, in ERRL, each update participant is also allowed to release the read locks held on behalf of a transaction once it receives the prepare message for the transaction. UUV is another read-only optimization that further reduces the costs associated with read-only participants. In UUV, each transaction starts as a read-only transaction at each participant and when the transaction executes the first operation that updates data at a participant, the participant sends an unsolicited update-vote. The "unsolicited update-vote" is a flag that is sent as part of the operation acknowledgment. Thus, at the end of a transaction, the coordinator precisely knows all update participants and infers that the rest of the participants are read only. In contrast to the traditional read-only optimization, this is accomplished, in UUV, without having to explicitly pull the vote of each participant. Consequently, the coordinator only needs to inform each read-only participant that the transaction has terminated without requiring the participant to send back any reply message, reducing the number of messages with read-only participants, compared with the traditional read-only optimization, to the half. The UDCCV mechanism can be used in conjunction with ERRL in a manner similar to its use with the traditional read-only optimization. That is, when a participant executes an operation that is associated with a deferred constraint, the participant sends an UDCCV flag as part of the successful operation acknowledgment. This flag informs the coordinator about a possible execution infection. Consequently, at commit processing time, the coordinator informs each other participant about this possibility using an UDCCV flag that it sends as part of each prepare message. Once a participant receives such a flag, it continues to hold the read locks until the end of the commit protocol (i.e., the second phase of the protocol). If the transaction does not perform any operation that is associated with deferred constraints, the participants can still utilize ERRL as usual. Thus, UDCCV prevents possible execution infections only with transactions that are associated with deferred constraints while still able to utilize ERRL with the other transactions. The UDCCV mechanism can be also used in conjunction with UUV but in a slightly different manner than its use with the traditional read-only optimization. This is because, in UUV, a coordinator does not pull the votes of read-only participants through prepare messages. Consequently, in the case of possible execution infections, the coordinator cannot request from any participant to continue to hold the read locks until the commit decision is made. Instead, the coordinator delays the termination message, which is called "read-only" in UUV, that it is supposed to send to each read-only participant until after it has received the votes of the update participants and made the final decision for the transaction. Thus, ensuring full termination of transactions across all participants before any locks are released. Similar to the previous two optimizations, in UUV, the UDCCV mechanism is used on a per transaction basis and only in the presence of potential execution infections.

REFERENCES

1. Gray, J. (1978) "Notes on Database Operating Systems", in Bayer, R., R.M. Graham & G. Seegmuller, (Eds.), Operating Systems: An Advanced Course, LNCS, Vol. 60, pp.393–481, SpringerVerlag.
2. Lampson, B. (1981) "Atomic Transactions", in Lampson, B., M. Paul & H.J. Siegert, (Eds.): Distributed Systems: Architecture and Implementation – An Advanced Course, Vol. 105, pp.246– 265, Springer-Verlag.
3. Al-Houmaily, Y. (2010) "Atomic Commit Protocols, their Integration, and their Optimisations in Distributed Database Systems", Int'l J. of Intelligent Information and Database Systems, Vol. 4, No.4, pp. 373-412.
4. Chrysanthis, P., G. Samaras & Y. Al-Houmaily (1998) "Recovery and Performance of Atomic Commit Processing in Distributed Database Systems", (Chapter 13), in Kumar, V. & M. Hsu (Eds.), Recovery Mechanisms in Database Systems, Prentice Hall.
5. Lee, I. & H. Yeom (2002) "A Single Phase Distributed Commit Protocol for Main Memory Database Systems", in Proc. of the 6th Int'l Parallel and Distributed Processing Symposium.
6. Ayari, B., A. Khelil & N. Suri (2011) "On the Design of Perturbation-Resilient Atomic Commit Protocols for Mobile Transactions", ACM Transactions on Computer Systems, Vol. 29, No. 3, pp.7:1–7:36.
7. Nouali-Taboudjemat, N., F. Chehbour & H. Drias (2010) "On Performance Evaluation and Design of Atomic Commit Protocols for Mobile Transactions", Distributed and Parallel Databases, Vol. 27, No. 1, pp. 53-94.
8. Obermeier, S., S. Böttcher, M. Hett, P. Chrysanthis & G. Samaras (2009) "Blocking Reduction for Distributed Transaction Processing Within MANETs", Distributed

and Parallel Databases, Vol. 25, No. 3.

9. Haritsa, J., K. Ramamritham & R. Gupta (2000) "The PROMPT Real-Time Commit Protocol", IEEE Transactions on Parallel and Distributed Systems, Vol. 11, No. 2.

10. Qin, B. & Y. Liu (2003) "High Performance Distributed Real-Time Commit Protocol", J. of Systems and Software, Vol. 68, No. 2.

11. Shanker, U., M. Mesra & A. Sarje (2008) "Distributed Real Time Database Systems: Background and Literature Review", Distributed and Parallel Databases, Vol. 23, No. 2, pp. 127-149.

12. Rocha, T., A-B. Arntsen, A. Eidsvik, M. Toledo & R. Karlsen (2007) "Promoting Levels of Openness on Component-Based Adaptable Middleware", in Proc. of the 6th Int'l Workshop on Adaptive and Reflective Middleware.

13. Al-Houmaily, Y. (2013) "An Intelligent Adaptive Participant's Presumption Protocol for Atomic Commitment in Distributed Databases", Int'l J. of Intelligent Information and Database Systems, Vol. 7, No. 3, pp. 242-277.

14. Mohan, C., B. Lindsay & R. Obermarck (1986) "Transaction Management in the R* Distributed Data Base Management System", ACM TODS, Vol. 11, No. 4, pp. 378-396.

15. X/Open Company Limited (1991) "Distributed Transaction Processing: The XA Specification", (X/Open Doc. No. XO/CAE/91/300).

16. Samaras, G., G. Kyrou & P. Chrysanthis (2003) "Two-Phase Commit Processing with Restructured Commit Tree", in Proc. of the Panhellenic Conf. on Informatics, LNCS, Vol. 2563, pp.82–99.

17. Lomet, D. (1993) "Using Timestamping to Optimize Two Phase Commit", in Proc. of the 2nd Parallel and Distributed Information Systems.

18. ISO (2008) "Information Technology - Database Languages - SQL - Part 2: Foundation (SQL/Foundation)", ISO/IEC 9075-2.

19. Garcia-Molina, H., J. Ullman & J. Widom (2008) "Database Systems: The Complete Book", 2nd edition, Prentice-Hall.

20. Al-Houmaily, Y., P. Chrysanthis & S. Levitan (1997) "Enhancing the Performance of Presumed Commit Protocol", in Proc. of the 12th ACM Annual Symposium on Applied Computing.

21. Al-Houmaily, Y., P. Chrysanthis & S. Levitan (1997) "An Argument in Favor of the Presumed Commit Protocol", in Proc. of the 13th ICDE.

CHAPTER 4 CONCURRENCY CONTROL IN MOBILE ENVIRONMENTS: ISSUES & CHALLENGES

Salman Abdul Moiz[1] , Supriya N.Pal[2] , Jitendra Kumar[3], Lavanya P[4] , Deepak Chandra Joshi[5] , Venkataswamy G[6]

[1] Research Scientist, Centre for Development of Advanced Computing, Bangalore

[2] Associate Director, Centre for Development of Advanced Computing, Bangalore

[3] Senior Staff Scientist, Centre for Development of Advanced Computing, Bangalore

[4, 5, 6] Staff Scientist, Centre for Development of Advanced Computing, Bangalore

ABSTRACT

The use of data services from handheld devices has increased exponentially resulting in several challenges. Transactions requiring the same shared data item may simultaneously perform a write operation leading to inconsistency of data items. The generic characteristics of mobile environments like variable bandwidth, disconnections, mobility etc makes transaction management more difficult thereby the traditional Isolation property may not be guaranteed. This paper analyzes and compares various concurrency control strategies in mobile environments proposed in literature. The design requirement for preserving isolation property in mobile environments is also presented.

INTRODUCTION

Transactions are key to structuring distributed applications. Concurrency control is one of the important building blocks of transaction management. The requirement of concurrency control arose to ensure correctness when shared data item is updated by multiple transactions at the same time. The traditional two phase locking protocol is not suitable in mobile database environment due to frequent mobility and disconnections. Further to manage the data correctly, the support of ACID (Atomicity, Consistency, Isolation & Durability) properties of transaction should be revisited with respect to the characteristics of mobile database environment. Atomicity is guaranteed by the commit protocols, Consistency is assured by DBMS or application programs if it can ensure certain specified constraints, Isolation is guaranteed by concurrency control manager and Durability is ensured by logging. Transaction management is characterized by the environment in which transaction gets executed. In the first group the transaction are completely or partially executed at mobile host. In this group the focus is on support of ACID properties. In the second group, transactions initiated at mobile hosts are executed at fixed host. In this group ACID properties are not compromised and the focus is on support of executing transactions successfully in presence of mobility and disconnections [1]. The remaining part of this paper is organized as follows: Section -2 describes the architecture of mobile database system, execution modes in mobile environments and the need of mobile middleware and its architecture. Section -3 presents the concurrent access anomalies and the lists the challenges in achieving Isolation

Citation: Salman Abdul Moiz, Supriya N.Pal, Jitendra Kumar, Lavanya P, Deepak Chandra Joshi, Venkataswamy G, Concurrency Control In Mobile Environments: Issues & Challenges, DOI: 10.5121/ijdms.2011.3411

property in mobile environments. Section-4 presents the pessimistic strategies for concurrency control in mobile environments and along with issues and challenges. Section -5 describes the optimistic strategies in mobile environments followed by issues and challenges and Section -6 concludes the paper.

MOBILE DATABASE ENVIRONMENT

The following figure describes the reference architecture of Mobile Database System. It resembles C&C (Component & Connector) view style architecture.

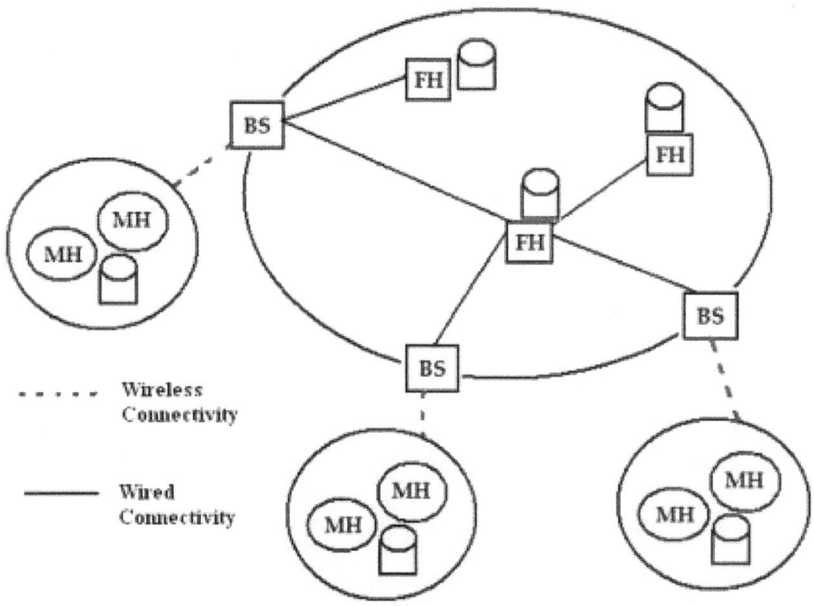

Figure 1. Reference architecture of Mobile Database System.

The Mobile database system consists of two major components and two major connectors. The two components are Mobile Host and Fixed Host respectively and the two connectors are Wireless and Wired Networks. Terminals, desktops, servers are the Fixed Host which are interconnected by means of a fixed network. Large databases can run on servers that guarantee efficient processing and reliable storage of database [1]. Mobile Hosts (MH) like Palmtops, Laptops, PDA's or Cellular phones is not always connected to the fixed network [1]. They may be disconnected for different reasons. Mobile host may differ with respect to the computing power and storage space; however MH can perform database transactions. The disconnections may be soft or hard. Hence disconnections are handled as normal situations and not as failures.

Advances in wireless technology and ubiquitous computing have created a new domain called mobile computing, where the users access the data irrespective of their physical location and movement behavior. The wireless technology provides users to logically retain the network connection even when there is a handoff i.e. when the mobile host is moving from one location to another. The geographical area covered by a base station is called a cell. Every time the mobile host communicates with the base station of the cell it belongs to. The process of entering new cell is said to be a handoff or handover.

Execution Modes

The transactions are initiated at mobile host but may be executed on mobile host or fixed host or the execution may be distributed between mobile host & fixed host [1] respectively.

- Complete Execution on the Fixed Network

In this execution mode, the transaction is initiated at mobile host but is completed executed at fixed network. In this model, the mobile host acts as a thin client.

- Complete Execution on a MH

In this mode, transactions are initiated at mobile host and are executed on mobile host. This approach requires mobile hosts to have processing & storage capabilities as well as managing data. However reconciliation is needed with the fixed host at some point in time.

- Distributed Execution on a MH and the Wired Network

In this mode, transactions are initiated at mobile hosts and the execution is distributed among mobile host and fixed host. A sub-transaction is executed at mobile host and another one at fixed host. This helps in minimizing the communication between the fixed host and mobile hosts respectively.

- Distributed Execution among several MHs

In this mode, the transaction is distributed among several mobile hosts for execution. It provides a peer-peer strategy. A mobile host acts as a server for other mobile hosts so that the execution is distributed between them. The selection of a mobile host for execution of a transaction is location based.

- Distributed Execution among MHs and FHs

This mode provides a fully distributed environment where a transaction execution is distributed among several mobile hosts and fixed hosts respectively. In this transaction execution, multiple parties may be involved. For example a customer who wishes to purchase products may connect to the supermarket and as well as bank and finally the results are to be reconciled successfully on individual fixed hosts.

Mobile Middleware

Mobile Middleware is software that acts as an interface between the Mobile host and wired fixed host. The functions of Mobile Middleware are

- It must deliver the information precisely to the right place irrespective of mobility, disconnections, interface constraints etc.,
- It has to enable deployment of a standardized mobile application on mobile devices with varied operating systems, screen sizes etc.
- Need to secure data on devices rather than just securing data communications

Figure 2 depicts the typical mobile middleware architecture. It resembles three-tier architecture and has to support cross platform characteristics. This is because the mobile devices works on different platforms and operating systems and the applications need to be accessed from any of the devices. Mobile middleware communicates with the fixed host on behalf of the mobile hosts. The mobile middleware also helps in providing location transparency thereby reducing the overhead of hard coding the applications on mobile devices.

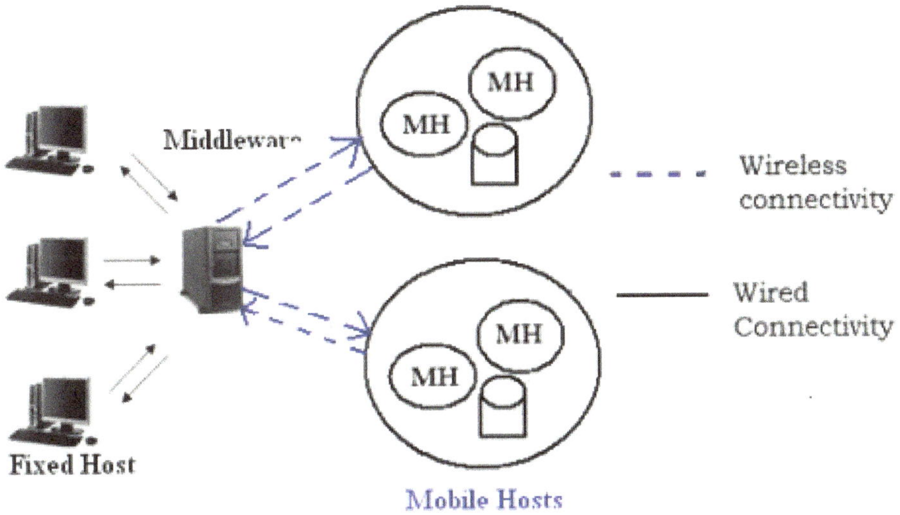

Figure 2. Mobile Middleware Architecture.

The mobile middleware helps in managing transactions, providing middleware security and support for cross platform implementation. The Cross platform middleware helps in supporting wide range of mobile applications. It also provides Device flexibility & Application flexibility. The transaction management in mobile environments can be implemented on the mobile middleware. The data synchronization strategies can be realized by mobile middleware.

CONCURRENT ACCESS ANOMALIES IN MOBILE ENVIRONMENTS

When multiple mobile hosts request for same data items, it may lead to concurrent access anomalies. To preserve Isolation property pessimistic and optimistic strategies are proposed in literature. In a pessimistic strategy, the traditional database uses locking protocol to overcome the problems of concurrent access. These protocols are not suitable for preserving consistency in presence of concurrent access of mobile hosts. A transaction initiated at a mobile host locks the required data items. If another mobile host requires the same data item it needs to wait till the mobile that requested the resource first unlocks the data item. If the mobile host doesn't commit the transaction, the second mobile host waiting in a queue has to wait for invariant time. This leads to starvation. Further as the disconnections are treated as normal behaviour in mobile environments, developing an efficient concurrency control strategy is a challenging problem. In an optimistic strategy, whenever multiple sites request for same data items, they are allowed to read the data item thus tolerating conflicts to occur. However at the time of global commit, conflict resolution strategy is applied to get back the system into consistent state. In mobile database environment, the global commit operation may increase the uplink bandwidth as the mobile host has to initiate the transactions again and again.

PESSIMISTIC STRATEGIES IN MOBILE ENVIRONMENT

Pessimistic strategy works on the following principle "Don't allow any transaction to use the same shared data item, unless it is completed". In Pessimistic strategy, the data items needed for executing a transaction are locked. Once the transaction is successfully completed, it is unlocked then the data items can be used by the transaction waiting in queue. Since disconnections are normal in mobile environments, a mobile host may lock the data item and may not release the locks invariantly. To overcome the problem of starvation, each transaction is associated with a timer. If the results of the offline transactions are not reconciled within a stipulated timer period, the transaction may be aborted and the data items are acquired by waiting transaction. Pessimistic strategies such as Two Phase Locking (2PL) require frequent message exchanges with fixed hosts [2]. This reduces the throughput of the system. Further unpredictable disconnections may also lead to undefined locking time.

Distributed High Priority Two Phase Locking (DHP-2L) Protocol

DHP-2L [3] is a distributed real time locking protocol based on high priority two phase locking (HP-2PL) to achieve concurrency control in mobile environments. Conventional concurrency protocols schedule transactions on equal basis. However, the HP-2PL [4] restarts a lower priority transaction if a higher priority transaction wants to set a lock which is held by higher priority transaction. A transaction is said to be local if it access data items available at only one base station. Otherwise it is a global transaction. DHP-2PL is a blocking protocol that resolves lock conflicts based on the priority of the transactions. Let T_r represents the lock requesting transaction and T_h the lock holding transaction, the following table specified the process of resolving lock conflicts in DHP-2PL.

Table 1. Lock Conflict resolution in DHP-2PL [3]

```
Lock Conflict (T_r. T_h)
Begin
  If Priority(T_r) > Priority(T_h)
     If T_h is not committing
         If T_h is a local transaction
             Restart T_h locally

Else
             Restart T_h globally
         End if

Else
         Block T_r until Th releases the lock
         Priority(T_h):= Priority(T_r) + fixed priority level
```

```
     Endif

Else
      Block T_r until T_h releases the lock
   End if
    End
```

However DHP-2PL uses transaction restart mechanism to resolve lock conflicts between noncommitting transactions. Further Global restarts takes more time than the local restart operations.

Timeout based Mobile Transaction Commit Protocol (TCOT)

TCOT [20] works on timeout based principle to reach the final state of the transaction execution by avoiding starvation of the shared data items. It works in an offline mode where the fragment needed for executing a transaction is read onto the mobile client and later the results are integrated with the server . If the transaction can't be executed within the time period "t", the timer value can be increased by sending the request again to the fixed host. This increases the uplink bandwidth. Further at the time of request of change in timer value, the mobile host may face the connectivity issues and it faces the issue of time lag between local and global commit operation.

Other Pessimistic Strategies

In [21] Mobile speculative locking protocol is introduced to reduce the blocking of transaction if two phase locking is employed. This approach requires extra resources at the mobile host to carry out speculative execution. In [22], a concurrency control scheme is proposed which in which the priority based scheme is used to serialize the transaction. Whenever a conflict occurs the priority is given to the older transaction. This is similar to the traditional locking and if the priority is given to the mobile host which cant execute the transaction for a long time, it not only suffers from starvation but the throughput decreases considerably. In [23], a concurrency control strategy is presented which sets the validity of data items based on the number of data items required. As the data items needed to execute a transaction might be distributed over several database servers, there is a need for a middleware which could handle such situations.

Issues & Challenges

Pessimistic protocols implemented in traditional environments are not suitable to mobile environments due to the inherent characteristics like mobility and Disconnections. Timeout based commit protocols are needed in mobile environments to avoid starvation problems as a result of indefinite locking of data items by a particular mobile host. The timer value may vary from one transaction to another. However if the transaction is aborted after expiry of timer, the transaction is to be requested again. This increases uplink bandwidth. To overcome this drawback if the transaction is not executed within specified time period it may be rolled back and may be executed again if no other transaction is waiting for same data items in the queue. Otherwise round-robin approach is followed. The qualitative analysis of the pessimistic strategies for guaranteeing concurrency control in mobile environments is presented in table 2.

Table 2. Qualitative analysis of Pessimistic Strategies for Concurrency Control

Pessimistic Strategy	Transaction Type	Waiting Time	Transaction throughput	Transaction Aborts	Transaction restarts
DHP-2L	Flat	Depends on transaction priority	Depends on priority of inheritance	Depends on firm deadline	More local/global restarts
TCOT	Nested	Depends on max time of execution	Decreases when there are frequent request for increase in timer value	Depends on threshold value	Transaction restarts if the execution is not completed in threshold limit
Mobile Speculative Locking	Nested	Depends on time taken by nested transaction	Less as more memory & computation capability is needed	Comparatively high as for every abort of nested transaction, an abort occurs	The intra and inter transaction parallelism may lead to high restarts due to disconnection s
Prioritized Concurrency Control scheme	Flat	Depends on time taken by high priority transaction	May decrease when the disconnection time is higher	Depends on current access time and data validity period	May reduce but execution time increases
Data count driven concurrency control scheme	Flat	Based on number of required data items	May reduce if transaction requires more data items and sever is heavily loaded	Depends on validity period and number of data items needed	May reduce but time taken for lookup of data items and counting them will be high

OPTIMISTIC STRATEGIES IN MOBILE ENVIRONMENT

Optimistic strategy works on the following principle:

"First perform operations, check for conflicts later".

In Optimistic Commit Protocols, conflict is tolerated in read phase. However to get back the system into a consistent state conflict resolution technique is applied at validation phase.

In this protocol multiple users are allowed to read the same shared data item simultaneously. When the transaction commits, the data items read by other users have to be invalidated. To implement this caching techniques are presented in literature which uses broadcasting i.e. whenever a commit is done locally, an invalidation report is broadcasted to all clients to invalidate the data items.

The Concurrency Control Mechanism (CCM

In CCM [5], a modified form of two tier replication scheme is proposed to reduce the no of transaction rejections and transaction commit time at the mobile hosts. In this approach the number of replicas allowed for shared data items are finite. If the possible number of replicas is set to "n", only "n" mobile hosts can locally store a copy of data item for execution. The validity of a data item is control by timeout parameter. If the data item is not updated or the results are not returned within specified period of time, it can't commit the transaction. The timeout values are assumed to be multiple of broadcast cycle time. If the transaction is not committed within specified time, it is blocked and has to wait till a new value of timer is assigned to the mobile host. It assumes that the value of timeout should be sufficiently large so that the updates can be propagated to the fixed host. However this may reduce the throughput of the system. Further in CCM if the transaction is committed within the specified time period it can update the data on fixed host without waiting for the result of base station. This increases the load on mobile host as it has to broadcast the status of data item to other mobile hosts which holds the same replica. Further in this approach after the expiry of timer value, DBS always has to send the new values of number of replicas and time for validity of data. Further if the number of applications deployed on a mobile increases, then the cache should also increase to maintain the data item information.

Sequential Order with Dynamic Adjustment (SODA) Strategy

SODA [6] guarantees consistency of concurrent transactions in mobile P2P databases. It reduces response time by applying the concept of sequential order and reduces the abort rate by dynamically adjusting the sequential order. SODA is a three phase commit protocol. In Read & Compute phase, transaction T reads the set of data items assigns a timestamp and stores them locally. T also computes the new values (write set) and maintains it locally. In Validation Phase, the read and write set are validated against set of committed transactions. If the transaction T passes the validation phase a new time stamp is assigned which is used as the commit time of transaction T. In Commit and Write Phase, if the transaction succeeds the validation phase, it can write values of write set into database. Otherwise it may be aborted. In a peer-peer strategy the transaction execution is distributed among mobile hosts. In these situations, every mobile host must possess the capability of managing transaction execution and integrated successfully with the fixed hosts. Further in mobile peer-peer systems, each host has to carry its own local database which is a challenge.

Concurrency control to support update transactions (CCUD)

In mobile commerce, browsing or querying database is not sufficient as some of the applications allow users to update the database. Local validation helps in achieving shorter response time, early detection of conflicts and reduced validation load on the fixed host [7]. However the broadcast errors might lead to ambiguity in making the commit decision. If a mobile host doesn't receive commit information correctly, it couldn't determine whether the local transactions must be committed or not. These broadcast errors can be reduced using reliable transmission protocol like a typical re-transmission and acknowledgement technique. Two types of broadcasts are used in this strategy viz. Notification broadcast for delivering the validation results of the transactions and Certification broadcast for broadcasting the invalidation information. In addition a confirmation protocol is used by mobile clients to receive the reliable results over a broadcast channel. The throughput of this strategy is less as it has to go through one additional level in making a final commit decision. This also increases the number of certification broadcast when many mobile hosts are requesting for the same shared data item as a result the uplink bandwidth increases.

Other Optimistic Strategies

In a mobile environment if the transaction validation is done on the server, it may lead to delayed response causing overhead at the server [8]. An Optimistic Concurrency Control with Dynamic Time stamp Adjustment Protocol requires client side write operations. However because of the delay in execution of a transaction, it may never be executed [14]. In [10,19], the conventional optimistic concurrency control algorithm in enhanced with an early termination mechanism on conflicting transactions. But because of early termination a transaction need to be initiated again and again. Optimistic concurrency control protocols (OCC) [13, 15, 17] are non-blocking and deadlock-free, which make them efficient to use in mobile computing and have been adopted in the Disconnected Operation [11] and Kangaroo Transaction model [16]. But, without locks to data items, transactions might access conflicting data items under an optimistic concurrency control protocol (OCC). Two concurrent transactions conflict if one of them performs a write on similar data items. Therefore, approaches to terminate conflicting transactions are proposed [18, 19]. In these approaches if the conflict rate increases, more and more transactions get aborted. In [14], author proposes A Timestamp-Based Optimistic Concurrency Control for Handling Mobile Transactions. However it [9,12,14] needs broadcasting of messages to send the invalidation reports which might unnecessary flood the network thereby reducing the transaction throughput. The approach followed in [14] uses broadcasting which is not suitable for some of the applications because of the rise in abort rates and unnecessary flooding of invalidation reports. For example in [1], the author proposes a scheme, to provide non-blocking protocol with restrained communication. But it faces the problem of time lag between the local and global commit. In [10] concept of non-conflicting transactions is introduced such that if a conflicting transaction is detected, it may be aborted.

Issues & Challenges

Optimistic commit protocol can be implemented for transaction processing in mobile environments. However the traditional optimistic protocol doesn't give good performance if it is implemented in mobile environments The invalidate report is sent to all the participants involved in some transaction execution. (The invalidation report may be sent only to the participants using the same shared data item and the data item is invalidated). Further in the traditional approach, once the data item becomes invalidated, a new request is to be initiated for execution of a transaction. In mobile environments this increases the uplink bandwidth. The qualitative analysis of the optimistic strategies for guaranteeing concurrency control in mobile environments is presented in table 3.

Table 3. Qualitative analysis of Optimistic Strategies for Concurrency Control

Optimistic Strategy	Trans Type	Data Validity	Conflict resolution	Uplink Bandwidth
CCM	Nested	Till the timer expires (can be utmost for limited no of concurrent request)	Through broadcasting of new values	Low, but less transaction throughput
SODA	Nested	Till the time of writing the write set onto fixed host	Through broadcasting done by mobile hosts (peers)	High, if the transaction fails in third phase, it has to be requested again.
CCUD	Flat	Data Item becomes valid when certification broadcast is invoked	Through broadcasting after local validation	Increases exponentially when access to shared data items increases because of the additional confirmation protocol
Time stamp based OCC	Flat	Till the invalidation report is received	Through broadcasting of invalidation reports	Since data items are read only on demand uplink bandwidth is sufficiently low
Improving CC in Mobile Databases	Flat	Till the invalidation reports are received	Conflicting transactions are terminated before reaching the validation phase	High as the transaction has to be started again once it receives invalidation report

CONCLUSION

Concurrency control forms a basic building block for transaction management in any database environments. However as disconnections are treated as normal situations in mobile environments, there is a need for relaxation of ACID properties in mobile environments. In this paper several concurrency control strategies to achieve the Isolation is discussed. In pessimistic strategy the transaction may be blocked due to locking. However the time based strategies made an attempt to resolve the starvation issues in presence of disconnections and mobility. To overcome the problem of blocking, optimistic strategies are presented in literature. However there is a need for good conflict resolution strategies which satisfies Serializability property.

REFERENCES

1. Patrical Serran-Alvarado et.Al, "A Survey of Mobile Transactions", Distributed & Parallel Databases, Kluwer Publishers, 16, pp.193-230, 2004
2. K.P. Eswarn, J. Gray, R.A. Lorie, and I.L. Triger, "The notions of consistency and predicate locks in a database system," Communications of the ACM (CACM), vol. 19, no. 11, 1976.
3. Kam-Yiu Lam, Tei-Wei Kuo et.Al, "Concurrency Control in Mobile Distributed Real-Time Database Systems", Elseiver Sciences, Information Systems Vol. 25, No.4, pp. 261-286, 2000.
4. R.J. Abbott and H. Garcia-Molina. "Scheduling real-time transactions: a performance evaluation. ACM Transactions on Database Systems", Vol. 17, No. 3, pp. 513-560, 1992.
5. Nitin Prabhu, Vijay Kumar et. Al, "Concurrency Control in Mobile Database System", Proceedings of 18th IEEE International Conference on Advanced Information Networking and Application (AINA),pp. 83-86, 2004.
6. Zhaowen Xing, Le Gruenweld, K.K Phang, "SODA: An Algorithm to Guarantee Correctness of Concurrent Transaction Execution in Mobile P2P Databases", 19th IEEE International Conference on Database and Expert Systems Applications" pp.337-341, 2008.
7. Zakil Koo, Songchum Moon, "Effects of broadcast errors on concurrency control in wireless broadcasting environments", pp. 13-21, 2002.
8. Victor C.S., Kwok wa Lam and Son, S.H., "Concurrency Control Using Time-stamp Ordering in Broadcast Environments", the Computer Journal,Vol.45, No.4 PP.410-422, 2002
9. Victor C.S.Lee, Kwok Wa Lam, Tei-wei Kuo,"Efficient Validation of Mobile Transactions in Wireless Environments", The Journal of Systems and Software 69(2004), 183-193.
10. Minsoo Lee, Sumi Helal, "HiCoMo: High Commit Mobile Transactions", Distributed and Parallel Databases, 11, 73-92, 2002, Kluwer Academic Publishers
11. J. Kisler, and M. Satyanarayanan, "Disconnected Operation in the Coda File System", ACM Transactions on Computer Systems, 10(1), 1992
12. Khalil M. Ahmed, Mohammed A Ismail, Navava M. El. Makky, Khaled M. Nagi, "A New Transaction Management Scheme for MobileComputing Environments", 2003.
13. H. T. Kung and J. T. Robinson, "On Optimistic Methods for Concurrency Control", ACM TODS, Vol.6, No. 2, June 1981.

14. Ho Chin Choi, Byeong-Soo Jeong, "A Timestamp-Based Optimistic Concurrency Control for Handling Mobile Transactions", Springer Verlag, LNCS 3981, PP. 796-805, 2006.

15. T. Härder. "Observations on optimistic concurrency control schemes". Information Systems, 9(2):111–120, 1984.

16. K. Eswaran, J. Gray, R. Lorie, I. Traiger, "The Notion of Consistency and Predicate locks in a database system", Communication of the ACM, 19 (11): 624-633, 1976.

17. Bernstein, P.A, Hadzilacos, V. and Goodman, N, "Concurrency Control and Recovery in Database System", Addison-Wesley 1987

18. Barbara D. and T. Imielinski. "Sleepers and Workaholics: Strategies in Mobile Environments", Proc. ACM pp. 1-12, May 1994.

19. Anand Yendluri, Wen-Chi Hou, and Chih-Fang Wang, "Improving Concurrency Control in Mobile Databases",Springer Verlag LNCS 2973, PP. 642-655, 2004.

20. Vijay Kumar, Nitin Prabhu, Maggie Dunham, Ayse Yasemin Seydim, "TCOT - A Timeout based Mobile Transaction Commitment Protocol", IIS 9979453, 2004.

21. P. Krishna Reddy, Masaru Kitsuregawa, "Speculative Lock Management to Increase Concurrency in Mobile Environments", MDA'99, LNCS 1748, pp, 82-96, 1996.

22. Mohammed Khaja Nizamuddin, Dr. Syed Abdul Sattar, "An Improved, Prioritized ConcurrencyControl Scheme with Performance Gain in Mobile Environments", pp. 34-40, Vol.1, No.1, ARPN Journal of Systems & Software, 2011.

23. Mohammed Khaja Nizamuddin, Dr. Syed Abdul Sattar, "Data Count Driven Concurrency Control Scheme With Performance Gain in Mobile Environments", pp. 106-112, JETCIS, Vol,2. No. 2, 2011.

SECTION II
QUERIES AND TRANSACTIONS IN A DISTRIBUTED ENVIRONMENT

CHAPTER 5 GENERAL FRAMEWORK FOR OPTIMIZATION OF DISTRIBUTED QUERIES

Dr. Sunita M. Mahajan[1] and Ms.Vaishali P. Jadhav[2]

[1]Mumbai Education Trust, Reclaimation,Bandra, Mumbai ,India
[2]NMIMS University, Mumbai, India

ABSTRACT

The paper suggests the heuristic approach for selecting the optimal evaluation plan and Semi-join approach for reducing the communication cost. Calculating the cost of each evaluation plan of a query takes lots of computational efforts as well as time. Initially the heuristic approach is used to find best evaluation plan among various plans of a single query. By considering only joins, queries are divided into two: tree and cyclic. Semi-join is a useful tool to reduce the cost of joins. The communication cost in distributed database is mainly depending upon the amount of data transferred from one site to another site. Semi-join approach is sufficient to fully reduce the tree queries while semi-joins are not the full reducers for cyclic queries. Cyclic queries are therefore converted into tree queries using different approaches such as addition of vertices, elimination of vertices, decomposition of vertices and elimination of edges. After conversion of cyclic to tree query, semi-join approach can be used.

INTRODUCTION

A heuristic is a rule of thumb, or a good guide to follow when making decisions. Heuristic refers specifically to algorithms in computer science. Algorithms have importance which works well in certain situations even though they may perform inefficiently for uncommon situations. Therefore, a heuristic is a problem solving technique may include running tests and getting results by trial and error. After testing more sample data, it becomes easier to create an efficient algorithm to process similar types of data. These algorithms are not always perfect, but work well most of the time. The goal of heuristics is to develop a simple process that generates accurate results in an acceptable amount of time. In case of Query Optimization, it is impractical to search evaluation plans exhaustively, when the optimization of joins involves many relations. Optimizers use heuristics to find best evaluation plan in addition with an exhaustive algorithm which generates alternative join order plans and terminates when cost budget is exceed [1-3]. Our framework includes the heuristic rules for finding optimal evaluation plan among various plans of a single query. This reduces the computational cost of each evaluation plan. Then for distributed query, semi-join approach is used. The queries which are not forming cycles in the query graph are called tree queries. Semi-join approach reduces the communication cost

Citation: Dr. Sunita M. Mahajan and Ms.Vaishali P. Jadhav, General Framework For Optimization Of Distributed Queries, DOI: 10.5121/ijdms.2012.4303

by reducing the amount of data transfer from one site to another site. If the query graph forms the cycle, then query is a cyclic query. To make the use of semi-join approach, cyclic queries are converted into tree queries by using different approaches such as addition or elimination or decomposition of vertices, elimination of edges etc. The approach of using semi-joins as reducers to process a distributed query has received a great deal of attention. This approach consists of the following three phases: (1) a local processing phase which involves all local processing such as selections and projections, (2) a semi-join reduction phase where a sequence of semi-joins is used to reduce the size of relations, and then, lessen the total communication cost required, and (3) a final processing phase in which all resulting relations are sent to the result site where the final query processing is performed. The problem of minimizing the communication cost for distributed query processing by a semi-join reduction approach has been shown as NP-hard.

The rest of the paper is organized as follows: Section 2 describes the related work. Section 3 describes the heuristic approach. Section 4 gives the tree query optimization. Section 5 describes the cyclic query optimization. Section 6 gives the concluding remarks.

RELATED WORK

There has been much work on distributed query processing and optimization. Most of the work has focused on minimizing the total communication cost for executing a single query by judiciously choosing the join order and possibly adding semi-join operators to the query plan [1- 4]. Hevner and Yao considered simple queries and suggested an optimal semi-join algorithm. They also extended their algorithm to produce efficient reducers for general queries [5]. Kambayashi Y. and Yoshikawa M. suggested horizontal decomposition as the one of the way of converting cyclic query into tree query [6][7]. Bernstein and Chiu showed that semi-joins are full reducers for tree queries. Tree queries are those queries whose query graphs are trees. They also give a proof that cyclic queries cannot be answered by the semi-joins alone [8][9]. Goodmann N. And Shemuli O. give different approaches of transforming cyclic query into tree query [10][11]. A survey article by Yu and Chang reviews many query processing algorithms. These algorithms can be characterised by several properties including timing of the optimization, replication of data, cost of the data etc [18-20][22]. System R* uses dynamic programming to find an optimal solution to the distributed query processing problem. The algorithm considers both processing and communication costs to arrive at an optimal strategy. However it does not use semi-joins as one of the options for reducing the relations [21]. Chen and Yu give different approach of semi-joins. They are showing that the approach of semijoin as reducers can lead to substantially larger reduction on data transmission required. They developed an efficient heuristic approach to determine an effective sequence of semi-join and join reducers. Semi-joins whose execution will reduce the amount of data transmission required to perform a join sequence are termed beneficial semi-joins for that join sequence.

Beneficial semi-joins include the conventional profitable semi-joins and the gainful semi-joins that are not profitable themselves but become beneficial due to the inclusion of join reducer. This type of dependency between semi-join and join reducers complicates the identification of beneficial semi-joins and the ordering in the reducer sequence. They first obtain a sequence of join reducers and map it into a join sequence tree. In light of the join sequence tree we derive important properties of beneficial semi-joins. These properties are then applied to develop an efficient algorithm to determine the beneficial semi-joins which can be inserted into the join sequence. The approach of interleaving a join sequence with beneficial semi-joins is not only efficient but also effective in reducing the total amount of data transmission required to process distributed queries [23]

HEURISTIC APPROACH

There are many rules for transforming relational algebra operations into equivalent ones. In relational algebra, there are several definitions and theorems the query optimizer can use to transform the query. For instance, the definition of equivalent relations states that the set of attributes (domain) of each relation must be the same— because they are sets, the order does not matter. Here is a partial list of relational algebra theorems [1-2].

General Transformation Rules for Relational Algebra Operations

1. **Cascade of σ**: A conjunctive selection condition can be broken up into a cascade (sequence) of individual σ operations:

$$\sigma_{c1 \text{ AND } c2 \text{ AND} \ldots \text{AND } cn}(R) = \sigma_{c1}(\sigma_{c2}(\ldots(\sigma_{cn}(R))\ldots))$$

2. **Commutativity of σ**: The σ operation is commutative:

$$\sigma_{c1}(\sigma_{c2}(R)) = \sigma_{c2}(\sigma_{c1}(R))$$

3. **Cascade of π:** In a cascade (sequence) of π operations, all but the last one can be ignored:

$$\pi_{List1}(\pi_{List2}(\ldots(\pi_{Listn}(R))\ldots)) = \pi_{List1}(R)$$

4. **Commuting σ with π:** If the selection condition c involves only the attributes A1, ..., An in the projection list, the two operations can be commuted:

$$\pi_{A1, A2, \ldots, An}(\sigma_c(R)) = \sigma_c(\pi_{A1, A2, \ldots, An}(R))$$

5. **Commutativity of ⋈ (and x):** The operation is commutative as is the x operation:

$$R \bowtie_C S = S \bowtie_C R; \quad R \times S = S \times R$$

6 **Commuting σ with ⋈ (or x):** If all the attributes in the selection condition c involve only the attributes of one of the relations being joined—say, R—the two operations can be commuted as follows:

a. $\sigma_c(R \bowtie S) = (\sigma_c(R)) \bowtie S$

Alternatively, if the selection condition c can be written as (c1 and c2), where condition c1 involves only the attributes of R and condition c2 involves only the attributes of S, the operations commute as follows:

b. $\sigma_c(R \bowtie S) = (\sigma_{c1}(R)) \bowtie (\sigma_{c2}(S))$

7. **Commuting π with ⋈ (or x):** Suppose that the projection list is L = {A1, ..., An, B1, ..., Bm}, where A1, ..., An are attributes of R and B1, ..., Bm are attributes of S. If the join condition c involves only attributes in L, the two operations can be commuted as follows:

a. $\pi_L(R \bowtie_C S) = (\pi_{A1, \ldots, An}(R)) \bowtie_C (\pi_{B1, \ldots, Bm}(S))$

b. If the join condition C contains additional attributes not in L, these must be added to the projection list, and a final π operation is needed.

8. **Commutativity of set operations:** The set operations U and ∩ are commutative but "–" is not.

9. **Associativity of ⋈ , x, U, and ∩:** These four operations are individually associative; that is, if q stands for any one of these four operations (throughout the expression), we have

   a. (R q S) q T = R q (S q T)

10. **Commuting σ with set operations:** The σ operation commutes with U, ∩, and –. If q stands for any one of these three operations, we have

    a. $\sigma_c (R\ q\ S) = (\sigma_c (R))\ q\ (\sigma_c (S))$

11. **The π operation commutes with U:**

    i. $\pi_L (R \cup S) = (\pi_L (R)) \cup (\pi_L (s))$

12. **Converting a (σ , X) sequence into ⋈:**

    i. $\sigma_c (R \times S) = (R \bowtie_c S)$

Figure 2: Outline of a Heuristic Algebraic Optimization Algorithm.

The below algorithm utilizes some of the rules of transform an initial query tree into an optimized tree that is efficient to execute during heuristic optimization.

Input: Relational Algebra Query
Output: Best Evaluation Plan
Algorithm:
Step 1: Design the initial canonical tree of the query
Step 2: Move the SELECT operation down the query tree
Step 3: Apply more restrictive SELECT operation first. If the two relations are residing at same site, they will be handled first.
Step 4: Replace CARTESIAN PRODUCT and SELECT with JOIN operation
Step 5: Move PROJECT operations down the query tree

Figure 3: Heuristic Query Optimization

Motivating Example

Consider the following relations [4]

R1(Prof, Dept, Research_Area)

R2(Course, Professor, Text, Department)

Retrieve the professor who is teaching Soft Computing course which includes the text as Fuzzy in

Computers department and whose research area is Neural Network.

Select Prof from R1,R2 WHERE Dept = Department AND Research_Area = "Neural Network" AND Course = "Soft Computing" AND Text ="Fuzzy" AND Department = "Computers" ;

To implement optimizer we have considered the Visual Studio 2008 and SQL Server 2008 R2.The above query in the relational algebra form is given as the input and the final query tree by using the heuristic rules is the output of the optimizer

Following is the query tree converted using heuristic:

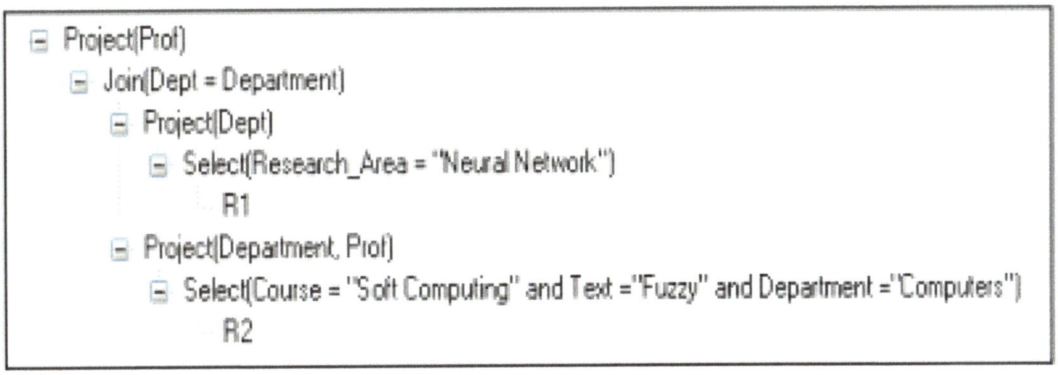

COST ESTIMATION APPROACH

In case of distributed query, along with the heuristic rules we need to apply cost estimation methods for reducing the transmission cost and for better optimization. The cost estimation methods are different for different types of queries. By considering only joins, the distributed queries are divided into tree query and cyclic query.

Tree Query and Cyclic Query

Consider the join graph and query graph given below. The query graph which forms the cycle is the graph of cyclic query and the query graph which does not form the cycle is tree query graph. We will consider the optimization of both the queries [4][5][6].

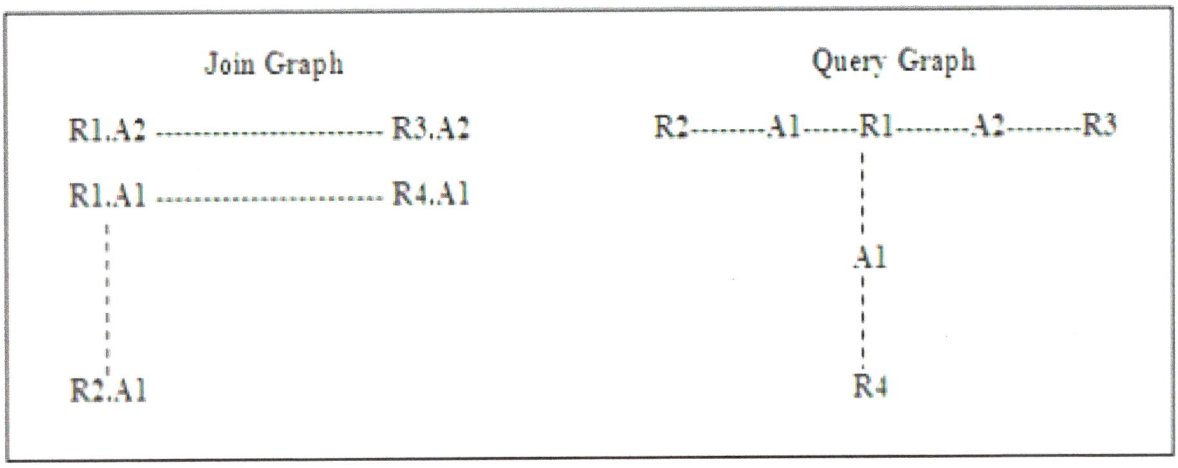

Figure 5: Tree Query Example.

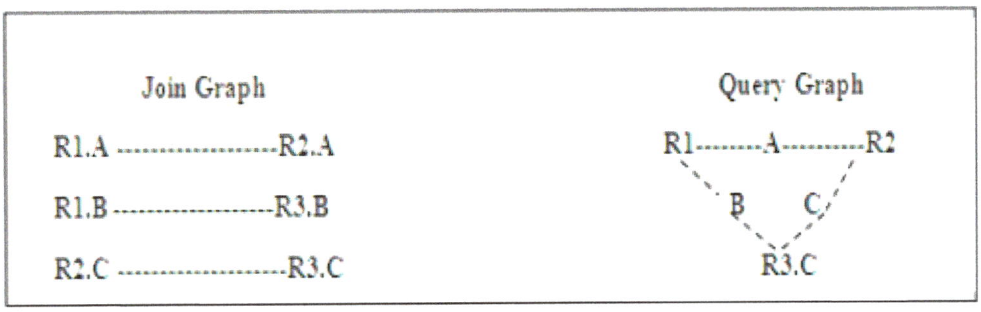

Figure 6: Cyclic Query Example.

Tree Query Optimization

Since the amount of data transferred affects the cost of a strategy, we should attempt to reduce it. A promising approach for optimizing tree queries is to make use of semi-joins. A semi-join from relation R2 to relation R1 on attribute A is denoted by R2---B--->R1 where R2 is the sending relation , R1 is the reduced relation and B is the joining attribute. It can be obtained by joining R1 and R2 on attribute B, then projecting the resulting relation on the schema of R1. The semi-join operation is denoted as $R_{i+1} \ltimes R_i$. For semi-join operation, we will consider the selectivity of relation on join attribute [7][8][9][10]. Selectivity: Let Pi be the probability that a value in attribute A appears in Ri, i = 1, 2. Pi is called the selectivity of Ri on attribute A. It is given by | Ri| / |A|.

Reduction of Simple Tree Queries Using Semi-Join Operation

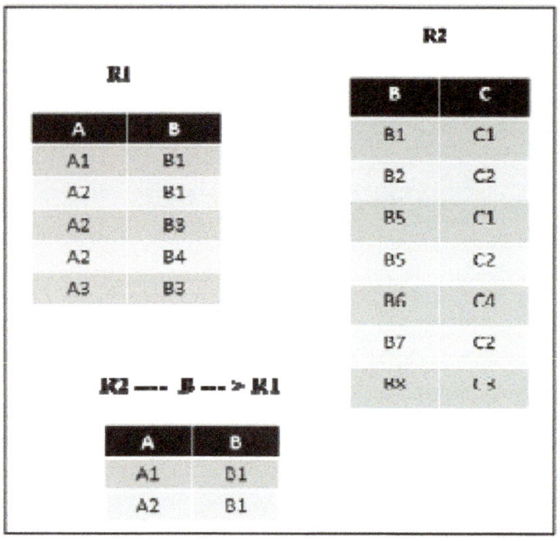

Figure 7. Semi-Join Operation.

A simple query consists of only one joining attribute. Since the simple query is a tree query, all the relations in the query may be reduced by using semi-join operation [11][12][13]. We are considering two strategies for implementing Semi-joins. Strategy 1: We will consider the relations which are in the ascending order of their size Strategy 2: We will consider the relation which is to be reduced, not in the ascending order but in the last semi-join operation. Consider the qualification of a simple query with n join clauses as for i = 1 to n , $R_i . A = R_{i+1}.A$ Consider relations R1, R2, R3, R4 and joining attribute as A. The relations are in the ascending order of their join attribute. Consider simple query is (R1.A = R2.A) and (R2.A=R3.A) and (R3.A = R4.A). Their Corresponding sizes are S1, S2, S3, and S4.Their corresponding selectivities are SEL1, SEL2, SEL3, and SEL4. The Cost of initiating a message is C0. The cardinality is C (Ri.A).

Strategy I:

Semi-join Operation will be as follows: We will consider the sequence of semi-joins $R_{i+1} \ltimes R_i$ where i is indexed from 1 to 4.

STEP 1:
R2 ⋉ R1
Cost 1= C_0 + S1
C (R2.A) = S2 * SEL1

STEP 2:
R3 ⋉ R2
Cost 2= C_0 + C (R2.A)
C (R3.A) = S3* SEL2 *SEL1

STEP 3:
R4 ⋉ R3
Cost 3= C_0 +C (R3.A)
C (R4.A) = S4 * SEL3 *SEL2 *SEL1

Moving the result to resultant site
Cost 4= C_0 +C (R4.A)

Therefore, Total Cost = Cost1 +Cost2 +Cost 3+Cost 4

Strategy II:

Relation R2 is to be reducible so we consider R2 at the end of semi join operation

STEP 1:
R3 ⋉ R1
Cost 1= C (R1.A)
C (R3.A) = S3 * SEL1

STEP 2:
R4 ⋉ R3
Cost 2= C (R3.A)
C (R4.A) = S4 * SEL3 *SEL1

STEP 3:
R2 ⋉ R4
Cost 3= C (R4.A)
C (R2.A) = S2 * SEL4 *SEL3*SEL1

Therefore, Total Cost = Cost1+Cost2+Cost3

After comparing the total costs obtained by strategy I and II, select the strategy having the lowest cost.

Motivating Example Consider the following example for illustration of both the strategies: Illustration: Consider the simple query with R1 , R2,R3 and R4 as relations and A as their joining attribute. Result should be at the site of relation 2.Size and Selectivity of each relation is given below:

	Size	Selectivity
R1.A	10000	0.1
R2.A	20000	0.2
R3.A	30000	0.3
R4.A	40000	0.4

Figure 8. Relation with size and selectivity.

Strategy I

Consider transmission cost =10. It is added to each calculation of cost.

R2 ⋉ R1
Cost = 10010
C(R2.A) = 20000 * 0.1 = 2000

R3 ⋉ R2
Cost = 2010
C(R3.A) = 30000 * 0.2 *0.1 = 600

R4 ⋉ R3
Cost = 610
C(R4.A) = 40000* 0.3 *0.2 *0.1 = 240

Moving the result to site of relation 2
Cost = 250

Therefore, Total Cost = 10010 +2010+610+250 = 12880 ------------- Strategy I

Strategy II:

Relation R2 is to be reducible so we consider R2 at the end of semi join operation

R3 ⋉ R1
Cost = 10010
C(R3.A) = 30000 * 0.1 = 3000

R4 ⋉ R3
Cost = 3010
C(R4.A) = 40000 * 0.3 *0.1 = 1200

R2 ⋉ R4
Cost = 1210

C(R2.A) = 20000 * 0.4 *0.3*0.1 = 240

Therefore, Total Cost = 10010+3010+1210 = 14230 -------------------- Strategy II Comparing the total costs obtained by strategy I and II, and selecting strategy I

So, Total Cost = 12880

Cyclic Query Optimization

There is no semi-join sequence which can reduce all relations in a cyclic query. So we cannot use semi-join strategies for cyclic query optimization. For processing a cyclic query, we first transform it into a tree query and then a tree query optimization procedure is applied. There are many ways of transformation from cyclic queries to tree queries. Some of the techniques are given below[10][14][15][16]:

Minimization of Vertices

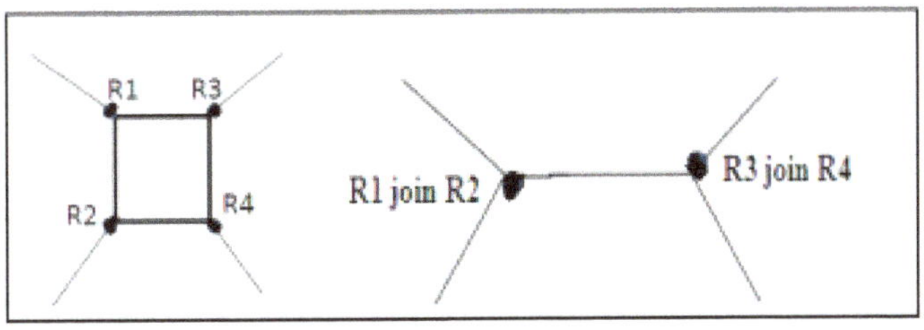

Figure 9. Removal of cycle using minimization of vertices.

Pseudo- Code:

Consider a graph having vertices as relations Ri, Rj, Rk

Check whether vertices of relations forms a cyclic graph

If (Cyclic Graph)

Start transformation

Merge the vertices of relations such that resulting vertex is connected to every vertex which is connected to vi or vj or vk

End Transformation

Else

Graph is not a cyclic graph

Technique 2: Minimization of Edge

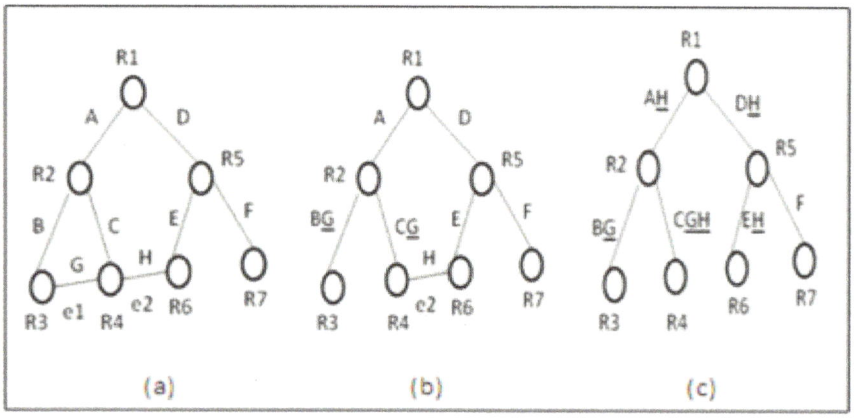

Figure 10. Removal of cycle using Attribute Addition Approach.

Pseudo-Code:

Consider relations Ri and Rj are joined on attribute A

Check one of the values common to Ri.A and Rj.A

If (common value exists)

Let common value be a

Replace the join on this value by two selection operations Ri [A = a] and Rj [A =a].

Repeat till all A-values from Ri and Rj are over

Technique 3: Addition of Vertices

Instead of adding attributes we can convert queries by adding extra relations. After adding relation, apply following transformation to the graph. Elementary Transformation: In a query graph, vertices acts as relations and edges are the joining attributes of two vertices.Consider three vertices as Vi, Vj, Vk and their edges be Y1, Y2 and Y3.If there is no edge between Vi and Vk, Y3 is assumed to be Ø. We can change the label Y3 to any Y4 satisfying the following condition, where Z = E1 E2 ≠ Ø. E3 –Z Y4 Y3 U Z. Here we assume Y1 ≠ Ø. and Y2 ≠ Ø. If Y3-Z is Ø, Y4 can be Ø. In such a case, the edge is removed. If Y3 is originally Ø, we can add edge eik whose label is a subset of Z. Consider the following relations: R1(ABC), R2(ADC), R3(EADB).The corresponding query graph forms the cycle, but addition of new relation R4(ACDB) removes the cycle.

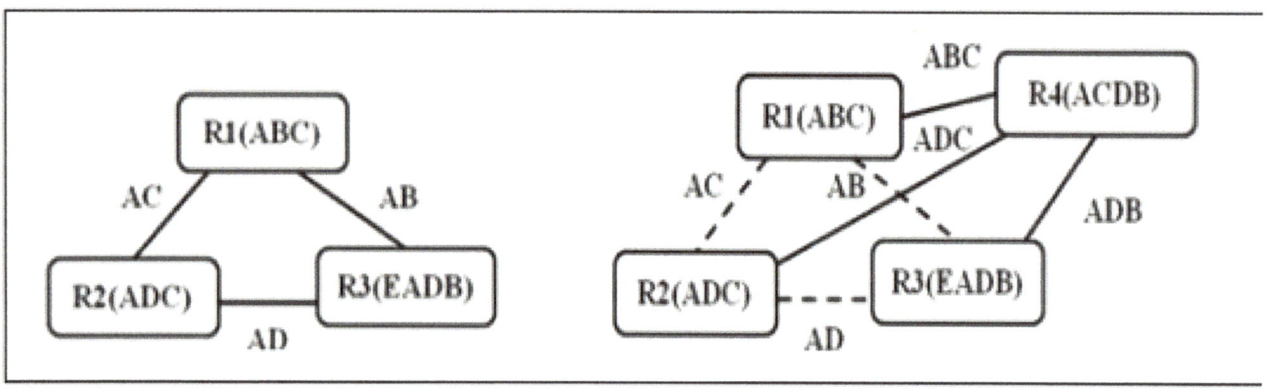

Figure 11. Removal of cycle using addition of vertices.

Pseudo-Code:

Add vertices corresponding to the extra relations to the query graph.

Add appropriate edges.

Apply the elementary transformation to the resulting graph

Apply operations to compute the instances of the extra relations.

Technique 4: Decomposition of Vertices

To remove the cycle from a graph, we can divide decompose the relation horizontally, or if a relation satisfies a functional or multi-valued dependency, relation can be vertically decomposed [6][16][19][20].

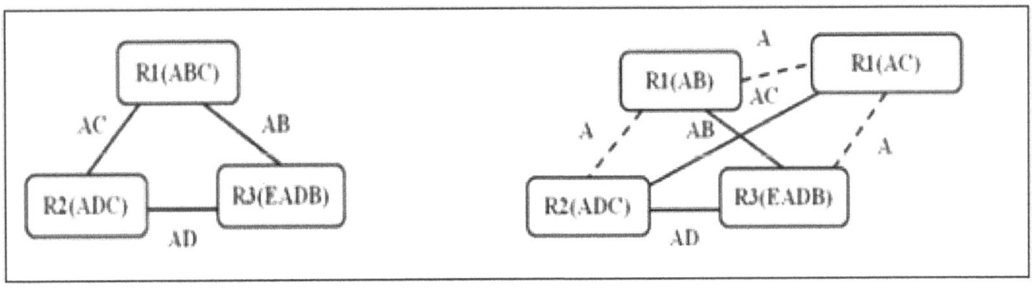

Figure 12. Removal of vertices using vertical decomposition of a relation.

Consider relation R(ABC) and the functional dependency FD : A → B is required in relation R. The given relation R is not satisfing the required functional dependency.Horizontal decomposition R1 and R2 of relation R satisfies the Functional Dependency.

R

A	B	C
1	1	1
1	2	2
2	1	3
2	3	2

R1'

A	B	C
1	1	1
2	1	3

R1''

A	B	C
1	2	2
2	3	2

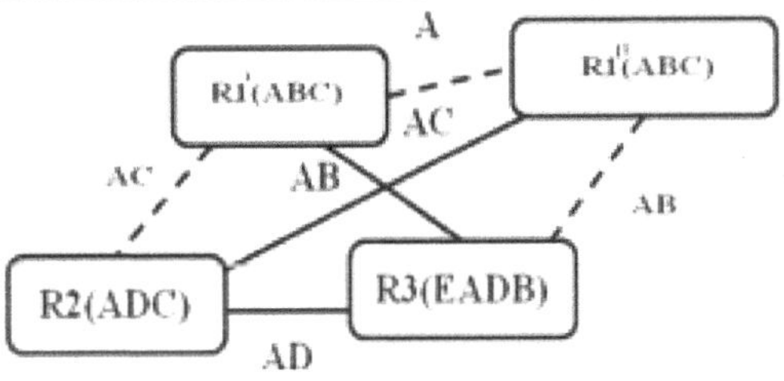

Figure 13. Removal of cycle using horizontal decomposition of a relation.

CONCLUSION

By using the heuristic approach, we can reduce the cost of query optimization. As we are considering join of distributed queries, queries are divided into tree queries and cyclic queries. Semi-joins are full reducers for tree queries. The conversion of cyclic queries into tree queries uses different approaches such as addition of vertices, elimination of vertices, decomposition of relations and elimination of edges etc. Horizontal and vertical decomposition of relations is the best method for conversion of cyclic queries into tree queries.

REFERENCES

1. Abraham Silberschatz, Hank Korth and S. Sudarshan. Database system concepts, 5th Edition. McGraw-Hill, 2006
2. Ramez Elmasri and Shamkant B. Navathe. Fundamentals of database systems, Fifth edition. Pearson Education ,2009.
3. http://www.techterms.com/definition/heuristic
4. Won Kim,David S. Reiner,Don s. Batory. Query processing in database systems. Springer Verlag, Berlin Heidelberg New York Tokyo.
5. Aper PMG, Hevner AR,Yao SB, "Optimization algorithms for distributed queries", IEEE Transactions on software Engineering, SE-9.1, January 1983, 57-68.
6. Kambayashi Y, Yoshikawa M, "Query processing utilizing dependencies and horizontal decomposition", Proc ACM SIGMOD conference, San Jose, May 1983, 55-57.
7. Kambayashi Y, Yoshikawa M, "Query processing for distributed databse using generalized semijoins", Proc. ACM SIGMOD International Conference on Management of Data, June 1982, 151-160.
8. Bernstein PA, Chiu DM, "Using semi-joins to solve relational queries", Journal of ACM, 28,1 ,January 1981, 25-40.
9. Bernstein PA, Goodman N, "Power of natural Semi-joins", SIAM Journal of Computing , 10, 4, November 1981, 751-771.
10. Goodman N,Shmueli O, "Transforming cyclic schemas into trees", ACM SIGACT Symposium on Principles of Database Systems, March 1982, 49-54.
11. Goodman N,Shmueli O," Tree Queries : a simple class of relational queries", ACM Transactions on Database systems, 7,4, December 1982, 653-677.

12. Gouda MG, Dayal UD, “Optimal semijoin schedules for query processing in local distributed database sytems”, Proc. ACM SIGMOD Conference , Ann Arbor, 1981, 164-175.
13. Goodman N, Shmueil O, “The tree property is fundamental for query processing”, Proc. ACM SIGACT-SIGMOD Symposium on Principles of Database Systems, March 1982, 40-48.
14. Fagin R, “Acylic Database schemes(of various degrees): a painless introduction”, IBM Research Report, RJ3800, February 1983.
15. Epstein R, Stonebraker M, Wong E, “Distributed query processing in a relational database system”, Proc. ACM SIG MOD Conference, Austin, TX, May 1978, 169-180.
16. Wong E, Youseffi K, “Decomposition – a strategy for query processing”, ACM Transactions on Database systems, 1, 3 ,September 1976, 223-241.
17. Yao SB, “Optimization of query evaluation algorithms”, ACM Transactions Database Systems,4,2,June 1979,133-155.
18. Yu CT, Lam K et al, “Distributed query optimization for tree queries”, Dept. of Information Engineering, University of Illinois at Chicago Circle, October 1979.
19. Yu CT, Chang CC, “ On the design of a query processing strategy in a distributed database environment”, Proc. ACM SIGMOD Conference, San Jose, 1983, 30-39.
20. [20] Yu CT, Chang CC et al, “Two surprising results in processing simple queries in distributed databases”, IEEE COMPSAC, November 1982.
21. Berstein, P.A. etal. “Query Processing in a system for distributed databases”, ACM Trans. Database
22. System Vol.6, No.4, Dec 1981.
23. C.T. Yu and C.C. Chang, “Distributed Query Processing,” ACM Computing Surveys, 16(4), 1984.
24. http://www.csd.uoc.gr/~hy460/pdf/chenyu.pdf

CHAPTER 6

DYNAMIC MANAGEMENT OF TRANSACTIONS IN DISTRIBUTED REAL-TIME PROCESSING SYSTEM

Y. Jayanta Singh [1] , Yumnam Somananda Singh [2] , Ashok Gaikwad [2] and S.C. Mehrotra [3]

[1] Faculty of Information Technology, 7 th October University, Misurata, Libya

[2] Faculty of Computer Application Institute of Management Studies & I. T (IMSIT), India

[3] Dept of Information Technology and Computer Science Dr. B. A. Marathwada University, Aurangabad, India

ABSTRACT

Managing the transactions in real time distributed computing system is not easy, as it has heterogeneously networked computers to solve a single problem. If a transaction runs across some different sites, it may commit at some sites and may failure at another site, leading to an inconsistent transaction. The complexity is increase in real time applications by placing deadlines on the response time of the database system and transactions processing. Such a system needs to process Transactions before these deadlines expired. A series of simulation study have been performed to analyze the performance under different transaction management under conditions such as different workloads, distribution methods, execution mode-distribution and parallel etc. The scheduling of data accesses are done in order to meet their deadlines and to minimize the number of transactions that missed deadlines. A new concept is introduced to manage the transactions in dynamic ways rather than setting computing parameters in static ways. With this approach, the system gives a significant improvement in performance.

INTRODUCTION

Real-Time Database Systems are becoming increasingly important in a wide range of applications, such as telecommunications, mobile communication systems, nuclear reactor control, traffic control systems, computer integrated manufacturing, robotics and military systems. A Real-Time Database System (RTDBS) is a transaction processing system that is designed to handle workloads where transactions have deadlines. The objective of the system is to meet these deadlines. As the world gets smarter and more informatics, demands on IT will grow. Many converging technologies are coming up like emerging IT delivery model-cloud computing. Demands of the real time distributed database are also increasing. Many transaction complexities are there in handling concurrency control and database recovery in distributed database systems. Two-phase commit protocol is most widely used to solve these problems [1]. To ensure such transaction atomicity, commit protocols are implemented in distributed database system. A uniform commitment is guarantee by a commit protocol in a distributed transaction execution to ensure that all the participating sites agree on a final outcome. Result may be either a commit or an abort condition.

Citation: Singh Y.J, Singh Y.S., Gaikwad A. and Mehrotra S.C., (2010), "Dynamic Management of Transactions in Distributed Real-time processing system", Inter. Journal of Database Management Systems, Vol. 2, no. 2, pp.161-170, DOI:10.5121/ijdms.2010.2210

Many real time database applications in areas of communication system and military systems are distributed in nature. In a real time database system the transaction processing system that is designed to handle workloads where transactions have complete deadlines. To ensure transaction atomicity, commit protocol are implemented in distributed database system. Experimental performances of transaction scheduling under variety of workloads and different system configuration are evaluated through this simulation. Many database researchers have proposed varieties of commit protocols like Two phase commit and Nested two phase commit [2, 3], Presumed commit [4] and Presume abort [3], Broadcast Two phase commit , Three phase commit [5,6] etc. These require exchanges of multiple messages, in multiple phases, between the participating sites where the distributed transaction executed. Several log records are generated to make permanent changed to the data disk, demanding some more transaction execution time [4, 7, 8]. Proper scheduling of transactions and management of its execution time are important factors in designing such systems. Transactions processing in any database systems can have real time constraints. The scheduling transactions with deadlines on a single processor memory resident database system have been developed and evaluated the scheduling through simulation [9]. A real time database system is a Transaction processing system that designed to handle workloads where transactions have complete deadlines. In case of faults, it is not possible to provide such guarantee. Real actions such as firing a weapon or dispensing cash may not be compensatable at all [10]. Proper scheduling of transactions and management of its execution time are the important factors in designing such systems. In such a database, the performance of the commit protocol is usually measured in terms of number of transactions that complete before their deadlines. The transaction that miss their deadlines before the completion of processing are just killed or aborted and discarded from the system without being executed to completion [11]. The section 2 describes the simulation details. In section 3, simulation model and simulation parameters are given. The detail experiments, results and analysis are given in section 4. The overall conclusions are discussed in section 5.

SIMULATION DETAILS This study is in continuation of our work in the same domain [12,13]. The study follows the real time processing model [14,15,16] and transaction processing addressing timeliness [17]. This model has six components:

(i) a source

(ii) a transaction manager

(iii) a concurrency control manager

(iv) a resource manager

(v) a recovery manager

(vi) a sink to collects statistics on the completed transactions.

A network manager models the behavior of the communications network. The definitions of the components of the model are given below.

(i) The source: This component is responsible for generating the workloads for a site. The workloads are characterized in terms of files that they access and number of pages that they access and also update of a file.

(ii) The transaction manager: The transaction manager is responsible for accepting transaction from the source and modeling their execution. This deals with the execution behavior of the transaction. Each transaction in the workload has a general structure consist of a master process and a number of cohorts. The master resides at the sites where the transaction was submitted. Each cohort makes a sequence of read and writes requests to files that are stored at its sites. A transaction has one cohort at each site where it needs to access data.

To choose the execution sites for a transaction's cohorts, the decision rule is: if a file is present at the originating site, use the copy there; otherwise, choose uniformly from among the sites that have remote copies of the files. The transaction manager also models the details of the commit and abort protocols

(iii) The concurrency control manager: It deals with the implementation of the concurrency control algorithms. In this study, this module is not fully implemented. The effect of this is dependent on algorithm that chooses during designing the system.

(iv) The resource manager: The resource manager models the physical resources like CPU, Disk, and files etc for writing to or accessing data or messages from them.

(v) The sink: The sink deals for collection of statistics on the completed transactions.

(vi) The Network Manager: The network manager encapsulates the model of the communications network. It is assuming a local area network system, where the actual time on the wire for messages is negligible.

EXECUTION MODEL AND SIMULATION PARAMETERS

The execution model is discussed below. A common model of a distributed transaction is that there is one process, called as Master, which is executed at the site where the transaction is submitted, and a set of processes, called Cohorts, which executes on behalf of the transaction at these various sites that are accessed by the transaction. In other words, each transaction has a master process that runs at its site of origination. The master process in turn sets up a collection of cohort's processes to perform the actual processing involved in running the transaction. When cohort finishes executing its portion of a query, it sends an execution complete message to the master. When the master received such a message from each cohort, it starts its execution process. When a transaction is initiated, the set of files and data items that, it will access are chosen by the source. The master is then loaded at its originating site and initiates the first phase of the protocol by sending PREPARE (to commit) messages in parallel to all the cohorts. Each cohort that is ready to commit, first force-writes a prepared log record to its local stable storage and then sends a YES vote to the master. At this stage, the cohort has entered a prepared state wherein it cannot unilaterally commit or abort the transaction but has to wait for final decision from the master. On other hand, each cohort that decides to abort force-writes an abort log record and sends a NO vote to the master. Since a NO vote acts like a veto, cohort is permitted unilaterally abort the transaction without waiting for a response from the master. After the master receives the votes from all the cohorts, it initiates the second phase of the protocol. If all the votes are YES, it moves to a committing state by force-writing a commit log record and sending COMMIT messages to all the cohorts. Each cohort after receiving a COMMIT message moves to the committing state, force-writes a commit log record, and sends an acknowledgement (ACK) message to the master. If the master receives even one NO vote, it moves to the aborting state by force writing an abort log record and sends ABORT messages to those cohorts that are in the prepared state. These cohorts, after receiving the ABORT message, move to aborting state, force-write an abort log record and send an ACK message to the master. Finally, the master, after receiving acknowledgement from all the prepared cohorts, writes an end log record and then forgets and made free the transaction. The statistics are collected in the Sink [Jayant et al'90,92,96]. The database is modeled as a collection of DBsize pages that are uniformly distributed across all the NumSites sites. At each site, transactions arrive under Poisson stream with rate ArrivalRate, and each transaction has an associated firm deadline. The deadline is assigned using the formula

$$DT = AT + SF * RT \quad (1)$$

Here DT, AT, SF and RT are the deadline, arrival rate, Slack factor and resource time respectively, of transaction T. The Resource time is the total service time at the resources that the transaction requires for its execution. The Slack factor is a constant that provides control over the tightness or slackness of the transaction deadlines. In this model, each of the transaction in the supplied workload has the structure of the single master and multiple cohorts. The number of sites at which each transaction executes is specifying by the Fileselection time (DistDegree) parameter. At each of the execution sites, the number of pages accessed by the transaction's cohort varies uniformly between 0.5 and 1.5 times CohortSize. These pages are chosen randomly from among the database pages located at that site. A page that is read is updated with probability of WriteProb. Summary of the simulation parameter is given in table I.

Parameter Settings

The values of the parameter set in the simulation are given in table II. The CPU time to process a page is 10 milliseconds while disk access times are 20 milliseconds.

TABLE1. SIMULATION PARAMETERS

Parameters	Description
NumSites orSelectfile	Number of sites in the Database
Dbsize	Number of pages in the database.
ArrivalRate	Transaction arrival rate/site
Slackfactor	Slack factor in Deadline formula
FileSelection Time	Degree of Freedom (DistDegree)
WriteProb	Page update probability
PageCPU	CPU page processing time
PageDisk	Disk page access time
TerminalThink	Time between completion of 1 transaction & submission of another
Numwrite	Number of Write Transactions
NumberReadT	Number of Read Transactions

TABLE II. VALUES OF SIMULATION MODEL PARAMETERS

Parameters	Set Values	Parameters	Set Values
NumSites	8	FileSelection Time	3
Dbsize	vary(max.2400)	PageCPU	10ms
ArrivalRate	6 to 8 job/sec	PageDisk	20ms
Slackfactor	4	TerminalThink	0 to 0.5 sec
WriteProb	0.5		

EXPERIMENTS AND RESULTS

The experiment has been performed using different simulation language like C++Sim, DeNet etc in reports [13,14,15]. For this study, GPSS World is used as a simulator [18]. Literatures are also collected from several recent studies [19, 1, 20, 21,22, 23]. The study for performance evaluation starts by first developing a base model. Further experiments were constructed around the base model experiments by varying a few parameters and process of execution at a time. The performance metric of the experiments is MissPercent that is the percentage of input transaction that the system is unable to complete before their deadline. The MissPercent values in range of 0% to 20% are taken to represent system performance under "Normal" loads, while ranges of 21% to 100% represent system performance under "heavy" loads. The study analyzes the performance of the system under different workload with varying the arrival rate of the transaction, dynamic slack factors, execution mode etc. The study analyzed the performance using this new concept of 'intelligent agent' technique. Only the statistically significant results are discussed. The experimental results are discussed below. This following section discusses the statistical results of this simulation under different environments.

Comparison of Centralized and Distributed systems

This experiment compares the performance of the system under centralized and distributed. The distributed systems have higher percentage of miss Transactions than centralized system. This higher miss percentage is due to distance between cohorts. This leads to design of a new perfect distributed commit processing protocol to have a real-time committing performance.

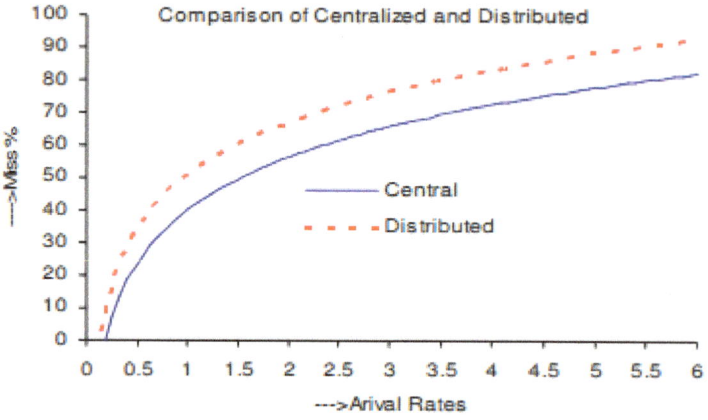

Figure 1 Comparison of Centralize and distributed performances.

Impact of distribution methods

This experiment is conducted to know the impact of difference between distribution methods to the performance of the system. As an example, we take Exponential distribution and Poisson distribution. The assignment and committing of transactions to cohorts are passed under scheduler using Exponential distribution and Poisson distribution and the statistics of the simulation outputs are noted. The Exponential give more uniform assignment and committing of transactions than Poisson. Poisson throws higher numbers of transactions giving more collisions of transactions and large number miss percentage of transactions than Exponential. So on many experiments of such similar types can be conducted by using more different distribution rules.

Impact execution mode: Distribution and Parallel

This experiment compares the output of the system putting the cohorts in parallel with that of distribution execution. From this we can conclude following points. Parallel execution of the cohorts reduces the transaction response time. The time required for the commit processing is partially reduced. This is because the queuing time is shorted in parallel and so there are much fewer chances of a cohort aborting during waiting phase. In the following figure, d1, d2 and d3 are representing cohorts connected in distributed and p1, p2 and p3 represents those connected in parallel.

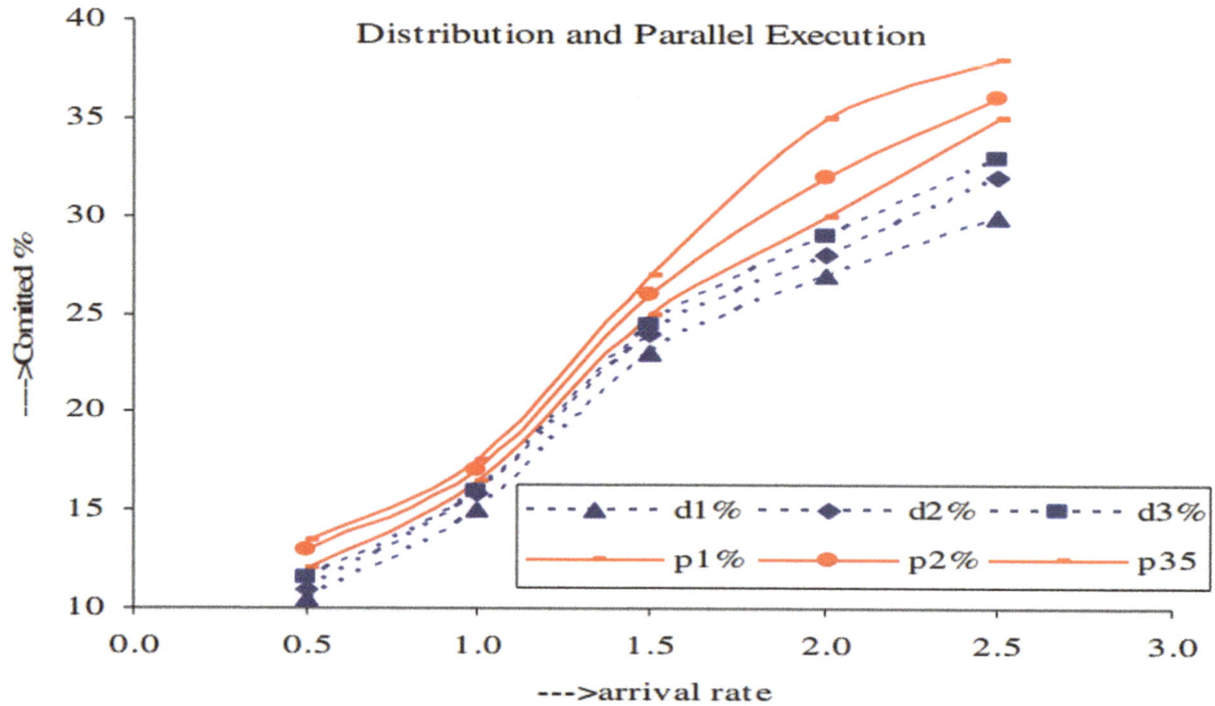

Figure 2 Impact of execution mode-distribution and Parallel.

Impact of slack to Throughput

In this set of experiments, the impact of slack factor to observed on the throughput of the system. The throughput initially increases with increase in slack factor –statically or dynamically. But it drops rapidly at very high loads. Here we collected only statically results, not the exact results. Still there are lots more to study required about other parameters to improve the throughput of the overall system. The following figure 3 shows impact of slack factors to throughput of all 8 sites.

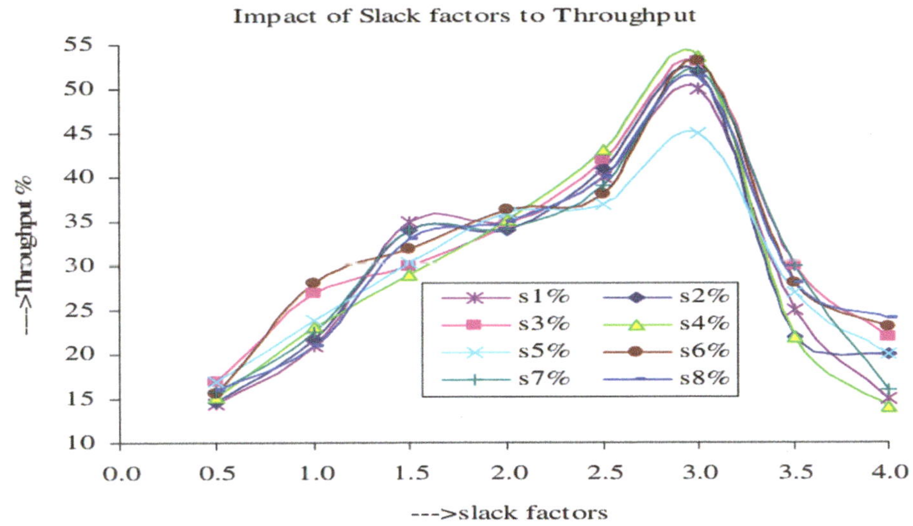

Figure 3. Impact of Slack factors to Throughput.

Dynamic Management

The transactions can be manage in many differet ways. In most of the earlier works done the transcations are management in static ways, where the parameter values are fixed to a constant value during execution of the experiments. Here in our work, we are introducing experiment done with dynamic manegments of transacions, where the values of the paremeters are changes or adjust automatically depending on the requirements during the execution the experiment. Here we are conducting two different experiments

Impact of Dynamic Intelligent agent

A dynamic intelligent agent is introduced to take sensory input from the environment, and produces as output actions that affect it. The agents act in rapidly changing, unpredictable or open environments and where their action can fail are known to the agents. Main advantages for the use of the mobile agents are the increased the autonomy of the system in many ways like flexibility to topological changes, to load balance changes. After knowing the status of transactions to be fail, extra slack factor can be apply to safe the transaction. The fig 4 shows the performance comparison between normal/base model and impact of the intelligent agent. By adding such agent can improved the performance of the system.

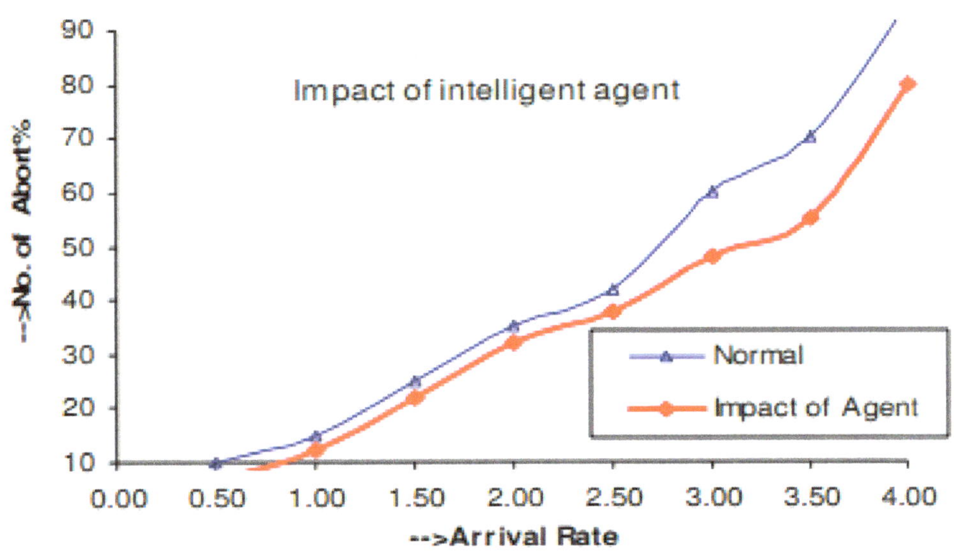

Figure 4. Impact of intelligent agent.

Impact of dynamic Slack factor

This set of experiment is conducted to safe some of the transactions before killing or aborting them. The Slack factor is provided to control over the tightness or slackness of the transaction deadlines. Normally the system aborts all transactions which are unlikely to be completed before their deadlines. If the slack factor value is nearly negative, it aborts the transaction and removed it from the queue. After computing the slack value of all transactions, the system will know possible total number of transactions which have +vet and -vet slack values. If there is large number of transaction with +vet slack values means that the system will have some bonus time. If the system is not having firmed slack condition, it can alter some of –vet slack value to next higher level to safe some of the killing transactions. In other words, the bonus time remains from the transactions that have +vet slack value are going to used to safe the transaction with -vet slack value. With the static slack value, it gives normal performance. By increasing the slack dynamically, it gives lower values of missed percentage of transactions. So on exchange of slack time between transactions increased the performance of the system.

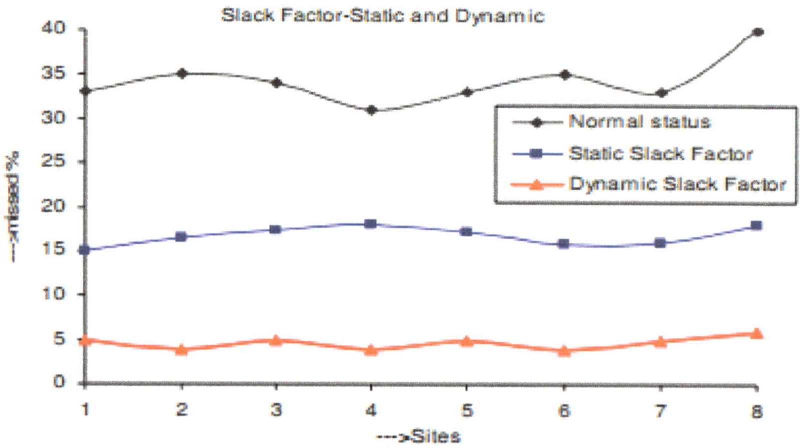

Figure5. Impact of Slack factor to Individual sites.

CONCLUSION

A series of simulation study have been performed to analyze the performance under different transaction management situation such as different workloads, distribution methods, execution mode-Distribution and Parallel, impact of dynamic slack factors to throughput. The scheduling of data accesses are done in order to meet their deadlines and to minimize the number of transactions that missed deadlines. Parallel execution of the cohorts reduces the transaction response time than that of serial or distributed execution. The time required for the commit processing is partially reduced, because the queuing time is shorted in parallel and so there are much fewer chances of a cohort aborting during waiting phase. The throughput initially increases with increase in slack factor. But it drops rapidly at very high work loads. The slack factors can be providing by static or dynamics ways. The new approach dynamic management either dynamic intelligent agent or dynamic slack management gives a significant improvement to the performance of the system. Dynamic intelligent agent keeps tracks of timing of the transactions to help them from aborts. This agent gives advance information about the remaining execution time of the transactions. This helps the system to inject extra time to such transactions. In all the conditions the arrival rate of transaction plays a major role in reducing number of miss percentage and improved performance.

REFERENCE

1. Silberschatz, Korth, Sudarshan,2002, Database system concept,4th (I.E), McGraow-Hill Pub. 698-709,903
2. Gray. J,1978,"Notes on Database Operating Systems", Operating Systems:An Advanced Course, Lecture notes in Computer Science
3. Mohan, C, Lindsay B and Obermark 1986, Transaction Management in the R* Distributed Database Management Systems, ACM TODS, 11(4).
4. Lampson B and Lomet D,1993, "A new Presumes Commit Optimization for Two phase Commit", Pro.of 19th VLDB Conference.
5. Oszu M, Valduriez P,1991, Principles of Distributed Database Systems, Prentice-Hall.
6. Kohler W, 1981,A survey of Techniques for Synchronization and Recovery in Decentralized Computer System, ACM Computing Surveys, 13(2)
7. Nystrom D, Nolin M,2006, Pessimistic Concurrency Control and Versioning to Support Database Pointers in Real-Time Databases, Proc. 16th Euromicro Conf. on Real-Time Systems
8. Ramamritham,Son S. H, and DiPippo L,2004, Real-Time Databases and Data Services, Real-Time Systems J., vol. 28, 179-216.
9. Robert A and Garcia-Molina H,1992, Scheduling Real-Time Transactions, ACM Trans. on Database Systems, 17(3).
10. Levy E., Korth H and Silberschatz,1991,An optimistic commit protocol for distributed transaction management, Pro.of ACM SIGMOD Conf.
11. Jayant. H, Carey M, Livney,1992, "Data Access Scheduling in Firm Real time Database Systems", Real Time systems Journal, 4(3)

12. Jayanta Singh and S.C Mehrotra, 2006,"Performance analysis of a Real Time Distributed Database System through simulation" 15th IASTED International Conf. on APPLIED SIMULATION & MODELLING, Greece
13. Jayanta Singh and S.C Mehrotra,2009 "A study on transaction scheduling in a real-time distributed system",EUROSIS's Annual Industrial Simulation Conference, UK.
14. Jayant H. 1991, "Transaction Scheduling in Firm Real-Time Database Systems", Ph.D. Thesis, Computer Science Dept. Univ. of Wisconsin, Madison.
15. Jayant H. Carey M and Livney M,1990 "Dynamic Real-Time Optimistic Concurrency Control", Proc. of 11th IEEE Real-Time Systems Symp.
16. Jayant H., Ramesh G. Kriti.R, S. Seshadri, "Commit processing in Distributed Real-Time Database Systems", Tech. Report-TR-96-01, Pro. Pro. Of 17th IEEE Real-Time Systems Symposium, USA,1996
17. Han Q, 2003, Addressing timeliness /accuracy/ cost tradeoffs in information collection for dynamic environments, IEEE Real-Time System Symposium,Cancun, Mexico
18. Minutesmansoftware, GPSS world, North Carolina, U. S. A. 2010.
19. Xiong M. and Ramamritham K.,2004, Deriving Deadlines and Periods for Real-Time Update Transactions, IEEE Trans. on Computers, vol. 53,(5).
20. Gustavsson S and Andler S 2005, Decentralized and continuous consistency management in distributed real-time databases with multiple writers of replicated data, Workshop on parallel and distributed real-time systems, Denver, CO
21. Xiong M, Han S., and Lam K,2005, A Deferrable Scheduling for Real-Time Transactions Maintaining Data Freshness, IEEE Real-Time Systems Symposium.
22. Jan Lindstrom,2006 "Relaxed Correctness for Firm Real-Time Databases," rtcsa,pp.82-86, 12th IEEE International Conference on Embedded and Real-Time Computing Systems and Applications (RTCSA'06).
23. Idoudi, N. Duvallet, C. Sadeg, B. Bouaziz, R. Gargouri, F,2008, Structural Model of Real-Time Databases: An Illustration, 11th IEEE International Symposium on Object-Oriented Real-Time Distributed Computing (ISORC 2008)

CHAPTER 7 FUZZY LOGIC BASED QUERY OPTIMIZATION IN DISTRIBUTED DATABASE

Abhijeet R Raipurkar[1] ,G.R.Bamnote[2]

[1]M.E. Final Year, Department of Computer Science & Engineering, PRMIT&R, Badnera, India
[2]Head & Professor, Department Of Computer Science & Engineering, PRMIT&R, Badnera, India

ABSTRACT

Structural Query Language (SQL) is very restrictive in data extraction. Classical SQL queries have remarkable capabilities in terms of data extraction and answer formation from information stored at widely dispersed databases. Human queries are rarely crisp which poses challenges in efficient answer formation and data retrieval. These are based on human perception which is grossly inexact and imprecise based on world knowledge. Integration of query languages with fuzzy logic can increase their capability in data retrieval based on human perception. Query optimization is a difficult task in a distributed client/server environment as data location becomes a major factor. The integration of a query processing subsystem into a distributed database management system with fuzzy logic is used for analyzing query response time across fragmentations of global relations. Fuzzy logic based query optimization in distributed database have an important impact on the performance of distributed query processing.

INTRODUCTION

Distributed database adds to the conventional centralized Database system [3] some other types of processing expenses, because of the additional design (hardware & software) to handle the distribution. These expenses present as the cost of data transfer over the network. Data transferred could be, intermediate files resulting from local sites, or final results need to be sent back to the original site that issued the query. Therefore, database designers are concerned about query optimization, which target minimizing the cost of transferring data across the network. Criteria for measuring the cost of a query evaluation strategy for centralized DBMSs number of disk accesses (# blocks read / written) and for distributed databases, additionally the cost of data transmission over the network and Potential gain in performance from having several sites processing parts of the query in parallel. Join queries [4] in distributed database are ship whole, fetch as needed, semi joins [4] and bloom joins and each of these join strategies are having their own advantages and disadvantages. Main considerations of query processing in distributed databases are: communication cost, if there is several copies of a relation, decide which copy to use, amount of data being shipped,

Citation: Raipurkar A.R., G.R. Bamnote, (2013), "Fuzzy Logic Based Query Optimization in Distributed Database", International Journal of Innovative Research in Computer and Communication Engineering, Vol. 1, no.2, pp. 422-426, ISSN (Online): 2320 – 9801.

relative processing speed at each site and site selection In a relational database [7] all information can be found in a series of tables. A query therefore consists of operations on tables. The most common queries are Select-Project-Join queries. Distributed query processing: Transform a high-level query (of relational calculus/SQL) on a distributed database (i.e., a set of global relations) into an equivalent and efficient lower-level query (of relational algebra) on relation fragments. Distributed query processing is more complex because of fragmentation/replication of relations, additional communication costs and parallel execution of operations. Query optimization is the process of producing an optimal (close to optimal) query execution plan which represents an execution strategy for the query. The main task in query optimization is to consider different orderings of the operations and minimize total cost associated with execution of request. Query optimization is a crucial and difficult part of the overall query processing.

RELATED WORK

In a relational database all information can be found in a series of tables. A query therefore consists of operations on tables. The most common queries are Select-Project-Join queries. For a given query, the search space can be defined as the set of equivalent operator trees that can be produced using transformation rules. Distributed query optimization process consists of transforming global queries from control sites to Fragment queries in local site. The process of transformation is as shown below:

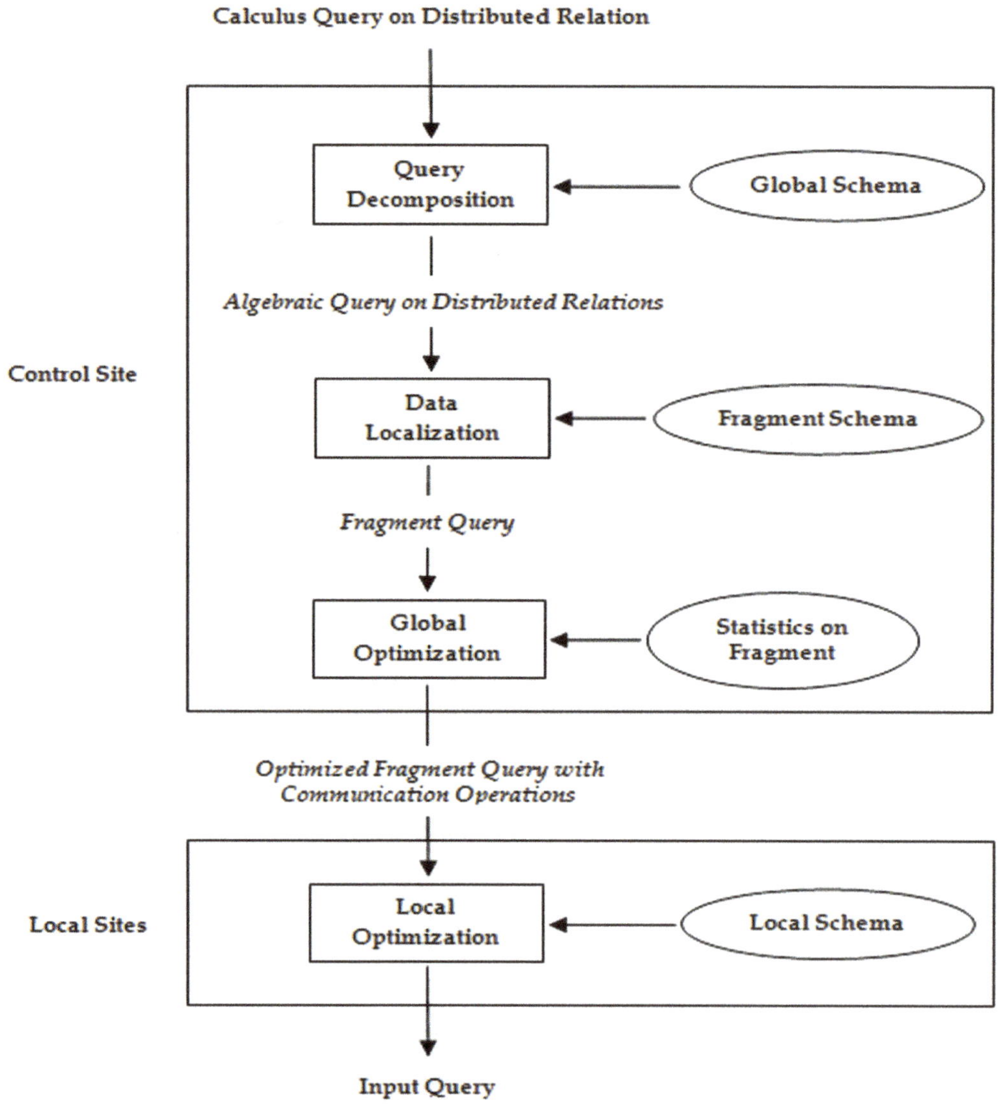

Figure.1 Distributed Query Optimization Process.

The input is a query on distributed data expressed in relational calculus. Four main layers are involved to map the distributed query into an optimized sequence of local operations, each acting on a local database. These layers perform the functions of query decomposition, data localization, global query optimization, and local query optimization. Query decomposition and data localization correspond to query rewriting. The first three layers are performed by a central site and use global information. Local optimization is done by the local sites. Ordering of the operators of relational algebra is crucial for efficient query processing so expensive operators should be moved at the end of query processing. Various unary and binary operations can be pushed to the leaves of the tree as per time complexity associated with it. Following are the various unary and binary operators used during query optimization process along with time complexity. In time complexity 'n' represents cardinality of relation..

Table 1: Comparison of Time Complexity for Various Relational Operations

Operations	Time Complexity
Select, Project (without duplicate elimination)	O(n)
Project (with duplicate elimination)	O(n log n)
Group Join Semi-join Division Set Operators	O(n log n)
Cartesian Product	O(n2)

PROPOSED SYSTEM

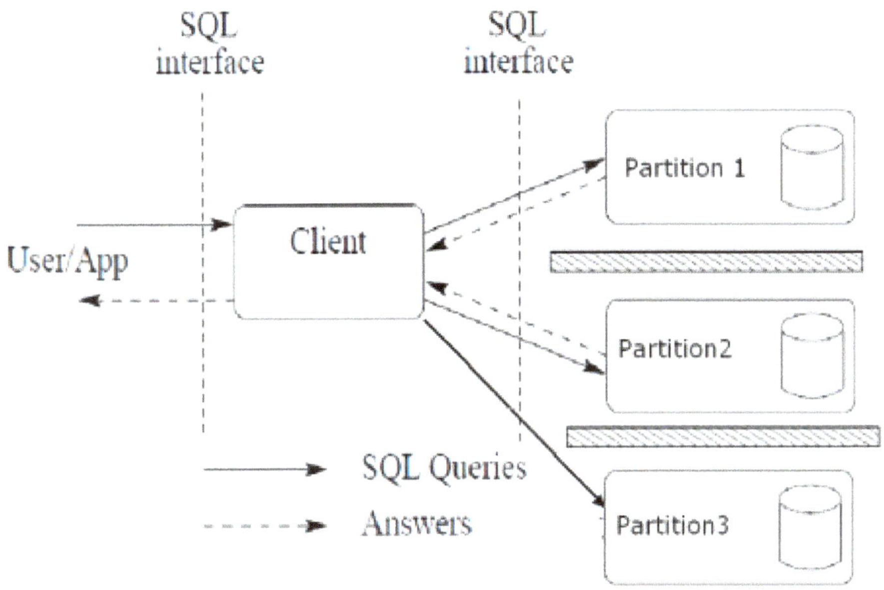

Figure. 2 Proposed System Architecture.

The general architecture of a distributed secure database service, as illustrated in Fig 2, consists of a trusted client as well as two or more servers that provide a database service. Client will execute the queries on various fragments and proposed algorithm will find out the best minimized query processing time. Also client can execute fuzzy queries on the fragments which are created by partitioning algorithm. Fuzziness in the database can be handled by transforming fuzzy queries into normal SQL queries. In the proposed system, database is partitioned into three partitions dbfpartition1, dbfpartition2 and dbfpartition3. In the database design, dbfpartition1 consists of two vertically fragmented relations on the basis of tupule Id (tid) from which original global relation can be recovered by applying simple join algorithm. Dbfpartition2 consists of three vertically fragmented relations on the basis of tupule id and dbfpartition3 consists of original global relation. In the proposed query processing and query optimization process, query response time is compared against these two vertically fragmented relations with global relation and fragments with minimum response time for read only and update application is selected for development distributed database applications. A. Fuzziness in database A database is an ordered collection of related data elements intended to meet the information needs of an organization and designed to be shared by multiple users. If a regular or classical database is a structured collection of records or data stored in a computer, a fuzzy database is a database, which is able to deal with uncertain or incomplete information using fuzzy logic. Basically, a fuzzy database is a database with fuzzy attributes, which may be defined as attributes of an item, row, or object in a database, which allows storing fuzzy information. The following is a brief definition of the characteristics of imperfect data:

Uncertain data - The uncertainty is related to the degree of truth of its attribute value, and it means that we can apportion some, but not all, of our belief to a given value or a group of values.

- Vague data - Lack of definite or sharp distinctions. Imprecise data - The imprecision and vagueness are relevant to the content of an attribute value, and it means that a choice must be made from a given range (interval or set) of values but we do not know exactly which one to choose at present.
- Inapplicable data - There may be some entities for which a piece of data relating to one of its properties cannot be acquired due to a lack of the property.

In the real time situation, people express their ideas using the natural languages. Normally natural language has a lot of vagueness and ambiguity. However, while applying one's thoughts as a query in terms of natural languages into the database, a lot of problems are experienced due to the inefficiency of RDBMS to handle such queries. Consider the query "Give names of the employees who have highest and lowest salary". This query cannot be processed directly by the SQL, since it contains a lot of vagueness like highest and lowest salary. The best remedy for modelling the above situation is by the use of fuzzy Sets.

The proposed scheme is implemented using Microsoft Visual Studio 2010 and Microsoft SQL server 2010.

The Working scheme is,

1. Create a different partitions for the database (here three database are created with different schemas).
2. Apply workload i.e. queries on all databases and estimate the cost of each query in terms of response time.
3. The number of queries applied on the partitions is varied from 1 to 100.
4. Different types of query operations such as Insert, Update, delete, fetch and fuzzy value based searching are applied on all the partitions
5. Fuzzy range is defined for the salary attributed defined in all the partitions
6. If user is fetching records of particular fuzzy ranges then query is classified into fuzzy range1, 2 or 3 as per the user input.
7. Then the comparison is done on the basis of cost of queries i.e. response time of the query

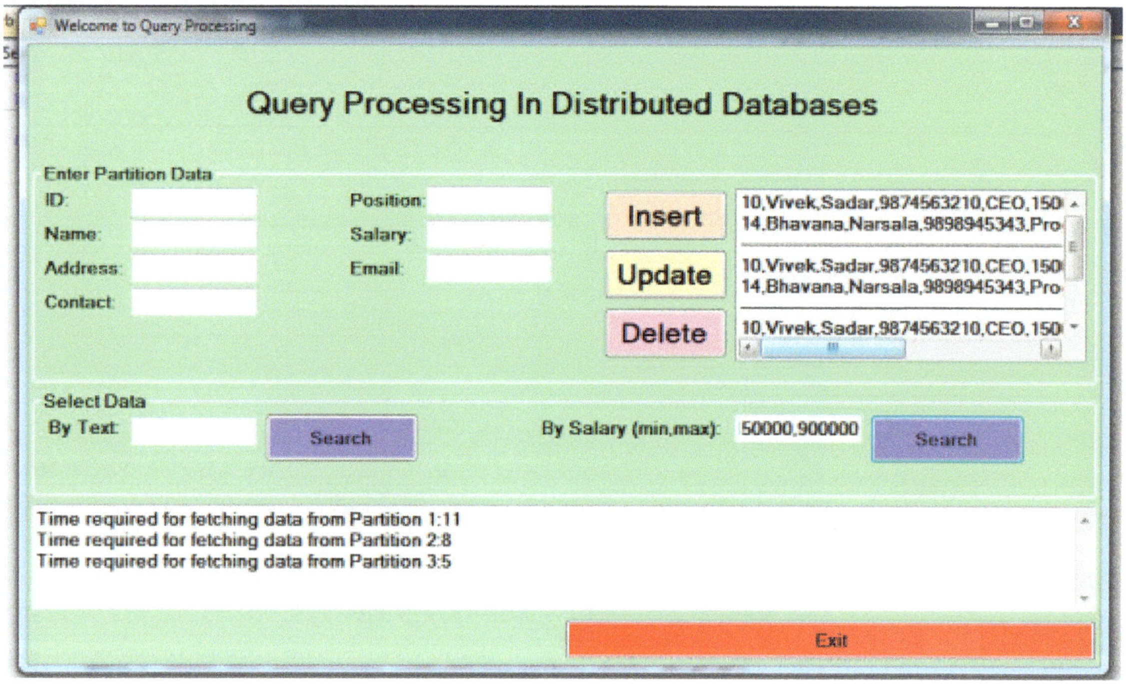

Figure. 3 Fuzzy Query for all partitions showing response time.

For Fuzzy queries which we had simulated on salary attribute of the partitions, partion3 is best candidate as it results in least response time. Fuzzy ranges are defined in terms of minimum and maximum salary which will be entered by user in main window of project and according salary will be assigned proper fuzzy ranges as defined in system. Comparison of simulating normal query and fuzzy query on all partitions shows that fuzzy queries will always take less response time as compared to normal SQL query. Reason for the least response time is that query evaluation engine does not have to search all the records in database; it has to search records in fuzzy range values. Hence fuzzy queries are most optimized queries in distributed databases.

CONCLUSION

We have proposed method of incorporating fuzziness in distributed database for accommodating fuzzy queries which are approximations based on human knowledge. Fuzzy queries to relational database are proposed as one candidate model and fuzzy relational database is presented as another relational model. With the help of example of employee distributed database, we have successfully implemented fuzzy logic based queries using dot net environment for GUI and SQL server for databases. This establishes feasibility of the concepts proposed. Distributed database systems provide an improvement on communication and data processing due to its data distribution throughout different network sites. Not only is data access faster, but a single-point of failure is less likely to occur, and it provides local control of data for users. However, there is some complexity when attempting to manage and control distributed database systems. A distributed database allows faster local queries and can reduce network traffic. With these benefits comes the issue of maintaining data integrity.

Proposed work for query processing handles two important issues in data distribution i.e. minimizing query response time through partitions and handling fuzziness in database by translating fuzzy queries into SQL.

REFERENCES

1. C. T. Yu, K. C. Guh, W. Zhang, M. Templeton, D. Brill, and A. L. P. Chen, "An Integrated Algorithm for Distributed Query Processing," in IFIP Conference on Distributed processingAmsterdam, 1987.
2. D. Chiang, L.R. Chow and N. Hsien, "Fuzzy information in extended fuzzy relational databases", Fuzzy Sets and Systems 92, pp.1-10. (1997).
3. G. Aggarwal, M. Bawa, P. Ganesan, H. Garcia-Molina, K. Kenthapadi, R. Motwani,U. Srivastava, D. Thomas, and Y. Xu. Two can keep a secret: A distributed architecture for secure database services. In Conference on Innovative Data Systems Research,2005.
4. G.J. Klir and B. Yuan [2001], "Fuzzy Sets and Fuzzy Logic: Theory and Applications", Prentice Hall, Inc. Englewood Cliffs, N. J., U.S.A.
5. G. Pelagatti and F. A. Schreiber, "A Model of an access Strategy in Distributed Database System," in International Conference of Database Architecture, Venice, Italy, 1979.
6. J. Callan, "Distributed information retrieval". In Advances in Information Retrieval, W. B. Croft, Ed. Kluwer Academic Publishers, 2000, pp. 127–150.
7.] K. T. Huang, "Query Optimization in Distributed Databases," in Laboratory for information and Decision Systems: MIT, 1982.
8. Li, Victor O. K. "Query processing in distributed data bases", MIT. Lab.for Information and Decision Systems Series/Report no.: LIDS-P ; 1107,1981
9. M. Tamer Ozsu, Patrick Valduries, "Principles of Distributed Database System", Second Edition, Pearson Education, pp 169.
10. N. Alon, W. F. de la Vega, R. Kannan, and M. Karpinski. Random sampling and approximation of max-csp problems. In J. Comput. Syst. Sci., pages 212–243,2003.
11. Nilarun Mukherjee, Synthesis of Non Replicated Dynamic Fragment Allocation Algorithm in Distributed Database System", Published in Proceeding of International conference on advances in Computer Science , 2010
12.] P. Valduriez and T. Ozsu, "Principle of Distributed Database Systems.," Prentice Hall,1999. P. A. Bernstein, N. Gooman, E. Wong, C.L. Reeve, and J.B. Rothie, "Query Processing in a system for Distributed Databases", ACM Transaction on Database Systems, Vol. 6, pp. 602- 625, (1981).
13. Ramez Elmasri, Shamkant B. Navathe, "Fundamentals of Database System", Fifth Edition,Pearson Education, Second Impression, pp 894, 2009.
14. P. A. Bernstein and W. C. D-M, "Using semi-joins to solve relational queries," ACM vol. 28:1, pp. 25-40,1981.
15. M. S. Chen and P. S. Yu, "Combining Join and Semi Operations for Distributed Query Processing," IEEE Trans. of Knowledge & Data Engineering, vol. 5:3, pp. 534-542, 1993.
16. M. S. Chen and P. S. Yu, "A Graph Theoritical Approach to Determine a Join Reducer Sequences in Distributed Query Processing," IEEE Trans. Of Knowledge & Data Engineering, vol. 6:1, pp. 152-165, 1994.
17. M. S. Chen and P. S. Yu, "Interleaving a Join Sequence with Semijoins in distributed Query Processing," IEEE Trans. on Parallel and Distributed Systems, vol. 3:5, pp. 611-621, 1992.
18. T. Ibaraki and T. Kameda, "On the Optimal Nesting Order for N-Relatioanl Joins," ACM (TODS), vol. 9:3, pp. 482-502, 1984.
19. P. A. Bernstein, N. Goodman, E. Wong, C. L. Reeve, and J. B. Rothie, "Query Processing in a System for Distributed Databases (SDD- 1)," ACM Transactions On Database Systems, , vol. 6: 4, pp. 602-625, 1981.

CHAPTER 8

COMMIT PROTOCOLS IN MOBILE ENVIRONMENTS: DESIGN & IMPLEMENTATION

Salman Abdul Moiz[1] , Dr. Lakshmi Rajamani[2] & Supriya N.Pal[3]

[1]Centre for Development of Advanced Computing, Bangalore, India

[2]University College of Engineering, Osmania University, Hyderabad, India

[3]Centre for Development of Advanced Computing, Bangalore, India

ABSTRACT

In any database environment either wired or wireless, if multiple host access similar data items it may lead to concurrent access anomalies. As disconnections and mobility are the common characteristics in mobile environment, preserving consistency in presence of concurrent access is a challenging issue. Most of the approaches use locking mechanisms to achieve concurrency control. This leads to increase in blocking and abort rate in mobile environments. However the dynamic timer adjustment strategies may use locking mechanism to efficiently implement concurrency control. To reduce deadlocks and blocking of resources an enhanced optimistic approach for concurrency control is proposed. To show the effectiveness of the commit protocols in mobile environments, a simulator is designed and implemented to demonstrate how the transactions are committed and how the data consistency is maintained when the transactions are executed concurrently. The simulator was tested for both pessimistic and optimistic approaches.

INTRODUCTION

Mobile computing is widely used in many applications such as mobile banking, traffic status, weather forecasting, etc., [10, 5]. In order to provide these services, required information is retrieved from database server via a wireless channel and is passed on to the mobile hosts. Concurrency Control is one of the important components of transaction management. Several valuable attempts were made to efficiently implement the concurrency control strategies in mobile environment. The concurrency control strategies presented in literature are based on three mechanisms viz., locking, timestamps and optimistic concurrency control. Due to various constraints in the mobile environment and nature of different online applications, these schemes may not work effectively. Several valuable attempts have been made to efficiently implement the commit protocols in traditional and mobile environments. The choice of a protocol depends on type of the mobile application and the choice of the data service provider. In this paper the design and implementation of both protocols are presented. The remaining part of this paper is organized as follows: Section 2 summarizes the survey of commit protocols proposed in the literature, section 3 describes the environment and the elements of mobile

Citation: Abdul Moiz S., Rajamani L. & S. N. Pal, (2010), "Commit Protocols in Mobile Environments: Design & Implementation", International Journal of Database Management Systems (IJDMS), Vol.2, No.3, August 2010, DOI: 10.5121/ijdms.2010.2310.

databases, section 4 specifies the conceptual architecture, section 5 describes the design & implementation of optimistic protocols, section 6 presents mobility issues, section 7 specifies the results and section 8 concludes the paper.

RELATED WORK

As long as the mobile clients are not involved in the concurrent access of data items, the database consistency can be preserved. When multiple mobile hosts initiate the transactions requesting for the same data item, it can be locked by only one of the transaction. After the execution of the transaction, the data items are unlocked and the same are acquired by the waiting transaction. When one transaction is being executed, the other transaction that needs the same data items, locked by the former has to wait for invariant time. The delay in acquiring the data items may further increase due to disconnections of mobile hosts for longer time. To solve these problems, following concurrency control techniques are proposed. The basic idea is that a transaction has to be executed within certain time period (Execution time). This information is maintained by fixed host. To achieve concurrency control, two phase locking protocol was used in the traditional environment. However this protocol requires clients to communicate continuously with the server to obtain locks and detect the conflicts. Hence it is not suitable for mobile environments. In [3], A Timeout based Mobile Transaction Commitment Protocol uses timeouts to provide non-blocking protocol with restrained communication. It faces the problem of the time lag between local and global commit. In [4] the proposed Mobile 2PC protocol preserves the 2PC principle and minimizes the impact of unreliable wireless communication. This protocol assumes that all communicating partners are stationary hosts, equipped with sufficient computing resources and power supply with permanently available bandwidth. In the pessimistic approaches, the items may be blocked for certain period of time. To avoid the blocking of data items and allowing multiple users to access the shared data items requires strong conflict resolution strategies. For this reason, an optimistic concurrency control technique is frequently used in wireless environments [13, 14, 15]. An optimistic concurrency control technique detects and resolves data conflicts in the phase of transaction validation. In a mobile environment the transaction validation is done on the server, it may lead to delayed response causing overhead at the server. An Optimistic Concurrency Control with Dynamic Time stamp Adjustment Protocol requires client side write operations. However because of the delay in execution of a transaction, it may never be executed [16]. In [17], the conventional optimistic concurrency control algorithm is enhanced with an early termination mechanism on conflicting transactions. However because of early termination a transaction need to be initiated again and again. Optimistic concurrency control protocols (OCC) [19, 20, 22] are non-blocking and deadlockfree, which make them efficient to use in mobile computing and have been adopted in the Disconnected Operation [21] and Kangaroo Transaction model. However, without locks to data items, transactions might access conflicting data items under an optimistic concurrency control protocol (OCC). Two concurrent transactions conflict if one of them performs a write on similar data items. Therefore, approaches to terminate conflicting transactions are proposed [17,18]. In these approaches if the conflict rate increases, more and more transactions get aborted. Pessimistic commit protocols suitable for mobile environments are presented from [5] to [8]. Further a Real Time optimistic Commit protocols with a conflict resolution strategy is presented in [9]. The Design & Implementation of Pessimistic Commit protocols is described in [10]. The design and implementation of the optimistic commit protocol is presented in this chapter.

MOBILE DATABASE MODEL

Mobile Database Architecture

The mobile computing environment generally consists of three entities Fixed Host (FH), Mobile Hosts (MH) and Base Stations (BS) respectively. Terminals, desktop, servers are the fixed host, which are interconnected by means of a fixed network.

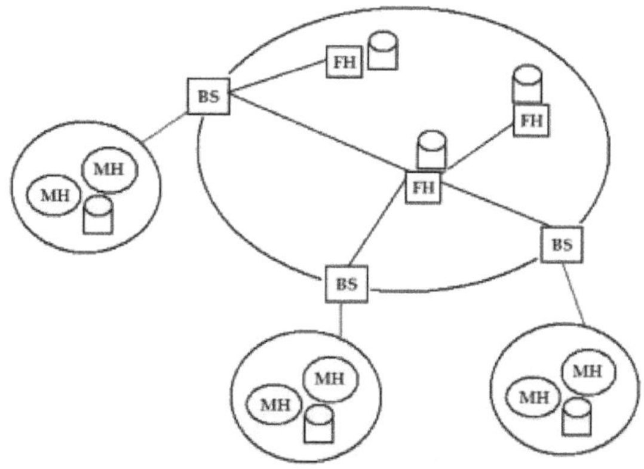

Figure 1. Mobile Database Architecture [9]

Large databases can run on servers that guarantee efficient processing and reliable storage of database. Fixed hosts perform the transaction and data management functions with the help of data base servers (DBS). Mobile units are the portable computers which can retain the network connections through the support of the Base Stations (BS). The request for execution of a transaction is initiated at a mobile host may but it may be executed at fixed host or mobile host. A Base station connects to a mobile unit and is equipped with a wireless interface. It is also known as a Mobile Support Station. Mobile Hosts (MH) may not always be connected to the fixed network. They may be disconnected for different reasons. Mobile host may differ with respect to the computing power and storage space; however MH can run a DBMS module. The commit protocols assume that the transaction request is sent to the Base Station which acts as the coordinator. The Mobile host and the Database systems act as the participants. The decision regarding the final commit, scheduling of transaction etc is done by the base station to which the mobile host was registered when it initiated the transaction request.

The component of the mobile transaction management system that are designed, implemented and tested includes the Pessimistic & Optimistic commit protocols.

Pessimistic Commit Protocols The pessimistic approach says "No one can cause concurrency violation with my data if I don't let them at the data which I have it" [1]. In pessimistic commit protocols a row is locked for execution of the transaction. Once the transaction completes it is unlocked and can be acquired by the waiting transaction which needs the shared resource. The pessimistic commit protocols uses locking of data items yet enhances throughput. Four variations of this pessimistic approach are presented. The Algorithmic approach uses static time out mechanisms to reduce the starvation of waiting process [8]. The Single Lock Manager Approach [5] uses the dynamic timer adjustment strategy to increase the overall commit rate. However to reduce the rollback operations the Concurrency control with reduced rollbacks [6] uses pre-emptive approach of scheduling the transactions and the strategy for concurrency control [7] uses predictive approach for scheduling the transaction execution. These approaches may be selected based on the business logic of the mobile application. The design and implementation of pessimistic commit protocols was presented in [10].

Optimistic Commit Protocols

In optimistic concurrency control strategy, the data items are not locked and can be used by more than one mobile host at the same time. The transaction executes in two phases: In the first phase the transaction is committed locally on mobile host using the on-demand approach [9]. In the second phase the results are updated onto the fixed host. In on demand multicasting , the data fragment needed by mobile host for executing the transactions is only requested from the mobile host and whenever the data conflict occurs, the invalidation reports along with request for re-execution of transactions is only sent to the mobile host using the shared data item. In optimistic replication, shared data is replicated on mobile hosts and users are allowed to continue their work while disconnected. Updates performed by fixed host and later propagated to servers. In the earlier approaches whenever a concurrency violation occurs i.e data items are updated at fixed host the conflicting transaction using the similar data items was aborted. In this approach the conflicting transaction is not aborted but it is restated with new state of the data items.

ARCHITECTURE OF OPTIMISTIC CONCURRENCY CONTROL STRATEGY

The generic architecture of optimistic concurrency control strategy is represented in figure 2. This architecture is suitable for both online and offline transactions. However the emphasis is on offline transactions in this paper, where the transactions are executed at mobile host and later on the results are reconciled with the fixed host.

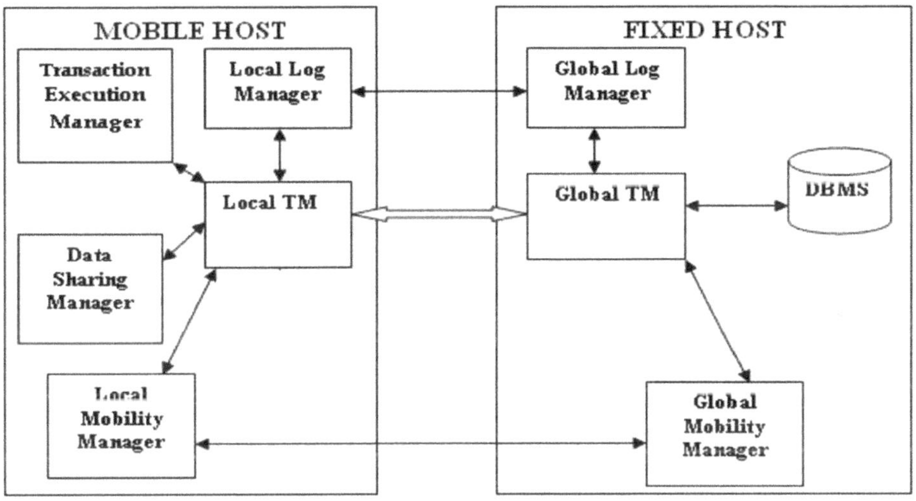

Figure 2. Architecture of Optimistic Concurrency Control Strategy.

At Mobile Host, the Local Transaction Manager is responsible for managing the transactions at respective mobile hosts. When a local transaction is committed, the Local Log Manager maintains log records to support Durability. The commit record in the log storage helps in reconciliation of the results onto the fixed hosts. The Data Sharing Manager or cache manager manages the shared data which is obtained to initiate the offline transactions. Transaction Execution Manager is responsible for executing offline transactions and the Local Mobility Manager manages the handoff information when mobile host moves from one cell to another. At Fixed Host, the Global Transaction Manager is responsible for managing the transactions submitted my mobile host after the offline processing. The Global Log Manager is responsible for making the final decision regarding the completion of a transaction and it is also responsible to maintaining durability after a failure. The Global Mobility Manager is responsible to manage sub-transactions to decide the final result of the transaction when the mobile host was on move during its execution. The optimistic concurrency control supports offline transactions. Hence the mobile host initiates the request for the transaction. The Base station acts as a Global Transaction Manager. The base station acts as the coordinator and the Mobile hosts and the Database System as participants. In figure 2 the architectural elements specified at fixed host i.e. Global Transaction Manager, Global Log Manager & Global Mobility Manager are logical components of the coordinator i.e. the base station.

DESIGN & IMPLEMENTATION OF OPTIMISTIC COMMIT PROTOCOLS

In the optimistic approaches, the data item requested for offline transactions are not locked, rather the transaction proceeds tolerating the conflicts. Later at the time of reconciliation of results the conflict is detected and respective resolution strategy is adopted.

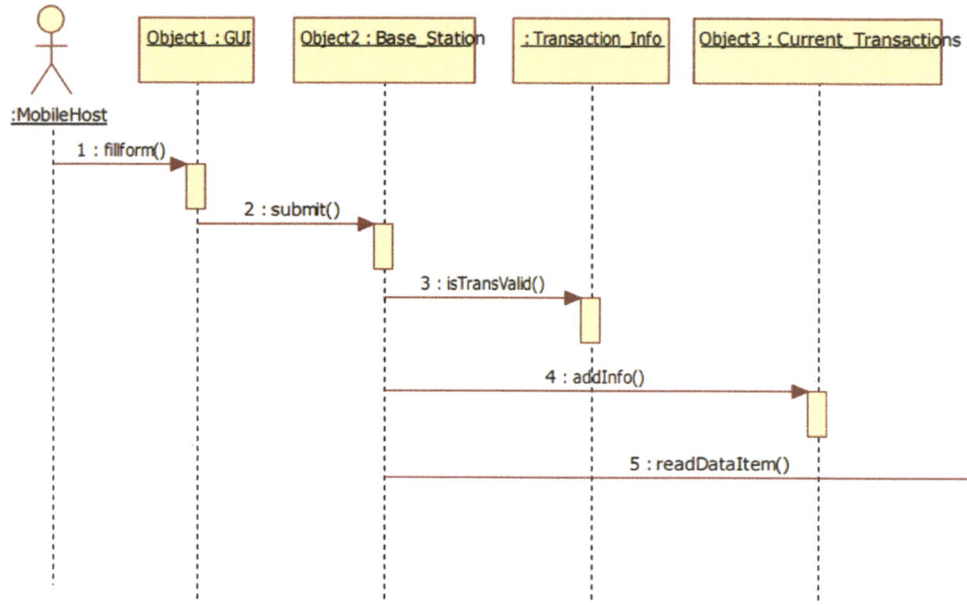

Figure 3. Behaviour of Initiating a Transaction.

Figure 3 depicts the behaviour of Initiate Transactions for Optimistic strategy for concurrency control. The implementation of optimistic protocols is divided into two phases. In the tentative phase, the data items are read by mobile host and the transaction is executed locally. In the commit phase, the final commit decision is made by resolving conflicts. In offline transactions, whenever a mobile host initiates the transaction (1: fillform()), the request is sent to the base station (2: submit()). The base station checks whether the requested transaction can be executed (3: isTransValid()), by comparing the Transaction_id with the one which is requested by the mobile host. Then the information regarding the new transaction request is entered in Current_Transaction relation (4: addInfo()). The data items are then read by the mobile host (5: readDataItem()). Figure 5 describes the behavior of executing a transaction. When the transactions are committed locally (1:localCommit()), the local transaction manager sends the result (2: Propagate()) to the coordinator. The Global Transaction Manager at the Base station makes a decision regarding committing the transaction (3: isCommit()) based on the forward or backward validation strategy.

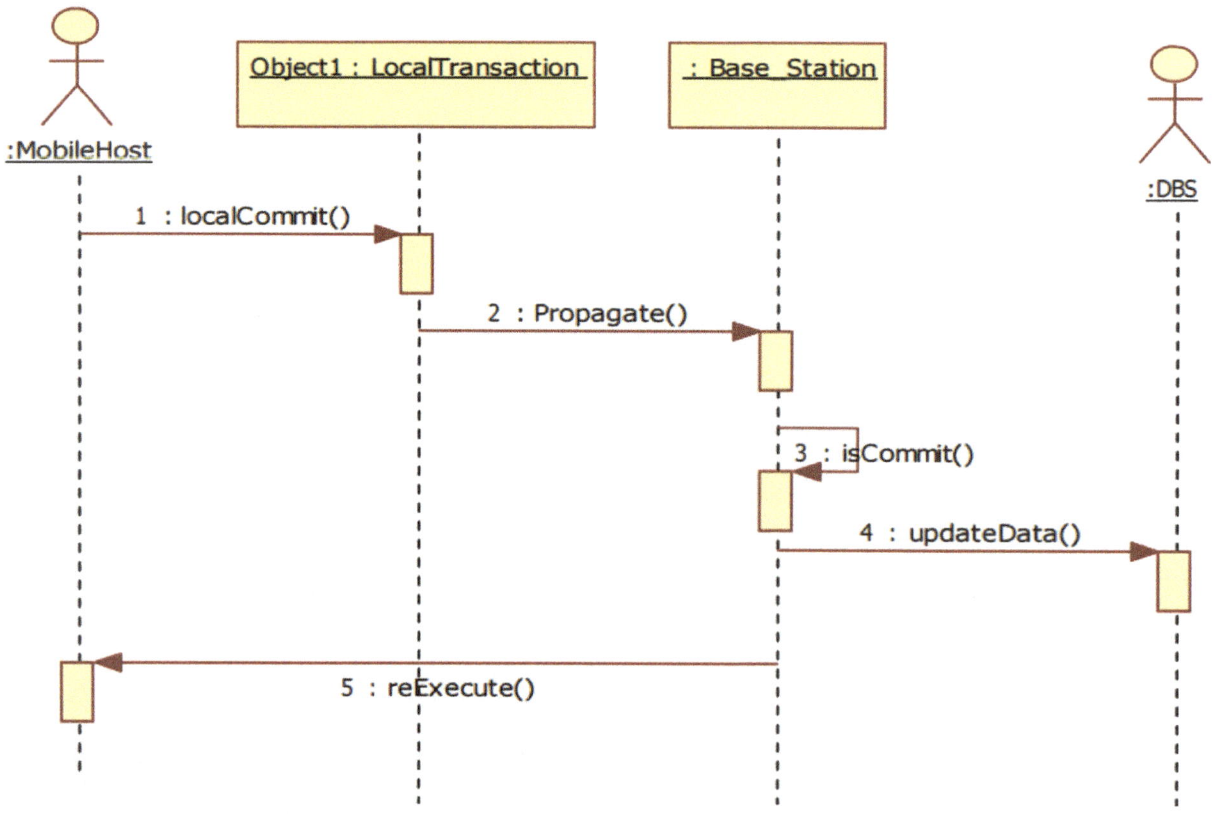

Figure 4. Behaviour of Executing A Transaction.

The result is then updated to the database (4: updateData()). If more than one mobile host were sharing the same data items, then there exists a conflict. Conflict is resolved by multicasting the updated values to those mobile host which are the vicitims of data conflict. The new value of the data is sent to the mobile host by instructions to restart the execution of the transaction (5: reExecute()) at the respective mobile host.

MOBILITY MANAGEMENT IN OPTIMISTIC STRATEGY FOR CONCURRENCY CONTROL

Whenever a mobile host moves from one cell to another during the execution of a transaction, it registers with the mobile host in foreign cell. Figure 5 describes the behavior of execute transaction for optimistic protocols when the mobile host moves from one cell to another When a mobile host completes the transaction in foreign cell (1: localCommit()), it sends the result to the base station to which it is registered to (2: propagate()) . The base station checks whether the mobile host started its execution in the same cell (3: isMhInHloc()) i.e in home location. Otherwise the result is propagated to the base station where the transaction started the execution (4: Propagate ()). The base station makes a final commit decision (5: isCommit()). Once the coordinator decides to commit the transactions the results are updated in the database (6: updateData()). In case of any conflicts with other mobile host, the new values of data items are propogated to the mobile host using the conflicting data items (7: reExecute()).

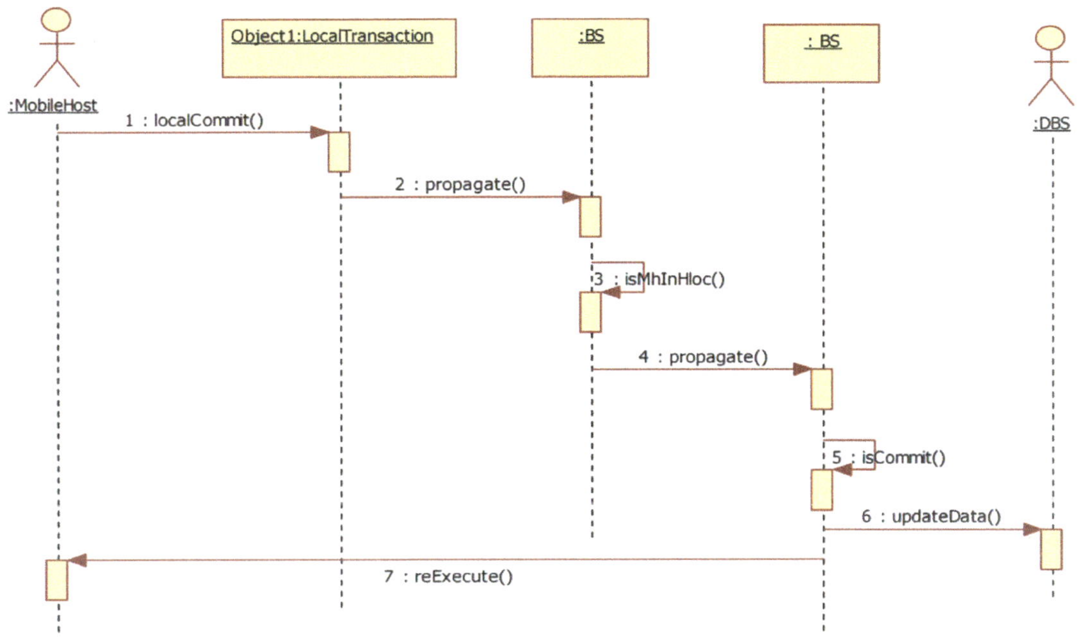

Figure 5 Handoff During Transaction Execution.

RESULTS

In this section we compare the results of the proposed Real Time Optimistic Concurrency Control strategy with the optimistic strategies proposed in the literature. In OCC/DTA (Optimistic Concurrency Control-Dynamic Timer Adjustment) [23], client side validation procedure is used that enhances the transaction throughput by adjusting the serialization order. In validation phase the mobile clients perform partial validation for committing a transaction. If the partial validation is successful global validation is performed. A transaction is expected to complete its execution within the specified time stamp. If the Lower bound crosses the higher bound value the transaction is aborted. As the mobile hosts have varying processing capabilities, restricting a transaction to be executed within certain timestamp may increase the abort rate. When a transaction is aborted, it may have to request for execution later, this unnecessary increase the uplink bandwidth too. As proposed in the real time optimistic strategy the when a conflict is detected the transaction may not initiate the transaction request again, instead the updated value of conflicting data items if any will be multicasted to those mobile hosts using the shared data item with a request to reexecute the transaction. Though there may be possibility of increase in re-execution request, but this reduces the abort rate, decreases the uplink bandwidth and also avoids sending irrelevant information to the mobile host by using multicasting. FBOCC [15] adopts optimistic concurrency control technique suitable for broadcast environments. In this technique the transaction is aborted immediately upon detection of conflict without adjustment of any serialization order. When the transactions are aborted immediately after detecting the conflicts, the abort rate is much higher and uplink bandwidth will almost be equivalent to the downlink bandwidth. The proposed optimistic concurrency control strategy is compared with FBOCC. To simulate the results the Mobile transactions were generated at each client to measure the number of aborted transactions due to data conflict. As the number of mobile clients gets increased, the frequency of data conflicts gets increased. The maximum numbers of clients used to generate different transactions were 20. At any instant of time 50% of transactions used the same shared data items.

Table 1. Comparison of FBOCC with the Proposed Optimistic Strategy

No. of Clients	Abort rate		No. of times uplink bandwidth is utilized	
	FBOCC	Proposed Strategy	FBOCC	Proposed Startegy
2	1	0	2	2
4	3	0	3	0
8	7	1	7	1
12	11	2	11	2
16	15	3	15	3
20	19	4	19	4

In FBOCC the transaction is aborted once a conflict is detected, whereas in proposed protocol, the transaction is re-executed with new values of data items. However it might be aborted after 3 attempts (say) of re-execution requests. The number of re-execution requests varies from one transaction to another and/or one application to another. The number of possible attempts for reexecution of a transaction is maintained at the fixed host. The results in table 7.3 are based on the speed of execution of a transaction & the execution request was sent to the coordinator dynamically. A mobile host might request for execution quiet later but can be committed earlier. In the first case 2 clients have requested for same shared data item. In the second case 4 clients have requested for same shared data items. There is a possibility the transaction which was aborted might have also requested for execution of transaction immediately. It is also obvious that as the abort rate increases the uplink bandwidth also increases.

CONCLUSION

The Optimistic Concurrency Control Strategy doesn't use any locking which doesn't block the shared resources. Further concurrency can be guaranteed by first executing transactions locally and later on propagating the results. In this scheme whenever a fixed host detects a concurrency violation, it propagates the updated shared data item to the mobile host using the same data item without aborting it. The mobile host which successfully completes the transaction locally will be committed irrespective of its arrival time. In this scheme there could be a possibility that the transaction which arrived quiet early might not get executed because the other mobile hosts are executing faster. The future work may introduce a priority field to give chance to the transaction which requested first or a hybrid approach for concurrency control that enters into pessimistic approach by partially locking data items to complete its execution is needed.

REFERENCES

1. Smith Wayne Plourede: "Handling Concurrency Issues in .NET", http://www.15seconds.com/issue/030604.htm, Web retreieve on February 19, 2005).
2. Samidip Basu & Syed M. Rahman, "Improving Optimistic Concurrency Control using Hybrid Techniques of Snapshot Isolation & ROCC", Proceedings of Mid-west Instruction & Computing Symposium, 2006.
3. Vijay Kumar, Nitin Prabhu, Maggie Dunham, Ayse Yasemin Seydim, "TCOT - A Timeout based Mobile Transaction Commitment Protocol", IIS 9979453, 2004.
4. Nadia Nouali, Anne Doucet, Habiba Drias, "A Two-Phase Commit Protocol for Mobile Wireless Environment", Vol. 39, 16th Australasian Database Conference, 2005.
5. Salman Abdul Moiz, Dr. Lakshmi Rajamani, "Single Lock Manager Approach for achieving Concurrency in Mobile Environments", 14th IEEE International Conference on High Performance Computing (HiPC), 2007. Springer LNCS 4873, ISBN 978-3-540-77219-4, pp. 650-660, 2007.
6. Salman Abdul Moiz, Dr. Lakshmi Rajamani, "Concurrency Control Strategy to Reduce frequent rollbacks in Mobile Environments", 2009 IEEE/IFIP International Symposium on Trusted Computing (TrustCom 2009), ISBN# 978-0-7695-3823-5, Vol 2. Pp. 709-714, 2009.
7. Salman Abdul Moiz, Dr. Lakshmi Rajamani, "An Efficient Strategy for achieving Concurrency Control in Mobile Environments", 12th IEEE Asia Pacific Network Operations & Management
8. (APNOMS) symposium, 2009. Springer LNCS 5787, ISBN# 978-3-642-04491-5, pp. 519-5222, 2009.
9. Salman Abdul Moiz, Dr. Lakshmi Rajamani, "An Algorithmic approach for achieving concurrency in Mobile Environments", 1st National Conference on Computing for Nation Development, INDIACom 2007, ISBN #978-81-094526-0-1, ISSN # 0973-7529.
10. Salman Abdul Moiz, Dr. Lakshmi Rajamani, "A Real Time Optimistic Strategy to achieve
11. Concurrency control in Mobile Environments using on-demand multicasting", International Journal of Wireless & Mobile Networks (IJWMN), Vol.2, No.2, May 2010, pp. 172-185, ISSN #0975-3834 (online), ISSN #0975-4679 (print).
12. Salman Abdul Moiz, Dr. Lakshmi Rajamani, Supriya N. Pal, " Design and Implementation of Pessimistic Commit Protocols in Mobile Environments", The First International Workshop on Database Systems (DMS-2010), Springer Verlag Berlin Hiedelberg, CNSA 2010, CCIS 89, pp. 603- 612, 2010
13. Barbara, D., "Mobile computing and databases-a survey", IEEE Transaction of Knowledge Data Engineering, volume 11 issue 1, pp.108-117, 1999
14. Imielinski, T. and Badrinath, B. R., "Mobile wireless computing: challenges in data management", Communications of the ACM 37(10), pp. 18-28, 1994

15. Mei-Wai Au, Edward Chan and Kam-Yiu Lam, "Concurrency Control for Mobile Systems with Data Broadcast", Journal of Interconnection Networks, pp.253-267, 2001

16. Pitoura E., "Supporting Read-Only Transactions in Wireless Broadcasting", Proc. DEXA Workshop on Mobility in Database and Distributed Systems, pp.428-433, 1998.

17. Victor C.S.Lee, Kwok Wa Lam, Tei-wei Kuo,"Efficient Validation of Mobile Transactions in Wireless Environments", The Journal of Systems and Software 69(2004), 183-193.

18. Ho Chin Choi, Byeong-Soo Jeong, , "A Timestamp-Based Optimistic Concurrency Control for Handling Mobile Transactions, Springer Verlag, LNCS 3981, PP. 796-805, 1996

19. Anand Yendluri, Wen-Chi Hou, and Chih-Fang Wang, "Improving Concurrency Control in Mobile Databases", Springer Verlag LNCS 2973, PP. 642-655, 2004.

20. Barbara D. and T. Imielinski. "Sleepers and Workaholics: Strategies in Mobile Environments," Proc. ACM pp. 1-12, May 1994.

21. Bernstein, P.A, Hadzilacos, V. and Goodman, N, "Concurrency Control and Recovery in database System", Addison-Wesley 1987

22. H. T. Kung and J. T. Robinson, "On Optimistic Methods for Concurrency Control," ACM TODS, 6(2), June 1981.

23. J. Kisler, and M. Satyanarayanan, Disconnected Operation in the Coda File System, ACM Transactions on Computer Systems, 10(1), 1992.

24. T. Härder. "Observations on optimistic concurrency control schemes". Information Systems, 9(2):111–120, 1984.

25. Ho Chin Choi, Byeong-Soo Jeong, "A Timestamp-Based Optimistic Concurrency Control for Handling Mobile Transactions", Springer Verlag, LNCS 3981, PP. 796-805, 2006.

CHAPTER 9

A SURVEY: FP TREE ALGORITHM WITH AND WITHOUT TRUSTED PARTY FOR ENVIRONMENTALLY DISTRIBUTED DATABASES

Raghvendra Kumar[1] , Ashish Jaiswal[2] ,Divyarth Rai[3]

[1,2,3] Dept of Computer Engineering LNCT Group of College Jabalpur, M.P., India

ABSTRACT

Data mining technology has emerged as a means of Identifying patterns and trends from large quantities of data. Mining rule is important data mining problem .To solve mining rule problem many technique are available example Apriori, FP Tree. FP Tree Algorithm has wide distribution to find relationship between among the attribute in database. The privacy concept arises when the data is distributed in the environment, concept of privacy arises here so that no any unauthorized person not able to decrypt the data and see the result. For this we used hash based secure sum cryptography technique because when the party to find the global result may be that result is frequent or infrequent. That's why privacy concept is arises with and without trusted party. In this paper we compare the result privacy preserving technique with and without trusted party for horizontal partitioned database with the help of FP Tree Algorithm. And provide high privacy to database with percentage of data leakage is zero percent.

INTRODUCTION

Data mining techniques are available to retrieve useful information from large database. Prediction and description are the two fundamental goals of data mining. To full fill these goals many data mining techniques [1] [2] [3] [4] exists such as FP Tree Algorithm, Apriori algorithm [7] [8] [9], classification, clustering and so on. Among these, FP Tree Algorithm has wide applications to discover interesting relationship among attributes in large databases. FP tree algorithm is used to find the rules which satisfy the user specified minimum support and minimum confidence. In the process of finding FP Tree Algorithm, the set of frequent item sets are computed as the first step and then FP Tree Algorithm are generated based on these frequent item sets. Two types of database environments exist namely centralized and distributed. A Centralized database [4] [5] [6] [7] is a database located and maintained in one location, unlike a distributed database. One main advantage is that all data is located in one place. The disadvantage is that bottlenecks may occur. Many FP Tree Algorithm struggle with their management information systems and their membership databases. One of their primary struggles is the lack of

Citation: Kumar R., Jaiswal A., Rai D. (2013), "A Survey: FP Tree Algorithm with and Without Trusted Party for Environmentally Distributed Databases", International Journal of Innovative Research in Computer and Communication Engineering, Vol. 1, no.9, pp. 2212-2220, ISSN (Online): 2320 – 9798.

centralized information. Too often, assns and nonprofits keep separate databases for membership, events, sales, and other processes. When at all feasible, these databases should be combined into a single, centralized database. There are several benefits to moving your data to a centralized system. Benefit in centralized database .data integrity, Valuable broad marketing information or history, Ease of training, Support. Distributed database [4] [5] [6] [7] is defined as collection of logically distributed database which are connected with each other through a network. A distributed database management system is used for managing distributed database. Each party has its own database and operating system. Charge in view of the motivation to have as a feature of privacy in data mining techniques to save from harm the confidential data of the user, there evolved an innovative stream in data mining period that is privacy preserving in data mining. There exists a key difference among regular data mining algorithms Under a variety of data mining techniques similar to classification, FP Tree Algorithm [6], clustering and privacy Preserving data mining algorithms that is the recognized algorithms deals with how to evaluate the Stored raw data and how to take out useful knowledge discovery patterns from the database Whereas in the afterward, it essentially deals with the sensitive information of the user records where privacy factor is the main concern and it is measured to be vital issue. The main aim in many scattered methods for privacy preserving data mining is to agree to useful aggregate computations on the complete data set through preserving the privacy of the individual parties' data or information. Each party owner is interested to work together in obtaining combined results, but not fully trust other parties in conditions of the distribution of their own data sets. Several data mining system should satisfy the important property that is privacy preserving of data or information. Particularly in distributed data mining, privacy preserving is individual crucial feature. Secure multi party computation is a useful approach to save the privacy in distributed data mining. Privacy preserving data mining utilizes a mining algorithm to obtain mutually beneficial global data mining objectives without helpful private data. Therefore, in many data mining applications privacy preserving has become a significant subject.

SECURE MULTI PARTY COMMUNICATION

Approximately all Privacy Preserving data mining techniques rely on Secure multi party communication protocol. Secure multi party communication is defined as a computation protocol at the last part of which no party involved knows anything else except its own inputs the outcome, i.e. the view of each party during the execution can be effectively simulated by the input and output of the party. In the late 1980s [1], work on Secure multi party communication verified that an extensive class of functions can be computed securely under reasonable assumptions without involving a trusted third party. Secure multi party communication has commonly concentrated on two models of security. The semi-honest model assumes that every party follows the rule of the protocol, but is free to later use [2] [12] what it sees during execution of the protocol. The malicious model assumes that parties can arbitrarily cheat and such cheating will not compromise moreover security or the outcome, i.e. the results from the malicious party will be correct or the malicious party will be detected. Most of the Privacy Preserving data mining techniques assume an intermediate model, Preserving Privacy with non-colluding parties. A malicious party May dishonest the results, but will not be able to learn the private data of other parties without colluding with another party. This is a practical hypothesis in most cases.

PRIVACY IN FP TREE ALGORITHM USING CRYPTOGRAPHY BASED TECHNIQUE

Lots of algorithms suggested like Apriori algorithms [1] [8] [9] [13]. It is based upon the challenging monotone property. Due to their two main troubles i.e. frequent database examine and superior computational cost, there is a need of flattened data structure for mining frequent item sets, which moderates the multi scan trouble and improve the candidate item set generation. Tree shelf is an efficient algorithm based upon the lexicographic tree in which each node represents a frequent pattern [1] [6]. FP-Growth algorithm [6] is a restricted algorithm for producing the frequent item sets without production of candidate item sets. It is based upon divide and conquers approach. It needs database scan to discover all frequent item sets. This approach compresses the database of frequent item sets into frequent pattern tree recursively in the same order of magnitude as the sequence of frequent patterns. Then in next step divide the compressed database into set of conditional databases. Privacy preserving FP tree algorithm is very necessary because when the data is distributed among different partitioned like horizontal partition, vertical partition and mixed partition but in this we will describe only privacy preserving in horizontal partition. In case of horizontal partition the data is distributed in among different party so to find the global support, global confidence and life. Then privacy is play very important role to find global result, there are mainly three important method to provide privacy in horizontal partition are cryptography technique, heuristic based technique and reconstruction based technique but in this we mainly focus only on cryptography technique to provide privacy to horizontal partitioned data. And why the cryptography technique is more useful because two main reasons behind that.

1. It has a well-recognized and well amorphous model meant for privacy which can essentially provide good number of methodologies for verifying and validating intention.
2. Cryptography branch has a broad mixture of tool set to incorporate privacy in data mining.

TECHNIQUES OF PRIVACY PRESERVING FP TREE ALGORITHM IN HORIZONTAL PARTITION DATA WITHOUT TRUSTED PARTY

In horizontal partition data is distributed in among party the number of party will be grater then 2 (n>2). And no party is consider as a trusted party [10] all the party have their individual private data and no other party will able to know other party data .in this method basically we are using hash based secure sum technique .in secure sum each party will calculate their own data value and send to next party that near to original party and this will going till the original party will collect all the value of data after that the parent party will calculate the global support and global confidence and it also not necessary that the result that found is globally frequent or infrequent its depend on value which will found after collect all the value may be that globally frequent and may not be locally frequent to say that item is globally frequent its consider that item may or may not be locally frequent. Figure 1 shows that how the data is distributed in among different parties.

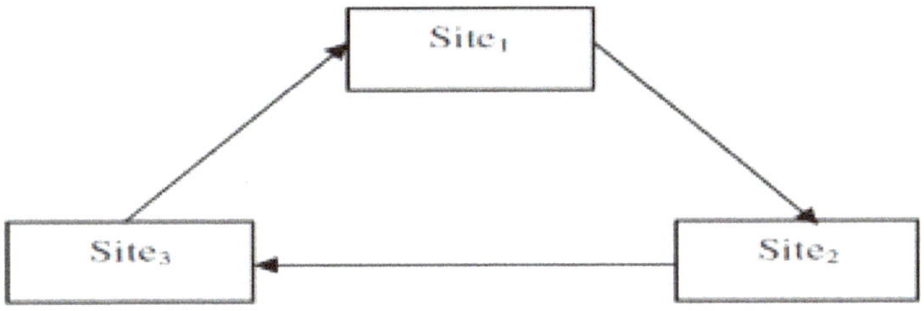

Figure 1: Communication among three sites.

For this we are using one of method to find the global result of confidence and support. There are mainly number of steps to find the global confidence and global confidence.

Algorithm1

Step1: Each party will calculate their frequent item sets and

Infrequent item sets and store the data value on memory.

Step2: Each party will generate their own random number because we are using hash based secure sum protocol so that each party have two random number one of its own and other is received by previous party.

Step3: Now the party 1 will calculate the partial support value by using the following formula.

Ps j= Xj .support – Min support*|DB|-RN1-RNn where RN is random number.

After that party1 calculate the mask value

PSj = PSj + mask value

Step4: Party 2 compute the PSj for each item received the list using the formula

PSj= PSj + xj. Sup - min*support |DB| +Rn1-Rn (i-1)

Step5: After that the value of PSj calculated by party 2 send to next coming party and after that all the value is send to the original party and that original party will calculate all global support.

Step6: Party 1 will find whether that global support is grater then zero or not if the value is grater then zero then it will be global frequent otherwise is infrequent.

Step7: Like that the entire party will calculate the will calculate the global support party 3 party 4 party 5…….party n.

Step8: Finally the party 1 calculates the actual support by using the formula

ASj = PSj + mask value

Step9: At last the party 1 will send the calculated value of actual support and global frequent item set to all other party in the horizontal partition.

Step10: Each party will generate the rule by using their confidence value.

Party 1 calculate the mask value by using the following formula

Mask value is calculated by using two different hash functions

Key1=Hash (key) =key mod N

And after that

Mask key = Hash2 (Key1) =Key+Mkey1

Double hash function is used to make the FP Tree

Algorithm rule more secure

Table1: Contain the dataset of first party having the minimum support is 40%

TID/ITEM	A1	A2	A3	A4
T1	1	1	0	0
T2	1	1	1	0
T3	1	1	1	1

Step1:-

TID	List
T1	A1, A2
T2	A1, A2, A3
T3	A1, A2, A3, A4

Step2:-

A1:3, A2:3, A3: 2, A4:1

Step3:-Arranging in decreasing order

A1:3, A2:3, A3:2, A4:1

Step4:-

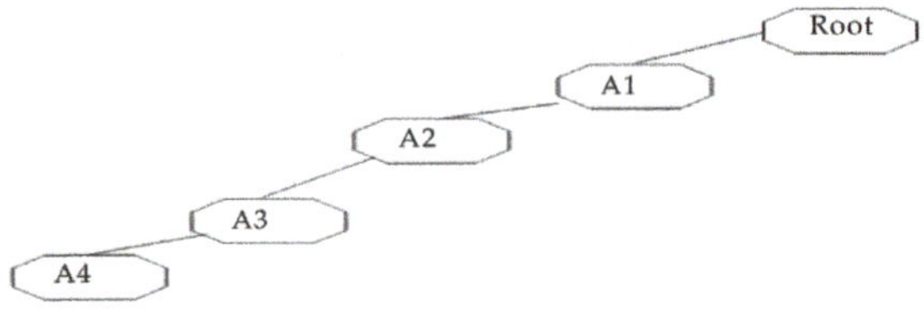

Step5:- A1 :{(A1: 3)}

A2 :{(A1: 3)}

A3 :{(A2: 2, A1:2)}

A4 :{(A3: 1, A2:1, A1:1)}

Step6:- As here is minimum support is 40% so no candidate item set is selected

Table2: Contain the dataset of second party having the minimum support is 40%

TID/ITEM	A1	A2	A3	A4	A5
T1	1	0	1	1	1
T2	0	1	1	0	0
T3	0	0	1	0	1
T4	1	0	1	0	1

Step1:-

TID	List
T1	A1, A3, A4, A5
T2	A2, A3
T3	A3, A4
T4	A1, A3, A5

Step2:-

A1:2, A2:1, A3: 4, A4:2, A5:2

Step3:-Arranging in decreasing order

A3:4, A1:2, A4:2, A5:2, A2:1

Step4:-

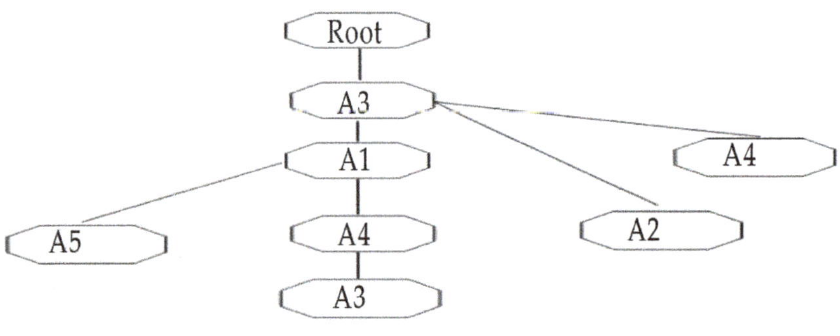

Step5:- A1 :{(A3: 1)}

A2 :{(A3: 1)}

A3 :{(A3: 4)}

A4 :{(A1: 1, A3:1), (A3:1)}

A5 :{(A4:1, A1:1, A3:1) (A1:1, A3:1)}

Step6:- A4= (A3:2)

A5= (A1:2, A3:2)

Step7:- A4A3:2, A5A1:2, A5A3:2

Step8:- Support (A4A3) = Count (A4A3)/ Total number of transaction= 2/4=50%

Support (A5A1) = Count (A5A1)/ Total number of transaction= 2/4=50%

Support (A5A3) = Count (A5A3)/ Total number of transaction= 2/4=50%

The candidate item set is selected = {A1, A3, A4, A5}

Table3: Contain the dataset of first party having the minimum support is 40%

TID/ITEM	A1	A2	A3	A4
T1	1	1	0	1
T2	1	1	1	0
T3	1	0	0	0
T4	0	1	0	1

Step1:-

TID	List
T1	A1, A2, A4
T2	A1, A2, A3
T3	A1
T4	A2, A4

Step2:-

A1:3, A2:3, A3:1, A4:2

Step3:-Arranging in decreasing order

A1:3, A2:3, A4:2, A3:1

Step4:-

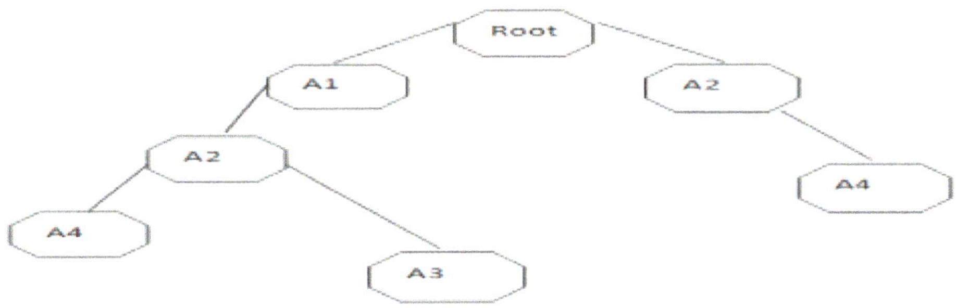

Step5:- A1 :{(A1: 3)}

A2 :{(A1: 2) (A2:1)}

A3 :{(A2: 1, A1:1)}

A4 :{(A2: 1, A1:1), (A2:1)}

Step6: A4– (A2.2)

Step7:- A4A2:2

Step8:- Support (A4A2) = Count (A4A2)/ Total number of transaction= 2/4=50%

The candidate item set is selected = {A2, A4}

IMPLEMENTATION OF PRIVACY PRESERVING FP TREE ALGORITHM WITHOUT TRUSTED PARTY

At party 1: At party 1 no any candidate item is selected

At party 2: The list of frequent item at party 2 {A1, A3, A4, A5}

At party 3: The list of frequent item at party 3{A2, A4}

Consider the item set {A1}

Select the random number RN1=10, RN2=20, RN3=10

Key =110, M=2

Hash key=key mod M

Mask key=hash key- M key

Hash key=110 mod 2=0

Mask key=110-2^0=109

FOR FIRST ITEM SET I= {A1}

PS=I1Support- minimum support*DB+ (RNi-RNi-1) + Mask key

STEP1:-

PS11= 3-.4*3+ (10-20) +109=100.8

PS12=2-.4*4+ (20-10) +100.8=111.2

ps13=3-.4*4+ (10-20) +111.2=102.6

Global encrypt support (GES) = partial support-mask key

GES= 102.6-110=-7.4

Actual support=global support+ database*minimum support

AS=-7.4+11*.4=-3

TECHNIQUES OF PRIVACY PRESERVING FP TREE ALGORITHM IN HORIZONTAL PARTITION DATA WITH TRUSTED PARTY

In this method all the task will done by help of trusted party [11] and trusted party play important role in this method as well as trusted party is helpful of providing privacy to the database in among party and also data leakage is zero percent. The following steps to calculate the FP Tree Algorithm in horizontal partition with the help of trusted party

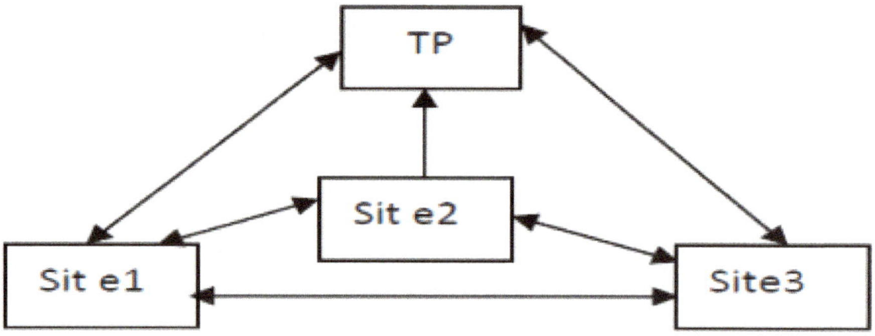

Figure 2: Communication between sites and Trusted Party.

Algorithm2

Step1: Trusted party will send a request to calculate the locally frequent item by the help of public key and hash function as well as minimum threshold support value.

Step2: After that each party will calculate the frequent item set and send to the trusted party without interfering of other party.

Step3: Trusted party will see all the frequent item set that coming from different party by help of private key and merged all frequent items set and remove all the duplicate item sets. For each party TP will generate the random number and sign (+ or -) and send to all the party that present to the database and that party is indicate weather that random number will added or subtracted its depend on the sign value.

Step4: Every party computes partial support for each item set in the merged list which is received from TP by using the formula

PS ij= Xj.sup – Min Sup × | D Bi | + (Sign i) RN i

Where i indicate the ith party, ranges from 1 to n and j indicates jth item set in the merged list, ranges from 1 to k. Each party then broadcast its computed PSij values for all the item sets in the merged list to all other parties.

Step5: Every party computes Total PS ij for each item set Xj by using the formula.

Total PS ij= $\sum_{i=1}^{n}(PSij)$ for each j = 1 to k and sends to the Trusted party.

Step6: Trusted party will send the value of total partial support to all parties that present in database if any duplication will occur then the step 5 will follow again to calculate the partial support.

Step7: Trusted party computes Global Excess Support for each item set Xj by using the formula

Global support j = TotalPS1j – Sign Sum RN

Where Sign Sum RN is computed by adding all the random numbers with their signs by trusted party. If the computed value of GES j ≥ 0 then the item set Xj is globally frequent otherwise it is globally infrequent.

Step8: For each global frequent item set Xj, Trusted party finds Actual Support as

Actual support j = Global support j + Minimum Support * |DB|

Where $|DB| = \sum_{i=1}^{n}(|DBi|)$

Step9: Trusted party will send the list of frequent item sets to all other parties present in distributed database.

Step10: Every party will generate FP Tree Algorithm by using the confidence to every parties and the minimum support that received by trusted party.

IMPLEMENTATION OF PRIVACY PRESERVING FP TREE ALGORITHM WITH TRUSTED PARTY

For implementation we will take above database that contain of three different tables. At party 1: At party 1 no any candidate item is selected

At party 2: The list of frequent item at party 2 {A1, A3, A4, A5}

At party 3: The list of frequent item at party 3 {A2, A4}

Consider the item set {A1}

Select the random number RN1=10, RN2=20, RN3=10

So that the size of database that contain |DB1|=3, |DB2|=4, |DB3|=4 so the size of global database is 11.

Trusted party will compute the signsumRN BY adding three random numbers

Signsum RN= (+) 10+ (+20) + (+) 10=40

Partial supports for A1 at different parties are computed as follows.

At Party1

PS11=A1.Support-40%of DB1+ (Sign1) RN1

PS11=3-.4*3+ (+) 10=11.8

At Party2

PS21=A1.Support-40%of DB2+ (Sign2) RN2

PS21=2-.4*4+ (+) 20=20.4

At Party3

PS31=A1.Support-40%of DB3+ (Sign3) RN3

PS31=3-.4*4+ (+) 10=11.4

Party1 broadcast 11.8 to all other party party2 and party3, party2 broadcast 20.4 to party3 and party1, party3 broadcast 11.4 to party 1 and party2.

Total PS11=PS11+ (PS21+PS31) =11.8+ (20.4+11.4) =43.6

Total PS11=PS21+ (PS11+PS31) =20.4+ (11.8+11.4) =43.6

Total PS11=PS31+ (PS21+PS11) = 11.4+ (20.4+11.8) =43.6

Trusted party receives 43.6 as total support of an item set A1 from three parties which ensures the computations performed by all others parties is correct. Trusted party when calculates the Global Excess Support by subtracting the

SignsumRN from the TotalPS11

Global Excess support=TotalPS11-SignsumRN=43.6-40=3.6

The value of global support is 3.6 then it means that the item sets are globally infrequent.

Actual support of A1 is computed by adding minimum support of the total database of global excess support

AS11=Global Excess Support+ minimum support*|DB|=3.6+.4*11=8

Hence the Global frequent item A1 Support is 8.

Without trusted party having the global support is -3 and with trusted party having the global support is 8 so that the without trusted party is more faster and more secure as well the data leakage is zero but in the with trusted party is a ideal model so we need to provide the highest privacy and minimum data leakage to the database.

CONCLUSION

The difficulty of preserving privacy in FP tree algorithm when the database is distributed horizontally among n (n>2) number of parties when no trusted party is considered. A replica which adopts a hash based secure sum cryptography technique to find the global FP Tree Algorithm is propose in this paper by preserving the privacy constraints. Double hashing function is adopted to enhance the privacy further. The proposed replica capably finds global frequent item sets even when no party can be treated as trusted. And next in this paper we compare with trusted party. The trusted party initiates the process and prepares the merged list. All the parties computes the partial supports and total supports for all the item sets in the merged list using the sign based secure sum cryptography technique and based on these results finally trusted party finds global frequent item sets. And after comparing the result of these we find output that data leakage with trusted party is more as compare to without trusted party so privacy also without trusted party is more as compare to with trusted party.

REFERENCES

1. Agrawal, R., et al.: Mining association rules between sets of items in large database. In: Proc. of ACM SIGMOD'93, D.C, 1993,pp. 207-216 ACM Press, Washington.
2. Agarwal, R., Imielinski, T., Swamy, A.: Mining Association Rules between Sets of Items in Large Databases. In Proceedings of the 1993 ACM SIGMOD International Conference on Management of Data, 1993, pp. 207-210.
3. Srikant, R., Agrawal, R.: Mining generalized association rules. In: VLDB'95,1994, pp.479-488 .
4. Agrawal, R., Srikant, R.: Privacy-Preserving Data Mining. In: proceedings of the 2000 ACM SIGMOD on management of data, 2000, pp. 439- 450.
5. Lindell, Y., Pinkas, B.: Privacy preserving Data Mining. In: Proceedings of 20th Annual International Cryptology Conference (CRYPTO) 2000.
6. Kantarcioglu, M., Clifton, C.: Privacy-Preserving distributed mining of association rules on horizontally partitioned data. In IEEE Transactions on Knowledge and Data Engineering Journal, IEEE Press, Vol 16(9), 2004, pp.1026-1037.
7. Han, J. Kamber, M.:Data Mining Concepts and Techniques. Morgan Kaufmann, San Francisco, 2006.
8. Sheikh, R., Kumar, B., Mishra, D, K.: A Distributed k- Secure Sum Technique for Secure Multi-Site Computations. Journal of Computing, Vol 2, 2010, pp.239-243.
9. Sugumar, Jayakumar, R., Rengarajan, C.:Design a Secure Multi Site Computation System for Privacy Preserving Data Mining. In International Journal of Computer Science and Telecommunications, Vol 3, 2012, pp.101-105.
10. Muthu Lakshmi, N. V., Sandhya Rani, K.: Privacy Preserving Association Rule Mining without Trusted Site for Horizontal Partitioned database. In International Journal of Data Mining & Knowledge Management Process (IJDKP) Vol.2, 2012, pp.17-29.
11. Muthu lakshmi, N.V., Sandhya Rani, K.. Privacy Preserving Association Rule Mining in Horizontally Partitioned Databases Using Cryptography Techniques. In International Journal of Computer Science and Information Technologies(IJCSIT), Vol. 3 (1),2012 , PP. 3176 – 3182.
12. Goldreich, O., Micali, S. & Wigerson, A.: How to play any mental game. In: Proceedings of the 19th Annual ACM Symposium on Theory of Computing, pp.218-229.
13. Franklin, M., Galil, Z. & Yung, M.:An overview of Secured Distributed Computing. Technical Report CUCS- 00892, Department of Computer Science, Columbia University

SECTION III
SECURITY IN DISTRIBUTED ARCHITECTURES

CHAPTER 10

PRIVACY PRESERVING IN DISTRIBUTED DATABASE USING DATA ENCRYPTION STANDARD (DES)

Jyotirmayee Rautaray[1] , Raghvendra Kumar[2]

[1]School of Computer Engineering, KIIT University, Odisha, India
[2]School of Computer Engineering, KIIT University, Odisha, India

ABSTRACT

Distributed data mining explores unknown information from data sources which are distributed among several parties. Privacy of participating parties becomes great concern and sensitive information pertaining to individual parties and needs high protection when data mining occurs among several parties. Different approaches for mining data securely in a distributed environment have been proposed but in the existing approaches, collusion among the participating parties might reveal responsive information about other participating parties and they suffer from the intended purposes of maintaining privacy of the individual participating sites, reducing computational complexity and minimizing communication overhead. The proposed method finds global frequent item sets in a distributed environment with minimal communication among parties and ensures higher degree of privacy with Data Encryption Standard (DES). The proposed method generates global frequent item sets among colluded parties without affecting mining performance and confirms optimal communication among parties with high privacy and zero percentage of data leakage.

INTRODUCTION

Data mining techniques is extract useful information for considered decision making from transactional dataset which is either centralized data base or distributed data base. The term data mining refers to extract or mine knowledge from an enormous amount of data. Data mining functionalities similar to association rule mining, cluster analysis, classification, prediction etc. specify the different kinds of patterns mined. Association Rule Mining [1] [2] [3] [4] [5] finds exciting association or correlation among a large set of data items. Finding association rules among huge amount of business transactions can help in making many business decisions such as index design cross marketing etc. A best example of Association Rule Mining is market basket analysis. This is the process of analysing the client buying behaviour from the association between the different items which is available in the shopping baskets. This analysis can help retailers to increase marketing strategies. Association Rule Mining involves two stages

Citation: Rautaray J., Kumar R. (2013), "Privacy Preserving in Distributed Database using Data Encryption Standard (DES)", International Journal of Innovative Research in Science, Engineering and Technology, Vol. 2, no.3, pp. 2212-2220, ISSN (Online): 2319-8753.

- Finding frequent item sets from a given transactional data set
- Generating strong association rule between the two or more attributes

But the Association Rule Mining take more number of steps to find the Association Rule between the two attribute. so the complexity Is also increased. That's why in this paper we used FP Tree algorithm [5] [6] [7] [8] which is advancement to the Association Rule Mining. In this the number of step is very less as compared to Association Rule Mining. And it's very easy to find the Association Rule between the given transactional item sets. Algorithm shows how to extract frequent item sets from a given transactional data set

Algorithm: FP Grouth

Allows frequent item set without candidate item set generation. This is two step approaches Step1:-Design a compact data structure called the FP tree using the 2 passes over the given data set.

Step2:- Extract frequent item sets from the FP tree this frequent item is extract after the traversing through FP tree.

Distributed Data Mining

Distributed Data Mining [5] [6] [13] [14] is measured as the exact solution for many applications, as it reduces several practical problems like huge data transfers, huge storage unit requirement, security or privacy issues etc. Distributed Frequent Rule Mining is a sub-area of Distributed data mining. Let D1, D2… Dn is data sources which are physically distributed. Let n be the number of items and I = {i1, i2…in} be a set of items. Global Support of an item set is defined as the ratio of the number of occurrences of the item set in all the data sources to the whole number of transactions in all the data sources. An item set is said to be globally frequent when the number of occurrences of that particular item set in all the data sources is larger than a user-specified minimum support. During global frequent item set generation, local frequent item sets of entity party need to be shared. So, the participating parties learn the exact support count of all other participating parties. However, in many situations the participating parties are not interested to release the support counts of some of their item sets which are considered as sensitive information. Thus, it is essential to share information pertaining to an entity data source without revealing sensitive information. Fig 1 shows the how the frequent rule mining finds the global rule in distributed database.

Secure Multi Party Computation

Secure Multi Party Computation [7] [8] [9] [10] solutions can be applied to maintain privacy in distributed rule mining. The main goal of Secure Multi Party Computation in distributed rule mining is to find global frequent item set without disclosing the local support count of participating sites to each other. In distributed privacy preserving data mining, the participating sites may be treated as honest, semi-honest. The semi-honest parties are honest but try to learn more from received information. Secure Multi Party Computation worked both real and ideal model this is very useful more than two parties to compute their global result without disclosing the individual result. In real model there is no any existence of the trusted third party but in Ideal model there is existence of trusted third party.

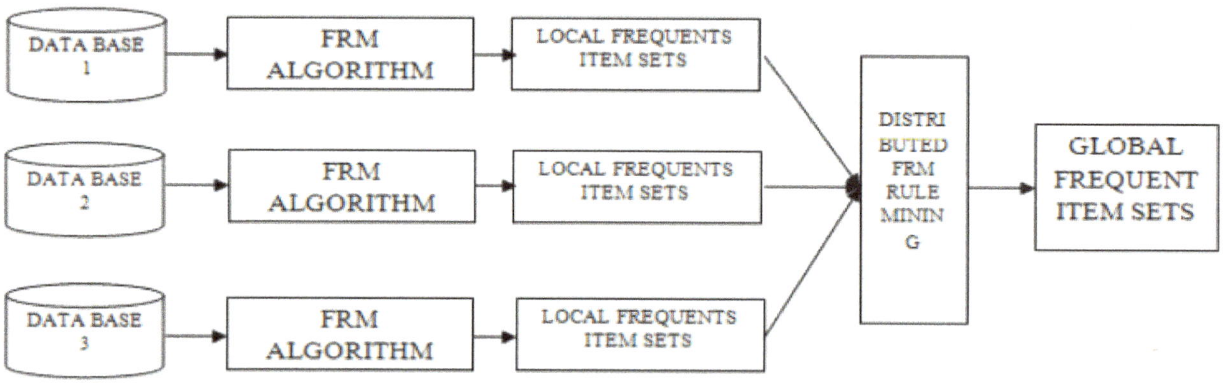

Figure 1: Distributed Frequent Rule mining.

Data Encryption standard for Two Key

Some researchers suggest double encryption [14] [15] that provide the high privacy to the database. The working of double encryption is as following. First consider two secrete key or random number Like Key1 and Key2. After that encrypt the first party data set using the key 1 value and after that the second that encrypted data set to the next party presents in the network and after that encryption the second party data set uses the second secrete key or second random number. so after that the data set is fully encrypted its becomes impossible to the hacker to hack that particular data sets. Fig2 shows the working step of data encryption standard in two key value cases.

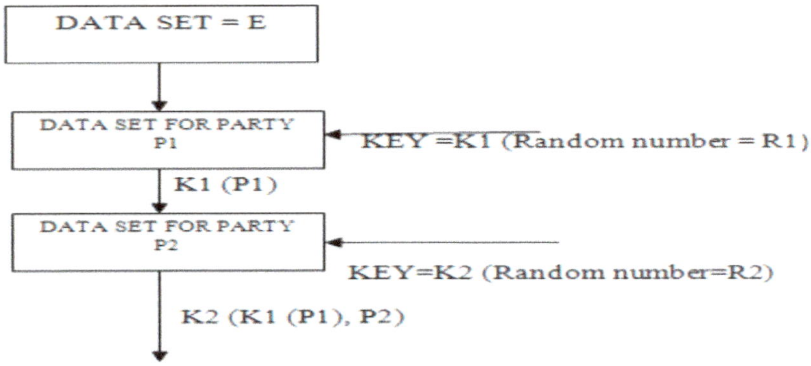

Figure 2: Data encryption in DES algorithm.

IMPLEMENTATION AND RESULT

In this implementation [10] [11] consider two different databases represented as Party P1 and Party P2 having minimum support count is 40 % and first calculate the partial support by using the following formula Partial support= X. support- Minimum support*|size of the database| and after that we calculate the global excess support by using the following formula that's is global excess support= Total partial support – key value. If global excess support if greater than zero it means that's its globally frequent item sets otherwise infrequent item set. Table 1 and Table 2 represent the data sets for party 1 and 2

Table: 1

			Set of data for Party1			MIN SUPPORT=40%
TID	A1	A2	A3	A4	A5	A6
T1	0	1	1	0	0	0
T2	1	0	1	1	0	1
T3	1	1	0	0	1	0
T4	1	0	0	1	0	1

STEP1:-

TID	LIST
T1	A2, A3
T2	A1, A3, A4, A6
T3	A1, A2, A5
T4	A1, A4, A6

STEP2:-
A1:3, A2:2, A3:2, A4:2, A5:1, A6:2

STEP3:-SORT IN DESENDING ORDER
A1:3, A2:2, A3:2, A4:2, A6:2, A5:1

STEP4:-

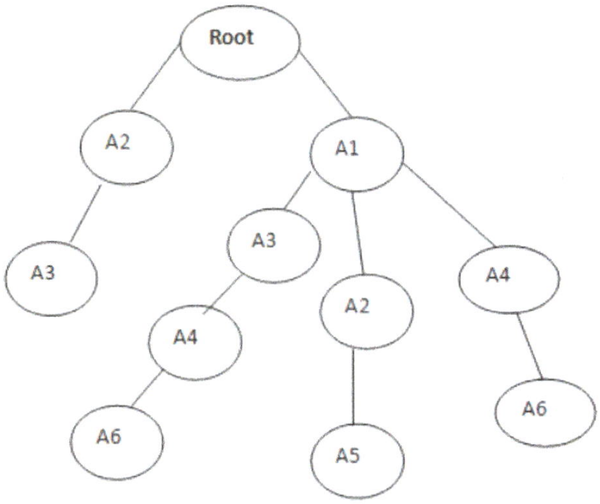

STEP5:- A1= {(A1:3)}

A2= {(A2:1), (A1:1)}

A3= {(A2:1) (A1:1)}

A4= {(A3:1, A1:1), (A1:1)}

A5= {(A2:1, A1:1)}

A6= {(A4:1, A3:1, A1:1) (A4:1, A1:1)}

STEP6:

A4= A1:2, A6= (A4:2, A1:2)

STEP7:

A4A1:2, A6A4:2, A6A1:2

STEP8:- SUPPORT (A4, A1) = COUNT (A4, A1)/ T=2/4=O.5=50%

SUPPORT (A6, A4) = COUNT (A6, A4)/T=2/4=O.5=50%

SUPPORT (A6, A1) = COUNT (A6, A1)/T=2/4=O.5=50%

CANDIDATE SET = {A1, A4, A6}

Table: 2

		Set of data for Party2		MIN SUPPORT=40%	
TID	A1	A2	A3	A4	A5
T1	1	1	0	0	1
T2	1	1	1	0	1
T3	0	1	1	0	0
T4	1	0	0	1	0

STEP1:-

TID	LIST
T1	A1, A2, A5
T2	A1, A2, A3, A5
T3	A2, A3
T4	A1, A4

STEP2:-

A1:3, A2:3, A3:2, A4:1, A5:2

STEP3:- SORT IN DESENDING ORDER

A1:3, A2:3, A3:2, A5:2, A4:1

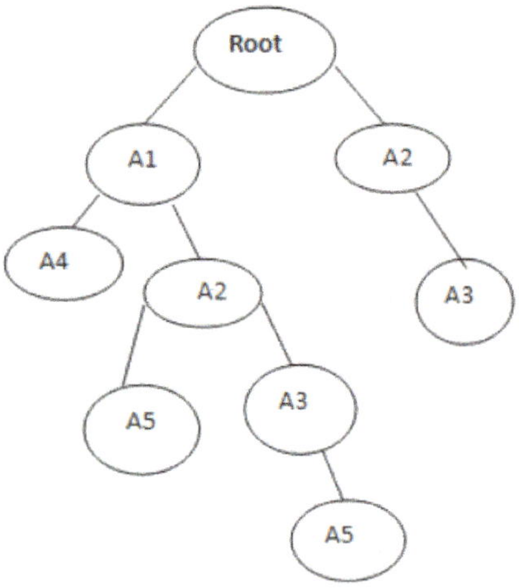

STEP5:

A1= {(A1:3)}

A2= {(A1:2), (A2:1)}

A3= {(A2:1, A1:1) (A2:1)}

A4= {(A1:1)} A5= {(A2:1, A1:1) (A3:1, A2:1, A1:1)}

STEP6:

A3= {A2:2} A5= {(A2:2) (A1:2)}

STEP7:

A3A2:2, A5A2:2, A5A1:2

STEP8:

SUPPORT (A3, A2) = COUNT (A3, A2)/T=2/4=0.5=50%

SUPPORT (A5, A2) =COUNT (A5, A2)/T=2/4=0.5=50%

SUPPORT (A5, A1) = COUNT (A5, A1)/T=2/4=0.5=50%

SUCH THAT CANDIDATE SET- {A1, A2, A3, A5}

At party P1 the number of candidate item sets is {A1, A4, A6}

At party P2the number of candidate item sets is {A1, A2, A3, A5}

Let us consider the item set {A1}

So that the partial support of party P1 is calculated by using the following formula

Ps1= X. support- minimum support*|size of the database|

Ps1=3-.4*4=1.4

So that the partial support of party P2 is calculated by using the same formula given above Ps2=3-.4*4=1.4 So that each party has their own partial support value then after that for providing the high privacy used random number or key value let the for party P1 have the key value is 1 and for party P2 have the key value 1 , after that encrypt the each party database by using the key value then the party party P1 send the value to the party P2 is Ps1+key value1=1.4+1=2.4 and the party P2 receive that value and adds its own partial support as well as the key value such that the party P2 send the value is Ps1value +Ps2+ Key value2=1.4+1+2.4=4.8 so that the global excess support is GES=Ps2-Key value=4.8-1-1=2.8 so that global excess support greater than zero it means that its globally frequent item sets.

CONCLUSION

Privacy preserving data mining techniques for distributed database environment have been studied and algorithm for finding global frequent item sets has been proposed and implemented. It is found that the proposed method securely determine global frequent item sets with minimal communication and time complexity. Secure multi party computation is used for global frequent item set generation. In this implemented work we provide the highest privacy to the database with zero percentage of data leakage but this is applicable for homogeneous database but in future this extended in heterogeneous database.

REFERENCES

1. Agrawal, R., et al.: Mining association rules between sets of items in large database. In: Proc. of ACM SIGMOD'93, D.C, pp.207-216, 1993.
2. Agarwal, R., Imielinski, T., Swamy, A.: Mining Association Rules between Sets of Items in Large Databases. In Proceedings of the 1993, ACM SIGMOD International Conference on Management of Data, pp. 207-210, 1993.
3. Srikant, R., Agrawal, R.: Mining generalized association rules. In: VLDB'95, pp.479-488, 1995.
4. Agrawal, R., Srikant, R.: Privacy-Preserving Data Mining. In: proceedings of the 2000 ACM SIGMOD on management of data, pp. 439-450, 2000.
5. Lindell, Y., Pinkas, B.: Privacy preserving Data Mining. In: Proceedings of 20th Annual International Cryptology Conference (CRYPTO) 2000.
6. Kantarcioglu, M., Clifton, C.: Privacy-Preserving distributed mining of association rules on horizontally

partitioned data. In IEEE Transactions on Knowledge and Data Engineering Journal, IEEE Press, Vol 16(9), pp.1026-1037, 2004.

7. Han, J. Kamber, M.:Data Mining Concepts and Techniques. Morgan Kaufmann, San Francisco, 2006.

8. B., Mishra, "Hybrid technique for secure sum protocol". WCSIT, Vol 1, pp.198-201, 2011.

9. Sugumar, Jayakumar, R., Rengarajan, C.:Design a Secure Multi Site Computation System for Privacy Preserving Data Mining. In International Journal of Computer Science and Telecommunications, Vol 3, pp.101-105. 2012.

10. Muthu Lakshmi, N. V., Sandhya Rani, K.: Privacy Preserving Association Rule Mining without Trusted Site for Horizontal Partitioned database. In International Journal of Data Mining & Knowledge Management Process (IJDKP) Vol.2, pp.17-29, 2012.

11. Muthu lakshmi, N.V., Sandhya Rani, K.: Privacy Preserving Association Rule Mining in Horizontally Partitioned Databases Using Cryptography Techniques. In International Journal of Computer Science and Information Technologies (IJCSIT), Vol. 3 (1) , PP. 3176 – 3182, 2012.

12. Goldreich, O., Micali, S. & Wigerson, A.: How to play any mental game. In: Proceedings of the 19th Annual ACM Symposium on Theory of Computing, pp.218-229.

13. Franklin, M., Galil, Z. & Yung, M.:An overview of Secured Distributed Computing. Technical Report CUCS- 00892, Department of Computer Science, Columbia University.

14. Dehao C. "Tree Partition based Parallel Frequent Pattern mining on Shared Memory Systems" IEEE.

15. Charles p. pfleeger, shri Lawrence pfleeger "security in computing"2011.

CHAPTER 11

A DISTRIBUTED SECURE MECHANISM FOR RESOURCE PROTECTION IN A DIGITAL ECOSYSTEM ENVIRONMENT

Ilung Pranata, Geoff Skinner, Rukshan Athauda

Faculty of Science and IT, University of Newcastle, Callaghan, Australia

ABSTRACT

The dynamic interaction and collaboration of the loosely coupled entities play a pivotal role for the successful implementation of a Digital Ecosystem environment. However, such interaction and collaboration can only be promoted when information and resources are effortlessly shared, accessed, and utilized by the interacting entities. A major requirement to promote an intensive sharing of resources is the ability to secure and uphold the confidentiality, integrity and non-repudiation of resources. This requirement is extremely important in particular when interactions with the unfamiliar entities occur frequently. In this paper, we present a distributed mechanism for improving resource protection in a Digital Ecosystem environment. This mechanism can be used not only for any secure and reliable transaction, but also for encouraging the collaborative efforts by the Digital Ecosystem community members to play a major role in securing the environment. Public Key Infrastructure is also employed to provide a strong protection for its access workflows.

INTRODUCTION

Information and resource protection is a de-facto requirement that must be advocated by every enterprise, organisation, and government entity. The importance of this requirement is further escalated when the entities are performing transactions in an online environment. Information security has been long considered as a crucial factor for e-commerce transactions. It is important to note that lack of sufficient security protection may limit the expansion of e-commerce technology [1]. However, although several e-commerce security mechanisms have been proposed and debated over a number of years, current internet technology still poses a number of incidents pertinent to the loss of information, unauthorized use of resources, and information hacking. These incidents generate an excruciating cost for the enterprises, ranging from the loss of revenue to the damage of their reputation. A recent survey [2] shows that the average cost resulted from the worst incident at about £280k - £690k per incident for a large organisation and £27.5k - £55k per incident for a small and medium organisation.

Similarly, Digital Ecosystem (DE) faces the identical issues due to its open environment where information and resources are exchanged over the network. With possibly thousands of Small and Medium Enterprises (SMEs) that form

Citation: I. Pranata, G. Skinner and R. Athauda, "A Distributed Secure Mechanism for Resource Protection in a Digital Ecosystem Environment," Journal of Information Security, Vol. 3 No. 1, 2012, pp. 25-38. doi:10.4236/jis.2012.31004.

series of communities in a DE environment [3], protecting enterprise resources and acknowledging which entities are trusted to access the resources become extensive tasks for each enterprise. While ensuring security protection is all about upholding the confidentiality, integrity, availability and non-repudiation of information, it is evident that the most consistent and effective way to ensure the preservation of these security properties is through the implementation of authentication, authorisation, encryption, and access control mechanisms [1,4]. Additionally, the provision of an efficient mechanism to measure the trustworthiness of entities will further strengthen the information and resource protecttion [5]. While authentication ensures only the right entities that are allowed to consume the resources, authorisation restricts the access over multiple hosted resources based on each entity's privileges. Nevertheless, current research in these areas for a DE environment is still very much limited or not attempted. This research gap further becomes our main motivation to focus our work in.

The remainder of this paper is structured as follows: Section 2 provides an introduction of Digital Ecosystem and its security challenges. Section 3 provides an overview of our proposed solution. Section 4 provides an implementation of our proposed solution. Section 5 presents an security analysis on the proposed solution. This is followed by Section 6 which shows the results of performance and scalability testing on our solution. To conclude the paper, Section 7 summarizes our present work and demonstrates several future works.

DIGITAL ECOSYSTEM & ITS SECURITY CHALLENGES

Since its first inception, the newly emerging concept of Digital Ecosystem (DE) has received increasing attentions from researchers, businesses, IT professionals and communities around the world. A wide variety of researches and initiatives have been undertaken that aimed at the realization and implementation of a Digital Ecosystem concept. The enthusiasms were revealed inside numerous projects funded by European Commission under FP6 framework programme followed by FP7 framework programme as well as in numerous pilot regional workplans in Aragon, Tampere, Piedmont and West Midland [6,7]. The derived objective of DE primarily focuses on dynamic formation of a knowledge based economy [8]. Further, it was proposed that a knowledge based economy will lead to a creation of more jobs and a greater social inclusion in sustaining the world economic growth [6]. To realize this objective, it is critical to form an open framework infrastructure in promoting a wide use of Information and Communication Technology (ICT), as well as to solve the digital divide issues of internet and e-business adoption by small and medium enterprises [9].

The term "ecosystem" used inside DE notion is a fundamental biological science terminology to represent a dynamic interrelation between organisms and species that actively interact to conserve the environment [10]. Therefore, the similarity in concept and an analogy can be drawn between Digital Ecosystem and natural ecology community [9,11]. In a fundamental perspective, Digital Ecosystem is described as a digital environment and infrastructure where multiple digital components form a synergic correlation and collaboration with an evolutionary ability to adapt with its local circumstances [12]. Such digital components, or digital species used in other literatures, encompass various applications, services, frameworks, ontologies, knowledge, laws, taxonomies, reputetion, training modules, trust relationships, and business models [9]. In a more technical term, Briscoe & Wilde [13] clearly define DE as the Multi-Agent Systems [14] that utilize distributed evolutionary computing [15,16] to combine the suitable agents in meeting user requests for applications. Further, the connectivity between the agents must be defined by the geography or spatial proximity unlike peer to peer [19] on which its peers' connectivity is based on bandwidth and information content.

In a DE environment where multiple interacting entities exist, the required efforts to enforce a strong authentication and authorisation mechanism are extensive. We identify three core issues that appear to be the challenging tasks to enforce such mechanisms. First, as the DE community expands its size to incorporate more entities, the resource providers face a challenge to identify the legal entities that are able to access their resources. Second, the fact that each entity would have different set of access permissions to access multiple resources further complicates the implementation of an efficient mechanism. Third, it is probable that each resource provider would host multiple resources and services in a DE environment. This situation, in turn, creates a great issue to authorize the right entities to the right resources with the right permissions. The failure to assign the right permissions to the authorized entities would compromise the usage of resources which would bring negative impact to the resource provider. Therefore, it is apparent that enforcing strong and efficient authentication and authorisation mechanisms in a DE environment needs in-depth solutions on the core issues.

However, the current internet mechanisms are still far from adequate to provide a reliable authentication and authorisation processes for a DE environment. This view is reflected from our literature analysis over a number of internet mechanisms. Several prominent authentication mechanisms such as Identity Provider (IdP) or Credential Provider [20], Credential Server (CRES) [21], Grid Security Infrastructure (GSI) MyProxy [22] utilizes a centralised approach for creating user credential although their implementation differs between one another. These mechanisms could be implemented in DE, however the conspicuous issue of single server failure must be carefully considered. In an event where the credential provider server is down, there possibly a chaos in a DE community due to the unavailability of credential services for client authentication. Apparently, several authorisation mechanisms such as CAS [23], Akenti [24], and PMI [25] also take a similar centralised approach.

These mechanisms inherit several issues pertinent to the centralised management. First, the central management would face real issue with the bottleneck and failure on its servers. Security breach would occur if the central servers fail to perform their authorisation processes over the clients. This situation exposes the resources to the malicious attacks as there is no other authorisation mechanisms are in place. Although it is possible to replicate the central server, the replication process will bring abundance administrative issues and higher chances for compromising the resources, considering a huge amount of data that needs to be replicated. Second, challenges occur when the central server attempt to assign the access permissions to the DE member entities. As a large number of resource providers that host one or more resources, the central server needs to register each resource and its access permissions individually. Further, this situation becomes even more challenging as a single resource could be associated with multiple different access permissions, and each client may have different access permissions assigned to him. Therefore, the central management is not practical when there is huge number of entities in a DE environment. Third, serious administration issues would occur as a DE environment grows in size and diversity due to the great benefits that they can achieve. A central server will be experiencing huge burden to manage all client and resource providers' accounts and permissions even with the use of super computers or grid collections of computers.

Several DE literatures in [6,10,13] clearly reveal that DE is characterized as an open environment on which a centralized structure is minimized. DE must be engineered to provide a high resilience infrastructure while avoiding single point of control and failure. Therefore, a completely distributed control mechanism is required that immune to the super control failure. It is evident that the aforementioned internet mechanisms are inappropriate to be implemented in a DE environment due to its centralized management. We have dedicated a paper in [26] that derive the analogy of DE concept and further discuss its security challenges and requirements in detail. In this paper, we focus at the implementation and validation of our proposed DRPM solution [27,28] to solve the identified issues.

AN OVERVIEW OF DRPM

In this section, we provide a brief explanation of the important elements and workflows in in DRPM. Full discussion on these workflows could be found in [27,28].

Important Elements of DRPM

Two important elements of DRPM are client profile and capability token. A client profile is created in registration workflow when a client registers himself to access the resources. Its main function is to allow resource provider to capture all required, but voluntarily provided, client's information before any access to the resources is granted. The data that is contained in a client profile provides necessary information about who the client is and about their intentions for using the requested resources. Therefore, it ensures the resource provider that resources are not going to the wrong entities which would further impose the confidentiality and integrity of the resources. The use of client profiles also facilitates auditing process for the clients that are accessing a resource. For example, there may be a situation where a resource provider needs to make a trace back to determine which client was delegated access to the resource in case there was an incident involving a dispute or counterfeiting of the resource in question. Such implementation would reduce the risk of stolen data by the unauthorized entities.

At the end of registration process, an entity that is deemed eligible to access the resources would be issued a capability token. The purpose of this token is to simplify the management of access permissions that appear to be the challenge in collaborative environment, as have been pointed out by the number of literature from the previous section. A capability token functions as the authentication token for any subsequent access requests as well as for granting the access permissions. It contains the necessary right permissions for each client to perform a set of operations on a particular resource. This capability is produced by the resource provider on which a particular resource is hosted. On subsequent access request, this token is used by the resource provider to grant the client access to the resources and further provide the authorization process for the clients. Our basic design of capability token, as shown in Figure 1, contains the client profile identifier, resource provider identifier, resource identifier and list of access permissions, and it is expressed in XML [43] due to its simplicity, wide usability and selfdescriptive characteristics. A time-stamp can be implemented in the capability token to determine the validity period of a user in accessing the resources. In the event where the trustworthiness of a new user is equivocal, a short-life capability token can be issued. Once the trustworthiness of the user gradually increases, resource provider can replace the short-life token with longer timestamp validity. Additionally, the Uniform Resource Locator (URL) of resources is embedded in the token to provide an automatic and seamless connection to resource servers.

A Secure Registration Workflow

The DRPM registration portal is used to generate a client profile during the initial resource provisioning. The registration process comprises of three main stages: client registration, public key exchanges, and secure transfer of capability token. The resource provider endorsed certificate is utilized to identify the authentic resource provider I. Pranata, G. Skinner and R. Athauda, "A Distributed Secure Mechanism for Resource Protection in a Digital Ecosystem Environment," Journal of Information Security, Vol. 3 No. 1, 2012, pp. 25-38. doi:10.4236/jis.2012.31004.

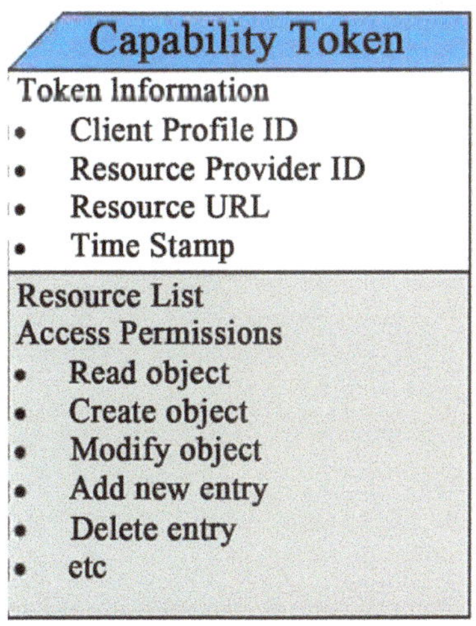

Figure 1: The structure of capability token.

The registration steps are detailed below:

- A new client contacts the resource provider for requesting a resource. Resource provider sends its WoT endorsed public key to the client. Once the client determines and accepts the trustworthiness of the public key, he stores the resource provider trusted public keys and fills his information on the registration portal.

- After the client information is filled, the registration portal creates a unique client and save this client profile.
- Resource provider then requests for client certificate and stores the client public key on its repository. If required, WoT verification could be performed on client certificate to ensure the trustworthiness of the client.
- The resource provider generates a client capability token based on client's allowed permissions.
- Resource provider uses its own private key to sign the capability token. This process enhances the integrity of capability token over the untrusted network.
- Resource provider then uses client's public key, received from step 3, to encrypt the signed message and send it to client end-point.
- Client uses his own private key to decrypt the encrypted capability token.
- Client then uses resource provider public key to generate the capability token from the signed message.

Note that at the final step of registration process, client will have his capability token and public key which was retrieved from the resource provider. The capability token and resource provider public key will be stored in client repository for subsequent requests. On another endpoint, the resource provider stores the client's public key in its own repository. We trust that the combination of both encryption and hashing mechanisms further uphold the confidentiality, integrity and non-repudiation of capability token during its transfer in the communication channel.

A Secure Resource Access Workflow

Once a client has been successfully registered with the resource provider, client will present his capability token to the resource provider on every access request. The capability token which contains client assertions and authorization permissions is primarily used as a base by the resource provider for authenticating the client and granting the resource access. Three foremost protection requirements for the resource access are the identification of resource provider, secured transfer of capability token, and authentication of a requesting client. A detailed workflow that ensures security protection on each resource access is provided in Figure 3.

The steps are as follow:

- Client retrieves the resource provider capability token. The capability token contains the client access permissions and the resource URL. At this stage, the client also determines a symmetric pass key which will be shared with the resource provider and generate an Authentication Token which consists both symmetric pass key and capability token.
- Client uses his private key to sign the capability token.
- Client then encrypts the signed capability token using resource provider public key and he sends the encrypted message to the resource provider.
- When resource provider received the encrypted message, it uses its own private key to de-crypt the message and retrieve the signed capability token.
- Resource provider then verifies the signature of capability token using client public key. It then verifies the integrity of the capability token by generating the hash number from capability token.
- Resource provider retrieves the access permissions listed in capability token.

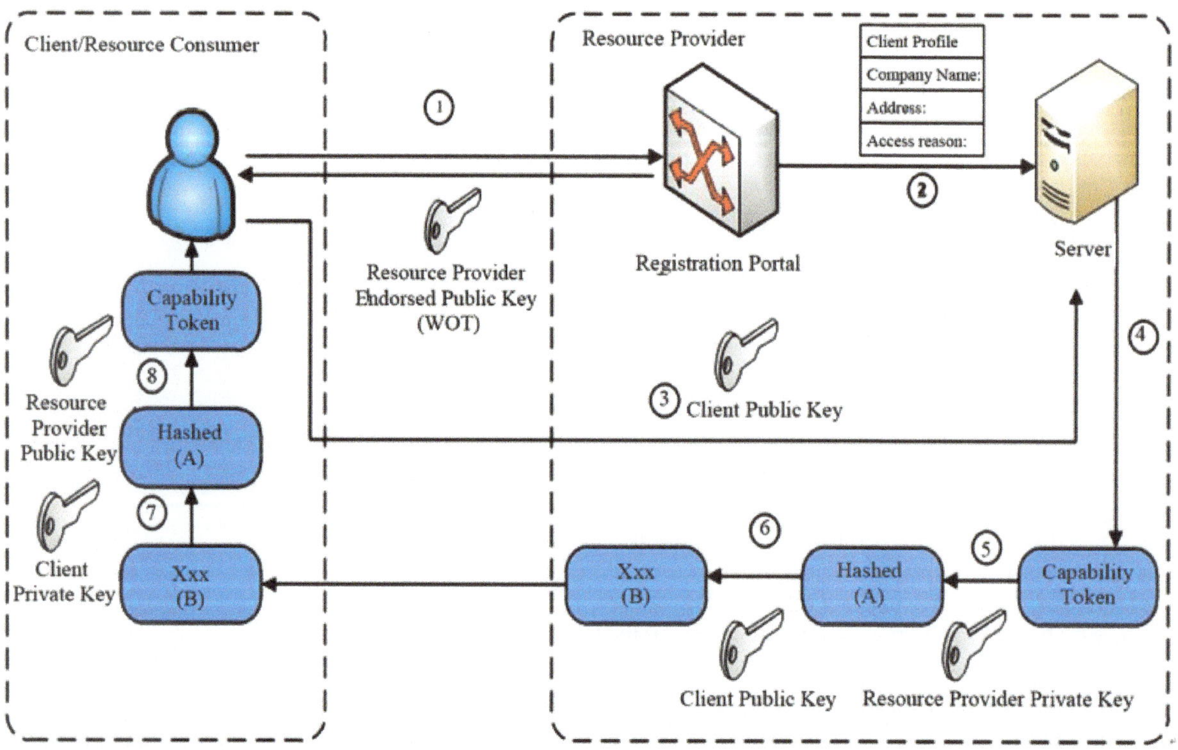

Figure 2: DRPM secure registration workflow.

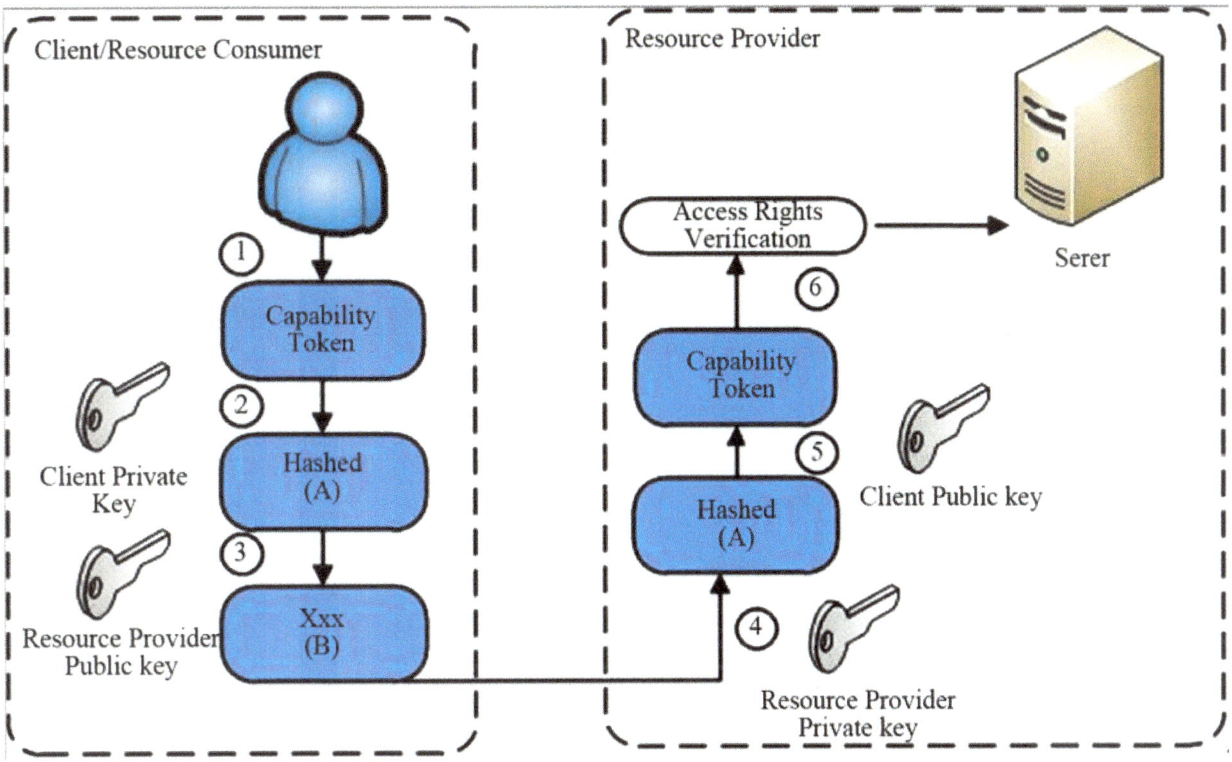

Figure 3: DRPM resource access protection.

Note that, on the step 1 of the workflow the client determines a symmetric pass key. This pass key will be utilized to generate a symmetric key for further communication after client is authenticated. In an event where the capability token is stolen due to man-in-middle attack, the unauthorized entity will still not be able to access the resource due as the symmetric key passphrase is shared between the legitimate client and resource provider only. This symmetric key would be used to secure communication after the authentication process. This is primarily due to the limitation of PKI which requires higher computation process. Further, a request for updating the resource provider public key could be made if the resource provider generates a new pair of public-private keys due to an unforeseeable security breach.

Engaging Community Protection

As discussed in Section 2, DE must limit its centralized structure and promotes the involvement of Small and Medium Enterprises (SMEs) for its successful implementation. It is evident that centralized approach using either a Certificate Authority (CA) or Credential Provider (CP) must be minimized. For DRPM, we propose an idea to integrate the community trust services, such as Web of Trust (WoT) into DRPM workflow, particularly in client registration process. We present this idea as an alternative approach for protecting resources in a DE environment. Further, the implementation of WoT in DRPM encourages active participation of DE member entities to protect their environment.

Web of Trust (WoT) is a community endorsed certificate which provides a decentralized trust management in a digital community. In WoT, there is no central authority (such as CA) that every entity trust, instead each entity is able to sign others certificates or public keys to build an interconnected web of public keys. The identifycation of an entity is provided primarily by his public key which is digitally signed by any number of "introducers". Three degree of trustworthiness is introduced to reveal the reliability of the entity public key certificate: undefined, marginal and complete. Final decision for trusting the entity is rely on the user after examining the degree of trustworthiness. The prominent application of WoT is in Pretty Good Privacy (PGP) [30], which is used extensively to secure emails. The implementation of WoT in DRPM and the mechanism to ensure the trustworthiness of WoT entities is not within the scope of this paper. This issue becomes an inspiration for our future work.

DRPM IMPLEMENTATION

Our DRPM prototype is divided into two major applications: the resource provider application and the client application. The resource provider application consists of three main system components: listener component, registration component and resource component. The respective tasks of these components are to listen for any incoming connection from the client, to automatically create client profile and capability token, to securely exchange and host multiple resources. In contrast, client application is primarily utilized by resource consumer to securely register and access the hosted resources. Further explanation of each of the components that builds up our prototype architecture is provided.

Resource Provider Architecture

Listener Server Component

The main functionality of listener server component is to accept any incoming HTTP requests from DE client members. Three main client requests on which this component handles are client registration, provider key signing and provider key retrieval. Upon receiving a client request, this listener component analyses the header of the incoming HTTP connection. This process has an objective to determine the nature of client request. Our client component, which would be discussed in detail in the following sub-section, was able to create unique HTTP headers to identify the objective of each request. Figure 4 explains the activity workflow that reflects full functionalities of this listener server component.

In a case where an incoming HTTP request contains a registration header, the listener component constructs a certificate object that contains resource provider information and its public key. This certificate object is then sent to the client together with the registration page URL for redirection purposes. When client receives a token, he may verify the certificate to ensure the trustworthiness of resource provider and subsequently, he is redirected to the registration page. In a case where an incoming HTTP request contains a signed key header, the listener component sends provider public key to the client for signing process. We implemented a transaction lock on which other clients are not able to retrieve provider key during the signing process. Further, a configurable timeout of 5 minutes were adopted for each signing process. If the timeout is reached and client has not returned the signed key, the transaction lock will be released. In the last case where the client request is to retrieve provider key, this listener component would response back with provider public key.

When starting the listener server component, the system administrator would need to configure three URL addresses: URL address where the listener server is located, URL address of registration page component, and URL address of resource login component. These URLs are used by the clients to connect to the resource provider server and its resources, and for the listener server to redirect the client to the registration components. Another functionality of the listener server component is to generate both public and private keys. The KeyManager module of this component presents the existing resource provider public and private keys. It has a functionality to re-create both public and private keys. If the new keys are created, these keys will be stored securely in the key repository on the resource provider server.

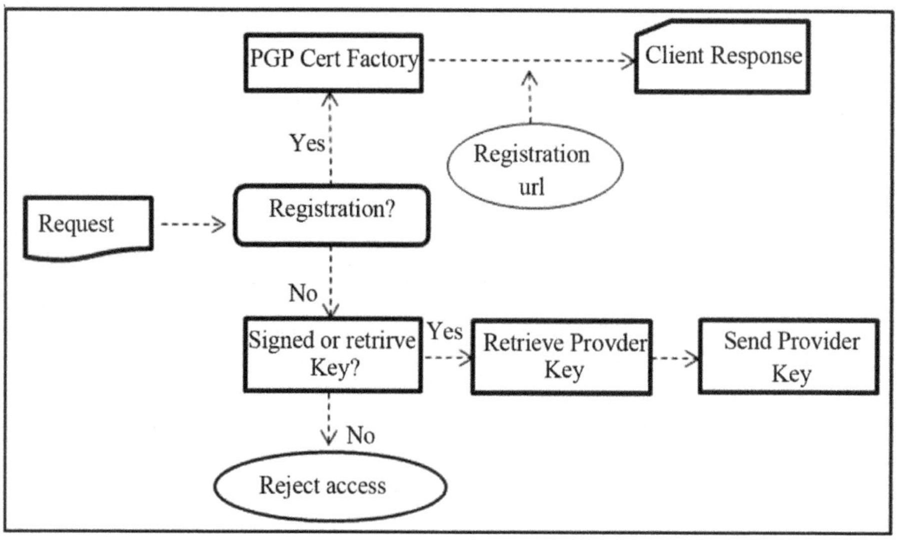

Figure 4: Listener server activity workflow.

Registration Page Component

The registration page component contains a set of minimum information which needs to be filled in by the client. For our testing, we uploaded 4 resources on which the access permissions of each resource could be requested. In real implementation, types of resources and their access permissions are highly dependent on the configuretion that is set by each resource provider. During the registration process, client public key is obtained and stored by resource provider in its server repository. The obtained public key will be used in future access requests. That is to verify the signature of the presented capability token. When a client submits his information and indicates which resources that he intends to consume the registration page component then creates a client profile based on the supplied information. This client profile will be stored in resource provider's database. After the creation of client profile, this component constructs a capability token and generates a hash no of this token. The hash no is then stored in the database for subsequent resource access verification. The newly created capability token goes through encryption and signing process (by calling the EncrypAndSignToken method). Figure 5 demonstrates the capability token that was taken before and after the encryption and signing process.

Resource Page Component

This is the critical component where the resources and critical information are hosted. Therefore, a considerable amount of security must be implemented. When this component is requested by client, a series of validation checks are conducted to determine the availability of capability token, its originality and integrity. This component contains a login module that performs these checks. When resource component receives a HTTP request with access header, login module checks the availability of capability token in the request. It obtains client capability token from the incoming request. The module then calls the decryptFile and the verifySignature method to decrypt and verify the signature as showed in Figure 3. If any of these processes fails, access request will be rejected as a failed authentication process, otherwise the client will be redirected to the resource page component where he will be given access based on the permissions that is contained in his capability token.

Note that, when a client is able to access the resource page component, it means that he has been authenticated by the resource provider as a genuine client. However, at this stage the access permissions which are presented by the client in his capability token have not been authorised. A hash no verification of capability token is performed for this purpose (through createVerifyHash module). The hash no will be compared with the hash no that was obtained during the registration process. If hash no verification succeeds, the resource page component retrieves all access permissions from client's capability token, and it further granted the resource access based on these listed permissions. If the verification fails, a notification would be presented to the client and access to the resource would be disallowed.

Client Architecture

Key Admin Component

Similar to the KeyManager module of resource provider listener component, this component allow clients to generate, manage and distribute his public and private keys.

Any created keys would be stored in keys repository which is kept in client workstation. This component was proved to be very useful for client administrator to manage his own keys.

Figure 5: The original (a) and the encrypted-signed (b) capability token.

Client Registration Component

This component is a critical module for a client to Register for new resources. A client provides his intended resource provider listener server URL and its port for a secure communication. When a client registers for resource, a new HttpWebRequest will be created and sent to the resource provider listener server. This HttpWebRequest serves as a request message from client to listener component to process and return the provider's certificate and its registration page URL. Upon receiving the response, the component processes and de-serializes this response. in order to obtain the certificate object. The requested client would then be able to view the WoT certificate, and simultaneously he is redirected to the resource provider registration page. Figure 6 shows our implementation of client registration component.

We built this secure component in a windows application with a simple web browser interface. This component is equipped with a capability to generate a HTTP protocol request for its initial communication. We set a temporary listener which is started when the client clicks on "register" button. This objective of temporary listener is to receive the encrypted token and further decrypts the token with resource provider public key which is obtained from its certificate object. The signature verification process follows after the decryption process. Figure 7 explains the entire activity workflow during resource registration from the client node point of view.

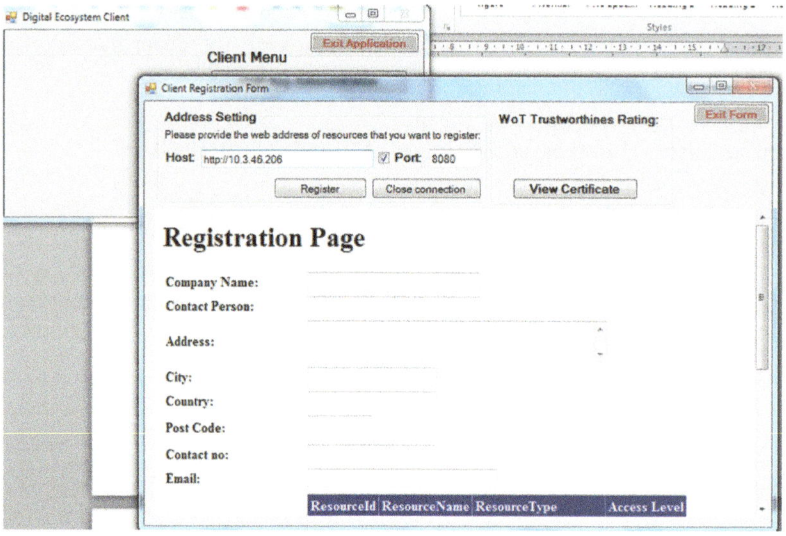

Figure 6: Client registration component.

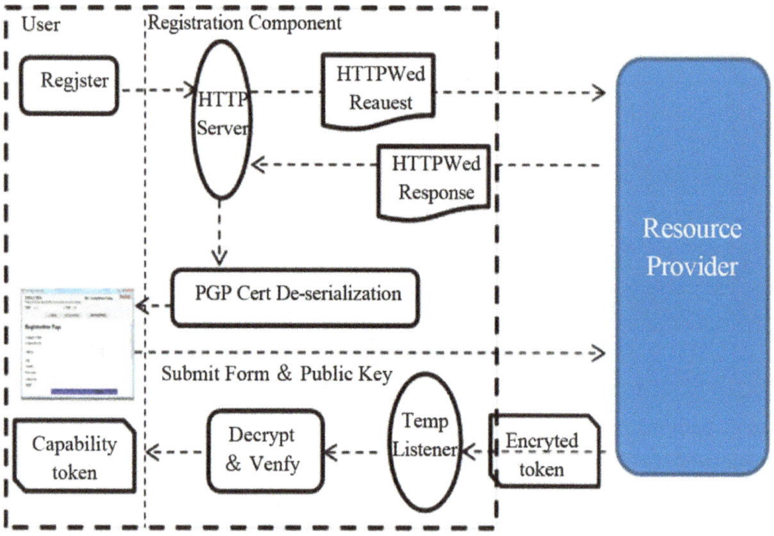

Figure 7: Activity workflow in client component.

Resource Access Component

DE client uses this component to access resources that are hosted in resource provider server. This component establishes communication and exchange processes of capability token and resources. A client is able to select which resource provider that he wants to access the resources based on his retrieved capability tokens. The component also lists all resources and their respective granted permissions. The lists of resource providers, resources, and permission types are retrieved from all capability tokens that are stored in client repository. When a client submits an access request, the capability token of its resource provider is retrieved and a symmetric key passphrase is generated. A temporary object will then be created to encapsulate this capability token and symmetric key passphrase. This object is further encrypted and signed as discussed previously in Figure 3.

SECURITY VALIDATION & ANALYSIS

In order to validate our proposed solution, we developed several scenarios that showed various unauthorised attempts to access the resources. In each scenario, we focussed at how the existing prototype could mitigate any threats that were attempting to access the resources. The test outcomes of these scenarios would further attest the ability of our proposed solution to uphold the confidentiality, integrity and availability of resources and information while strengthening the authentication and authorisation mechanisms in a DE environment. These scenarios are detailed below:

- Scenario 1: If a capability token is stolen, would the unauthorised entity be able to read its content?
- In our solution, a capability token is always encrypted and signed before it is being transferred in the network. The strongest encryption algorithm for e-commerce transactions (RSA algorithm) is utilized to prevent the unauthorised entity to read the content of capability token. Moreover, the Public Key Infrastructure (PKI) is fully utilized in our solution. With these measures in place, the confidentiality of capability token is always enforced. The unauthorised entity is only able to read the scramble data unless it has the corresponding private key to decrypt it. Figure 7 above has showed the encrypted capability token before it is being sent in the network.

- Scenario 2: If an unauthorised entity attempts to use the stolen capability token to camouflage himself as a legitimate client, would he be able to access the resources?

In this situation, the unauthorised entity would not be allowed to access the resource for two reasons:

- Resource provider always verifies the signature of capability token with the client public key on every access requests. Unless the unauthorised entity successfully obtained the client private key, the verification process of this capability token will be failed, and access will not be granted. Figure 8 shows the failed verification processes of capability token signature.
- In an event when an unauthorised entity performs the man-in-middle or relay attack during an active communication between client and resource provider, he would be able to obtain the capability token. However, the unauthorised entity will still not be able to access the resource due to the symmetric key passphrase that is shared between the legitimate client and resource provider only.
- Scenario 3: If an unauthorised entity or client modifies the capability token by adding or removing the resources or permission types, would he be able to consume the resources?

We implement a hashing mechanism for the resource provider to check the integrity of capability token. If there is any change, either minor or major change, in the capability token, the hash verification process will fail and the resource access will not be granted, as shown in Figure 9. This verification process further upholds the integrity of a capability token before any access to the resources is given.

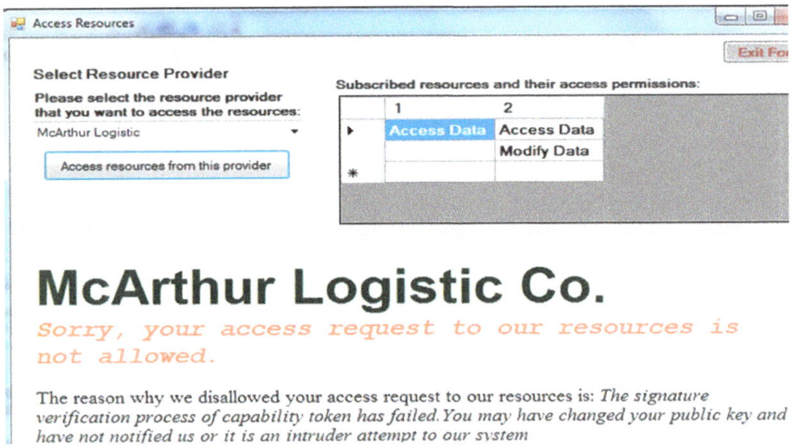

Figure 8: Access disallowed as failure to verify token signature.

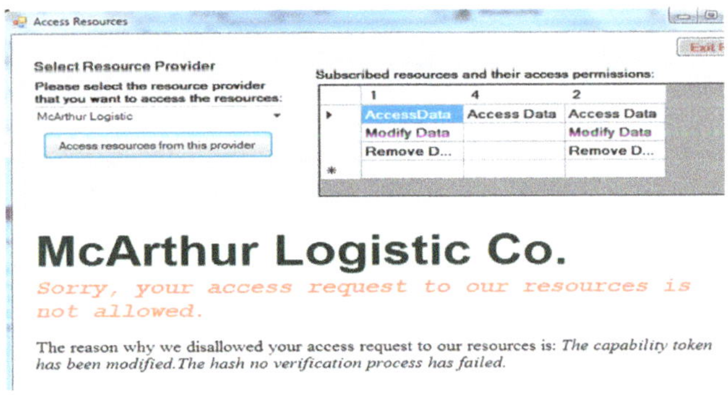

Figure 9: Access disallowed as failure to verify the hash no.

- Scenario 4: It is possible that a client is redirected to the unauthorized sites that claim to be the legitimate resource provider, how would DRPM prevent such situation?

This situation is known as phishing attack on which the client is redirected to the fraudulent link where he enters the personal details to the fraudster without any knowledge that he is the victim of the crime [31]. Our proposed capability token contains a ResourceURL field which functions to automatically redirect the client to the legitimate resource provider website. Further, the encryption method that is implemented before any token transfer is performed further upholds the confidentiality of a capability token during the transfer process. Therefore, our solution further reduces the possibility of phishing attack in a DE environment.

The verification and evaluation of DRPM proved to be successful, and it further resolved our main research issue of "authenticating the genuine client and managing multiple authorisation permissions over various resources". Our prototype implementation and testing has proved to solve several security concerns which were derived in section V as well as various threat scenarios that are likely to occur in a DE environment. Finally, the unique authentication and authorisation mechanisms offered by DRPM in conjunction with its secure architecture provide a complete and full fledge security solutions for a DE environment.

PERFORMANCE AND SCALABILITY ANALYSIS

Performance Testing

In this section, we briefly review our analysis on the computational cost of DRPM prototype. To measure the performance impact of DRPM, three different scenarios from the workflows are identified. They are: the overhead cost during initial registration process where provider's public key and its registration page are sent to the client, the overhead cost in processing client's registration that includes generating capability token and secureing communication, and the overhead cost during resource access workflow. In addition, we compare the overhead cost of cryptography between two sets of machine.

All performance tests were conducted in two machines, and these machines respectively act as client and server. Our client machine run on a 1.86 GHz Intel Centrino with 1 Gb of RAM while our provider server machine run on a 2.26 GHz Intel Core2 Duo processor with 2 Gb of RAM and IIS 7 web server. Both machines were using NET framework 2.0 and MSSQL Server 2008 for the database. It is important to note that both client and provider server machines are below today's average of client and server computer standards. This configuration was taken to measure the performance of using DRPM prototype on the low end machines. As both client and provider server were connected via local high speed Ethernet LAN with 100 Mbps, we assume that the network latency during testing was insignificant. Therefore, it was not considered on the final performance results.

We conducted 52 repeated experiments for each scenario to obtain various performance results of DRPM. The result of the first two results was omitted due to the need for the application prototype to be compiled and the process workers to be started by the Just in Time (JIT) compiler in Net Framework 2.0. Therefore, only the results of subsequent 50 experiments were obtained. Due to the length limitation of the paper, we only present the mean and standard deviation of the experiment results. Further, the overhead costs derived from each scenario are calculated by applying the mean scores to the formula below:

$$\text{Overhead Cost} : \frac{\text{Processing Time}}{\text{Total Time Taken}} \times 100\%$$

The result of our performance testing on DRPM prototype is shown in Table 1.

The average total time take for initial registration reest was 226.18 milliseconds. This timing accounted for loading registration page and processing provider cerficate. Furthermore, the average total time for client regtration in our test was 593.24 milliseconds. This timing accounted for 134.56 milliseconds of server process and 458.68 milliseconds of client process. Our findings showed that token creation process accounted was accounted for the lowest time needed compare to other server processes such as encryption and signing process. The highest overhead cost (61.88%) was needed by other server process such as running complex stored procedures in database, forming response to client, and etc. In client process, the highest overhead cost was token decryption process. It was followed by signature verification process which was almost 88% faster than the former process. The rest client process accounted for 31.05 milliseconds (6.77%) was for processing response, storing token to repository, and etc.

As shown in Table 2, the overall time needed for accessing resource in our test was 701.28 milliseconds. This timing was account for 55.92 milliseconds for server login process and 645.36 milliseconds for client process and resource page loading. The result for server login process showed that the decryption process took the majority of server login time. This was followed by signature verification which was almost 88% faster than the decryption process aligned with the registration workflow decryption-signature process. Overall time take to retrieve the access permissions from token was 1.46 milliseconds for 1 Kb token size. As the capability token is intended for storing the access permissions in lightweight XML format, we expect that it only contains limited information; therefore its file size should not over than 5 Kb. Hash verification performance was a surprising result in our DRPM prototype testing. This was due to the process of hash verification method which involves generating hash no from the token (using SHA-1 algorithm) and comparing it with the original hash that is obtained from the database. The rest 5.34 milliseconds (9.54%) was needed for other server login processes such as reading private keys from key ring, forming HttpWebResponse message, writing logs, creating sessions and etc.

Table 1: Registration workflow overhead cost (in milliseconds).

Scenario	Steps on Workflow	Processing Type	Mean	Standard Deviation	Overhead Cost
Registration: initial request	Server (Step 1)	Loading Page	226.18	89.08	N/A
Registration: processing		Creating Token	6.84	6.89	5.08%
	Server (Steps 2-6)	Encrypt and Sign	44.46	6.84	33.04%
		Total Server Time	134.56	48.17	N/A
		Decrypt	375.78	46.19	81.92%
	Client (Steps 7-8)	Verify Signature	51.86	46.77	11.31%
		Total Time	458.68	55.32	N/A

Table 2: Resource access workflow overhead cost (in milliseconds).

Scenario	Steps on Workflow	Processing Type	Mean	Standard Deviation	Overhead Cost
Resource Access	Server (Steps 4-6)	Decrypt	43.48	4.04	77.75%
		Verify Signature	5.08	1.90	9.08%
		Verify Hash	0.52	0.71	0.93%
		Retrieve Permissions From token	1.5	0.50	2.68%
		Total Server Time	55.92	5.15	N/A
	Client (Steps 1-3)	Encrypt & Sign	435.84	55.75	67.53%
		Total Client Time	645.36	70.15	N/A

Token encryption and signature process accounts for the majority of total client process time. The rest 209.52 milliseconds (32.47%) was needed for other client processes including the activity to form HttpWebRequest, to retrieve token from repository, to process HttpWebResponse that was obtained from server, to redirect to resource page, to load resource page from server side and etc. Another finding from our testing was the overhead cost of cryptography processes which include decryption, encryption, sign and verification was reduced by almost 89% by doubling up the machine specification. This could be found by comparing any cryptography process between the client machine and server machine. Figure 10 shows the overhead percentage of each process.

Scalability Testing

We tested the scalability of the listener server component to handle multiple HttpWebRequest requests as shown Figure 11. This test was conducted by utilizing the Apache JMeter [32] tool that specializes on the web scalability and performance testing. The purpose of this test was to review the scalability of the listener component to handle multiple client registration requests.

In our test bed, 1000 users were generated to access the listener component concurrently. Our test shows that the average elapsed time of this set of results was 162 milliseconds with the aggregate highest elapsed time of 327 milliseconds and the aggregate lowest elapsed time of 5 milliseconds. The scalability testing on other components such as registration, login, resource page, etc. were not able to be conducted by JMeter. This is primarily due to the need to utilize the prototype to create the request stream that holds the encrypted and signed capability token. We tested the scalability of other components only with a small number of machines (5 or less) and only a small number of clients (4 or less). Therefore, scalability of these components was not addressed in the experiment.

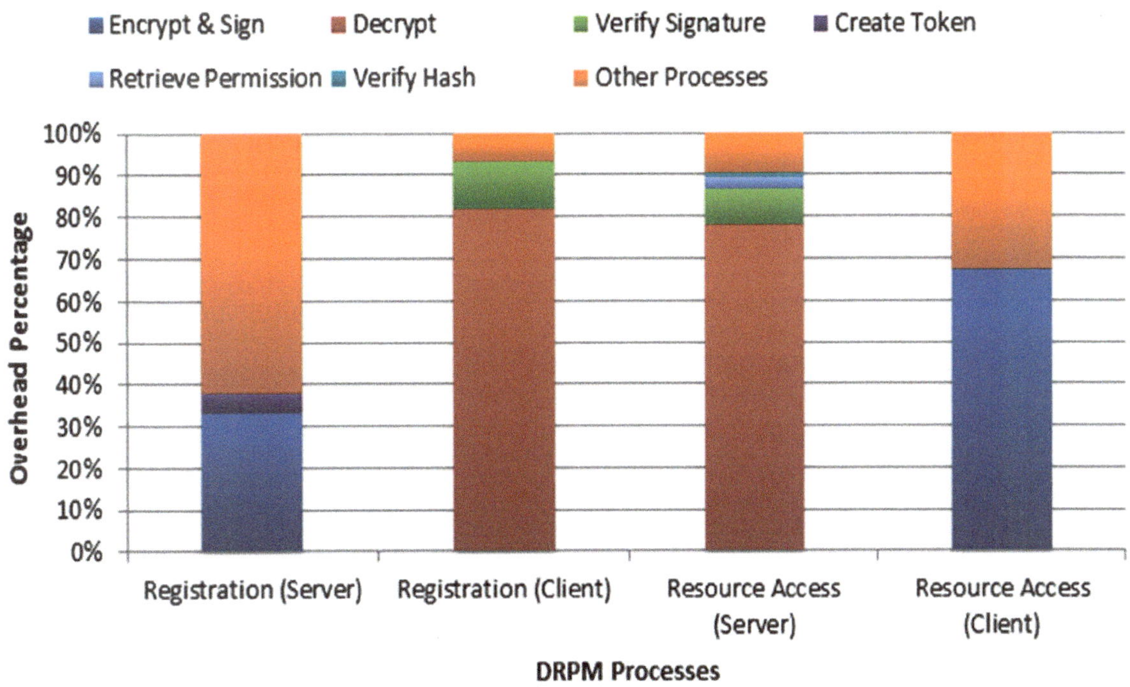

Figure 10: Overhead cost on DRPM prototype.

Figure 11: DRPM listener component scalability testing.

CONCLUSIONS

In this paper, we introduced the concept of Digital Ecosystem (DE), and we also outlined the challenges that are faced by DE, in particular the authentication and authorisation mechanism. We have also highlighted the requirement of DE to minimize the centralized structure and promoting the engagement of Small and Medium Enterprises (SMEs) for its successful adoption. We further propose a unique solution the Distributed Resource Protection Mechanism (DRPM) that attempt to solve the identified challenges. DRPM focuses on the creation of client profile and capability token to protect the critical resources. Moreover, we propose a secure DRPM architecture with adoption of Public Key Infrastructure (PKI). This further allows DRPM functions as a complete and full fledge security solution for Digital Ecosystem.

This paper also provides our implementation of secure DRPM which consists of two major system architectures: resource provider system and client system. Several scenarios of security threats are provided in this paper to analyse and evaluate the ability of our secure DRPM implementation to mitigate these threats. The analysis shows that the secure DRPM proposal is able to uphold the confidentiality, integrity, and non-repudiation of the resources. In addition, the performance and scalability analysis of DRPM are presented. Future works include the investigation of an effective trust mechanism in DRPM. As pointed in this paper, the utilisation of Web of Trust (WoT) would engage the interacting entities to actively protect their DE environment. At this point, however, DRPM does not include any trust mechanism that could allow the interacting entities to determine which resource providers are honest and which are not. The inclusivity of trust mechanism would significantly improve the overall security protection in DE environment. Therefore, investigation on the effective trust mechanism to improve the overall DRPM security is needed.

REFERENCES

1. D. Boughaci and H. Drias, "A Secure E-Transaction model for E-Commerce," IEEE GCC Conference (GCC), Manama, 20-22 March 2006. doi:10.1109/IEEEGCC.2006.5686242 .
2. C. Potter and A. Beard, "Information Security Breaches Survey 2010," Technical Report, PricewaterhouseCoopers, 2010. .
3. P. ltner and T. Grechenig, "A Joint Infrastructure of 'Digital Corporate Organisms' as Facilitator for a Virtual Digital Retail Ecosystem," 4th IEEE International Conference on Digital Ecosystems and Technologies (DEST), Dubai, 12-15 April 2010. .
4. Y.-L. Fang B. Han and Y.-B. Li, "Research and Implementation of Key Technology Based on Internet Encryption and Authentication," International Conference on Networking and Digital Society (ICNDS'09), Guiyang, 30-31 May 2009.
5. X. Tian and W. Dai, "Study on Information Management and Security of E-commerce System," International Symposium on Intelligence Information Processing and Trusted Computing (IPTC), Huanggang, 18-20 November 2010. .
6. P. Dini, M. Darking, N. Rathbone, M. Vidal, P. Hernandez, P. Ferronato, G. Briscoe and S. Hendryx, "The Digital Ecosystems Research Vision: 2010 and Beyond," 2011. www.digital-ecosystems.org/events/2005.05/de_ position_ paper_vf.pdf .
7. EComm, "Technologies for Digital Ecosystems," 2005. www.digital-ecosystems.org/doc/flyer-de-sector.doc.
8. F. Nachira, P. Dini and A. Nicolai, "A Network of Digital Business Ecosystems for Europe: Roots, Processes and Perspectives," 2011. http://www.digital-ecosystems.org/book/DBE-2007.pdf .
9. F. Nachira, E. Chiozza, H. Ihonen, M. Manzoni and F. Cunningham, "Towards a Network of Digital Business Ecosystems Fostering the Local Development," Discussion Paper, Bruxelles, 2002. [Paper reference:2]
10. H. Boley and E. Chang, "Digital Ecosystem: Principles and Semantics," Inaugural IEEE International

Conference on Digital Ecosystems and Technologies (IEEE DEST 2007), Cairns, 12-23 February 2007. .

11. M. Hadzic, E. Chang and T. Dillon, "Methodology Framework for the Design of Digital Ecosystem," ISIC IEEE International Conference Systems, Man and Cybernetics, Montreal, 7-10 October 2007.
12. DigitalEcosystem.org, "Digital Ecosystems: The New Global Commons for SMEs and Local Growth," 2011. http://www.digital-ecosystems.org/de/refs/ref_books.html .
13. G. Briscoe and P. Wilde, "Digital Ecosystems: Evolving Service-Oriented Architectures," 1st International Conference on Bio Inspired Models of Network, Information and Computing Systems, New York, June 2006. .
14. M. Wooldridge, "Introduction to MultiAgent Systems," Wiley, New York, 2002 .
15. E. Cantu-Paz, "A Survey of Parallel Genetic Algorithms," Reseaux et Systemes Repartis, Calculateurs Paralleles, Vol. 10, 1998, pp. 141-171.
16. J. Stender, "Parallel Genetic Algorithms: Theory and Applications," IOS Press, Amsterdam, 1993.
17. A. Berson, "Client/Server Architecture," 2nd Edition, McGraw-Hill Companies, Upper Saddle River, 1996.
18. W3C, "Web Services Architecture," 2011. http://www.w3.org/TR/ws-arch/
19. R. Schollmeier, "A Definition of Peer-to-Peer Networking for the Classification of Peer-to-Peer Architectures and Applications," Proceedings of 1st IEEE International Conference on Peer to Peer Computing, Linkoping, 27-29 August 2001. .
20. H. Koshutanski, et al., "Distributed Identity Management Model for Digital Ecosystems," International Conference on Emerging Security Information, Systems and Technologies (Securware'07), Valencia, 14-20 October 2007. .
21. J. M. Seigneur, "Demonstration of Security through Collaborative in Digital Business Ecosystem," Proceedings of the IEEE SECOVAL Workshop, Athens, September 2005. .
22. J. Novotny, "An Online Credential Repository for the Grid: MyProxy," Proceedings of the IEEE 10th International Symposium on High Performance Distributed Computing (HPDC-10), San Fransisco, 7-9 September 2001. .
23. L. Pearlman, et al., "A Community Authorization Service for Group Collaboration," Proceedings of the 3rd International Workshop on Policies for Distributed Systems and Networks, Monterey, 5-7 June 2002. doi:10.1109/POLICY.2002.1011293 .
24. M. Thompson, et al., "Certificate-Based Access Control for Widely Distributed Resources," Proceedings of the 8th Conference on USENIX Security Symposium, Washington DC, 23-26 August 1999.
25. J. Weise, "Public Key Infrastructure Overview," Sun Microsystem, Sun BluePrints Online 2001. .
26. I. Pranata, G. Skinner and R. Athauda, "A Survey on the Security Requirements for a Successful Adoption of Digital Ecosystem Environment," 2nd International Conference on Information Technology Security (ITS 2011), Singapore, 24-25 November 2011. .
27. I. Pranata, G. Skinner and R. Athauda, "Community Based Authentication and Authorisation Mechanism for Digital Ecosystem," 5th IEEE International Conference on Digital Ecosystems and Technologies (DEST'11), Seoul, 31 May-3 June 2011.
28. I. Pranata, G. Skinner and R. Athauda, "Distributed Mechanism for Protecting Resources in a Newly Emerged Digital Ecosystem," 11th International Conference on Algorithms and Architectures for Parallel Processing (ICA3PP 2011), Melbourne, 24-26 October 2011.
29. W3C, "Extensible Markup Language (XML)," 2011. http://www.w3.org/XML/
30. P. R. Zimmermann, "The Official PGP User's Guide," MIT Press, Cambridge, 1995. .
31. FTSC, "FSTC Counter-Phising Initiative," Financial Services Technology Consortium, New York, 2004. .
32. Apache JMeter, 2011. http://jakarta.apache.org/ jmeter/

CHAPTER 12

TECHNOLOGY OF SECURE FILE ARCHIVING IN THE UNIFORMLY RANDOM DISTRIBUTED ARCHIVE SCHEME

Ahmed Tallat, Hiroshi Yasuda, Kilho Shin

Applied Information Engineering, Tokyo Denki University, Tokyo, Japan

ABSTRACT

This paper investigates the security features of the distributed archive scheme named Uniformly Random Distributed Archive (URDA). It is a simple, fast and practically secure algorithm that meets the needs of confidentiality and availability requirements of data. URDA cuts a file archived into fragments, and distributes each fragment into randomly selected n − k + 1 storages out of n storages. As the result, users only need to access at least k storages to recover original file, whereas stolen data from k − 1 storages cannot cover original file. Thus, archived files are nothing but sequences of a large number of fixed length fragments. URDA is proved of disappearing both characters and biased bits of original data in archived files, indicating the probabilities of both a fragment and a bit appearing at particular position are uniformly constant respectively. Yet, through running experiments, we found out the risk of likelihood that URDA might be vulnerable to bit pattern attack due to the different ratios of characters appearing in real world files. However, we solved the problem by modifying URDA with variable fragment lengths, which results in that all the bits in revealed sequences are distributed uniformly and independently at random.

INTRODUCTION

Cloud computing is attracting attentions of people of a wide variety of fields including users, service providers and facility manufacturers. From the users' point of view, the most attractive advantages of cloud computing must be the ubiquity and affordability of services that cloud computing can realize. Since cloud computing is constructed on top of the Internet, users can take advantage of services anytime and anywhere. The recent rapid spread of mobile computing certainly enhances the demands for the ubiquity of service provision. On the other hand, the affordability of cloud computing is based on exploitation of public infrastructures. The Internet itself is apparently public good, and cloud computing is enlargeing its scope to computational powers and storages that are available in the Internet. For example, the data backup services provided by data center companies are very expensive, and small and middle-sized enterprises cannot afford them. In contrast, the same services are now being provided at significantly lower prices based on cloud computing.

Citation: A. Tallat, H. Yasuda and K. Shin, "Technology of Secure File Archiving in the Uniformly Random Distributed Archive Scheme," Journal of Information Security, Vol. 4 No. 1, 2013, pp. 42-53. doi: 10.4236/jis.2013.41006.

Thus, the advantages of cloud computing are due to the fundamental idea of exploiting the Internet and public goods existing in the Internet. This, however, can produce disadvantages as well. In particular, in terms of security, the Internet has serious problems. ISO 17799 [1] determines that confidentiality, integrity and availability (CIA) are the three important factors in considering security issues, and the Internet has vulnerability in all of them: Communication over the Internet is in principle subject to eavesdropping and tampering; Nobody controls the overall the services of the Internet, and cutoff and delay of communication can happen anytime. Furthermore, we cannot deny the possibility that the providers of services are malicious. Although cryptographic technology will provide us with strong countermeasures with respect to confidentiality and integrity, we need different technologies to solve the issue of availability.

Let's consider a data backup service based on cloud computing. A user uploads his or her data to the Internet for the backup purpose, and the data are distributed across many inexpensive storages unknown to the user. Different storage providers operate different storages under different policies. Even their connectivity may vary. Thus, the user can have a problem when he or she needs to restore the data. In the worst case scenario, it is still possible that some of storage providers have ceased their services without notification, and therefore, a part of the backup data has been lost forever.

To solve this problem of availability, storing data with redundancy is probably the only solution, and we have already had technologies to realize availability by redundant storing.

RAID [2] (Redundant Array of Inexpensive Disks) is daily use technology, and combines more than one physical hard disks into a single logical unit by distributing the whole data mostly with redundancy across multiple disks, which is necessary in case of data lost; A failed disk is replaced by a new one, and the lost data will be built from the remaining data and the redundancy such as parity data. This technology enables computer users to achieve high level storage reliability from PC-class components.

Although RAID is appropriate to apply to "home" servers, it has evidently issues in its scalability. In particular, RAID can accept failures of only one (RAID 3 and 5) or two disks, and will not be able to apply to the Internet, where users may lose access to more than two storages.

The technology known as "secret sharing" also provide a method to distribute secret information with redundancy: For $n > k > 0$, n members have their shares derived from a secret, and the secret will be completely reconstructed when k members exhibit their own shares; By contrast, collusion of (k − 1) members will reveal none or only a few bits of the secret. This property of secret sharing is referred to as k-out-of-n threshold secrecy. The initial (k, n) threshold secret sharing scheme (SSS) known in the literature were independently invented by Adi Shamir [3] and George Blackley [4] in 1979, and since then the scheme has been widely studied and applied on a variety of fields. (for example, Rabin [5], Bai [6,7], Blundo [8], He [9], Wang [10]).

Although these schemes support the severe requirement of k-out-of-n threshold secrecy, their computational complexity is extremely high, and it cannot show practical performance when applied to archive of bulky data: data should be fragmented into a number of fragments so that they are short enough to be dealt with by the secret sharing algorithms, and the algorithms need heavy computation such as modular exponentiation and matrix manipulation in calculating shares from each fragment.

The recent technology of P2P also provides the function of storing data with redundancy. P2P aims at sharing decentralized resources (CPU, storage, bandwidth and contents) of each participant, while eliminating conventional centralized unit to provide browsing and downloading, and thus the participants are both consumer and provider of the resources in distributed networks. The principle is simply uploading and downloading simultaneously and continuously, and the acceleration of data transferring can be improved significantly by downloading desired pieces simultaneously with random order from multiple providers that treat distributed contents as sequence of pieces through fragmenting them into sequences. We already have several P2P based global storage products (for example, OceanStore [11] and PAST [12]).

The most important problem of the P2P technology when applying to our purpose should be its extremely low efficiency in storage spaces and bandwidth. The initial aim of P2P is to realize sharing data among an unspecified number of people, and hence, data are exchanged and stored with very high redundancy exceeding the necessity for the backup purpose.

In our previous work [13], we investigated a simple scheme, called the uniformly random distributed archive scheme (URDA). The algorithm of URDA is extremely simple and easy: The original data is fragmented into a number of tiny fragments (several bits long), and each fragment is distributed across n − k + 1 storages out of n storages: The most important feature of URDA consists in that the selection of the n − k + 1 storages is dominated by a completely random process: Storages are selected uniformly and independently at random per fragment. By this, URDA meets the condition of k-out-of-n threshold robustness: that is, even if the owner of the data loses access to k − 1 storages of the entire n storages, the user can restore the original data from the data fragments retrieved from the remaining k storages.

In terms of confidentiality, it has been revealed in previous work that URDA has a couple of remarkable properties.

1) Except for bits existing in the very narrow neighborhood of the start and the end of the original file, the probability that a guess on the position where a particular fragment of the original file appears in a distributed backup file is very small, and almost constant.
2) When assuming that the original data consists of ASCII characters selected at random from the entire possible values, the probability that a particular bit pattern appears at a particular position in a distributed backup file is independent of the position. To be precise, we can theoretically derive the following formula.

$$\Pr\left[b_t = \cdots = b_{t-l} = 0\right] \approx \frac{1}{8}\left(\frac{l+1}{2^l} + \frac{7-l}{2^{l+1}}\right) = \frac{l+9}{2^{l+4}} \quad (1)$$

The symbol b_t represents the t-th bit from the head of the backup data, and the formula holds unless the bit falls into narrow neighborhoods of the head and the tail of the distributed backup file.

The first property implies that, if attackers do not take advantage of biases of bit patterns in the original data, they cannot guess the contents of the original data from the distributed backup data. On the other hand, in the second property, we take ASCII data as an instance, and show that the evident bias of bit patterns, that is, 0 appears every eight bits, disappears in distributed backup files. Thus, these properties indicate the possibility that URDA can provide confidentiality of a certain degree, without relying on cryptographic techniques. This would be an important advantage of URDA in terms of time efficiency of the scheme.

In this paper, we further investigate the second property. In the real world, any text files have particular biases in the distributions of bit patterns, and the theoretical conclusion of URDA might not hold true for data in the real world. We struggle with this problem through experiments.

In the experiments, we downloaded 200 ASCII files from the Internet, applied URDA to these files to generate 1000 backup files, and looked into the statistical features of the backup files. First, we found that the Equation (1) still holds true for the backup files we investigated in our experiments. This was verified by performing the one-sample t-test: It has turned out that the "null" hypothesis that the Equation (1) does hold cannot be rejected even with a large significance level. Secondly, we synthetically generated 200 random ASCII files and 1000 backup files in the same way as for the downloaded ASCII files. Then, we compared between the synthetic and the real backup files in terms of the variance of the distributions of the particular bit pattern. The result this time showed that the null hypothesis can be rejected with the significance level 0.05 by the F-test. This means that the distributions of bit patterns between the real and synthetic backup files are different, and therefore, we cannot deny the possibility that a clever attacker can invent an effective pattern analysis to guess the original contents from the contents of the backup files.

Based on the result of this experiment, we modified the algorithm of URDA so that the length of fragments are to be determined at random per fragment, and performed the same experiment using this modified URDA. The result was surprising. The two groups of distributions, one for the real backup files generated by the modified URDA and the other for the synthetic backup files, are concluded to be the same. To be precise, even with a large significance level, we could not reject the null hypotheses that claim that the distributions are the same as Gaussian distributions. This consequence is significant: The backup files of real ASCII files generated by the modified URDA are indistinguishable from the synthetic backup files. By definition, the synthetic backup files show the uniform randomness in terms of bit pattern distributions, and hence, we can conclude backup files generated by the modified URDA are secure against bit pattern analysis.

Following Section 2 describes some related studies followed by URDA scheme proposed in previous paper for the consistency of the paper, and it also includes analyses of security feature of URDA. Section 3 clarifies problem that the paper is tackling, and provides solution by running experiments and applying statistical methods. We conclude the paper with future work in section 4.

DISTRIBUTED ARCHIVE SCHEMES

In this section, we provide a brief review over the data storage techniques of redundancy known in the literature, and then describe URDA proposed in our previous work.

Distributed Schemes in Storage Pools

Digital high density recording technologies have made a variety of data recorded in storage medium. As a result, the form of utilizing storage devices has been greatly changed, and a variety of home appliances, computers/ servers, and even micro device in mobiles have become to have their own storages and to utilize them at a higher level.

However, with the advent of the Internet the need of sharing information made rapid increase of data in terms of variability and amount, which in turn led to creation of high technical processing power of computers and also posed strong demand to the scale of flexibility of storages for these ever-increasing data. Since there are limits of computational power and capacity within conventional devices having attached to individual storages inside, they are no longer able to meet the need the way of data being accessed, stored and shared. Furthermore, tracking and backing up files distributed into a variety of storages constitute significant hardship. Some storage techniques [14] try to address these problems by allowing all the files to be stored in a single, secure storage that can be accessed by other clients and servers regardless of the operating systems from anywhere within the same domain.

However, independency of storages and servers is costly in terms of updating, managing and running. Thus, the conception of "storage pool" [15] aims at providing the scale of flexibility to solve the problems by allowing servers to utilize storage capacity from the pool so that virtual hard disk drives can be dedicated to servers based on their needs without buying extra storage to each of them individually. The storage pool is also known as a dedicated storage network, because it is separated and independent from servers, allowing several servers to connect one drive and vise verse. Same as the independent storage, drive enclosure in the storage pool can hold any number of drives with a variety of types and expand on demand. Mostly the variety of drives has a central control unit to manage all the Input/output and they are equipped with some technical schemes for providing security and recoverability in case of disaster or system failure.

However, to guarantee the availability, integrity and confidentiality of the data stored in storage medium is not easy task. Because every system is vulnerable to certain damages caused by natural, physical and technical attacks, and thus these data can be lost, delayed or even stolen. Redundancy probably is the only feasible solution to address the issues. The fastest method to realize redundancy is replication [16], which distributes redundantly copied fragments of data across infrastructure, but it is space inefficient, and p2p is a typical example of the replication-based systems. Another resilient method is erasure coding that splits data into n fragments, which are then further redundantly encoded into k additional fragments using parity, matrix, polynomial etc. Thus, k specifies the level of resiliency or Maximum Distance Separable (MDS), where k = MDS.

Despite their values, widespread utilities, and reliabilities due to the capabilities of meeting the various needs for disaster recoveries, they all have drawbacks in terms of heavy cost and complex computational procedures. Because they use matrices, cryptography and heavy mathematical calculation etc. for producing redundancy, and applying them to large amount of data is very expensive, due to extremely time-consuming computational requirements, and even they are relatively inflexible, due to the complexity and difficulty of meeting various levels of desired security requirements as needed. What is more, dealing with cloud computing environment, for example for the purpose of backup of datacenter, is not easy with these schemes, due to lack of utilization of cost-effect readiness to use available storages provided. Thus, the currently heavy set-up cost and computational complexity cause significant hardship to utilize currently available storage services in order to realize secure backup services.

URDA-Uniformly Random Distributed Archive Scheme

In order to address aforementioned issues of current techniques when applying them to cloud computing in the context of robustness and security, and to provide affordable backup techniques, we have introduced URDA in our previous work.

The outline of the algorithm of URDA is as follows: URDA first fragment the source file to archive into multiple tiny fragments, and then distributes each fragment to n − k + 1 destination storages selected out of the entire n storages. The n − k + 1 storages are selected uniformly and independently at random per fragment. Thus, the source file is distributed across n storages, and each fragment is archived at exactly n − k + 1 different storages. The simple image of URDA is shown in Figure 1.

To be specific, URDA consists of a smartcard and a host (e.g. client/server software), and they communicate with each other through a standardized interface like IC card interface [17], Near Field Communication [18] and Infrared Link Access Protocol [19]. The role of the smartcard is to generate random distribution keys taking advantage of the key generator RNG_K receiving seeds from the seed generator RNG_S, both RNG_K and RNG_S are installed inside the smartcard, whereas the host fragments the source file, duplicates the fragments, and distributing the copies generated across multiple storages, following the indication by the random distribution keys. In the following, we give a brief description of the archival and retrieval phases of URDA. The flow chart of the algorithm is shown in Figure 2.

Archival phase: The role of the smart card in the archival phase is to generate a series of distribution keys and to transmit them to the host. The algorithm of the smart card in the archival phase is as follows;

- Receive the START_ARCHIVAL signal accompanying the identifier of the source file through the cardhost interface. The identifier is denoted by crr_fid.
- Generate a random seed taking advantage of RNG_S. The seed is denoted by crr_seed.
- Store the pair of crr_fid and crr_seed in the internal database. The pair will be used in the retrieval phase.
- Input crr_seed into RNG_K.
- Let RNG_K generate a random number, which is an index to determine the (n; k)-distribution key to be used by the host. The smart card outputs the random number to the host program.
- Repeat Step 5 until it receives the END_OF_FILE signal from the host program.

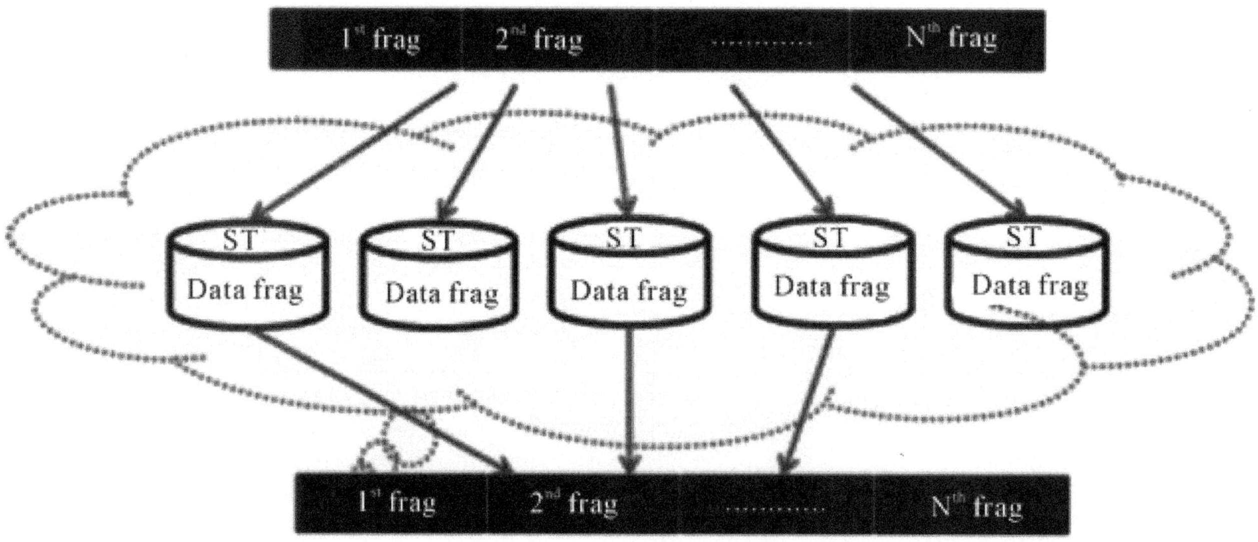

Figure 1: The simple image of URDA (n = 5, k = 3).

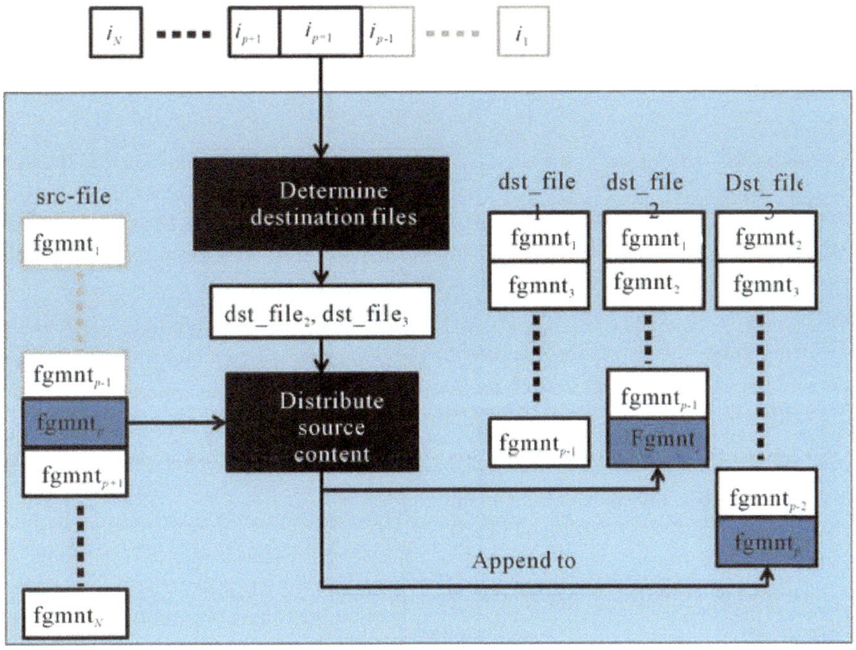

Figure 2: The flow chart of URDA.

On the other hand, the role of the host program in the archival phase is to distribute the contents of the source file over n destination files.

- Fragment the source file into the b-bit long fragments of $fgmnt_1,\cdots,fgmnt_{last}$, and create a pointer p to indicate the current fragment $fgmnt_p$. The initial value of p is 1.
- Send the START_ARCHIVAL signal to the smart card.
- Receive an index i_p from the smart card.
- Identify the distribution with index i_p. The distribution key determines the set of n − k + 1 destination files to which the current fragment $fgmnt_p$ is to be appended.
- Take away the current fragment $fgmnt_p$ from the source file, and increment the pointer p by 1.
- Append the fragment $fgmnt_p$ to the destination files determined in Step 4.
- Repeat the steps from 3 to 6 until all the fragments are taken away from the source file.
- Send the END_OF_File signal to the smart card.
- The host program sends the resultant n destination files to n storages via networks.

Retrieval phase: The algorithm of the smartcard in the retrieval phase is as follows:

- Receive the START_RETRIEVAL signal accompanying the identifier crr_fid of the target file from the host program.
- Look up crr_fid in the internal database, and retrieve the seed crr_seed paired with crr_fid.
- Input crr seed into RNGK.
- Output the random numbers i_p that RNGK generates to the host program.
- Repeat Step 4 until the END_OF_FILE signal is received.

On the other hand, algorithm of the host is described as follows.

- Fragment the destination files into b-bit length fragments, create a pointer for each destination file. Initially, each pointer is set so that it indicates the first fragment.
- Send the START_RETRIEVAL signal to the smart card.
- Receive an index i_p from the smart card. The initial value of p shall be 1.
- Determine the set of n − k + 1 destination files in which the current fragment $fgmnt_p$ are included.
- For each of the destination files determined in Step 4, take away the fragment indicated by the pointer associated with the destination file, and change the pointer so that it points the next fragment.
- Append $fgmnt_p$ to the source file, and increment p by 1.
- Repeat the steps of 3 to 6 until all of the destination files are empty.

The size of the resultant destination files is exactly $(n-k+1)$ times as great as the original size of the source file and the expected size of each destination file is $(n-k+1)/n$ times smaller than the size of the source file, and thus it supports (k,n) robustness and (k,n) security, which means that downloading from k storages is enough to recover original file and that even $(k-1)$ storages are attacked, the stolen data cannot cover total amount of the file.

Security Features of URDA

In this clause, we summarize the security features of URDA that are presented in our previous work.

The probability that a specific fragment is not included in any of specific r storages is

$$\frac{n-k+1}{n} * \frac{n-k}{n-1} * \cdots * \frac{n-k-r}{n-r-1}$$

Thus, if r storages are compromised, the probability that all of the fragments are revealed is

$$\left(1-\prod_{i=1}^{r}\frac{n-k-i}{n-i-1}\right)^{N} \qquad (2)$$

N is the total number of the fragments. When $r \geq k$, the Equation (2) is 1, whereas, when r < k, it approaches 0, as N increases. This implies the k-out-of-n threshold secrecy: Even if k − 1 storages are compromised, the entire original contents will not be revealed.

Definition 1. Let N and m denote the number of fragments in a source file and a revealed sequence, and a and j denote the positions of a fragment in both the source file and the revealed sequence $(N \geq a \geq 1, m \geq j \geq 1)$ respectively. Then we define that $\mathbf{Match}(a, j; N, m)$ denotes the probability that a fragment at the position of a in the source file appears at the position of j in the revealed sequence.

When a is fixed and j moves, following holds for the maximum value of $\mathbf{Match}(a, j; N, m)$.

$$\underset{j\in\{1,\cdots,m\}}{\mathbf{argmax}}\,\mathbf{Match}(a, j; N, m) = \left\{\left\lceil\frac{am}{N+1}\right\rceil, \left\lfloor\frac{am}{N+1}\right\rfloor+1\right\}$$

Thus, the maximum of $\mathbf{Match}(a, j; N, m)$ when a is fixed and j moves, is given by the following formula.

$$\mathbf{Match}\left(a, \frac{am}{N+1}; N, m\right) \approx \frac{m}{N\sqrt{\pi}}\cdot\left(\frac{N-1}{(a-1)(N-a)}\right)^{1/4} \qquad (3)$$

The minimum value of the equation can be reached at $a=\frac{N-1}{2}$, and Figure 3 is its simulation result for the value of $N = 10^3, 10^4, 10^5, 10^6$ and $\frac{m}{N}=\frac{3}{4}$.

Thus, we can conclude that the security against identifying the position of a fragment is uniformly small except the fragments located in heads and tails. Furthermore, obtaining further safety can be possible by adding dummy data at the heads and tails.

Next, we run a thought experiment. In the experiment, we see that the certain significant pattern of the bit distribution of ASCII text files disappears in archived backup files. For the ASCII text files to use in the experiment, we assume that ASCII characters in the files are selected uniformly and independently at random per character from the entire possible values. Therefore, the bit distribution of the files is as follows: The most significant bit (MSB) of every byte is always 0, whereas the remaining bits are distributed uniformly and independently at random. Then, we define

$$\bar{q}(j,\rho) = \sum_{a \bmod 8=\rho} \mathbf{Match}(a, j; N, m)$$

to represent the probability that $a \bmod 8 = \rho$ holds when $\overline{\mathrm{fgmnt}}_j$ is a copy of fgmnt_a. Then, the probability that the ρ-th bit $(\rho = 1,\cdots,7)$ of $\overline{\mathrm{fgmnt}}_j$ is 0 turns out to be

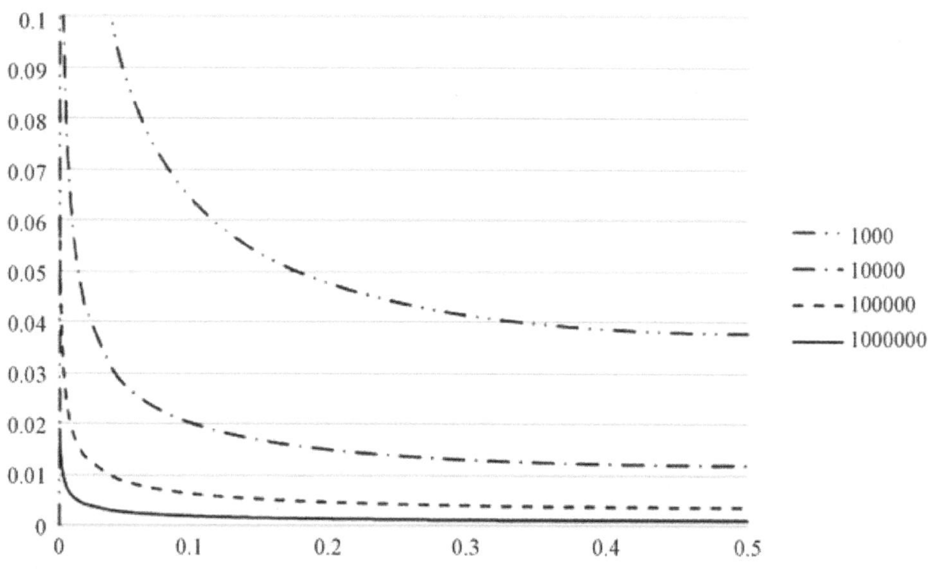

Figure 3: Simulation result

$$\Pr\left[b_{7j+\rho} = 0\right] = \bar{q}(j,\rho) + (1-\bar{q}(j,\rho))\cdot\frac{1}{2} \qquad (4)$$

A remarkable fact is that $\bar{q}(j,\rho) \approx \frac{1}{8}$ holds except for narrow neighborhoods of $j = 1$ and $j = m$. Hence, when t is not close to 1 or m, we have the following approximation.

$$P\left[b_t = \cdots = b_{t-l} = 0\right] \approx \frac{1}{8}\left(\frac{l+1}{2^l} + \frac{7-l}{2^{l+1}}\right) = \frac{l+9}{2^{l+4}}$$

Through the same computation as above, we have the following.

Corollary 1. When t is not close to 1 or m, $\Pr[b_t = \beta_t, \cdots, b_{t+l} = \beta_{t+l}]$ is approximately constant.

Corollary 2. When t is not close to 1 or m, $\Pr[b_t = \beta_t, \cdots, b_{t+l} = \beta_{t+l}]$ is approximately constant.

Corollary 1 and 2 imply that most of the bits in the revealed contents look almost the same in the attacker's eye.

PROBLEM AND SOLUTION

In following sections, through identifying the problem, we provide particular solutions to address it. To proceed, we investigate experimentally on ASCII characters to see if bit patterns of source files can be disappeared in archived files, and further demonstrate that practical security of plain text archiving can be obtain by varying fragment length in bit distribution.

IDENTIFIED PROBLEMS

Our previous work, assuming that source files include only ASCII characters selected uniformly and independently at random, we mathematically proved that an archived file consisting of seven-bit-long fragments shows uniformly constant distributions with respect to the probabilities that particular bit patterns appear in it. To be precise, we let $C_1 \cdots C_L$ be the byte contents of a file, where C_i is an ASCII character selected uniformly at random from the entire space of ASCII characters. Then, we apply URDA to this file by setting the fragment length to be seven bits, and hence, the file content is fragmented into seven-bit-long fragments. The resulting archived files are collections of these fragments. Focusing on one of the archived files, we proved that the probability $\Pr[b_{t-\ell} = \beta_{-\ell}, b_{t-\ell+1} = \beta_{-\ell+1}, \cdots, b_t = \beta_0]$ is approximately constant regardless of the choice of t, unless t is too small or too large. b_t denotes the bit at the position t in the archived file, and $\beta_{-\ell}\beta_{-\ell+1}\cdots\beta_0$ is an arbitrary bit pattern with $\beta_i \in \{0,1\}$. This means that we can view the archived file as secure against bit pattern analysis, since the source file does not include any bit pattern except that the bit 0 appears every 8 bits, and this pattern proves to disappear in the archived file.

On the other hand, text files found in the real world, even when they consist of ASCII characters, cannot help including biases in the distribution of characters. Thus, the hypothesis of the aforementioned investigation does not necessarily hold, and hence, it is not certain that the conclusion of the investigation holds true for the real files.

The problem that we solve in this paper is first to investigate whether the property that we proved in our previous work also holds true for real files that include biases in the distributions of characters. Then, we will answer the question whether URDA is secure against bit pattern analysis when applied to real files.

How to Solve the Problem

To solve this problem, we run experiments with a large number of files that we obtain from the internet.

To be specific, we download ASCII files from diverse sites to apply URDA to these files, and then investigate the distributions of bit patterns that appear in the resulting archived files. We first examine whether the mean of the probabilities that particular bit patterns (in the experiments, we focus on four bit patterns that are sequences of 0) is identical to what was theoretically derived in Equation (1).

When we naturally assume that the probabilities observed follow Gaussian distributions, it is not sufficient to investigate only the means. We have to investigate the variances as well. For this purpose, in addition to the files obtained from the Internet, we generate synthetic ASCII files based on the uniformly random process: For each position in a file, an ASCII character is selected uniformly and independently at random. Then we compare the distributions of the probabilities of the same bit patterns between the archived files generated from the downloaded files and those derived from the synthetic files. The comparison will be made in terms of the means and the variances, since we assume that the distributions follow Gaussian distribution. Since the synthetic files are generated based on the same probabilistic model as what Equation (1) was based on, and since we concluded that such files are secure against bit pattern analysis, this comparison shows an answer to the question whether the same conclusion with respect to confidentiality holds true for real ASCII files.

URDA with the Setting of the Fragment Length = 7 bits

The procedures to run the experiment are given as follows.

1) Find 200 ASCII files in the Internet, and download them.
2) Apply URDA to the downloaded files with n = 5 and k = 3, and hence, obtain 1000 archived files, each of which is at least 100 KB length. Here, we set the fragment length to be seven bits as specified in Section 2.2.
3) For t = 1 to 400,000, count the number n_t of occurrence of $b_t = \cdots = b_{t-\ell} = 0$ for $\ell = 0,1,2,3$ over the 1,000 archived files, and calculate $\Pr[b_t = \cdots = b_{t-\ell} = 0]$

by $\frac{n_t}{1000}$. Thus, we have 400,000 scores of $\Pr[b_t = \cdots = b_{t-\ell} = 0]$ for each $\ell = 0,1,2,3$ respecttively.

We plot these scores in the graphs of Figure 4.

Yet we are still unable to estimate whether the mathematical formula can also apply to the real world biased ASCII files with fixed fragment length, without evaluating dispersion of the scores from means.

Statistical Tests

According to the mathematical evaluation given in URDA in previous work, the scores vary drastically when t is small (the position is close to the head of the files), but they quickly converge to Equation (1).

In fact, when looking at Figure 4, the scores observed in this experiment seem to follow this rule: The values of

$\frac{l+9}{2^{l+4}}$ are 0.5625, 0.3125, 0.1719 and 0.0938 respectively for l = 0,1,2,3. In the following, we will investigate this, that is, whether the scores observed in fact follow the statistically calculated mathematical formula proved in previous work.

Examining the Means

By the one-sample t-test, we investigate whether the population means underlying the observed scores are identical to the test means calculated by Equation (1).

The null hypothesis here is of course that the population means are identical to the test means.Table 1 shows the results of one-sample t-test.

The t statistics are calculated from the equation

$$t = \frac{\bar{x}-\mu}{s/\sqrt{n}}$$

, where $\bar{x}, \mu, n$ and s stand for the sample mean, test mean, sample size and standard deviation of the sample respectively. From Table 1, we see that we cannot reject the null hypothesis even with very large significance level, say 0.2: Typically, we use the signifycance level 0.05 or 0.01. Hence, we can reasonably guess that the null hypothesis is right, that is, the population means are identical to the theoretical value calculated by Equation (1).

Examining the Variances

In the previous clause, we see that the population means are identical to the theoretical means calculated from Equation (1). This result alone, however, is insufficient, since this result tells nothing about how the scores vary around the means. Thus, we have to investigate whether the population variances are sufficiently small. The problem here is that, unlike the calculation of means, we do not have a formula to give the theoretical expectation for the variances. As an alternative method, we generate synthetic files that are generated based on the same probability model as the mathematical model that underlies Equation (1), and compare the scores obtained from the experiment and the scores derived from these synthetic files.

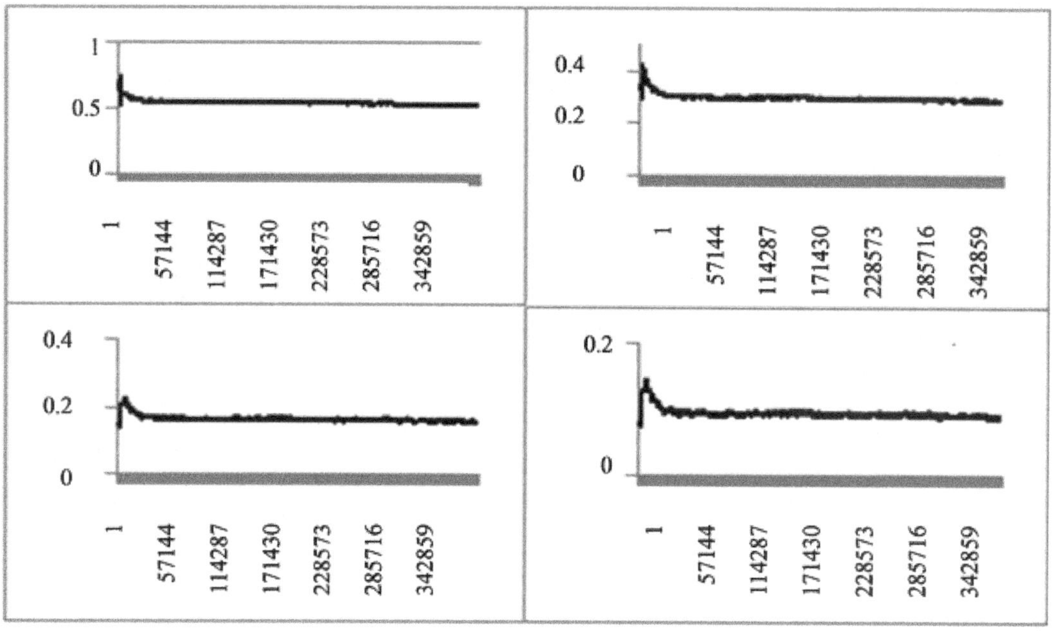

Figure 4: Fixed-fragment-length Pr[$b_t = \cdots = b_{t-l} = 0$] (l = 0,1,2,3, t = 1, ⋯ , 400,000).

Table 1: Comparing of observed scores and test means.

	$\Pr[b_t = 0]$	$\Pr[b_t, b_{t+1} = 0]$	$\Pr[b_t, \cdots, b_{t+2} = 0]$	$\Pr[b_t, \cdots, b_{t+3} = 0]$
Sample Mean	$\bar{x}_f = 0.5707$	$\bar{x}_f = 0.3082$	$\bar{x}_f = 0.1718$	$\bar{x}_f = 0.0948$
Test Mean	$\bar{x}_f = 0.5625$	$\bar{x}_f = 0.3125$	$\bar{x}_f = 0.1719$	$\bar{x}_f = 0.0938$
T-Statistics	$T_f = -0.706$	$T_f = 0.4928$	$T_f = 0.0107$	$T_f = -0.167$
TINV	$T = 1.66$	$T = 1.66$	$T = 1.66$	$T = 1.66$
P-Value	$T_{tail} = 0.482$	$T_{tail} = 0.623$	$T_{tail} = 0.992$	$T_{tail} = 0.868$

To be specific, we generate 200 files that include only ASCII characters selected uniformly and independently at random regardless of the position of the characters. Then, we apply Step 2 and 3 of Section 3.3 to obtain 400,000 scores for each of $\ell = 0,1,2,3$. We call these scores test scores to distinguish them from the sample scores generated in Section 3.3.

To verify this statistically, we apply two-sample F-test to the sample scores and the test scores. Consequently, the null hypothesis to use should be that the population variances underlying the sample scores are identical to those underlying the test scores.

Table 2 shows the result of the test, where σ_f^2 and $\sigma_t^2, \bar{x}_f$ and $\bar{x}_t$ are the variances and the means of the sample scores and the test scores, respectively. According to Table 2, we see that the variance σ_f^2 is greater than σ_t^2, while the means x_f and x_t are very close to each other. When investigating the P-values presented in the table with the significance level 0.05, we see that the null hypothesis should be rejected for all cases of $\ell = 0,1,2,3$. Thus, when we apply URDA to ASCII files downloaded from the Internet with the fixed fragment length seven bits, the resulting archived files will not be explained by the mathematical model that is a basis of Equation (1). In other words, we cannot prove that the archived files generated by URDA with the aforementioned setting are secure against the bit pattern analysis, and we cannot recommend use of URDA with this setting.

URDA with the Setting of the Fragment Length = Variable

As seen in the above, using URDA with the fixed fragment length cannot be recommended from the security point of view. In this clause, we investigate the security of URDA with a different setting, that is, we assume that the fragment length is variable, and is selected at random per fragment in the range of 1 to 32 bits.

For the experiment, we use the same ASCII files stated in Section 3.3. The difference consists in Step 2, and we run URDA with the setting of the fragment length = variable.

In the same way as Section 3.3, we obtain 400,000 sample scores for each of $\ell = 0,1,2,3$, and plot them in Figure 5.

At a glance, the means of the sample scores are identical to their theoretically expected values of $\Pr[b_t = \cdots = b_{t-\ell} = 0] = \frac{l+9}{2^{l+4}}$, and the variances have become smaller compared with the case of the fixed fragment length. In the following, we verify these observations by means of statistics.

Examining the Means

In the same way as the previous subsection, we apply the one-sample t-test to verify that the population means of the sample scores are identical to the theoretical expectation.

Table 3 shows that the P-values obtained are large (the minimum is 0.188), and we cannot reject the null hypotheses with a small significance level, for example, 0.05. Hence the population means of the target probabilities are identical to the values given by $\frac{l+9}{2^{l+4}}$ for $\ell = 0,1,2,3$.

Examining the Variances

As shown in Table 4, the variances of the sample scores are close to those of the test scores, which are the scores generated in Section 3.3 using the synthetic ASCII files. If this is true, this will be a clear contrast with the former case where we ran URDA with the fixed fragment length. In the following, we verify that the population variances of the sample scores and the test scores are identical to each other by means of the two-sample F-test.

Table 4 shows that the P-values obtained are large (the smallest is 0.1704), and we cannot reject the null hypotheses with a small significance level, for example, 0.05.

As a consequence, we can conclude that the population variances that underlie the sample scores and the test scores are identical to each other.

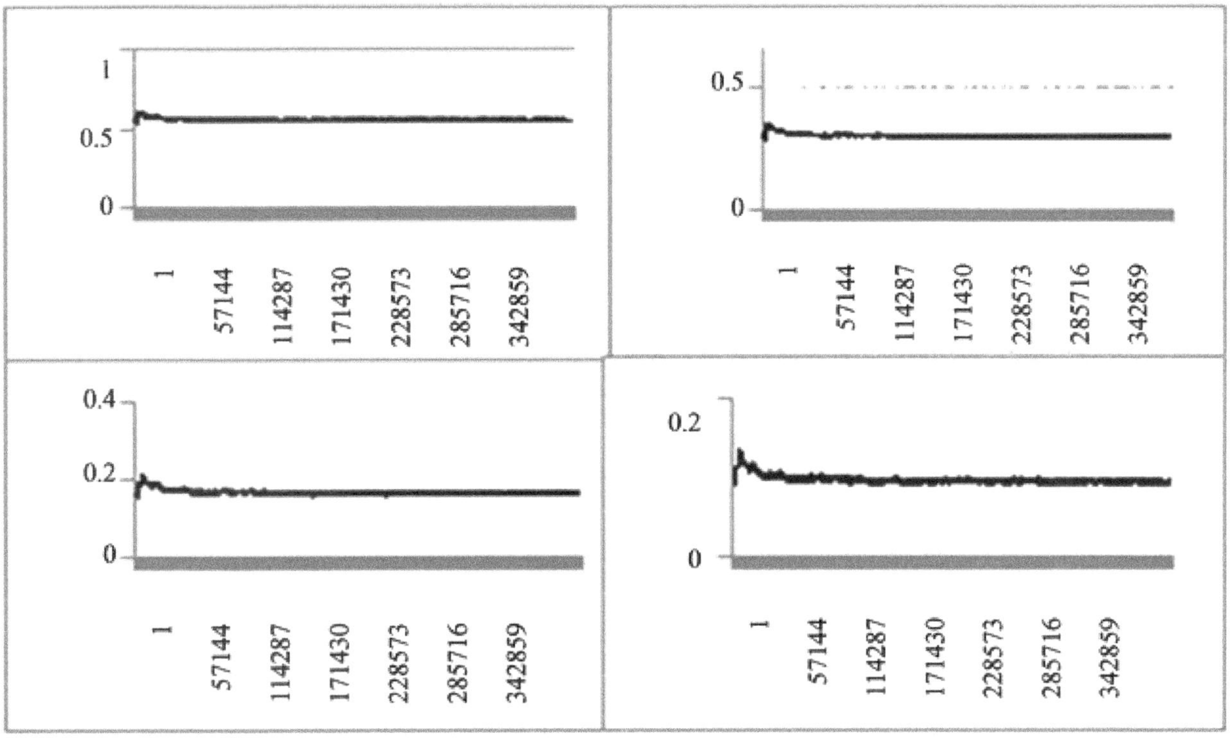

Figure 5: Variable-fragment-length $\Pr[b_t = \cdots = b_{t-l} = 0]$ ($l = 0,1,2,3$, $t = 1, \cdots, 400{,}000$).

Table 2: Comparing of fixed variances and test variances.

	$\Pr[b_i = 0]$	$\Pr[b_i, b_{i+1} = 0]$	$\Pr[b_i, \cdots, b_{i+2} = 0]$	$\Pr[b_i, \cdots, b_{i+3} = 0]$
Sample Variance	$\sigma_f^2 = 0.0135$	$\sigma_f^2 = 0.0078$	$\sigma_f^2 = 0.0078$	$\sigma_f^2 = 0.0036$
Test Variance	$\sigma_f^2 = 0.0036$	$\sigma_t^2 = 0.0045$	$\sigma_t^2 = 0.0019$	$\sigma_t^2 = 0.0014$
Sample Mean	$\bar{x}_f = 0.5707$	$\bar{x}_f = 0.3082$	$\bar{x}_f = 0.1718$	$\bar{x}_f = 0.0948$
Test Mean	$\bar{x}_t = 0.5617$	$\bar{x}_t = 0.3103$	$\bar{x}_t = 0.1721$	$\bar{x}_t = 0.0923$
F-Value	1.53	1.72	2.64	2.61
Critical Value	$O_{tail} = 1.39$ $T_{tail} = 1.49$	$O_{tail} = 1.39$ $T_{tail} = 1.49$	$O_{tail} = 1.39$ $T_{tail} = 1.49$	$O_{tail} = 1.39$ $T_{tail} = 1.49$
P-Value	$T_{tail} = 0.036$	$T_{tail} = 0.007$	$T_{tail} = 0.000002$	$T_{tail} = 0.000004$

Table 3: Comparing of variable means and test means.

	$\Pr[b_i = 0]$	$\Pr[b_i, b_{i+1} = 0]$	$\Pr[b_i, \cdots, b_{i+2} = 0]$	$\Pr[b_i, \cdots, b_{i+3} = 0]$
Test Mean	$\bar{x}_t = 0.5625$	$\bar{x}_t = 0.3125$	$\bar{x}_t = 0.1719$	$\bar{x}_t = 0.0938$
Sample Mean	$\bar{x}_r = 0.5511$	$\bar{x}_r = 0.3031$	$\bar{x}_r = 0.1712$	$\bar{x}_r = 0.0938$
TINV	$T = 1.66$	$T = 1.66$	$T = 1.66$	$T = 1.66$
T-Statistics	$T_r = 1.067$	$T_r = 1.3261$	$T_r = 0.1437$	$T_r = -0.021$
P-Value	$T_{tail} = 0.288$	$T_{tail} = 0.188$	$T_{tail} = 0.886$	$T_{tail} = 0.983$

Table 4: Comparing of variable variances and test variances.

	$\Pr[b_i = 0]$	$\Pr[b_i, b_{i+1} = 0]$	$\Pr[b_i, \cdots, b_{i+2} = 0]$	$\Pr[b_i, \cdots, b_{i+3} = 0]$
Sample Variances	$\sigma_r^2 = 0.0115$	$\sigma_r^2 = 0.0051$	$\sigma_r^2 = 0.0025$	$\sigma_r^2 = 0.0015$
Test Variances	$\sigma_t^2 = 0.0088$	$\sigma_t^2 = 0.0045$	$\sigma_t^2 = 0.0019$	$\sigma_t^2 = 0.0014$
Sample Mean	$\bar{x}_r = 0.5511$	$\bar{x}_r = 0.3031$	$\bar{x}_r = 0.1712$	$\bar{x}_r = 0.0938$
Test Mean	$\bar{x}_p = 0.5617$	$\bar{x}_p = 0.3103$	$\bar{x}_p = 0.1721$	$\bar{x}_p = 0.0923$
F-Value	0.7694	0.89	0.7583	0.9458
Critical Value	$O_{tail} = 1.39$ $T_{tail} = 1.49$	$O_{tail} = 1.39$ $T_{tail} = 1.49$	$O_{tail} = 1.39$ $T_{tail} = 1.49$	$O_{tail} = 1.39$ $T_{tail} = 1.49$
P-Value	$T_{tail} = 0.194$	$T_{tail} = 0.549$	$T_{tail} = 0.1704$	$T_{tail} = 0.7823$

Summary of This Experiments

In our previous work, assuming that source files include ASCII characters selected uniformly and independently at random per character, we have mathematically proved that an archived file consisting of seven-bit-long fragments shows uniformly constant distributions with respect to the probabilities that particular bit patterns appear. In other words, we can view the archived file as secure against the bit pattern analysis. On the other hand, the distributions of characters that appear in files of the real world are certainly biased, and hence, it was not certain that the same conclusion holds true when applying URDA to files of the real world with the same setting. To investigate this problem, we first compared the following two scenarios in terms of the means and variances of the probability distribution of some particular bit patterns.

- Apply URDA to files taken from the Internet with the setting of seven-bit-long fragments.
- Apply URDA to synthetic files generated so that every ASCII character appears with the same probability regardless of the position in the files.

As we expected, the means of the probability are identical to their theoretical expectation of $\frac{l+9}{2^{l+4}}$ for $\ell = 0,1,2,3$, but the variances for the first scenario are significantly larger than those for the second scenario. Therefore, we cannot deny the possibility that there exist some clever attacks that take advantage of this difference in the variance.

Hence, we ran the same experiments after modifying the first scenario. In the new scenario, the length of each fragment is not fixed, but is determined at random between 1 bit to 32 bits per fragment. The results of the comparison is surprising, we cannot detect statistically significant differences in either the means or the variances between the scores for the downloaded and randomly fragmented ASCII files and those for the synthetic ASCII files. In other words, we cannot statistically distinguish between the archived files generated from the downloaded files and the synthetic files.

Thus, we cannot conclude that use of URDA with the fixed fragment length is secure, while use of URDA with the randomly variable fragment length is secure against bit pattern analysis.

CONCLUSION AND FUTURE WORK

We investigated whether the formula

$$P[b_l = \cdots = b_{l-l} = 0] \approx \frac{l+9}{2^{l+4}}$$

applies to real ASCII text files that include biases in the distributions of characters. Applying URDA to downloaded text files by fragmenting the files into seven bit long, we found that the resulting archived files might be vulnerable to bit pattern analysis attacks. Thus, in the same way as the previous experiment, we ran another experiment by modifying URDA in the way how to select fragment lengths, that is, the length of each fragment is determined at random per fragment between 1 bit to 32 bits, and showed this modified URDA with the randomly variable fragment length is secure against the bit pattern analysis.

As the next step, we will investigate the security of URDA when applied to text files that include a variety of character sets and their corresponding code units. We will specify the significance of biased bits in these code units, which includes their actual representation in storages and how it affects security issues in plain text archiving. Consequently we need to testify, by stochasticcally determining the size b per fragment, whether we can obtain similar conclusion for various kinds of source files with various bit distributions. In addition, we also investigate some sorts of file existed in the real world that are said close to random files like video, image and compressed files etc.

REFERENCES

1. http://www.iso.org/iso/iso_catalogue/catalogue_tc/catalogue_detail.htm?csnumber=39612 .
2. P. M. Chen, E. K. Lee, G. A. Gibson, R. H. Katz and D. A. Patterson, "Aid: High-performance, Reliable Secondary Storage," ACM Computing Surveys, Vol. 26, No. 2, 1994, pp. 145-185. .
3. A. Shamir, "How to Share a Secret," Communication of ACM, Vol. 22, No. 11, 1979, pp. 612-613. .
4. G. Blakley, "Safeguarding Cryptographic Keys," 1979 Proceedings of the National Computer Conference, New York, 4-7 July 1979, p. 313. .
5. M. O. Rabin, "Efficient Dispersal of Information for Security, Load Balancing, and Fault Tolerance," Journal of the ACM, Vol. 36, No. 2, 1989, pp. 335-348. doi:10.1145/62044.62050 .
6. L. Bai, "A Strong Ramp Secret Sharing Scheme Using Matrix Projection," Proceedings of the 2006 International Symposium on a World of Wireless, Mobile and Multimedia Networks, New York, 26-29 July 2006, pp. 652-656.
7. L. Bai and X. K. Zou, "A Proactive Secret Sharing Scheme in Matrix Projection Method," International Journal of Security and Networks, Vol. 4, No. 4, 2009, pp. 201- 209.
8. C. Blundo, "Alfredo de Santis and Ugo Vaccaro, Efficient Sharing of Many Secrets," Springer Verlag, Berlin, 1993. .
9. J. M. He and E. Dawson, "Multistage Secret Sharing Based on One-Way Function," Electronic Letters, Vol. 30, No. 19, 1994, pp. 1591-1592. doi:10.1049/el:19941076 .
10. K. Wang, X. K. Zou and Y. Sui, "A Multiple Secret Sharing Scheme Based on Matrix Projection," Proceedings of the 33rd Annual IEEE International Computer Software and Applications Conference, Seattle, 20-24 July 2009, pp. 400-405. .
11. S. Rhea, C. Wells, P. Eaton, D. Geels, B. Zhao, H. Weatherspoon and J. Kubiatowicz, "Maintenance-Free Global Data Storage," IEEE Internet Computing, Vol. 5, No. 5, 2001, pp. 40-49. doi:10.1109/4236.957894 .
12. A. Rowstron and P. Druschel, "Storage Management and Caching in PAST, a Large-Scale, Persistent Peer-to-Peer Storage Utility," Proceeding SOSP'01 Proceedings of the Eighteenth ACM Symposium on Operating Systems Principles, Banff, 21-24 October 2001, pp. 188-201. .
13. A. Tallat, K. Shin, H. Lee and H. Yasuda, "Some Remarkable Property of the Uniformly Random Distributed Archive Scheme," Advances in Information Sciences and Service Sciences, Vol. 4, No. 11, 2012, pp. 114-124. .
14. Cisco System, "Storage Networking 101," Cisco System, San Jose, 2001. .
15. International Business Machines Corporation, "Introduction to Storage Area Networks," 2012. http://www.redbooks.ibm.com/ .

16. S. Ratnasamy, P. Francis, M. Handley, R. Karp and S. Shenker, “A scalable Content-Addressable Network”, SIGCOMM ‘01 Proceedings of the 2001 Conference on Applications, Technologies, Architectures, and Protocols for Computer Communications, 2001, pp. 161-172. .

17. International Organization for Standardization, “ISO/IEC 7816 Series: Identification Cards-Integrated Circuits(s) Cards with Contacts,” International Organization for Standardization, Geneva, 1999. .

18. International Organization for Standardization, “ISO/IEC 18092-3: Information Technology-Telecomunications and Information Exchange between Systems-Near Field Communication-Interface and Protocol (NFCIP-1),” International Organization for Standardization, Geneva, 2004. .

19. IBM Corporation, “Infrared Data Association: Serial infrared Link Access Protocol (IrLAP) Version.1.1,” IBM Corporation, New York, 1996.

CHAPTER 13

RELIABLE CONTENT DISTRIBUTION IN P2P NETWORKS BASED ON PEER GROUPS

Elias P. Duarte Jr and Ana Flavia B. Godoi

Department of Informatics, Federal University of Parana (UFPR), Curitiba, Brazil

ABSTRACT

Peer-to-Peer (P2P) networks are highly dynamic systems which are very popular for content dis- tribution in the Internet. A single peer remains in the system for an unpredictable amount of time, and the rate in which peers enter and leave the system, i.e. the churn, is often high. A user that is obtaining content from a selected peer is frequently informed that particular peer is not available anymore, and is asked to select another peer, or will have another peer assigned, often without enough checks to confirm that the content provided by the new peer presents the same quality of the previous peer. In this work we present a strategy based on group communication for transparent and robust content access in P2P networks. Instead of accessing a single peer for obtaining the desired content, a user request is received and processed by a group of peers. This group of peers, called PCG (Peer Content Group) provides reliable content access in sense that even as members of the group crash or leave the system, users continue to receive the content if at least one group member remains fault-free. Each PCG member is capable of independently serving the request. A PCG is transparent to the user, as the group interface is identical to the interface provided by a single peer. A group member is elected to serve each request. A fault monitoring component allows the detection of member crashes. If the peer is serving request crashes, another group member is elected to continue providing the service. The PCG and a P2P file sharing applications were implemented in the JXTA platform. Evaluation results are presented showing the latency of group operations and system components.

INTRODUCTION

P2P (peer-to-peer) networks and applications are very popular content distribution systems [1] . Typical P2P applications go beyond content sharing, and include distributed computing and collaboration [2] . A peer is a process that can serve requests and, at the same time, can issue requests to other peers [3] - [5] . A P2P system is usually highly dynamic, in the sense that the set of peers of a system varies with time, as they continuously enter and leave the system. The rate in which the system composition varies is called the system churn. Because of their very nature, P2P applications present potentially good intrinsic properties such as availability, user and resource anonymity,

Citation: Duarte Jr., E. and Godoi, A. (2014), "Reliable Content Distribution in P2P Networks Based on Peer Groups". International Journal of Internet and Distributed Systems, 2, 5-14. doi: 10.4236/ijids.2014.22002.

and scalability. On the other hand, their dynamic nature creates challenges for effectively deploying traditional distributed abstractions, such as distributed agreement [6] .

Because of their intrinsic redundancy, P2P systems can naturally lead to high availability. Nevertheless, most current systems do not offer continuous service and data in the presence of failures and reconfigurations. In this way, interruptions and abrupt variations of performance are frequent. In fact, in most systems it is common to have the client or even the end-user to be responsible for selecting the specific peer from which service or content is obtained. If the peer that is providing the content fails or leaves the system, the client peer not only stops receiving the content but also usually has to select another peer to continue receiving the content. In general, there is no verification of whether the quality of the new serving peer content has not changed.

In this paper we propose a new approach to build robust P2P systems which increases the availability of content provision, providing transparent recovery after serving peers fail or leave the system. The main goal of the proposed system is to place the responsibility of keeping the quality of service on the P2P infrastructure itself, being transparent to the end-user. The proposed approach is based on the fact that most content is naturally replicated in a P2P system. Group communication [7] is a useful approach that can be employed to support consistent replication in distributed systems. A group consists of a set of processes that share a common state and cooperate to execute tasks. From the point of view of the users, the group represents a single logical entity. The group communication service guarantees the availability and the consistency of the distributed application that relies on the group, even after faults occur. A key component of the group service is the module responsible for keeping a view of which members are in the group.

In this work we introduce a novel abstraction called Peer Content Groups (PCG) to deploy transparent content delivery despite of churn, based on a group service for P2P systems. All members of a PCG maintain the same content. A PCG provides reliable content access if at least one group member remains fault-free. The group interface is transparent, identical to the interface provided by a single peer. A group member is elected to serve each request. A fault detection component allows the detection of member crashes. If the peer that is serving a request crashes or leaves the system, another group member is elected to continue providing the service. Peer election and replacement are transparent to client peers. Both the PCG and a P2P file sharing application were implemented in the JXTA platform [8] . This application allows a file to be continuously and transparently transferred from the P2P system even when the serving peers crash or leave the system. Case studies are presented showing representative values for the latency of several system components. To the best of our knowledge this is the first strategy proposed to create and maintain transparent peer groups for continuous content delivery in P2P networks.

The rest of this paper is organized as follows. Section 2 presents the Peer Content Groups, describing the PCG architecture, functionality and algorithms. Section 3 describes the JXTA resources employed to implement the PCG and the file-sharing application. Section 4 presents related work. Finally, Section 5 concludes the paper.

PEER CONTENT GROUPS

A Peer Content Group (PCG) consists of a set of peers all of which maintain a specific content, each can provide this content to other client peers, and maintain information on which peers are currently in group (group composition). We employ the terms peer, node and process interchangeably and with the same meaning in this work. The network topology can be represented by a complete graph, i.e. each peer can communicate directly with any other peer. We consider an asynchronous system, i.e. bounds on the time required for the execution of an action by a process or for a channel to deliver a message are unknown [6] . Peers fail by crashing, i.e. a faulty process ceases all activities. However a peer can also simply leave the system, and in this case the effect on the group is the same as if it had crashed. A peer that fails can later recover, but it does not maintain any state information about its previous computations. In the same way, a process that left the system explicitly, can later rejoin the system again. Peers communicate through reliable channels: if a process p sends a message m to process q and assuming that process q does not fail, then q receives m.

The PCG service allows member peers to communicate among themselves and also provides the group interface for peers outside the group to interact with the group. The group membership component is responsible for detecting faulty members, and for keeping an up-to-date list of peers that are fault-free, called the group view [7] [9] [10] . Furthermore there are also mechanisms for members to join and to leave a PCG. The next subsection presents the protocols and functionalities of this component, shown as Algorithm 1.

Algorithm 1: PCG Composition Management.

```
/* Variables: */
ListOfPeers agreementGroupView <- empty;
ListOfPeers localGroupView <- empty;
List of ListOfPeers lViews <- empty;
Join(GroupId):
/* peer i executes this function to join group GroupId */
search for group GroupId;
if group is found
then send join message to the members
else create group with GroupId;
ReceiveMessageFromGroup(msg):
/* peer i receives a message from peer j */
Case msg is:
a join message:
send reply with localGroupView to peer j;
insert peer j in the localGroupView;
a reply to the first join message:
insert peer j in the localGroupView;
store peer j's group view in lViews;
a heartbeat message from peer j :
insert peer j in localGroupView;
store peer j's group view in lViews;
```

UpdateView():

/* Executed by peer i at each heartbeat interval */

send heartbeat message with localGroupView to group members;

if peer i has not received a heartbeat from peer j;

then remove peer j from localGroupView

agreementGroupView = peers in all views of lViews;

Joining/Creating a Peer Content Group

The procedure executed by a peer to join a PCG starts when the peer sends an initial request to become a group member. The request carries the PCG identifier, which must be related to the content provided (id's are detailed later in the context of the implementation). If no reply is received, the peer creates the PCG, as it concludes the group does not exist. Otherwise, the peer updates its local view with the identifiers of all peers from which it received replies to the original request. We assume every member correctly sends a reply to a join request. Furthermore every peer i that received the join request from peer j, inserts the peer j's identifier in its local view and sends an acknowledgement to peer j.

Updating the Peer Content Group View

The group management service allows peers to dynamically maintain the PCG view. Every time a message is received by a given peer, its local PCG view is updated with information about the peer that sent the message. All messages exchanged among peers, except the initial join message, carry the local view of the peer that sent the message. All peers of the PCG keep the views of the other members of the group. These views are used to construct an agreement group view, which is described below. An agreement group view consists of a list of all fault-free members of the PCG, ordered lexicographically.

A heartbeat is sent by every peer to other PCG members periodically, at a heartbeat interval. Heartbeats are used by a peer as a means to inform all group members it is alive. Heartbeats also carry the group view. A peer also sends its local group view to all group members every time its local view changes by the detection of an event, which is either a new peer that entered the group or one that has left or crashed.

Local Group View & Agreement View

Each peer keeps a local group view, which is a set of peer identifiers. As the system is asynchronous and dynamic, and peers join and leave the PCG continuously, each peer may have a local group view different from the views kept by other members. Nevertheless the PCG as a whole can offer dependable services if members share a unique agreement view. A peer builds the agreement view from the local views received from other peers in the group, as follows. Peer j is in the group view of peer i if peer j is in all local views maintained and received by peer i. In other words, only peers that are not considered to be faulty by all members are kept in the agreement view. Thus the agreement view is an intersection of all local views. It must be noted that, as the system is highly dynamic, the agreement view presents weak guarantees of consistency.

Each peer periodically checks whether it received heartbeats from the peers that are in its local view. In case peer i does not receive heartbeats for long enough from some peer j, peer i removes this peer j from its local view. As the system is asynchronous, a slow peer can be considered to be faulty by some member, and may be eventually removed from the agreement view. When the slow peer receives a local view in which it is not listed, it executes the initialization procedure, i.e. it leaves and joins the group again.

Observe that the protocol presented above allows the existence of several distinct agreement views at some point, again because the system is highly dynamic. However, if for a large enough interval of time the system remains stable (without members joining/leaving the group) and if there are no undue suspects, the proposed protocol allows that the several local group views to converge to a unique agreement view. We assume that the systems goes through stable periods frequently enough. During these periods the agreement view is unique and lists the actual fault-free members in the group.

An API (Application Programmer Interface) is also defined to the group management service, which allows applications to be constructed with the proposed system. The interface allows messages to be sent and received to/from an individual peer or to the group as a whole, and also provides means to obtain PCG composition information.

Peer Election

A distributed leader election protocol is executed to select the peer that will serve a request. The election is executed after a client peer sends a request to the PCG. This request is received by all members but only one member replies. All members maintain a list with all pending requests. This list also contains information about which peer is serving each request. When a new request arrives, PCG members must decide which peer will serve the request, and inserts the information in the list.

A server peer is elected based on the agreement group view and on the number of the requests received. Each request received is assigned an identifier, which is the same at all peers. The request identifier is the number of requests received by the file group plus one. The id of the last request received is exchanged by all PCG members in the heartbeat message. Each peer computes locally the remainder of the division of the request id by the amount of peers in the agreement view of the file group. The result identifies the peer of the agreement view elected to serve the request. When a peer decides it is a server of some request, this peer starts to send of the file to the client peer.

In case this server peer becomes faulty or leaves the system, the group elects a new server to replace the previous one. Each peer of the file group determines the new server, based on the agreement view and the request id. The new server starts to the send the file from the point the download had stopped. After a request has been served, all group members remove the request id from their lists of pending requests.

A JXTA-BASED FILE SHARING APPLICATION

The proposed Peer Content Group service was implemented in the JXTA platform [8] version 2.5, using Java language. Besides the PCG service itself, an example file sharing application was implemented, called JXTA Content Group.

JXTA Implementation

Figure 1 shows how the application and group service fit within the JXTA architecture. The JXTA network overlay, as well as several JXTA components and services were used to implement and run both the group service and the application. The JXTA core provides essential services, including basic operations such as the creation of peers with unique identifiers. The JXTA service layer provides non-essential but nevertheless important services, for example: peer authentication and content indexing. Another key JXTA component is the pipe, which corresponds to a communication channel between peers. The native JXTA peer groups were also used, as well as JXTA advertisements, employed to publish and find resources in the JXTA network.

Although JXTA does have a "peer group" primitive, which was employed in the implementation of the proposed PCG, it is important to make clear that these groups are different from each other. Every JXTA peer takes part of some JXTA peer group. When a peer is first created and starts running, it is already part of the main JXTA World Peer Group. From then on a peer can create new groups, or join other existing JXTA groups. The proposed PCG or its JXTA implementation JXTA Content Group is actually an application group, which peers can join and leave, depending on the content they have available and are willing to share. The PCG structure is described in the next subsection.

Peers communicate through communication channels called pipes. In order to create a pipe, a peer needs information about the identification of the pipe of the other peer with which communication is desired. This information is obtained from JXTA advertisements. Each resource of the JXTA P2P network is described by an advertisement. In order to share a resource, a peer that has that resource needs to create an advertisement for that resource and publish this advertisement on the JXTA network. Other peers can then search and locate the resource.

The publication and search of advertisements in the JXTA network are executed with the help of super-peers, called rendezvous. A rendezvous keeps indexes that allow the location of resources across the network. When a peer publishes an advertisement, the rendezvous keeps information about both the advertisement and the identification of the advertised peer. Each peer needs to be connected to at least one rendezvous. To start a search, one peer sends a request to the rendezvous to which it is connected and waits for responses. The rendezvous checks local indexes and may propagate the search request to its neighbours. If the resource is found, the rendezvous sends a reply, with information about the requested resource.

All searches are deployed in the context of the JXTA groups. This means that if a peer executes a search inside a JXTA group to which the peer belongs, only resources published in this JXTA group will be returned.

A PCG File Sharing Application

In this section we describe an example application based on the proposed PCG. The application allows peers that keep a given file to form a PCG. Not only can a client can download the file reliably and transparently from the group, but also the group interface is identical to a single peer interface, thus the group is transparent to the client. Changes in the group composition are also transparent to clients, service is automatically recovered by the group if peers join/leave the group or fail/recover. The group is capable of recovering from service interruptions, providing continuous download, even if only one peer is available.

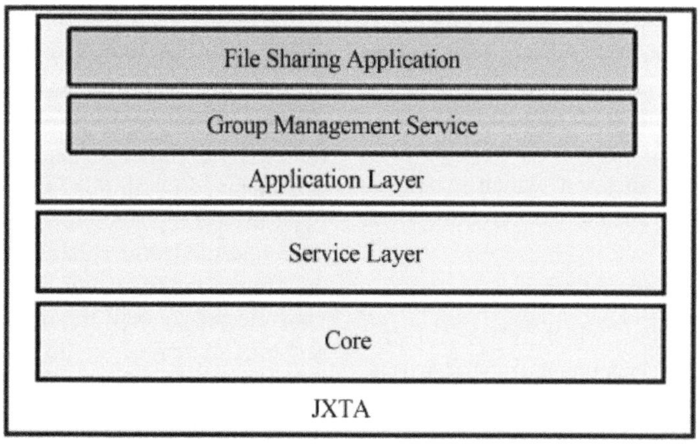

Figure 1: PCG composition management.

JXTA Content Groups in the JXTA Group Hierarchy

Peers are grouped hierarchically in a JXTA network. The main JXTA group is the World Peer Group, as shown in Figure 2. All other JXTA groups are created from this one. When a peer initiates the execution of JXTA protocols, it automatically becomes part of the main group. If the peer wants to access the content sharing application, it issues a search for the application group and then joins this group. At the lower layer, file groups are defined within the application group, three examples of which are shown in Figure 2: groups A, B and C. A file group is composed of peers that maintain a file they are willing to share. Each file group is responsible for keeping and making just one file available to other peers, peers can take part of as many file groups as they wish to, according to the number of files they are willing do share. The application groups are also JXTA groups. All members of these groups execute the content sharing application.

Group management procedures are executed in order to maintain the file group. Maintenance tasks include continuously monitoring and updating the group composition, taking account of peers that join and leave the group, either intentionally or because of faults. Another task is the election of peers that will serve client requests. Request management is also another group task. After a peer initializes, it executes a search for the application group, hierarchically below the JXTA main group. In case the peer does not find the group, it creates one. Otherwise the peer joins the group, becoming a member of the application group. The next steps depend on whether the peer wishes to share files (server peer) or to download files (client peer). Both cases are described in the subsections below. If a client peer wishes to obtain a file, this peer searches for the corresponding file group and requests the file. If a server peer wishes to share a file, it searches for the corresponding group and joins that group, or creates a new one in case the group does not exist.

The identifier of a file group is the hash of the shared file. The id of each group is the hash. A server peer that wishes to share a file computes the hash and searches for a group with id equal to that hash. A client peer searches for file groups using the group description in the corresponding JXTA advertisement. The PCG description contains the file name-not the hash. In this way, a client can find more than one file group with the same file name, these groups keep different versions of the file, the hashes are thus different.

Server Peer

The server peers have files to share with other peers. After they connect to the application group, the server peers join the file group of the corresponding file they desire to offer. If the group does not exist, the first peer creates and publishes the group advertisement.

The peers that are members of file groups execute the group management service which includes the group management tasks and the leader election protocol that designates a peer to serve each download request received by the group. For each file group of which the peer is a member, it executes one instance of the group management service.

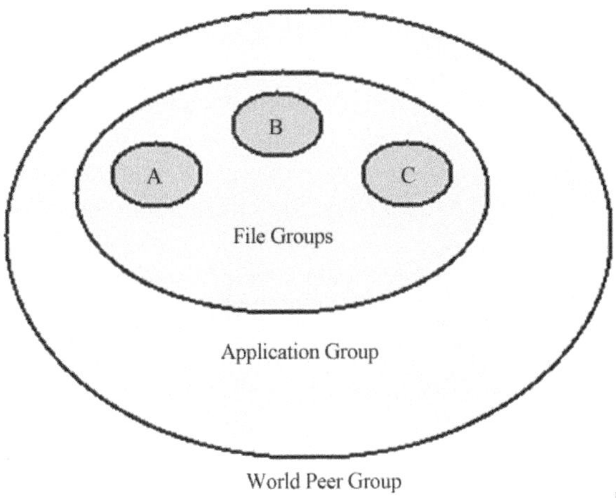

Figure 2: The JXTA group hierarchy.

The file groups provide the interface through which other peers can get the file. Client peers use this interface to reply to download requests. When a group receives a request, a member is elected to send the file to the client. After the election, the peer designated to serve the request, i.e. the server peer, starts the transmission of the file to the client. In case this server becomes faulty or leaves the group before the transmission is complete, the other members elect a replacement after the group composition is updated. After the transmission is finished, the group members receive a confirmation message sent by the client, and remove the request id from the pending requests list.

Client Peer

Client peers connect to the application group to search for available file groups. These peers are only in the application group, and use the download functionality of content groups. For each file that a client desires, the client must search for a peer or group from which the file can be obtained. The group interface is identical to a single peer interface, thus a search may return both. If the client finds the file group, a request is sent to the group. The request has the advertisement of the client's communication channel, which the server has to use to send the file to the client. After sending the request, the client creates a communication channel and waits to receive the file from the group. After the file is completely received, the client closes the channel and sends a confirmation message to the group.

Evaluation

This section shows experimental results obtained from the execution of a case study described below. The environment consisted of five hosts based on Pentium 2.8 GHz processors, running Ubuntu Linux, connected on a 100 Mbps Ethernet. Eight server peers were executed on four hosts, i.e. each host executed two server instances. The fifth host executed both the rendezvous peer and the client. Client peers were employed to allow the evaluation of the leader election module.

A single file was used in the measurements, i.e. the eight server peers all belong to the same PCG. The clients requested downloads of this file. The group management module was configured so that peers would send heartbeat/local view messages periodically in a 10 seconds heartbeat interval. Experiments were repeated several times and results presented below are representative of the set of results obtained.

In order to make the execution of more than one peer on a single host possible, each peer used a different communication port. Furthermore each peer must be executed from a different directory. In order to simulate a realistic P2P scenario, a random artificial delay was inserted as each message was transmitted. Without this delay all messages would be delivered within less than 1 millisecond in our system. The inserted delay varied from zero to a hundred milliseconds, uniformly distributed on this interval.

Latency of the Group Communication Service

This section describes the latency measured for a peer to join and also leave the group. In order to measure this latency the eight peers were initialized one by one. The procedure we adopted was to allow one peer to join the group after the other peers had successfully been detected by all group members. The latency consisted of the time elapsed between the initial join request message was sent until the peer appeared in the local views of all group members. We then computed the average of all measured latencies. The experiment can be roughly divided in two parts: in the first part, one peer was executed per host until four hosts were running peers. After this part, a second peer was started on each host. Results are shown in Figure 3. The graph shows the number of members in the group as a new joining peer is detected.

Figure 3 shows the average latency for all group members to detect that a new member has joined the group. The x-axis corresponds to the number of peers already in the group. It is clear that the latency increases significantly when the fifth peer joins the group—this corresponds to the second part of the experiment, as described above, when more than one peer is instantiated per host. The average latency for all members to detect a new member was 11.8 seconds. It is important to keep in mind that the group management service depends on the heartbeat interval to determine any change in the group composition. In the case study this interval was set to 10 seconds. It is thus possible to state that the latency to detect a new member is, in average, 1.2 times the heartbeat interval.

The latency for detecting that a member has become faulty or has left the group was also measured by making members leave the group one by one. Each member was removed from the group after the remaining peers had already detected all the members that had previously left the group.

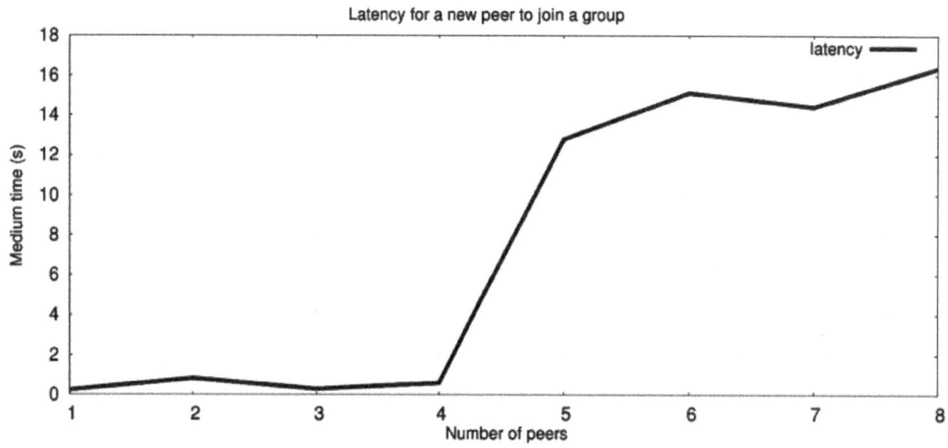

Figure 3: Latency for peers to join a group.

The impact of a peer fault on other modules, such as the leader election protocol, was also measured. The graph in Figure 4shows the average latency obtained as the number of group members varied.

It is possible to conclude that the latency to detect that a member became faulty/left the group increases slowly as the number of members in the group increases. The latency was, in most cases, between 11 and 13.5 seconds, with an average of 12.8 seconds, or 1.3 heartbeat intervals.

Latency to the Start Downloading a File

The leader election module is used to designate a group member to serve a download request. The time it takes to elect a leader starts when the request is received and completes when the file starts to be transmitted. This latency was also measured in the presence of faults, i.e. the elected peer becomes faulty and another member is elected to replace the faulty server. This latency was measured for a varying number of peers in the group. The graph in Figure 5 shows the results we obtained. It is clear from the figure that the latency increases when the server peer becomes faulty and is replaced. In this experiment, the latency varied between 7 and 13 seconds, with an average of 11 seconds, which corresponds to 1.1 heartbeat intervals.

RELATED WORK

The implementation of reliable distributed algorithms in P2P systems is still a research challenge. Due to their dynamic nature, i.e. processes enter and leave the system continuously, it is not possible to implement solutions developed for traditional static systems [6] . In particular, reaching agreement in a dynamic distributed system is still an open problem. In this section we make a review of related research efforts. We start mentioning that this work is a extended version of our previous conference paper [11] .

SWIM (Scalable Weakly-consistent Infection-style Process Group Membership Protocol) [12] proposes process groups that have weakly-consistent membership knowledge. SWIM is based on a randomized probing protocol, being thus probabilistic. The system employs gossip for disseminating failure detection and membership information. As the size of content-based groups grows, adopting a probabilistic strategy may be an option for guaranteeing scalability. SCAMP (Scalable Membership Protocol) [13] is another probabilistic peer-to-peer membership protocol which is based on partial views which support a gossip style of dissemination.

The approach proposed in [14] relies on a super-peer overlay which is built based on the semantic similarity of content provided. The main purpose is to use the overlay to reduce the cost of queries in unstructured P2P networks. Another related work is the strategy proposed in [15] for deploying fault-tolerant super-peers in structured P2P networks; the proposed strategy is also evaluated with a file sharing application but peers are organized in hierarchical groups that rely on a top-level super-peer. The proposed approach is to make each regular peer logically connect with two or more super peers in other groups so that the failure of a super-peer does not disrupt the provided service.

The evaluation of group membership under churn is reported in [16]. A related problem is reaching agreement in mobile ad hoc networks. In [17] group members are at first unknown, so that before any membership or failure detection protocol is executed there is a phase in which participants themselves are identified.

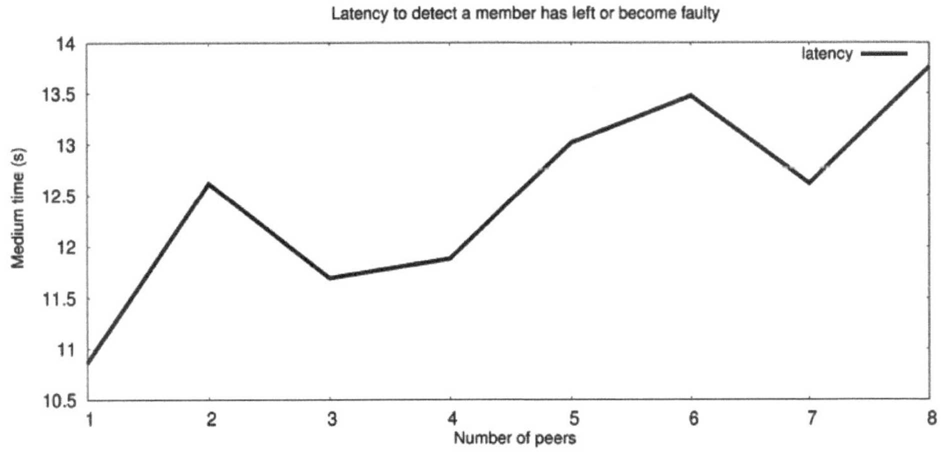

Figure 4: Latency to detect that a member has left or become faulty.

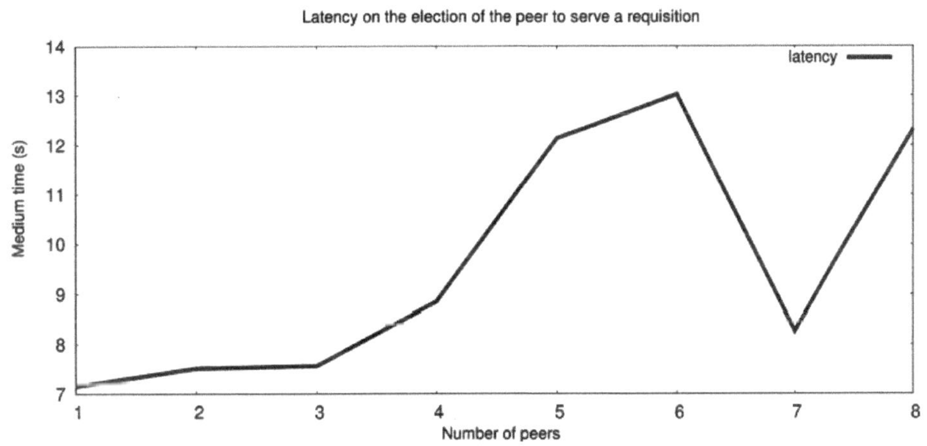

Figure 5: Peer election latency.

The authors show basic conditions on participant knowledge and system synchrony required to achieve consensus in such a system.

In [18] the authors propose a multi-layered hierarchical fully distributed group model. Groups support causal delivery of messages, which is achieved by having each peer to hold information on the accuracy of physical clock of all peers and minimum delay time among every pair of peers. The authors evaluate the hierarchical model in terms of the group information size and delay time compared with a flat group model.

Finally, the recent survey [19] gives an overview of different strategies for defining groups in P2P systems, this includes groups formed by user interest or technical criteria such as proximity. The authors present an evalation that does take robustness in consideration, besides other criteria such as suitability and security.

CONCLUSIONS

The Peer Content Groups (PCGs) defined in this work allow reliable and transparent content access in JXTA- based P2P networks. PCG is based on content-based group abstraction, which allows peers that maintain and are willing to share a given content to cooperate to serve client requests. This abstraction consists of a group management service and a distributed leader election module that designates the server for each request. If this server fails or leaves the system, the group elects a replacement. The service is transparent in the sense that the group interface is identical to a single peer interface, and furthermore server replacement in case of faults is not visible to the client. An example file sharing application was implemented and is described. Evaluation results are shown for the latency for detecting a new joining member, faulty members and the time to download a file.

Future work includes defining a reputation scheme for groups, and defining an approach for distributing load among group members.

REFERENCES

1. Theotokis, S.A. and Spinellis, D. (2004) A Survey of Peer-to-Peer Content Distribution Technologies. ACM Computing Surveys, 36, 335-371.http://dx.doi.org/10.1145/1041680.1041681 .
2. Zhang, Q., Cheng, L. and Boutaba, R. (2010) Cloud Computing: State-of-the-Art and Research Challenges. Journal of Internet Services and Applications, 1, 7-18. http://dx.doi.org/10.1007/s13174-010-0007-6 .
3. Lua, E.K., Crowcroft, J., Pias, M., Sharma, R. and Lim, S. (2005) A Survey and Comparison of Peer-to-Peer Overlay Network Schemes. IEEE Communications Surveys and Tutorials, 7, 986-988. .
4. Clark, D. (2001) Face-to-Face with Peer-to-Peer Computing. IEEE Computer, 34, 18-21.
5. Schollmeier, R. (2001) A Definition of Peer-to-Peer Networking for the Classification of Peer-to-Peer Architectures and Applications. The 1st IEEE International Conference on Peer-to-Peer Computing (P2P), August 2001, 101-102. .
6. Charron-Bost, B., Pedone, F. and Schipper, A., Eds. (2010) Replication: Theory and Practice. Springer, Berlin. http://dx.doi.org/10.1007/978-3-642-11294-2 [Paper reference:3]
7. Chockler, G.V., Keidar, I. and Vitenberg, R. (2001) Group Communication Specifications: A Comprehensive Study. ACM Computing Surveys, 33, 427-469. http://dx.doi.org/10.1145/503112.503113 [Paper reference:2]
8. JXTA (2014) The Language and Platform Independent Protocol for P2P Networking.http://jxta.kenai.com [Paper reference:2]
9. Bünzli, D., Fuzzati, R., Mena, S., Nestmann, U., Rutti, O., Schiper, A. and Wojciechowski, P.T. (2006) Advances in the Design and Implementation of Group Communication Middleware. In: Dependable Systems, 172-194. .
10. JGroups (2014) http://www.jgroups.org .
11. Godoi, A.F.B. and Duarte Jr., E.P. (2011) Peer Content Groups for Reliable and Transparent Content Access in P2P Networks. The 5th International Workshop on Peer-to-Peer Network Virtual Environments, The 17th IEEE International Conference on Parallel and Distributed Systems (ICPADS), 776-781. .
12. Das, A., Gupta, I. and Motivala, A. (2002) SWIM: Scalable Weakly-Consistent Infection-Style Process Group Membership Protocol. The 32nd IEEE/IFIP International Conference on Dependable Systems and Networks (DSN), 303-312. .
13. Ganesh, A., Kermarrec, A.-M. and Massoulie, L. (2003) Peer-to-Peer Membership Management for Gossip-Based Protocols. IEEE Transactions on Computers, 52, 139-149. http://dx.doi.org/10.1109/TC.2003.1176982 .
14. Garbacki, P., Epema, D. and van Steen, M. (2007) Optimizing Peer Relationships in a Super-Peer Network. The 27th IEEE International Conference on Distributed Computing Systems (ICDCS), Nuremberg, 25-27 June 2007, 31. .
15. Lin, J.-W., Yang, M.-F. and Tsai, J. (2007) Fault Tolerance for Super Peers of P2P Systems. The 13th IEEE International Symposium on Reliable Distributed Systems (SRDS), Beijing, 17-19 December 2007, 107-114. .
16. Baldoni, R., Mian, A.N., Scipioni, S. and Piergiovanni, S.T. (2005) Churn Resilience of Peer-to-Peer Group Membership: A Performance Analysis. The 7th International Workshop on Distributed Computing (IWDC), Lecture Notes in Computer Science, 3741. .
17. Greve, F. and Tixeuil, S. (2007) Knowledge Connectivity vs. Synchrony Requirements for Fault-Tolerant Agreement in Unknown Networks. The 37th IEEE/IFIP International Conference on Dependable Systems and Networks (DSN), Edinburgh, 25-28 June 2007, 82-91. .
18. Tsuneizumi, I., Aikebaier, A., Ikeda, M., Enokido, T. and Takizawa, M. (2011) A Multi-Layered Model for Scalable Group Communication in P2P Overlay Networks. The 25th IEEE International Conference on Advanced Information Networking and Applications (AINA), Biopolis, 22-25 March 2011, 324-331. .
19. Koskela, T., Kassinen, O., Harjula, E. and Ylianttila, M. (2013) P2P Group Management Systems: A Conceptual Analysis. ACM Computing Surveys, 45, Article No. 20. http://dx.doi.org/10.1145/2431211.2431219

SECTION IV
DISTRIBUTED DATABASES APPLICATIONS

CHAPTER 14

A UNIFIED MONITORING FRAMEWORK FOR DISTRIBUTED ENVIRONMENT

Xiaoguang Wang[1], Hui Wang[2], Yongbin Wang[1]

[1]Computer School, Communication University of China, Beijing, China

[2]Information Engineering School, Communication University of China, Beijing, China

ABSTRACT

Distributed computing is a field of computer science that studies distributed systems. With the increasing computing capacity of computers it is widely used to solve large problems. Monitoring system is one of the key components in distributed computing. Although there have been varieties of monitoring systems developed by different organizations, it is still a great challenge to monitor a heterogeneous distributed environment in a unified and transparent way. In this paper, we present a unified monitoring framework for distributed environment (UMFDE) with heterogeneous monitoring systems, and then propose a comprehensive method based on the Enterprise Service Bus (ESB) to integrate the monitoring systems in the environment as a unified monitoring system. A representative case study is given to show the feasibility of this framework.

INTRODUCTION

Distributed computing is a field of computer science that studies distributed systems that consist of multiple autonomous computers or clusters that communicate through a network.

Distributed systems have been in the mainstream of high performance computing with the increasing computing power of computers. They have been primarily used for solving comprehensive application problems such as parallel rendering, weather modeling, nuclear simulations, and data mining.

A scalable and unified resource monitoring system is one of the key components for the effective utilization of the massive computing power in distributed environment. Due to the considerable diversity of resources in the distributed environment, the monitoring of the environment is much more difficult than that of a group of homogenous computers. There have been a variety of monitoring systems developed by different organizations, such as ganglia, Relational Grid Monitoring Architecture (RGMA). Although some of them can be used in distributed environment, there are still some constraints. For example, we need to replace the existing monitoring systems and deploy the same monitoring system in all the clusters or computer sites. To address such challenges, [1] proposes an integrated framework (UGMF) which is compatible with other monitoring systems in the grid environment, however,

Citation: X. Wang, H. Wang and Y. Wang, "A Unified Monitoring Framework for Distributed Environment," Intelligent Information Management, Vol. 2 No. 7, 2010, pp. 398-405. doi: 10.4236/iim.2010.27049.

there are still some problems not addressed, such as message transformation, content-based routing and flexibility.

In this paper, we present a loosely-coupled, scalable and non-intrusive monitoring framework for distributed environment with heterogeneous monitoring systems. Here we use an integrative method based on Enterprise Service Bus (ESB) to integrate the existing monitoring systems into a unified monitoring framework without redeploying or modifying the systems themselves. The proposed architecture is capable of providing clients with standard-based interfaces, and implementing uniform access to different monitoring data sources through ESB in a transparent fashion. Besides that, we implement a representative case study in a distributed environment to verify the feasibility and scalability of the proposed framework.

The rest of the paper is organized as follows. In Section 2, we introduce several monitoring systems and present an overview of the Enterprise Service Bus. In Section 3, the proposed unified monitoring architecture is discussed in detail. A representative case study based on the proposed architecture is introduced in Section 4. The final conclusion is presented in Section 5.

RELATED WORK

Monitoring Systems

Resource monitoring is one of the fundamental components in distributed systems. Monitoring data plays a key role in various tasks of distributed computing such as fault detection, performance analysis, performance tuning, performance prediction, and task scheduling. Resources monitored in distributed environment include the CPU load, the memory usage, the network status, the disk usage, and etc.

In this section we present a brief introduction of several existing monitoring systems for distributed systems.

Grid Monitoring Architecture (GMA)

The Grid Monitoring Architecture (GMA) [2] is developed by the Global Grid Forum Performance Working Group. The goal of the architecture is to provide a minimal specification that will support required functionality and allow interoperability.

The Grid Monitoring Architecture consists of three types of components, as shown in Figure 1:

- Directory Service: The directory service stores the information about producers and consumers, and accepts requests, supports information publication and discovery.
- Producer: A producer is any component that uses the producer interface to send monitoring data to a consumer.
- Consumer: A consumer is any component that uses the consumer interface to receive monitoring data from a producer.

The GMA architecture supports three interactions for transferring data between producers and consumers: publication/subscription, query/response, and notification. In any case, the communication of control messages and transfer of performance data occur directly between each consumer/producer pair without further involvement of the directory service.

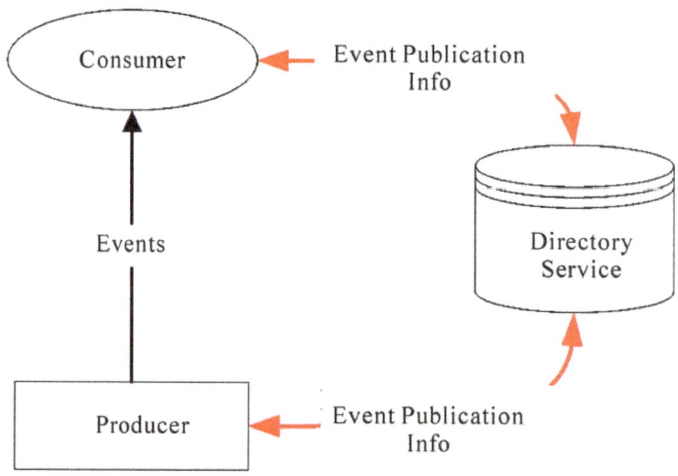

Figure 1: Components of the grid monitoring architecture.

Ganglia

The Ganglia [3] is a scalable distributed monitoring system for high-performance computing systems such as clusters and Grids. It is based on a hierarchical design targeted at federations of clusters, and relied on a multicast-based listen/announce protocol to monitor state within clusters and uses a hierarchy of point-to-point connections amongst representative cluster nodes to federate clusters and aggregate their state. It has been used to interconnect clusters across university campuses and around the world and can scale to handle clusters with 2000 nodes.

Compared with the Grid Monitoring Architecture, there is not a directory service for Ganglia to store and discover the information of producers and consumers.

Literature [4] presents a structure for monitoring a large set of computational clusters over wide-area networks using Ganglia. It illustrates methods for scaling a monitor network comprised of many clusters while keeping processing requirements low.

Windows HPC Server

Windows HPC Server 2008 [5] (HPCS) is the Microsoft high performance computing (HPC) platform built on Windows Server 2008 64-bit technology. HPCS can efficiently scale to a large number of processing cores and computers. HPCS includes a new, integrated management console that integrates the new network configuration wizard, template-based provisioning based on the Windows Server 2008 Windows Deployment Services technology, a new scheduler, cluster health monitoring at a glance along with built-in diagnostics, and a faster Microsoft Message Passing Interface (MS-MPI) that includes new NetworkDirect support.

HPC Server 2008 provides administrators and users with several tools to effectively monitor IT resources in the cluster, including the Node Management section in the Administration Console, System Center Operations Manager and Microsoft HPC Class Library.

Enterprise Service Bus

Enterprise Service Bus [6] (ESB) is a software infrastructure that can be used to connect heterogeneous applications and IT resources. It brings flow-related concepts such as transformation and routing to a Service-Oriented Architecture (SOA). It mediates incompatibilities among various applications, coordinates their interactions, and makes them broadly available as services for additional uses.

Despite various definitions used by different users, there are common components in the architecture of an ESB as below:

- Message transformation: To transform messages from one format to another based on open standards like XSLT and XPath.
- Message routing: To determine the destination of an incoming message based on user-defined rules and logic.
- Security: Mechanisms such as authentication, authorization, and encryption should be provided by an ESB to ensure the integrity and privacy of both the ESB runtime and the messages.
- Management: A management environment is necessary for the configuration of the ESB to be reliable and also to monitor the runtime execution of the message flows in the ESB.
- Transport Management: To convert incoming transport protocols to different outgoing transport protocols.
- Message Broker: ESB acts as a broker between service consumers and service providers.

OVERVIEW OF THE ARCHITECTURE

An overview of the proposed architecture (UMFDE) is shown in Figure 2. It is a four-tier framework that consists of the Service Provision Layer, the Service Interface Layer, the Integration Layer and the Application Layer.

Generally, there are two ways to monitor a distributed environment with a number of heterogeneous computers and clusters in the internet. One way is to deploy a new monitoring system to substitute all of the existing systems. This way is simple but impossible in most cases, because owners of the existing systems are in general not the same one. The other way is to integrate the existing systems by their exposed service interfaces without replacing the existing systems. Developers can reuse the monitoring services or develop new services.

The proposed architecture uses the integration method to achieve the goal of monitoring a distributed system.

Service Provision Layer

Service Provision Layer is comprised of a group of clusters or sites with their monitoring systems. Most of existing monitoring systems provide some kind of services that can be used by the Service Interface Layer.

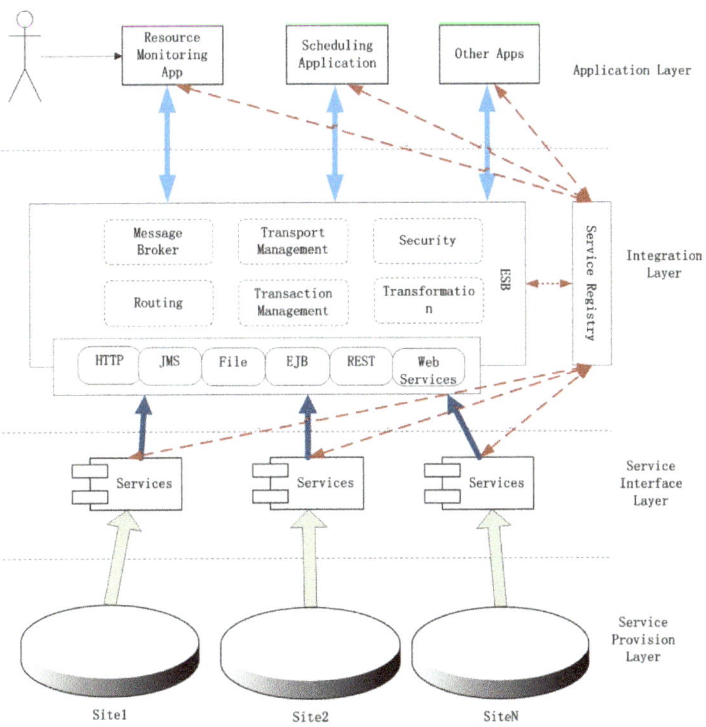

Figure 2: Architecture of the proposed monitoring framework.

Service Interface Layer

This layer is in charge of the encapsulation of the functionalities of existing monitoring systems into services, which can be connected to components and used in the Integration Layer. In this layer we may develop new monitoring services for clusters or sites without monitoring system. Since services may be offered by different systems, they may be developed based upon various protocols, such as HTTP, JMS, TCP, and SMTP.

Integration Layer

The aim of this layer is to integrate and thus provide reusability of original monitoring services defined in the Service Interface Layer, and to provide consumers with composite monitoring services. The Integration Layer is made up of two components: a Service Registry, an ESB.

Service Registry is a platform for publishing and discovering information about producers and consumers of the services, including the encapsulated services in the Service Interface Layer, the composite services in the Integration Layer, and consumer services in the Application Layer. However, it will not be further involved in the interactions between the publishers and the consumers.

ESB provides a reliable and scalable infrastructure that connects services of heterogeneous monitoring systems, mediates their incompatibilities, transforms their responses, and makes them broadly available as uniform services for different users. It is responsible for routing requests, invoking original services in Service Integration Layer, integrating and returning results and other fundamental functionalities including content-based routing, message transformation and location transparency. It also enables disparate applications and services to communicate using different protocols through transport protocol conversion.

The main features of the UMFDE are provided by the Integration Layer.

Application Layer

This layer consists of a variety of applications utilizing the monitoring data provided by the services in the Integration Layer instead of gathering raw data directly from the existing monitoring systems. These applications contain resource management applications, scheduling applications and so on.

The proposed framework supports two interaction types between producers and consumers, namely publication/subscription, and query/response.

IMPLEMENTATION

In this section, we discuss the implementation of a case study using the architecture proposed in last section. We will begin with the description of the scenario, and then continue into the details of implementation.

Overview

The context of the case study is that the client application sends a request to the UMFDE for the response of "the status of computers the client has access to in this environment".

The distributed environment used in this case study is comprised of two clusters, and a group of computers, site A. One cluster is Rocks cluster with monitoring system ganglia, the other one is Windows HPC Cluster. Site A has no monitoring system.

Here we choose the open source Mule ESB which is widely used by many enterprises to implement the case study. Key elements of Mule ESB are explained below [7-9]:

Service component: A service component is nothing more than a Java object that is hosted and contained by Mule. These components become services within the Mule instance. Components contain the business logic. Each service is configured using an inbound router collection, a component, and an outbound router collection.

- Endpoint: An endpoint is responsible for the receiving or sending of messages via associated transport.
- Router: Based on the Message Router pattern [8], routers exist to be able to decouple individual processing steps when messages are received from, or are dispatched to, endpoints.
- Transformer: Transformers are used to convert data from one format to another, such as type transformation, message transformation, and so on.

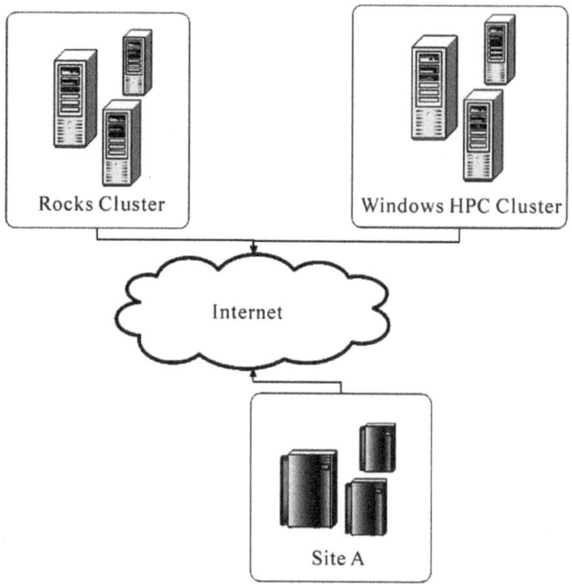

Figure 3: The distributed environment in the case study.

Besides that, we use Mule Service Registry to provide a full complement of registry and repository features, including service and artifact management, governance, lifecycle and dependency management.

The main services used in the case study include:

- Monitor Broker Service: Receives requests from and returns responses to client applications. It is hosted by the mule ESB.
- Authorization Service: As an external web service, it provides an interface for the Monitor Broker Service to obtain a list of clusters or sites whose monitoring data the current user is authorized to access.
- Original Monitor Services: Three services are developed to act as brokers to monitor two clusters and site A.

Implementation Details

Service Interface Layer

We develop web services for the monitoring systems of the two clusters. We design and develop a monitoring web service for Site A from scratch because there is no monitoring system in Site A. These services will return the status of its machines.

All of the three monitoring services will be published to the Mule Service Registry.

The response of web service of ganglia contains a list of machine's status which includes Id, Hostname, Ip, Mem_free, Cpu_num, cpu_speed, cpu_idle.

The response of web service of Windows HPC Cluster also contains a list of machine's status, but the status has different format and information. The status mainly includes Id, Name, NumberOfCores, CpuSpeed, State, Memory-Size, OnlineTime, NodeGroups, and Reachable. And the web service for Site A has similar response format as these computers are also built on windows platform.

It is obviously that the formats of responses are different, so we propose a unified response format to unify and integrate all of the response messages.

We list key properties of the unified format as follows:

- OsName: Name of the operating system.
- Cluster name: Name of cluster the node belongs to.
- ClusterType: Rocks or Windows HPC, Site A.
- CpuNum: Number of cpu.
- CpuSpeed: Speed of cpu.
- CpuLoad: The current cpu load.
- MemorySize: The total size of memory.
- MemoryFreePercent: The percent of free memory.

Integration Layer

The message flow of the case study is divided into two parts: a request flow for handling the request message, and a response flow for dealing with the response message.

Request Flow As shown in Figure 4, at first, client application calls the MonitorBroker Service in Mule ESB.

The MonitorBroker Service uses a component msglogger to log the request message into log files. Here we define a class to implement the log service. Then, the request message is forwarded to AuthService.

In the service AuthService, we define a ReflectionMessageBuilder component which will try and set the response of the authorization service as a bean property on the request message using reflection. The remaining part of AuthService is a filtering router which contains two outbound endpoints.

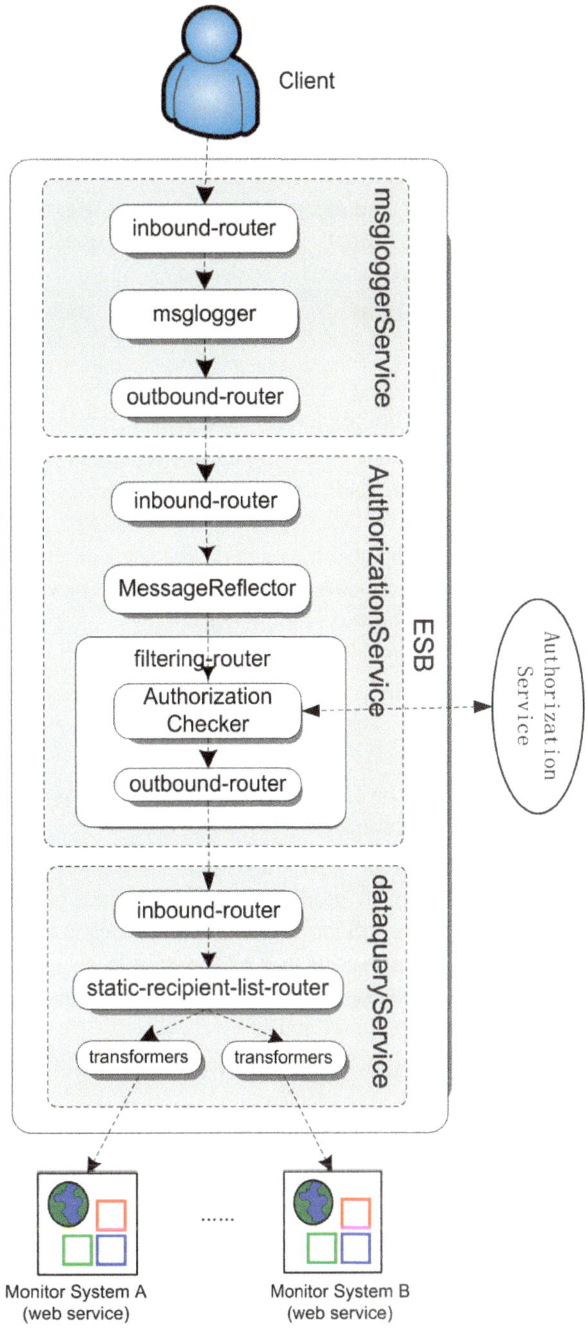

Figure 4: An overview of the Mule configuration of the request flow.

The first outbound endpoint invokes the external authorization service. After receiving the response, the ReflectionMessageBuilder will set the list of authorized clusters as a property called recipients on the request message. Then the second outbound endpoint will send the updated request message to the DataQueryService.

The static-recipient-list-router in the DataQueryService will apply a transformer to the request message, and then invoke external monitor services whose inbound endpoint is defined in the property recipients of the request message.

Response Flow In the response flow, the monitor broker service will aggregate the response messages from different monitor services. And because the response messages are based on different formats, the broker service will transform them with the unified format.

The procedure of the response flow is described as following:

- The monitoring services process requests from the Mule ESB broker service, and return responses to the broker service.
- In the broker service, transferService serivce component will record the reponse activity, and then transform reponse messages using the unified format. After that, reponse messages will be forwarded to aggregationService component.
- AggregationService Service mainly contains a custom asynchronous reply router component, result Aggregator. The resultAggregator will retrieve the reponse message, and aggregate them into one reponse.
- Finnaly, the broker service will return the reponse to the client application.

Application Layer We build a web application based on ASP.NET for users to monitor the status of the distributed environment. This client application is responsible for controlling user access and users' requests. It also provides multiple views of the status of the environment for users, such as the status of a computer and some cluster.

For this case study, we build a web form to collect users' requests, call the broker service in Mule ESB and display the results.

Sequence Graph The sequence graph as shown in Figure 6 is described in detail below:

- The client sends a request to the monitor broker service hosted by the ESB to get the status of computers in the distributed environment;
- The monitor broker service receives the request, and retrieves the authorized clusters of the client through the third party service authorizationService;
- After receiving the response from authorization-Service, the broker service individually calls the monitoring services of the authorized sites;
- The broker service asynchronously receives the responses from monitoring services, and then integrates them into one response message;
- ESB sends the integrated message to the client.

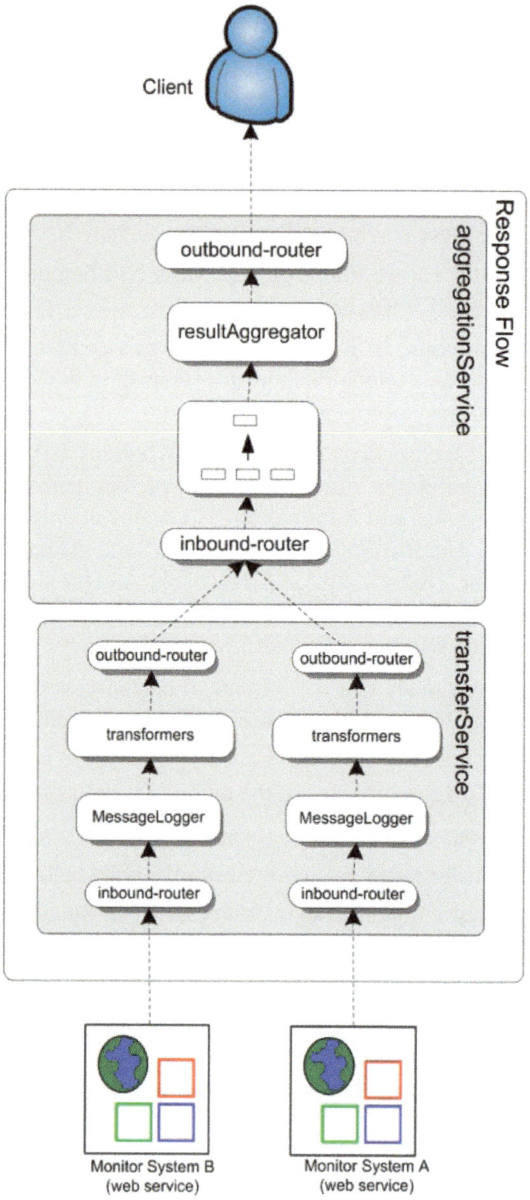

Figure 5: An overview of the Mule configuration of the response flow.

Summary

As shown in the case study, the proposed architecture is loose-coupled and scalable. It is advantageous in senses of:

- Compared with traditional unified monitoring technologies, the integration method based on enterprise service bus makes it easier to integrate the existing monitoring systems.
- Reducing the cost of software development and maintenance.
- Rapid response to changing requirements. For example, if requirement changes, we just need modify the broker service hosted by ESB.
- Improving system flexibility, scalability, availability and robustness.

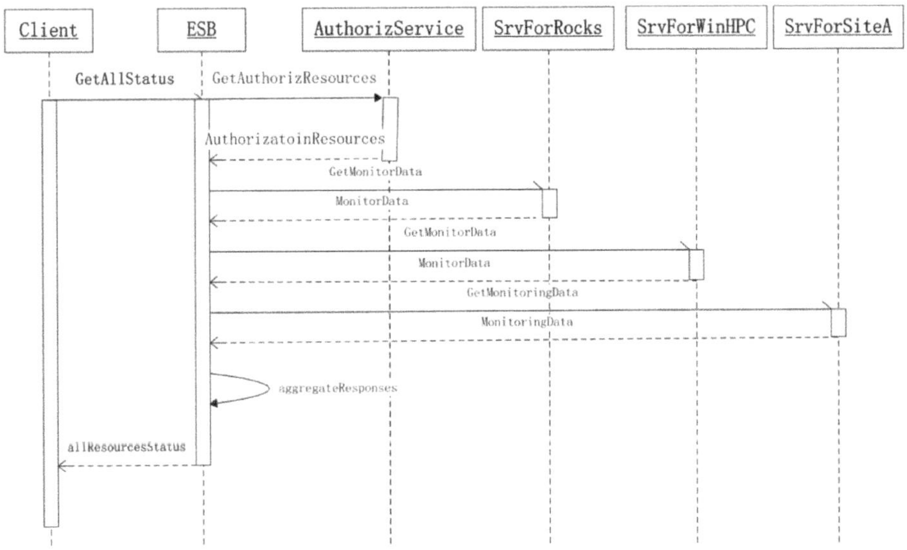

Figure 6: The sequence graph.

CONCLUSIONS

This paper proposes a unified monitoring framework for distributed environment that contains clusters or computer sites with heterogeneous monitoring systems. This framework provides a loosely-coupled, scalable and nonintrusive way to monitor a largely distributed environment.

We use an integration method based on Enterprise Service Bus to monitor computers which belong to different clusters in a unified and transparent way. For clusters with monitoring systems, we can reuse or develop services based on the legacy systems. For clusters without monitoring systems, we need develop new monitoring systems and services. By this approach, it is not required to redeploy or modify the legacy monitoring systems. The proposed framework provides standardbased interfaces to clients, and uniform access to different monitoring data sources through ESB in a transparent fashion.

The implemented case study has shown the feasibility and scalability of the proposed framework.

REFERENCES

1. K. Shen, S. Yang, M. Tian and P. Liu, "Towards a Uniform Monitoring Framework Supporting Interoperability in Grid," Proceedings of the Fifth International Conference on Grid and Cooperative Computing, Changsha, China, 2006, pp. 50-53.
2. B. Tierney, R. Aydt, D. Gunter, W. Smith, V. Taylor, R. Wolski and M. Swany, "A Grid Monitoring Architecture," Technical Report GWD-Perf-16-1, GGF, 2002.
3. M. Massie, B. Chun and D. Culler, "The Ganglia Distributed Monitoring System: Design, Implementation, and Experience," Parallel Computing, Vol. 30, No. 7, 2004, pp. 817-840.
4. F. Sacerdoti, M. Katz, M. Massie and D. Culler, "Wide Area Cluster Monitoring with Ganglia," IEEE International Conference on Cluster Computing, Hong Kong, 2003, pp. 289-298.
5. C. Russel and S. Crawford, "Windows Server 2008 Administrator's Companion," Microsoft Press, 2008.
6. X. G. Wang, H. Wang and Y. B. Wang, "A Monitoring Framework for Multi-Cluster Environment Using Enterprise Service Bus," International Conference on Management and Service Science, Beijing, China, 2009, pp. 1-4.
7. T. Rademakers and J. Dirksen, "Open-Source ESBs in Action," Manning Publications, 2008.
8. G. Hohpe and B. Woolf, "Enterprise Integration Patterns: Designing, Building, and Deploying Messaging Solutions," Addison-Wesley Longman Publishing Co. Inc., Boston, MA, USA, 2003.
9. P. Delia and A. Borg, "Mule 2: A Developers Guide," 1st Edition, Apress, 2008.

CHAPTER 15

ONLINE FINGERPRINT VERIFICATION ALGORITHM AND DISTRIBUTED SYSTEM

Ping Zhang[1] , Xi Guo[1] , Jyotirmay Gadedadikar[2]

[1]Department of Mathematics and Computer Science, Alcorn State University, Lorman, USA

[2]Department of Advanced Technologies, Alcorn State University, Lorman, USA

ABSTRACT

In this paper, a novel online fingerprint verification algorithm and distribution system is proposed. In the beginning, fingerprint acquisition, image preprocessing, and feature extraction are conducted on workstations. Then, the extracted feature is transmitted over the internet. Finally, fingerprint verification is processed on a server through web-based database query. For the fingerprint feature extraction, a template is imposed on the fingerprint image to calculate the type and direction of minutiae. A data structure of the feature set is designed in order to accurately match minutiae features between the testing fingerprint and the references in the database. An elastically structural feature matching algorithm is employed for feature verification. The proposed fingerprint matching algorithm is insensitive to fingerprint image distortion, scale, and rotation. Experimental results demonstrated that the matching algorithm is robust even on poor quality fingerprint images. Clients can remotely use ADO.NET on their workstations to verify the testing fingerprint and manipulate fingerprint feature database on the server through the internet. The proposed system performed well on benchmark fingerprint dataset.

INTRODUCTION

Biometrics refers to the automatic identification of a person based on his/her physiological or behavioral characteristics. Identification based on biometrics is preferred over traditional methods with the advantage that biometrics identification techniques obviate the need to remember a PIN/password which may be forgotten, or the need to carry the tokens like passports and driver's licenses which may be forged, stolen, or lost. For example, in the e-commerce application, the biggest concern is security problem. Currently, the common security method for online transaction consists of using one's password or PIN. However, PIN is cumbersome and insecure as people are afraid of passwords being stolen and the transaction process being invaded by adept hackers. With the increasing use of computers as vehicles of information, it is necessary to restrict access to sensitive/personal data. The biometric techniques can potentially prevent unauthorized access to or the fraudulent use of ATM, cellular phones, smart cards, desktop PCs, workstations, and computer networks.

Citation: P. Zhang, X. Guo and J. Gadedadikar, "Online Fingerprint Verification Algorithm and Distributed System," Journal of Signal and Information Processing, Vol. 2 No. 2, 2011, pp. 79-87. doi: 10.4236/jsip.2011.22011.

As a result, online biometric identification is enjoying a renewed interest. Since manual fingerprint identification is extremely tedious and time consuming, automatic and reliable fingerprint identification systems are in great demand. Many research achievements on fingerprint recognition and identification have been published in literature recently [1-4]. For example, fingerprint recognition and verification techniques include point set matching [5,6], graph matching [7], simulated annealing and genetic algorithms [8], relaxation [9], neural network based method for classification [10], and structural method for fingerprint recognition [11], etc. To capture the texture information of fingerprint image, Gabor filter with eight orientations is proposed by Jain et al. [12]. Patil et al. [13] used four orientations of Gabor filters for extracting fingerprint features from gray scale fingerprint image. The image is cropped to the size of 128 × 128 pixels using its core point as the center. Huang and Aviyente [14] and Khan and Javed [15] employed wavelet based analysis in order to provide rich discriminatory texture structure for fingerprint verification. To capture global transformation between two fingerprint images, genetic algorithm is adopted by Tan and Bhannu [16]. The combination of fingerprint minutiae and texture information performs the better recognition rate than individual methods. In the reference paper [17], the global structure (orientation field) and the local features (minutiae) are combined so that the global orientation field is beneficial to the alignment of the fingerprints which are either incomplete or poor quality. Ross et al. [18] proposed a new technique to estimate the nonlinear distortion in fingerprint pairs based on ridge curve correspondences. The nonlinear distortion, called thin plate spline (TPS) function, is used to estimate the "average" deformation model for a specific finger when several impressions of that finger are available. Experimental results demonstrated that incorporating their proposed model resulted in an improvement in the matching performance.

Although texture-like feature can improve fingerprint verification performance, minutiae pattern is the most important feature. Generally speaking, minutiae extraction from distorted images is not reliable and often gives erroneous results in matching. In this paper, we will focus on online fingerprint verification over the internet. First, the basic concept of fingerprint verification is reviewed in the introduction section. Then, an online fingerprint verification distributed system is drawn in Section II. Fingerprint acquisition and image preprocessing are discussed in Section III. Both minutiae feature extraction and dynamic matching algorithm are proposed in Section IV while experiments are conducted in Section V. A conclusion ends this paper.

ONLINE FINGERPRINT VERIFICATION DISTRIBUTED SYSTEM

Feature extraction plays an important role in the fingerprint verification system. Reliable and significant features are extracted from fingerprint image. The local features (ridge ending and ridge bifurcation) and global features (core point) of fingerprint are defined as follows:

- Ridge Ending: the point where a ridge ends abruptly.
- Ridge Bifurcation: the point where a ridge forks or diverges into two branch ridges.
- Core: The maximum curvature point. Some fingerprint has two cores.
- Minutiae: ridge ending, bifurcation, and core are called as the minutiae points.

The minutiae are shown in Figure 1. Advanced features like loops, islands, and delta (triangular portion) on the fingerprint image can be formed by combining all of the above minutiae points. In the proposed system, live-scan fingerprint devices are used as fingerprint acquisition. A live-scan fingerprint is directly obtained from the finger without the in termediate use of paper. For example, the Thompson CFS chip-based sensor works through thermal sensor to detect temperature difference across the ridges and valleys. Siemens sensors are based on differential capacitance.

The captured fingerprint image is a grayscale image with 256 levels and different sizes (512 × 512, 256 × 256, or 128 × 128) depending on application requirement. A benchmark fingerprint database can be obtained from National Institute of Standards and Technology (NIST), USA. The NIST Special Fingerprint Database 4 [19] includes 2000 fingerprint image pairs, which was used to test the proposed fingerprint algorithm. In the proposed system, fingerprint image preprocessing and feature extraction are conducted on computer workstations. In order to effectively manage fingerprint database on a server through the internet, the most advanced ActiveX Data Objects for .NET (ADO.NET) are employed to conduct fingerprint database query. For example, the operations of fingerprint enrollment, insertion and deletion of a record, etc. are carried out on the workstation sides and the changes in the database stored on the server side.

The fingerprint verification is processed over the internet in such a way that the workload of server is decreased. Multiple workstations share one database on the server. The fingerprint distributed system is shown in Figure 2.

FINGERPRINT IMAGE PREPROCESSING

Image filtering, image enhancement, and thinning are indispensable to fingerprint image processing. In this section, we will address these issues.

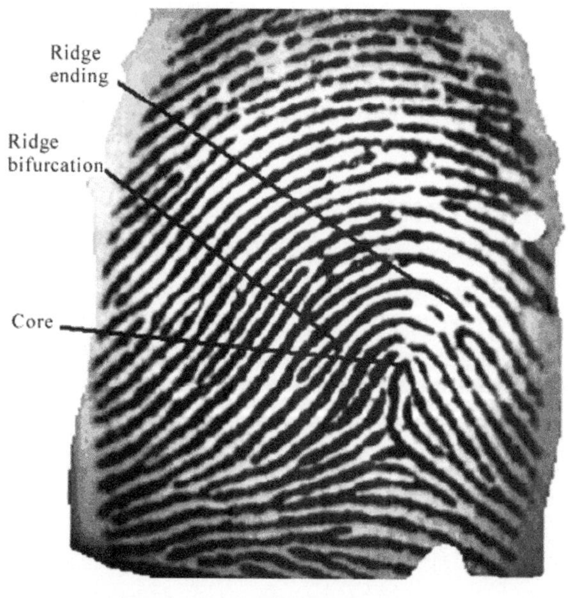

Figure 1: Fingerprint image with minutiae points.

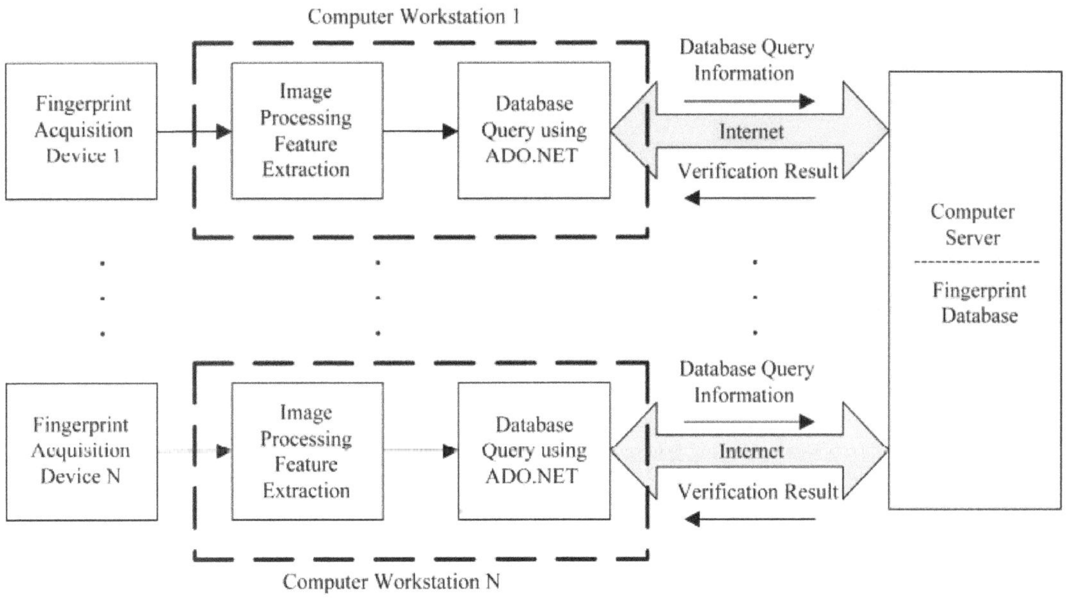

Figure 2: Online fingerprint verification distributed system.

IMAGE NOISE REMOVAL AND ENHANCEMENT

Median filter [20] is used to remove salt-and-pepper noises or spot-like noises. If a pixel is accidentally changed to an extreme value caused by various reasons, then the result of filter can achieve excellent result. The advantage of median filter is to keep the edge of the image and to remove salt-and-pepper noises in the images.

Histogram Equalization [20] is applied to enhance the ridges of the fingerprint images. Histogram Equalization reassigns a new value of a pixel based on the image histogram. The algorithm works by dividing the image into overlapping subimages with size of L × L; where L is the length and width of the subimage. Histogram information is obtained from local area of the fingerprint image.

Thinning Fingerprint Image

Fingerprint images consist of ridges. The position and direction of the ridges and the relationship among ridges convey unique information. The extra pixels usually comprise the thickness of the lines that need to be removed in order to accurately extract minutiae points.

According to Zhang and Suen's thinning algorithm [4], a thinning process is much like erosion. The pixels to be removed are marked in the first instance and then removed in a second pass over the image. This process is repeated until there are no more redundant pixels left. The remaining pixels are those belonging to the skeleton of the ridges and no minutiae points have been removed. This is called thinning by successive deletion. The skeleton must remain intact and must have a few basic properties listed below:

- It should consist of thin regions, one pixel wide;
- The pixels comprising the skeleton should lie in the centre of the ridges;
- Skeleton pixel must be connected to each other to form the same number of regions as existed in the original image.

Figure 3 shows the processed result of one original fingerprint image. Figure 3(a) is an original low-quality fingerprint image scanned by an optical senor, Figure 3(b) shows the result image after median filter, histogram equalization, thinning procedure.

Spur Detection and Refinement Procedure

After thinning, there exist either some spurs in the thinning image or broken lines in the ridges. A ridge smoothing algorithm is employed to delete the spurs and to link the broken lines with following criteria:

- If a branch in a ridge map is roughly orthogonal to the local ridge direction and its length is less than a specified threshold, then it will be removed.
- If a break line in a ridge is short enough and no other ridges pass through it, then it will be connected.
- If several minutiae form a cluster in a small region, then remove all of them except for the one nearest to the cluster center.
- If two minutiae are located close enough, facing each other, but no ridge lie between them, then all of them are removed.

FINGERPRINT CLASSIFICATION

Coarse Feature Classification

A fingerprint image can be classified as one of five categories [2]:

- Arch
- Left loop
- Right Loop
- Tented Arch
- Whorl

Figure 3: Original low-quality fingerprint image and the preprocessed images. (a) Original fingerprint image1; (b) Preprocessed image 1.

A human expert can easily perform coarse finger classification. For an automatic system, the problem becomes much more difficult due to poor image quality and impression distortion. Two hierarchical classifications are applied in our recognition system, namely, one coarse classification and one fine classification. The first step is to employ coarse classification method [2] to classify fingerprint image into one of the five categories. For the fine classification, further feature extraction method needs to be investigated. Two most stable and easily extracted features are ending points and bifurcation, which are used as fine features in this paper.

Fine Feature Extraction

After image pre-processing and the coarse feature extraction, a thinned fingerprint image will be applied to following process: Minutiae extraction: In order to extract minutiae in the thinned fingerprint image, a 5 × 5 pattern template is imposed on the image as shown in Figure 4. In the minutiae extraction, the thinned image is scanned twice to locate two kinds of points (ridge-ending and bifurcation).

Assuming Point M is a detecting point, the set of B(0), B(1), , B(7) are its 3 × 3 neighboring points in a clockwise direction beginning at top-left position; whereas the set of A(0), A(1), A(2), , A(15) are its 5 × 5 neighboring points, which directions are shown in Figure 4. L L If M is a ridge ending, the following criteria must be satisfied:

Criterion 1:

$$C_1 = \sum_{k=0}^{7} \left| \langle B(k+1),8\rangle - \langle B(k),8\rangle \right| = 2$$

and

$$C_2 = \sum_{k=0}^{15} \left| \langle A(k+1),16\rangle - \langle A(k),16\rangle \right| = 2 \quad (1)$$

Criterion 2:

$\text{if}\left(B(j) \neq 0\right)$
then

$$\sum_{k=-1}^{1} \left(\langle A(2j-k),16\rangle\right) = 1, \ \textit{if } j = 1,3,5,7$$

and

$$\sum_{k=-2}^{2} \left(\langle A(2j-k),16\rangle\right) = 1, \ \textit{if } j = 0,2,4,6 \quad (2)$$

where $\langle B(j),8\rangle$ presents the modulo operation of B(j) with 8, where 8 is the total number of pixels in the 3 × 3 neighboring ring; whereas $\langle A(j),16\rangle$ denotes the modulo operation of A(j) with 16, where 16 is the total number of the 5 × 5 neighboring ring. The direction of the ending point M is assigned as one of the directions A(0) ~ A(15), in which the direction of the correspondence A(i) is non-zero. The position and the direction are considered as ending point feature set. For the bifurcation extraction, criterion 3 is applied.

A0	A1	A2	A3	A4
A15	B0	B1	B2	A5
A14	B7	M	B3	A6
A13	B6	B5	B4	A7
A12	A11	A10	A9	A8

Figure 4: A minutiae extraction mask.

Criterion3:

$$C_3 = \sum_{k=0}^{7} \left| \langle B(k+1),8\rangle - \langle B(k),8\rangle \right| = 6$$

and

$$C_4 = \sum_{k=0}^{15} \left| \langle A(k+1),16\rangle - \langle A(k),16\rangle \right| = 6 \quad (3)$$

We can modify the criterion 2 accordingly. The direction of the bifurcation is assigned as one ridge direction that has the maximum distance to the other two ridges. It can be expressed by Criterion 4 below: If $(A(j)=1)$ Then r_1 and r_2 are calculated based on the following equation:

$$D_l = r_1 + r_2 \left| \left(\sum_{i=1}^{r_1} \langle A(j+i), 16 \rangle = 0 \right) \right. \text{ and } \left(\sum_{i=0}^{r_2} \langle A(j-i), 16 \rangle = 0 \right) \quad (4)$$

$$l \in (1,2,3),\ 0 \le j \le 15,$$
$$DIR = D_{max}\ iff.\ D_{max} = \max\{D_1, D_2, D_3\}$$

where r_1 is the number of the binary pixels, which values are continuously equal to 0 on the 5 × 5 neighboring ring counting in the clockwise direction, and starting from the point A(j); whereas r_2 has the same meaning in the anticlockwise direction. l represents one of three ridges on the bifurcation area. DIR is the direction of the bifurcation. For example, in Figure 5, the central point is point M, which is a bifurcation point with three ridges: Line M-A14, Line M-A4, and Line M-A8. The number of 0's counted by Equation(4) in the its 5 × 5 neighboring pixels for Line M-A14 is 10; the number of 0's for Line M-A4 is 8; and the number of 0's for Line M-A8 is 8. So the direction of the bifurcation is the direction of Line M-A14. If there are two lines that have the same number of 0's in the 5 × 5 neighboring pixels, then first ridge line direction counted from top-left in the clockwise direction will be considered as bifurcation direction.

A0	*A1*			*A4*
A14		*M*		
A12				*A8*

Figure 5: Bifurcation point in the 5×5 neighboring area.

Fine Feature Match

An efficient and effective algorithm for feature matching is the central theme of an automatic fingerprint identification system. As its name implies, the matching process deals with two fingerprint impressions captured at different times and in different environments. It will verify whether or not the two fingerprints are identical. The matching of two fingerprint impressions has proved to be difficult. Three areas of concerns might be that:

- the minutiae of fingerprint impressions captured might have different coordinates and relative angles;
- the shape of two fingerprint impressions taken at different places might not be the same due to the effect of stretching;
- same fingerprint might have different impression images as the different parts of fingerprint enrolled or as noises introduced while enrolling.

An ideal automatic fingerprint system must satisfy the following criteria:

- the size of feature file must be small in order to minimize search time and space;
- matching algorithm must be fast as well as accurate;
- matching algorithm must cope with the problems of rotation, distortion, false minutiae, and omitting minutiae of matching pairs;
- matching algorithm must be robust if two matching fingerprints only have partial images.

Based on the criteria mentioned above, a novel hybrid matching approach is proposed in this paper. The algorithm is divided two steps:

- All minutiae are ordered according to the distance from the fingerprint's core.
- The distance is represented by the number of ridges between two feature points in the fingerprint image.

All the minutiae are listed according to the distance to the core: $\{P_0, P_1, P_2, , P_{m-1}\}$. Here m is the number of minutiae. L Each feature set includes the following information: Information of each minutia in the fingerprint image must be recorded. The details of encoding information are described as data structures below:

Struct Fingerprint Feature

{
unsigned char Type; *// type of calculating minutia: ending point* (1) *or bifurcation* (2)
int ***DIR***; *// direction of the calculating minutia*
***struct Neighborhood_Minutiea_Feature P*[6]**;
POINTS Coordinates_xy; *// coordinates of testing minutia*
}

Struct Neighborhood_Minutiea_Feature

{
unsigned char Type; *// type of neighboring minutiae: ending point* (1) *or bifurcation* (2)
int ***LDIS***;
// distance between the neighboring minutia and the calculating minutia
int ***LDIR***;
// direction difference between the neighboring minutia and the calculating minutia
}

For each minutia Pi, five neighboring minutiae which are nearest to the minutia Pi are sorted. The five sorted minutiae are represented by $P_{i1}, P_{i2}, P_{i3}, P_{i4}, P_{i5}$ respectively. The distance between the P_i and one of the neighborhoods P_{ij} is defined as: LDIS[i,j] = the number of ridges between P_i and P_{ij}; j = 1, 2, 5. The local direction difference between P_i and P_{ij} is calculated as follows:

$$LDIR[i,j] = DIR[i] - DIR[j]$$

where DIR[i] is the direction of calculating point P_i. LDIR[i,j] is the directional difference between the calculating minutia P_i and its neighboring minutia P_{ij}.LDIS[i,j] and LDIR[i,j] are saved into the data structure: Neighborhood_Minutiea_Feature. Based on our definition, the extracted features (distance and direction) are insensitive to fingerprint image distortion and rotation. Let the testing fingerprint $\bar{F}$ be represented as a set of m minutiae features as follows:

$$\bar{F} = \{F_1, F_2, \cdots, F_m\} \tag{5}$$

Note that each of the elements in the feature set is a feature data structure containing the following components:

$$F_i = \{Type, DIR, Type.P_{i1}, P_{i1}.LDIS, P_{i1}.LDIR, Type.P_{i2}, P_{i2}.LDIS, P_{i2}.LDIR, Type.P_{i3}, P_{i3}.LDIR, Type.P_{i4}, P_{i4}.LDIS, P_{i4}.LDIR, Type.P_{i5}, P_{i5}.LDIS, P_{i5}.LDIR, \text{Coordinates\_xy}\} \tag{6}$$

Similarly, let the feature set of kth fingerprint image in fingerprint database be represented as a set of n minutiae points. Each minutiae point is represented by two data structures defined in the Struct Fingerprint Feature and Struct Neighborhood_Minutiea_Feature.

$$\overline{R_k} = \{R_{k1}, R_{k2}, \cdots, R_{kn}\} \tag{7}$$

It is assumed that the two fingerprint images are roughly aligned. The matching algorithm seeks to find the number of matched minutiae between the testing fingerprint and the reference fingerprint. The proposed matching algorithm is elaborated as follows: The distance between the ith minutia of testing fingerprint F_i and the jth minutia of the reference fingerprint R_{kj} in the database can be calculated according to the distance integral norm:

$$\begin{aligned} D(i,j) &= abs(F_i.Type - R_{kj}.Type) \\ &+ w_1 * (F_i.DIR - R_{kj}.DIR) \\ &+ \sum_{l=1}^{5} \{w_2 * abs(F_i -> P_{il} \cdot LDIS - R_{kj} -> P_{jl} \cdot LDIS) \\ &+ abs(F_i -> P_{il} \cdot LDIR - R_{kj} -> P_{jl} \cdot LDIR) \end{aligned} \tag{8}$$

The symbol "->" represents the data structure pointer operation; parameters w_1 and w_2 are weight factors which are empirically determined to give the maximum similarity matching. In our experiments, w_1 is set to 1.0 and w_2 is set to 0.5.

Input: A set of structural features of the testing fingerprint $\bar{F} = \{F_1, F_2, \cdots, F_m\}$ and a set of structural features in the kth reference fingerprint $\overline{R_k} = \{R_{k1}, R_{k2}, \cdots, R_{kn}\}$ Output: the ratio of the matched pair of two fingerprint images to the average minutiae number of two fingerprint images (MF).

Count = 0;
*Loop*1: *FOR* (i = 1; $i \le m$; ++i) {
*Loop*2: *FOR* (j = 1; $j \le$ n; ++j) {
If((*Type of* F_i ==*Type of* R_{kj}). *and*. $|F_i.DIR\text{-}R_{kj}.DIR| < \phi$)
{
Compute $D[i,j]$;
$D[i]min = min(D(i,j-1), D(i,j))$;
// *Write down the value j of reference fingerprint, which has minimum distance with minutiae i in testing fingerprint*;
}
} // *end of Loop* 2
If ($D[i]min < \sigma$)
Count = *Count* + 1;
// *increment the matched minutiae numbers; A paired testing minutia will not be paired again;*
} // *end of Loop* 1
MF = 2**Count*/(*m***n*);
End

Here f and s are two parameters depending on the image resolutions and application conditions. In our experiments, f is set to 0.75 and s is set to 5.0. MF is a parameter to judge the matching degree. The higher the MF is set, the higher possibility the two fingerprints will get matched.

Discussion of Proposed Algorithm

As the distance between two feature points on a finger print image is measured by the number of ridge/valley, the distance feature is therefore insensitive to scale and distortion. In addition, direction feature is the difference between the direction of testing minutia and that of its neighboring minutia, which is image-rotation insensitive. As a result, the proposed fingerprint feature extraction method is insensitive to image distortion and rotation. Another advantage is that an elastically structural feature matching method proves to be a fast and reliable solution for fingerprint verification and identification.

EXPERIMENTS

NIST Special Fingerprint Database IV [19] is used in the experiment. The database contains 2000 fingerprint image pairs with 8-bit grayscale images. Some poor quality fingerprints images are severely deformed due to rolling and/or inking problems of the distorted ridges. In the first experiment, 200 fingerprints from NIST Special Database 4 Fingerprint Database were chosen to test the proposed system. By using PC computer with 4 MB of internal memory and 2.50 GHz, The system shows that the image preprocessing which includes image filtering, enhancement, and thinning for a 256 × 256 grayscale fingerprint image, needs about 150 ms.

The minutia feature extraction and encoding takes 100 ms. It takes about 200 ms to match a testing fingerprint with 200 enrolled fingerprints in the database. As shown in Figure 2, image preprocessing and feature extraction were conducted on individual workstation computers. The fingerprint match (verification) is through the internet and conducted on a computer server, where enrolled fingerprint features were saved into database. ActiveX Data Objects for .NET was used for web-based database query. Clients can use ADO.NET on their workstation computer to remotely control the fingerprint feature database on the server, such as fingerprint feature enrollment, deletion, fast sorting, query, etc.

Figure 6 gives two examples of original fingerprint images and image preprocessed (noise removal, image enhancement and thinning) images. In the Figures 6(c) and 6(d), the blue points highlight the ending points and the bifurcation points are marked in red. In each thinned image, one feature point and its five nearest neighboring points are linked for visualizing feature extraction data structure. As for the deteriorated fingerprint image pairs in the data set, it is very difficult to match all the five neighboring feature points using Equation (8) due to missing minutiae and false minutiae occurring in the processed image. A flexible scheme is proposed in the applications. The different numbers of neighboring feature points are chosen to conduct fingerprint verification in order to achieve the highest recognition rate. Table 1 shows the relationship of the False Acceptance Rate (FAR), False

(a)

(b)

(c)

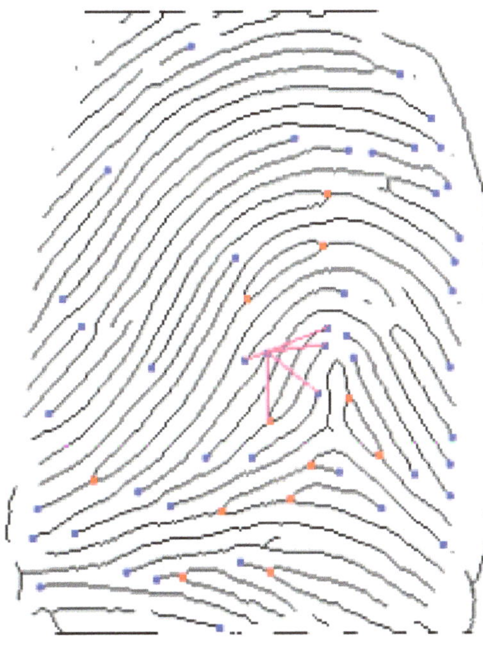

(d)

Figure 6: Original fingerprint images and feature extracted images. (a) original fingerprint image1; (b) original fingerprint image 2; (c) feature extracted image 1; (d) feature extracted image 2.

Table 1: FAR and FRR with different number of neighboring feature points in the fingerprint matching.

No. of Neighboring Feature Points	False Acceptance Rate (FAR)	False Reject Rate (FRR)
1	20.00%	0.50%
2	15.50%	1.00%
3	4.50%	2.50%
4	1.50%	5.00%
5	0.5%	6.00%

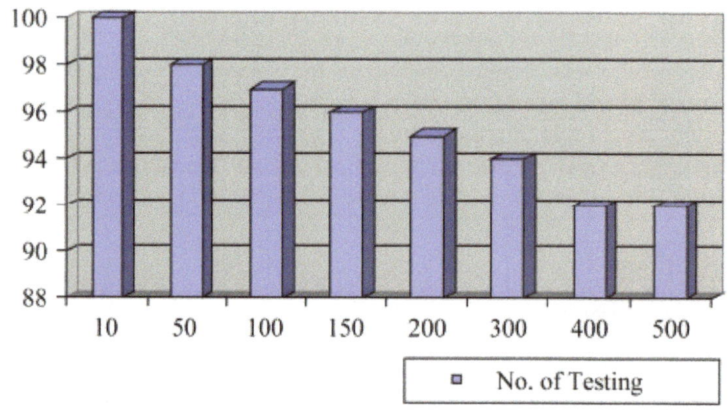

Figure 7: Fingerprint verification rates on different enrollment number of images.

Reject Rate (FRR) with the different number of neighboring feature points in the fingerprint image matching. In the second experiment, a comparative experiment on the different number of fingerprints was conducted. The recognition performance with different enrollment numbers of fingerprint is shown in Figure 7. For 200 fingerprint images, the verification rate (correct passing rate) can be as high as 95%.

CONCLUSIONS

Fingerprint verification over the internet is a new research topic as it will deal with web-based database query and fingerprint feature transmission over internet. A web-based fingerprint verification algorithm and its distributed system is presented in this paper. Based on internet transmission, no extra hardware system is needed. A new fingerprint feature extraction method and a flexible structural feature matching algorithm are proposed in the system. Experiments show that the proposed fingerprint verification algorithm is insensitive to fingerprint image distortion, scale, and rotation. The web-based online distributed system performs well on the benchmark fingerprint dataset and practical applications. Further research will be conducted on how the network security can be applied to fingerprint feature transmission over the internet. The feature data should be encrypted before transmission in order to protect the system from being invaded by adept hackers.

REFERENCES

1. Z. Miklos and K. Vajna, "A Fingerprint Verification System Based on Triangular Matching and Dynamic Time Warping," IEEE Transaction on Pattern Recognition and Machine Intelligence, Vol. 22, No. 11, November 2000, pp. 1266-1276. doi:10.1109/34.888711
2. N. K. Ratha, K. Karu, S. Chen and A. K. Jain, "A Real-Time Matching System for Large Fingerprint Database," IEEE Transaction on Pattern Analysis and Machine Intelligence, Vol. 18, No. 8, August 1996, pp. 799- 813. doi:10.1109/34.531800
3. A. K. Jain, L. Hong and R. Bolle, "On-line Fingerprint Verification," IEEE Transaction on Pattern Analysis and Machine Intelligence, Vol. 19, No. 4, April 1997, pp. 302-314. doi:10.1109/34.587996
4. T. Y. Zhang and C. Y. Suen, "A Fast Parallel Algorithm for Thinning Digital Patterns," Communication of the ACM, Vol. 27, No. 3, March 1984, pp. 236-239. doi:10.1145/357994.358023
5. J. H. Wegstein, "An Automated Fingerprint Identification System," Technical Report 500-89, National Bureau of Standards, Bethesda, 1982.
6. S. Umeyama, "Parametterized Point Pattern Matching and its Application to Recognition of Object Families," IEEE Transactions on Pattern Analysis and Machine Intelligence, Vol. 15, No. 2, February 1993, pp. 136-144. doi:10.1109/34.192485
7. D. K. Isenor and S. G. Zaky, "Fingerprint Identification Using Graph Matching," Pattern Recognition, Vol. 19, No. 2, 1986, pp.113-122.
8. N. Ansari, M. H. Chen and E. S. H. Hou, "A Genetic Algorithm for Point Pattern Mattering, Dynamic,

Genetic, and Chaotic Programming," John Wiley and Sons, New York, 1992, pp. 353-371.

9. J. Ton and A. K. Jain, "Registering Landsat Images by Point Matching," IEEE Transaction on Geoscience and Remote Sensing, Vol. 27, No. 5, September 1989, pp. 642-651. doi:10.1109/TGRS.1989.35948

10. V. S. Srinivasan and N. N. Murthy, "Detection of Singular Points in Fingerprint Images," Pattern Recognition, Vol. 25, No. 2, February 1992, pp. 139-153. doi:10.1016/0031-3203(92)90096-2

11. A. K. Hrechak and J. A. Mchugh, "Automated Fingerprint Recognition Using Structural Matching," Pattern Recognition, Vol. 23, No. 8, 1990, pp. 893-904. doi:10.1016/0031-3203(90)90134-7

12. A. K. Jain, S. Prabhakar and S. Pankanti, "Filterbankbased Fingerprint Mtching," IEEE Transactions on Image Processing, Vol. 9, No. 5, 2000, pp. 846-859. doi:10.1109/83.841531

13. P. M. Patil, R. S. Suralkar and H. K. Abhyankar, "Fingerprint Verification Based on Fixed Length Square Finer Code," Proceeding of IEEE Conference on Tools withArtificial Intelligence, Hong Kong, 16 November 2005, pp. 657-662.

14. K. Huang and S. Aviyente, "Choosing Best Basis in Wavelet Packets for Fingerprint Matching," Proceedings of IEEE Conference on Image Processing, East Lansing, 24-27 October 2004, pp. 1249-1252.

15. N. Y. Khan and M. Y. Javed, "Efficient Fingerprint Matching Technique Using Wavelet Based Features," Proceedings of Digital Image Computing Techniques and Applications, 2007, pp. 253-259.

16. X. Tan and B. Bhanu, "Fingerprint Verification Using Genetic Algorithm," Proceedings of 6th IEEE Workshop on Applications of Computer Vision, 2002, pp. 79-83.

17. J. Gu, J. Zhou and X. Tang, "Fingerprint Recognition by Combining Global Structure and Local Cues," IEEE Transactions on Image Processing, Vol. 15, No. 7, 2006, pp. 1951-1964.

18. A. Ross, S. C. Dass and A. K. Jain, "Fingerprint Warping Using Ridge Curve Correspondences," IEEE Transactions on Pattern Analysis and Machine Intelligence, Vol. 28, No. 1, 2006, pp. 19-30. doi:10.1109/TPAMI.2006.11

19. C. J. Watson and C. L. Wilson, "NIST Special Database 4 Fingerprint Database," National Institute of Standards and Technology Advanced Systems Division Image Recognition Group, 17 March 1992.

20. R. C. Gonzalez and R. E. Woods, "Digital Image Processing," 3rd Version, Pearson Prentice Hall, 2008.

CHAPTER 16

FAULT TOLERANCE MECHANISMS IN DISTRIBUTED SYSTEMS

Arif Sari and Murat Akkaya

Department of Management Information Systems, Girne American University, Kyrenia, Cyprus

ABSTRACT

The use of technology has increased vastly and today computer systems are interconnected via different communication medium. The use of distributed systems in our day to day activities has solely improved with data distributions. This is because distributed systems enable nodes to organise and allow their resources to be used among the connected systems or devices that make people to be integrated with geographically distributed computing facilities. The distributed systems may lead to lack of service availability due to multiple system failures on multiple failure points. This article highlights the different fault tolerance mechanism in distributed systems used to prevent multiple system failures on multiple failure points by considering replication, high redundancy and high availability of the distributed services.

INTRODUCTION

A faulty system creates a human/economic loss, air and rail traffic control, telecommunication loss, etc. The need for a reliable fault tolerance mechanism reduces these risks to a minimum. In distributed systems, faults or failures are limited or part. A part failure in distributed systems is not equally critical because the entire system would not be offline or brought down, for example a system having more than one processing cores (CPU), and if one of the cores fails the system would not stop functioning as though that's the one physical core in the system. Hence, the other cores would continue to function and process data normally. Nevertheless, in a non-distributed system when one of its components stops functioning, it would lead to a malfunction of the entire system or program and the corresponding processes would stop. Fault tolerance is the dynamic method that's used to keep the interconnected systems together, sustain reliability, and availability in distributed systems. The hardware and software redundancy methods are the known techniques of fault tolerance in distributed system. The hardware methods ensure the addition of some hardware components such as CPUs, communication links, memory, and I/O devices while in the software fault tolerance method, specific programs are included to deal with faults. Efficient fault tolerance mechanism helps in detecting of faults and if possible recovers from it. There are various definitions to what

Citation: Sari, A. and Akkaya, M. (2015), "Fault Tolerance Mechanisms in Distributed Systems". International Journal of Communications, Network and System Sciences, vol. 8, pp.471-482. doi: 10.4236/ijcns.2015.812042.

fault tolerance is. In dealing with fault tolerance, replication is typically used for general fault tolerance method to protect against system failure [1] [2].

Sebepou et al. highlighted three major forms of replication mechanism which are [1] [2]:

- The State Machine;
- Process Pairs;
- Roll Back Recovery.

1) State Machine

In this mechanism, the process state of a computer system is replicated on autonomous computer system at the same time, all replica nodes process data in analogous or matching way and also there's coordination in their process among the replica nodes and all the inputs are sent to all replica at the same time [2] [3]. An active replica is an example of state machine [3] [4].

2) Process Pairs

The process pairs functions like a master (primary)/ slave (secondary) link in replication coordination. The primary workstation acts in place of a master to transmit its corresponding input to the secondary node. Both nodes maintain a good communication link [3]-[5].

3) Roll Back Recovery (Check-Point-Based)

This mechanism collects check point momentarily and transfers these checkpoint states to a stable storage device or backup nodes. This enables a roll back recovery to be done successfully when or during recovery process. The checkpoint is been reconstructed prior to the recent state [3]-[6].

DISTRIBUTED SYSTEM

Distributed system are systems that don't share memory or clock, in distributed systems nodes connect and relay information by exchanging the information over a communication medium. The different computer in distributed system have their own memory and OS, local resources are owned by the node using the resources. While the resources that is been accessed over the network or communication medium is known to be remote resources [5]-[7]. Figure 1 shows the communication network between systems in the distributed environment. In distributed system, pool of rules are executed to synchronise the actions of various or different processes on a communication network, thereby forming a distinct set of related tasks [6]-[9]. The independent system or computers access resources remotely or locally in the distributed system communication environment, these resources are put together to form a single intelligible system. The user in the distributed environment is not aware of the multiple interconnected system that ensures the task is carried out accurately. In distributed system, no single system is required or carries the load of the entire system in processing a task [8] [9].

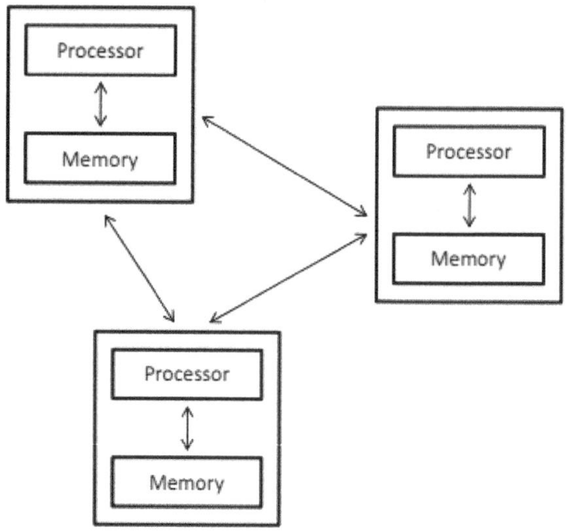

Figure 1: Distributed system.

DISTRIBUTED SYSTEM ARCHITECTURE

The architecture of distributed system is built on existing OS and network software [8]. Distributed system encompasses the collection of self-sufficient computers that are linked via a computer network and distribution middleware. The distribution middleware in distributed system, enables the corresponding computers to manage and share the resources of the corresponding system, thus making the computer users to see the system as a single combined computing infrastructure [9] [10]. Middleware is the link that joins distributed applications across different geographical locations, different computing hardware, network technologies, operating systems, and programming languages. The middleware delivers standard services such as naming, concurrency control, event distribution, security, authorization etc. Figure 2 shows the distributed system architecture, with the middleware offering its services to the connected systems in the distributed environment [10] [11]. In distributed system, the structure can be fully connected networks or partially connected networks [12]-[15]. As shown in Figure 3, a full connected network, is a network where each node is connected together. The disadvantage of this network is that when a new computer added, it physically increase the number of nodes connected to nodes, because the network connects node to node. Because of the increase in nodes, the number of file descriptors and difficulty for each node to communicate are increased heavily. File Descriptors is an intellectual indicator used to access a file or other input/output resource, such as a pipe or network connection [15]- [17]. Hence, the ability for the networked systems to continue functioning well is limited to the connected nodes ability of open the file descriptors and also the capability to manage new connections. The fully linked network systems are reliable because the message sent from one node to another node goes through one link, and when a node fails to function or a link fails, other nodes in the network can still communicate with other nodes.

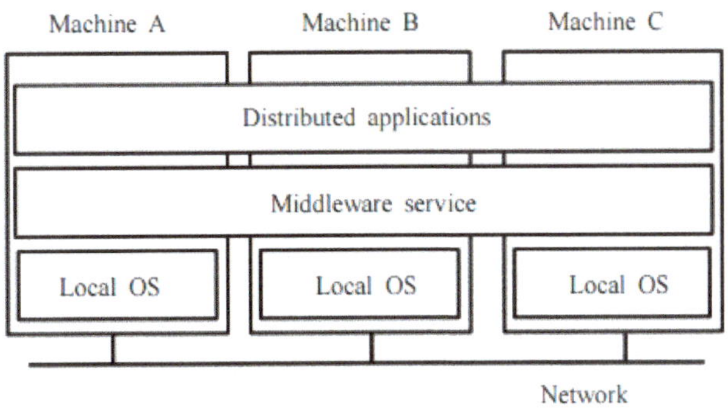

Figure 2: A simple architecture of a distributed system.

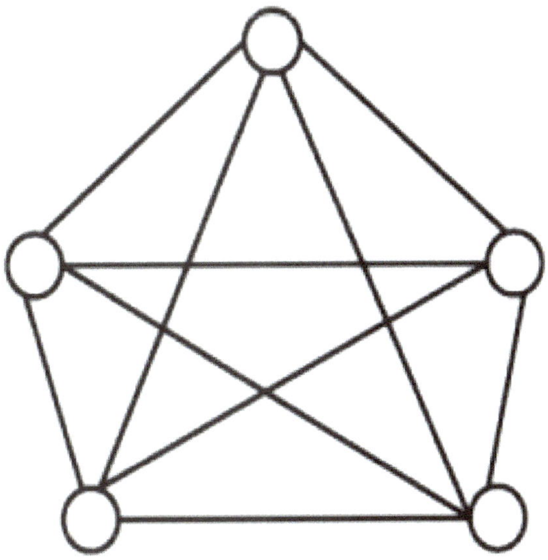

Figure 3: Fully connected network.

In the partially connected network, some node have direct links while others don't. Some models of partially connected networks are star structured networks, multi-access bus network, ring structured network, and tree structured network. In Figures 4-7 illustrates the corresponding networks. The disadvantages in these network in are: in the Star designed network, when the main node fails to function the entire networked system stops to function they collapse.

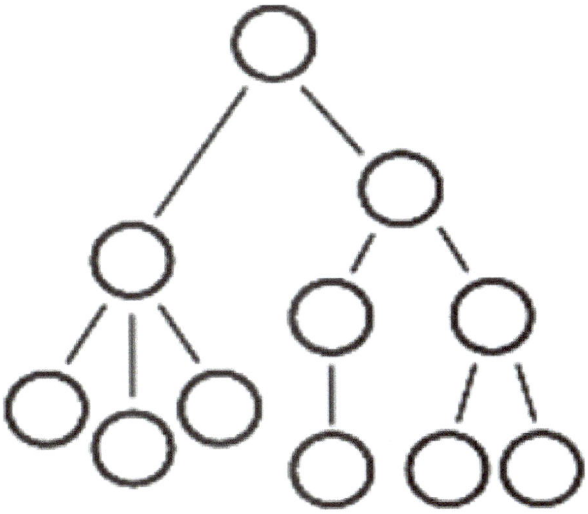

Figure 4: Tree structured network.

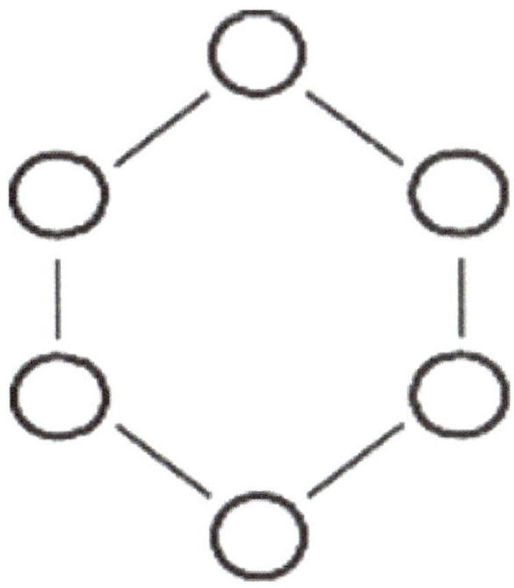

Figure 5: Ring structured network.

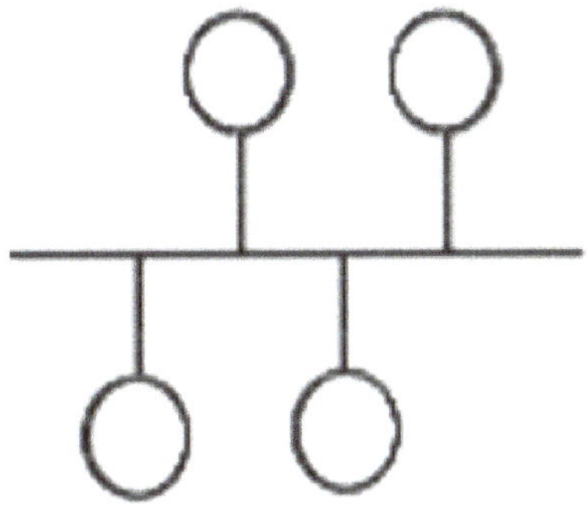

Figure 6: Multi-access bus network.

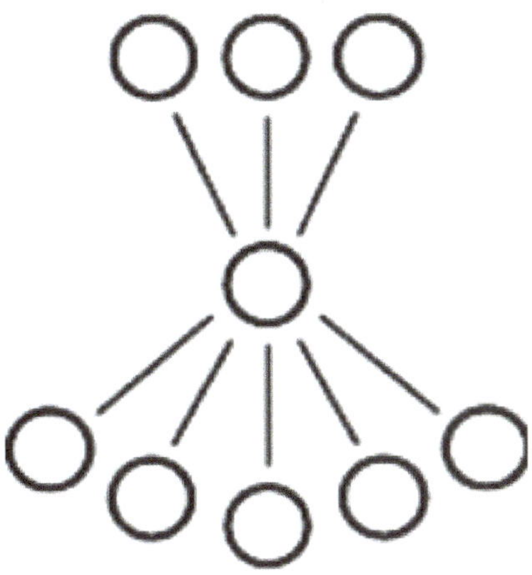

Figure 7: Star structured network.

In multi-access bus network, nodes are connected to each other through a communication link "a bus". If the bus link connecting the nodes fails to function, all other nodes can't connect to each other, and the performance of the network drops as more nodes or computers are added to the system or heavy traffic occurs in the system. In the ring network, nodes are connected at least to two other nodes in the network creating a path for signals to be exchanged between the connected nodes. As new nodes are added to the network, the transmission delay becomes longer. If a node fail every other node in the network can be inaccessible. In the tree structured network, this is like a network with hierarchy, each node in the network have a fixed number nodes that is attached to it in the sub level of the tree. In this network messages that are transmitted from the parent to the child nodes goes through one link. For a distributed system to perform and function according to build, it must have the following characteristics; Fault Tolerant, Scalability, Predictable Performance, Openness, Security, and Transparency.

FAULT TOLERANCE SYSTEMS

Fault tolerance system is a vital issue in distributed computing; it keeps the system in a working condition in subject to failure. The most important point of it is to keep the system functioning even if any of its part goes off or faulty [18]-[20]. For a system to be fault tolerant, it is related to dependable systems. Dependability covers some useful requirements in the fault tolerance system these requirements include: Availability, Reliability, Safety, and Maintainability. Availability: This is when a system is in a ready state, and is ready to deliver its functions to its corresponding users. Highly available systems works at a given instant in time. Reliability: This is the ability for a computer system run continuously without a failure. Unlike availability, reliability is defined in a time interval instead of an instant in time. A highly reliably system, works constantly in a long period of time without interruption. Safety: This is when a system fails to carry out its corresponding processes correctly and its operations are incorrect, but no shattering event happens. Maintainability: A highly maintainability system can also show a great measurement of accessibility, especially if the corresponding failures can be noticed and fixed mechanically. As we have seen, fault tolerance system is a system which has the capacity of or to keep running correctly and proper execution of its programs and continues functioning in the event of a partial failure [21] [22].

Although sometimes the performance of the system is affected due to the failure that occurred. Some of the fault is narrowed down to Hardware or Software Failure (Node Failure) or Unauthorised Access (Machine Error). Errors caused by fault tolerance events are separated into categories namely; performance, omission, timing, crash, and fail-stop [22]-[24].

- Performance: this is when the hardware or software components cannot meet the demands of the user.
- Omission: is when components cannot implement the actions of a number of distinctive commands.
- Timing: this is when components cannot implement the actions of a command at the right time.
- Crash: certain components crash with no response and cannot be repaired.
- Fail-stop: is when the software identifies errors, it ends the process or action, this is the easiest to handle, sometimes its simplicity deprives it from handling real situations.

In addition to the error timing, three situations or form can be distinguished:

- Permanent error; these causes damage to software components and resulting to permanent error or damage to the program, preventing it from running or functioning. In this case a restart of the program is done, an example is when a program crashes.
- Temporary error; this only result to a brief damage to the software component, the damage gets resolved after some time and the corresponding software continues to work or function normally.
- Periodic errors; these are errors that occurs occasionally. For example when there's a software conflict between two software when run at the same time.

In dealing with this type of error, one of the programs or software is exited to resolve the conflict. Most computers if not all have some fault tolerance technique such as micro diagnosis [25] [26], parity checking [27]-[29], watchdog timers [30]-[34], etc. an incompletely fault tolerant system have inbuilt resources to cause a reduction in its specified computing capability and reduce to a smaller or lower system by removing some programs that have been used previously or by reducing the rate at which specified processes are executed.

The reduction is due to the decrease or slowdown in the operational hardware configuration or it may be some design faults in the hardware.

BASIC CONCEPT OF FAULT TOLERANCE SYSTEMS

Fault tolerance mechanism can be divided into three stages; Hardware, Software, and System Fault [34]. Hardware Fault Tolerance: This involves the provision of supplementary backup hardware such as; CPU, Memory, Hard disks, Power Supply Units, etc. hardware fault tolerance can only deliver support for the hardware by providing the basic hardware backup system, it can't stop or detect error, accidental interfering with programs, program errors, etc. In hardware fault tolerance, computer systems that resolves fault occurring from hardware component automatically are built. This technique often partition the node into units that performance as a fault control area, each module is backed up with a defensive redundancy, the reason is that if one of the modules fails, the others can act or take up its function. There are two approach to hardware fault recovery namely; Fault Masking and Dynamic Recovery [35]-[37].

Fault Masking: This is an important redundancy method that fully covers faults within a set of redundant units or components. Other identical units carry out or implement the same tasks, and their outputs were noted to have removed errors created by a defective module. Commonly used fault masking module it the Triple Modular Redundancy (TMR). The TMR triplicate the circuitry and selected [38] [39]. The selected electrical system can also be triplicated so that the selected circuitry failures can be corrected by the same process. The selected system in the TMR needs more hardware, this enables computations to continue without been interrupted when a fault is detected or occurs, tolerating the operating system to be used [40] [41].

Dynamic Recovery: In dynamic recovery, special mechanism is essential to discover faults in the units, perform a switch on a faulty module, puts in a spare, and carryout some software actions necessary to restore and continue computation such as; rollback, initialization, retry, and restart. This requires special hardware and software to make this work in single computer, but in a multicomputer situation, the function is carried out by other processors [42]-[45].

Software Fault Tolerance: This is a special software designed to tolerate errors that would originate from a software or programming errors. The software fault tolerance utilize the static and dynamic redundancy methods similar to those used for hardware fault [46]. N-version programming approach uses the static redundancy like an independently program that does the same function creating out that are selected at special checkpoint. Another approach is the Design Diversity which this adds both hardware and software fault tolerance by deploying a fault tolerant system using diverse hardware and software in the redundant channels. In the Design diversity, every channel is intended to carry out the same function and a mechanism is in check to see if any of the channels changes from others. The aim of the Design Diversity is to tolerate faults from both hardware and software. This approach is very expensive, its use mainly is in the aircraft control applications.

Note: Software Fault Tolerance also consists of checkpoints storage and rollback recovery. Checkpoints are like a safe state or snapshot of the entire system in a working state. This is done regularly. The snapshot holds all the required information to restart the program from the checkpoint. The usefulness of the software fault tolerance is to create an application that would store checkpoints regularly for targeted systems. System Fault Tolerance: This is a complete system that stores not just checkpoints, it detects error in application, it stores memory block, program checkpoint automatically. When a fault or an error occurs, the system provides a correcting mechanism thereby correcting the error. Table 1 shows the comparison of three fault tolerance mechanism.

Table 1: Comparison of fault tolerance mechanism

Mechanism	**Hardware Fault Tolerance**	**Software Fault Tolerance**	**System Fault Tolerance**
Major technique	Hardware backup	Checkpoint storage Rollback recovery	Architecture with error detecting & correcting
Design complexity	Low	Medium	High
Time/cost expenditure	Low	Medium	High
Fault-tolerance Level	Low	Medium	High

FAULT TOLERANCE MECHANISM IN DISTRIBUTED SYSTEMS

Replication Based Fault Tolerance Technique

The replication based fault tolerance technique is one of the most popular method. This technique actually replicate the data on different other system. In the replication techniques, a request can be sent to one replica system in the midst of the other replica system. In this way if a particular or more than one node fails to function, it will not cause the whole system to stop functioning as shown in Figure 8. Replication adds redundancy in a system.

There are different phase in the replication protocol which are client contact, server coordination, execution, agreement, coordination and client response. Major issues in replication based techniques are consistency, degree of replica, replica on demand etc.

Consistency: This is a vital issue in replication technique. Several copies of the same entity create problem of consistency because of update that can be done by any of the user. The consistency of data is ensured by some criteria such as linearizability [47], sequential consistency and casual consistency [48] etc. sequential and linearizability consistency ensures strong consistency unlike casual consistency which defines a weak consistency criterion. For example a primary backup replication technique guarantee consistency by linerarizability, likewise active replication technique.

Degree or Number of Replica: The replication techniques utilises some protocols in replication of data or an object, such protocol are: Primary backup replication [49], voting [50] and primary-per partition replication [51]. In the degree of replication, to attain a high level of consistency, large number of replicas is needed. If the number of replica is low or less it would affect the scalability, performance and multiple fault tolerance capability. To solve the issue of less number of replica, in [51] adaptive replicas creation algorithm was proposed.

Process Level Redundancy Technique

This fault tolerance technique is often used for faults that disappears without anything been done to remedy the situation, this kind of fault is known as transient faults. Transient faults occurs when there's a temporary malfunction in any of the system component or sometimes by environmental interference. The problem with transient faults is that they are hard to handle and diagnose but they are less severe in nature. In handling of transient fault, software based fault tolerance technique such as Process-Level Redundancy (PLR) is used because hardware based fault tolerance technique is more expensive to deploy. As shown in Figure 9, the PLR compares processes to ensure correct execution and also it creates a set of redundant processes apiece application process. Redundancy at the process level enables the OS to schedule easily processes across all accessible hardware resources.

The PLR provides improved performance over existing software transient fault tolerance techniques with a 16.9% overhead for detection of fault [53]. PLR uses a software-centric approach which causes a shift in focus from guaranteeing hardware execution correctly to ensuring a correct software execution. Check Pointing and Roll Back: This is a popular technique which in the first part "check point" stores the current state of the system and this is done occasionally. The check point information is stored in a stable storage device for easy roll back when there's a node failure. Information that is stored or checked includes environment, process state, value of the registers etc. these information are very useful if a complete recovery needs to be done [50] [51]. Figure 10 illustrates the check pointing techniques. The two most known type or roll back recovery are the checkpoint and log based roll back recovery technique.

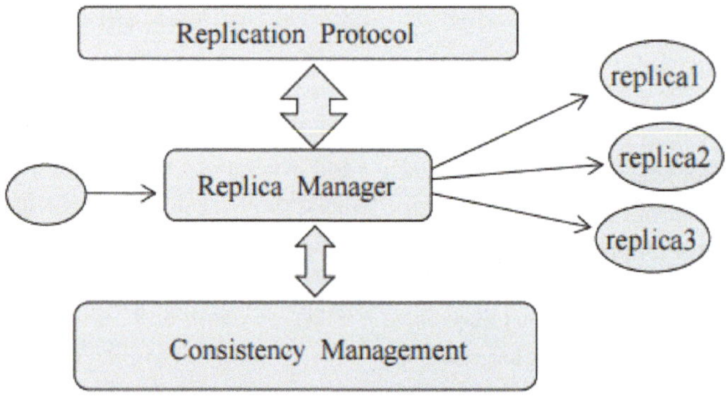

Figure 8: Replication based technique in distributed system.

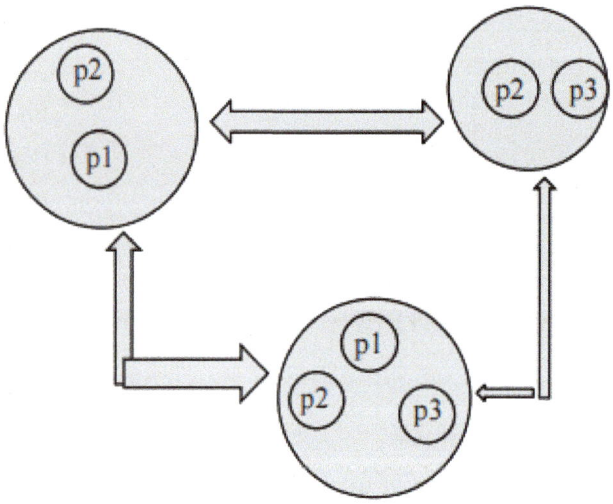

Figure 9: Process redundancy.

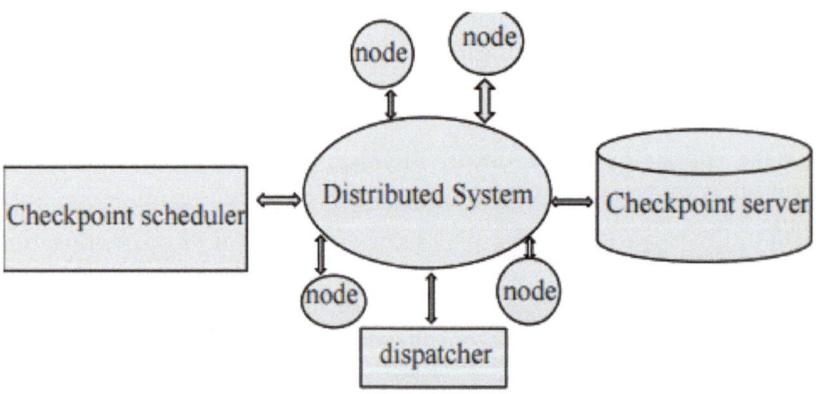

Figure 10: Check pointing technique.

Each of the type of rollback recovery technique uses different mechanism; the checkpoint based uses the checkpoints states that it has stored in a stable storage device, while the log based rollback recovery techniques combines both check pointing and logging of events [51].

In recovery form system failures, there are two type of check point technique that is used; coordinated and uncoordinated checkpoint techniques, these techniques are related with message logging [34]. Coordinated Check Point: In this technique, check are coordinated to save a consistent state because the coordinated checkpoint are consistent set of checkpoint. If the checkpoints are not consistent a full and complete rollback of the system can't be done [52]. In a situation where there's frequent failure, coordinated check point technique can't be used. The recovery time can be set to a higher value or lower value, when set to a lower value, it improves performance of the technique because it only select the recovery to last correct state of the system instead from the very first state or checkpoint.

Uncoordinated Check Point: This technique combines the message logging to ensure that the rollback state is correct. The uncoordinated check point technique executed checkpoints independently as well as recovery. There are three type of message logging protocols: optimistic, pessimistic and casual. In the optimistic protocol ensures all messages are logged. The pessimistic protocol makes sure that all the message that is received by a process are logged appropriately and stored in a stable and reliable storage media before it is forwarded into the system. While the causal protocol just log the message information of a process in all processes that are causally dependent [53].

Fusion Based Technique

Replication is the most widely used method or technique in fault tolerance. The main downside is the multiple of backups that it incurs. Because the backups increase as faults increase and the cost of management is very expensive, the fusion based technique solves that problem. Fusion based technique stands as an alternative because it requires fewer backup machines compared to the replication based technique. As shown in Figure 11, the backup machines are fused corresponding to the given set of machines [53] [54]. The fusion based technique has a very high overhead during recovery process and it's acceptable in low probability of fault in a system. From Table 2, it is clear that all methods having capability to handle multiple faults. In all methods performance can be improved by focusing on or addressing the serious aspects involved. In all the techniques involved, there is strong need for reliable, accurate and pure adaptive multiple failure detector mechanism [53], [54].

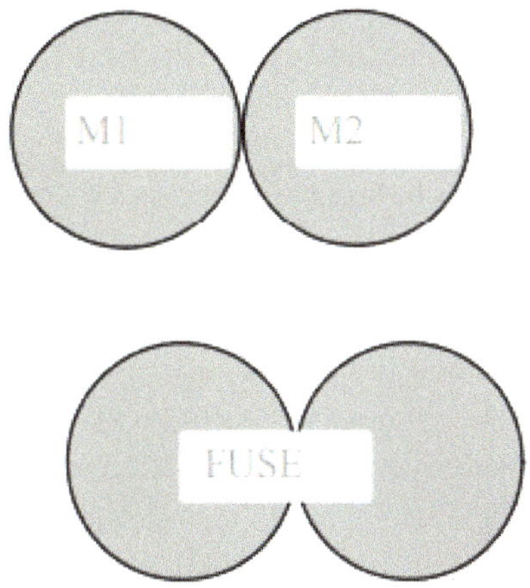

Figure 11: Fusion process technique.

Table 2: shows compares the different fault tolerance technique or mechanism in distributed system

Major Factors	Replication Based Technique	Checking Point/Roll Back Technique	Fusion Based Technique	Process Level Redundancy Technique
Working	Redirected to replica	State saved on stables to rage used for recovery	Back up machine	A set of redundant process
Consistency	Some criterion, linearizability.	Avoiding orphan messages	Among backup machines	Not a major issues
Multiple Faults Handling	Depend upon number of replica.	Depend upon Check pointing scheduling	Depends upon number of back machine	Depends upon set of redundant process
Performance	Decreases as number of replica increases.	Decrease with frequency and size of checkpoint	Decrease in case of faults as recovery cost is high	Decrease as faults appears disappear
N-Faults	N replicas ensure n-1 faults	Uncoordinated Pessimistic and N level disk less used for N-1 Faults	In order handle Extra N faults N backups machine are required	Scaling the number of process and Majority voting
Multiple Failure Detector	Reliable, Accurate, Adaptive	Reliable, Accurate, Adaptive	Reliable, Accurate, Adaptive	Reliable, Accurate, Adaptive

CONCLUSION

Fault tolerance is a major part of distributed system, because it ensures the continuity and functionality of a system at a point where there's a fault or failure. This research showed the different type of fault tolerance technique in distributed system such as the Fusion Based Technique, Check Pointing and Roll Back Technique, and Replication Based Fault Tolerance Technique. Each mechanism is advantageous over the other and costly in deployment. In this paper we highlight the levels of fault tolerance such as the hardware fault tolerance which ensures that additional backup hardware such as memory block, CPU, etc., software fault tolerance system comprises of checkpoints storage and rollback recovery mechanisms, and the system fault tolerance is a complete system that does both software and hardware fault tolerance, to ensure availability of the system during failure, error or fault. Future research would be conducted on comparing the various data security mechanisms and their performance metrics.

REFERENCES

1. Sebepou, Z. and Magoutis, K. (2011) CEC: Continuous Eventual Checkpointing for Data Stream Processing Operators. Proceedings of IEEE/IFIP 41st International Conference on Dependable Systems and Networks, 145-156. http://dx.doi.org/10.1109/dsn.2011.5958214

2. Sari, A. and Necat, B. (2012) Impact of RTS Mechanism on TORA and AODV Protocol's Performance in Mobile Ad Hoc Networks. International Journal of Science and Advanced Technology, 2, 188-191.
3. Chen, W.H. and Tsai, J.C. (2014) Fault-Tolerance Implementation in Typical Distributed Stream Processing Systems.
4. Sari, A. and Necat, B. (2012) Securing Mobile Ad Hoc Networks against Jamming Attacks through Unified Security Mechanism. International Journal of Ad Hoc, Sensor & Ubiquitous Computing, 3, 79-94. http://dx.doi.org/10.5121/ijasuc.2012.3306
5. Balazinska, M., Balakrishnan, H., Madden, S. and Stonebraker, M. (2008) Fault-Tolerance in the Borealis Distributed Stream Processing System. ACM Transactions on Database Systems, 33, 1-44. http://dx.doi.org/10.1145/1331904.1331907
6. Sari, A. (2014) Security Approaches in IEEE 802.11 MANET—Performance Evaluation of USM and RAS. International Journal of Communications, Network, and System Sciences, 7, 365-372. http://dx.doi.org/10.4236/ijcns.2014.79038
7. Elnozahy, E.N.M., Alvisi, L., Wang, Y.M. and Johnson, D.B. (2002) A Survey of Rollback-Recovery Protocols in Message-Passing Systems. ACM Computing Surveys, 34, 375-408. http://dx.doi.org/10.1145/568522.568525
8. Sari, A. (2014) Security Issues in RFID Middleware Systems: A Case of Network Layer Attacks: Proposed EPC Implementation for Network Layer Attacks. Transactions on Networks & Communications, 2, 1-6. http://dx.doi.org/10.14738/tnc.25.431
9. Andrew, S. (1995) Tanenbaum Distributed Operating Systems. Prentice Hall, Upper Saddle River.
10. Sari, A. (2015) Lightweight Robust Forwarding Scheme for Multi-Hop Wireless Networks. International Journal of Communications, Network and System Sciences, 8, 19-28. http://dx.doi.org/10.4236/ijcns.2015.83003
11. Coulouris, G., Dollimore, J. and Kindberg, T. (2001) Distributed Systems: Concepts and Design, 4th Edition, Pearson Education Ltd., New York.
12. Carter, W.C. and Bouricius, W.G. (1971) A Survey of Fault-Tolerant Computer Architecture and Its Evaluation. Computer, 4, 9-16.
13. Short, R.A. (1968) The Attainment of Reliable Digital Systems through the Use of Redundancy—A Survey. IEEE Computer Group News, 2, 2-17.
14. Sari, A. (2015) Two-Tier Hierarchical Cluster Based Topology in Wireless Sensor Networks for Contention Based Protocol Suite. International Journal of Communications, Network and System Sciences, 8, 29-42. http://dx.doi.org/10.4236/ijcns.2015.83004
15. Cooper, A.E. and Chow, W.T. (1976) Development of On-Board Space Computer Systems. IBM Journal of Research and Development, 20, 5-19. http://dx.doi.org/10.1147/rd.201.0005
16. Tanenbaum, A. and Van Steen, M. (2007) Distributed Systems: Principles and Paradigms. 2nd Edition, Pearson Prentice Hall, Upper Saddle River.
17. Koren, I. and Krishna, C.M. (2007) Fault-Tolerance Systems. Elsevier Inc., San Francisco.
18. Sari, A. and Onursal, O. (2013) Role of Information Security in E-Business Operations. International Journal of Information Technology and Business Management, 3, 90-93.
19. Avizienis, A., Kopetz, H. and Laprie, J.C. (1987) Dependable Computing and Fault-Tolerant Systems, Volume 1: The Evolution of Fault-Tolerant Computing. Springer-Verlag, Vienna, 193-213.
20. Sari, A. and Çağlar, E. (2015) Performance Simulation of Gossip Relay Protocol in Multi-Hop Wireless Networks. Social and Applied Sciences Journal, Girne American University, 7, 145-148.
21. Harper, R., Lala, J. and Deyst, J. (1988) Fault-Tolerant Parallel Processor Architectural Overview. Proceedings of the 18st International Symposium on Fault-Tolerant Computing, Tokyo, 27-30 June 1988.
22. Sari, A. and Rahnama, B. (2013) Addressing Security Challenges in WiMAX Environment. In: Proceedings of the 6th International Conference on Security of Information and Networks, ACM Press, New York, 454-456. http://dx.doi.org/10.1145/2523514.2523586
23. Briere, D. and Traverse, P. (1993) AIRBUS A320/A330/A340 Electrical Flight Controls: A Family of Fault-Tolerant Systems. Proceedings of the 23rd International Symposium on Fault-Tolerant Computing, Toulouse, 22-24 June 1993.
24. Charron-Bost, B., Pedone, F. and Schiper, A. (2010) Replication: Theory and Practice. Lecture Notes in Computer Science, 5959.
25. Sari, A. (2015) Security Issues in Mobile Wireless Ad Hoc Networks: A Comparative Survey of Methods and Techniques to Provide Security in Wireless Ad Hoc Networks. New Threats and Countermeasures in Digital Crime and Cyber Terrorism, IGI Global, Hershey, 66-94.
26. Sari, A. and Rahnama, B. (2013) Simulation of 802.11 Physical Layer Attacks in MANET. Proceedings of the Fifth International Conference on Computational Intelligence, Communication Systems and Networks (CICSyN), Madrid, 5-7 June 2013, 334-337. http://dx.doi.org/10.1109/cicsyn.2013.79
27. Tanenbaum, A.S. and van Steen, M. (2002) Distributed Systems: Principles and Paradigms. Pearson Education Asia.
28. Sari, A., Rahnama, B. and Caglar, E. (2014) Ultra-Fast Lithium Cell Charging for Mission Critical Applications. Transactions on Machine Learning and Artificial Intelligence, 2, 11-18. http://dx.doi.org/10.14738/tmlai.25.430
29. Ebnenasir, A. (2005) Software Fault-Tolerance. Computer Science and Engineering Department, Michigan State University, East Lansing. http://www.cse.msu.edu/~cse870/Lectures/SS2005 /ft1.pdf
30. Birman, K. (2005) Reliable Distributed Systems: Technologies, Web Services and Applications. Springer-Verlag, Berlin.

31. Obasuyi, G. and Sari, A. (2015) Security Challenges of Virtualization Hypervisors in Virtualized Hardware Environment. International Journal of Communications, Network and System Sciences, 8, 260-273. http://dx.doi.org/10.4236/ijcns.2015.87026
32. Avizienis, A. (1975) Architecture of Fault-Tolerant Computing Systems. Proceedings of the 1975 International Symposium on Fault-Tolerant Computing, Paris, 18-20 June 1975, 3-16.
33. Sari, A. (2015) A Review of Anomaly Detection Systems in Cloud Networks and Survey of Cloud Security Measures in Cloud Storage Applications. Journal of Information Security, 6, 142-154. http://dx.doi.org/10.4236/jis.2015.62015
34. Short, R.A. (1968) The Attainment of Reliable Digital Systems through the Use of Redundancy—A Survey. IEEE Computer Group News, 2, 2-17.
35. Sari, A. (2014) Influence of ICT Applications on Learning Process in Higher Education. Procedia—Social and Behavioral Sciences, 116, 4939-4945. http://dx.doi.org/10.1016/j.sbspro.2014.01.1053
36. Huang, M. and Bode, B. (2005) A Performance Comparison of Tree and Ring Topologies in Distributed Systems. Proceedings of the 19th IEEE International Parallel and Distributed Processing Symposium, Denver, 4-8 April 2005, 258.1. http://dx.doi.org/10.1109/IPDPS.2005.57
37. Huang, M. (2004) A Performance Comparison of Tree and Ring Topologies in Distributed System. Master's Thesis. www.osti.gov
38. Minar, N. (2001) Distributed Systems Topologies: Part 1. http://openp2p.com
39. Wiesmann, M., Pedone, F., Schiper, A., Kemme, B. and Alonso, G. (2000) Understanding Replication in Databases and Distributed Systems. Research Supported by EPFL-ETHZ DRAGON Project and OFES.
40. Herlihy, M. and Wing, J. (1990) Linearizability: A Correctness Condition for Concurrent Objects. ACM Transactions on Programming Languages and Systems, 12, 463-492. http://dx.doi.org/10.1145/78969.78972
41. Ahamad, M., Hutto, P.W., Neiger, G., Burns, J.E. and Kohli, P. (1994) Causal Memory: Definitions, Implementations and Programming. TR GIT-CC-93/55, Georgia Institute of Technology, Atlanta.
42. Rahnama, B., Sari, A. and Makvandi, R. (2013) Countering PCIe Gen. 3 Data Transfer Rate Imperfection Using Serial Data Interconnect. Proceedings of the 2013 International Conference on Technological Advances in Electrical, Electronics and Computer Engineering (TAEECE), Konya, 9-11 May 2013, 579-582. http://dx.doi.org/10.1109/TAEECE.2013.6557339
43. Budhiraja, N., Marzullo, K., Schneider, F.B. and Toueg, S. (1993) The Primary-Backup Approach. In: Mullender, S., Ed., Distributed Systems, ACM Press, New York, 199-216.
44. Gifford, D.K. (1979) Weighted Voting for Replicated Data. Proceedings of the Seventh ACM Symposium on Operating Systems Principles, Pacific Grove, 10-12 December 1979, 150-162. http://dx.doi.org/10.1145/800215.806583
45. Osrael, J., Froihofer, L., Goeschka, K.M., Beyer, S., Galdamez, P. and Munoz, F. (2006) A System Architecture for Enhanced Availability of Tightly Coupled Distributed Systems. Proceedings of the First International Conference on Availability, Reliability and Security, Vienna, 20-22 April 2006.
46. Cao, H.H. and Zhu, J.M. (2008) An Adaptive Replicas Creation Algorithm with Fault Tolerance in the Distributed Storage Network. Proceedings of the Second International Symposium on Intelligent Information Technology Application, Shanghai, 20-22 December 2008, 738-741.
47. Shye, A., Blomstedt, J., Moseley, T., Reddi, V. and Connors, D.A. (2008) PLR: A Software Approach to Transient Fault Tolerance for Multicore Architectures. IEEE Transactions on Dependable and Secure Computing, 6, 135-148. http://dx.doi.org/10.1109/TDSC.2008.62
48. Agarwal, V. (2004) Fault Tolerance in Distributed Systems. Indian Institute of Technology, Kanpur. www.cse.iitk.ac.in/report-repository
49. Jung, H., Shin, D., Kim, H. and Lee, H.Y. (2005) Design and Implementation of Multiple Fault Tolerant MPI over Myrinet (M3). In: Proceedings of the 2005 ACM/IEEE Conference on Supercomputing, IEEE Computer Society, Washington DC, 32. http://dx.doi.org/10.1109/SC.2005.22
50. Elnozahy, M., Alvisi, L., Wang, Y.M. and Johnson, D.B. (1996) A Survey of Rollback-Recovery Protocols in Message Passing Systems. Technical Report CMU-CS-96-81, School of Computer Science, Carnegie Mellon University, Pittsburgh.
51. Alvisi, L. and Marzullo, K. (1995) Message Logging: Pessimistic, Optimistic, and Causal. Proceedings of the 15th International Conference on Distributed Computing, Systems (ICDCS 1995), Vancouver, 30 May-2 Jun 1995, 229-236. http://dx.doi.org/10.1109/ICDCS.1995.500024
52. Garg, V.K. (2010) Implementing Fault-Tolerant Services Using Fused State Machines. Technical Report ECE-PDS- 2010-001, Parallel and Distributed Systems Laboratory, ECE Department, University of Texas, Austin.
53. Xiong, N., Cao, M., He, J. and Shu, L. (2009) A Survey on Fault Tolerance in Distributed Network Systems. Proceedings of the 2009 International Conference on Computational Science and Engineering, Vancouver, 29-31 August 2009, 1065-1070. http://dx.doi.org/10.1109/CSE.2009.497
54. Tian, D., Wu, K. and Li, X. (2008) A Novel Adaptive Failure Detector for Distributed Systems. Proceedings of the 2008 International Conference on Networking, Architecture, and Storage, Chongqing, 12-14 June 2008, 215-221. http://dx.doi.org/10.1109/NAS.2008.37

CHAPTER 17

DECENTRALIZATION OF A MULTI DATA SOURCE DISTRIBUTED PROCESSING SYSTEM USING A DISTRIBUTED HASH TABLE

Grzegorz Chmaj, Shahram Latifi

Department of Electrical and Computer Engineering, University of Nevada Las Vegas, Las Vegas, USA

ABSTRACT

A distributed processing system (DPS) contains many autonomous nodes, which contribute their own computing power. DPS is considered a unified logical structure, operating in a distributed manner; the processing tasks are divided into fragments and assigned to various nodes for processing. That type of operation requires and involves a great deal of communication. We propose to use the decentralized approach, based on a distributed hash table, to reduce the communication overhead and remove the server unit, thus avoiding having a single point of failure in the system. This paper proposes a mathematical model and algorithms that are implemented in a dedicated experimental system. Using the decentralized approach, this study demonstrates the efficient operation of a decentralized system which results in a reduced energy emission.

INTRODUCTION

Distributed Processing Systems (DPS) are used to process data over multiple nodes that are not located in one geographical location. The structure of a DPS usually consists of the central element, which performs the control tasks; the intercommunication structure (IS); and machines that join the structure in order to contribute with their computation resources. This type of organization is easy to implement and manage; however, it introduces the problem of a single point of error: the central element, without which system is unable to operate. The same issues were addressed for peer-to-peer media sharing systems, which at some point became the target of intellectual properties agencies. Centralized systems, such as Napster, could be closed easily because the only thing required was to shut down the central element. The design of decentralized systems, such as Gnutella, showed that this approach was very challenging, as broadcasting participants with system messages flooded the system and made it inoperable. Further, the data-locating aspect was found to be problematic; as in the case of decentralized system, there was no central server that could be simply asked for data location. DPS suffer from the same problems as do their centralized counterparts, additionally, in DPS, all nodes are active system elements and perform vital functions (what introduces additional problems). Therefore, the system management in DPS has to be reliable and efficient.

Citation: G. Chmaj and S. Latifi, "Decentralization of a Multi Data Source Distributed Processing System Using a Distributed Hash Table," International Journal of Communications, Network and System Sciences, Vol. 6 No. 10, 2013, pp. 451-458. doi: 10.4236/ijcns.2013.610047.

A distributed hash table (DHT) is an approach that allows data to be located in the fully distributed system, based on the data's identification number or content. DHTs are reliable and self-managed, and are often used in peer-topeer systems, such as Bit Torrent. We propose to use a DHT for a DPS containing many data sources. In such multi-data-source system, each system participant offers data from its data sources. Data at data sources change over time, so data have to be fetched at the time it is needed. The example of such a system is the structure of Unmanned Aerial Vehicles (UAVs), where each UAV provides geographic and environment data to other UAVs. A set of UAVs may be separated from the command center, so the use of a distributed control provides the independency. By using a DHT, high reliability and a maximum level of decentralization can be achieved.

MOTIVATION AND CONTRIBUTION

Many applications of DPS are not critical; thus, a design involving a single point of failure (the central element) is sufficient. Often, self-organization and energy consumption are not a concern, especially if the system is based on stationary nodes. However, a trend of mobilization can be observed in such a system in which nodes operate using battery power. More and more applications require high reliability, the absence of single point of failure, and the ability to self-reorganize, in case any system element becomes disconnected. The main motivations for this study were:

- Create mathematical foundation for all data transmission aspects described, using expressions and formulas. The complete description is strictly clear; many of the system's properties can be formulated as lemmas and theorems, and proved mathematically. Further extension of such description can be easily verified for compatibility, relying on mathematical properties and using new proofs.
- Easy implementation. The mathematical description proposed is easy to implement in both the simulation and real systems, often using the expressions in the code directly.
- A decentralized system, with an architecture that will be resistant to attacks and random disturbances, and will not have any single point of failure.
- Self-organization. The goal is to make a system that is able to reorganize in case of any structural change, such as any of its components joining or leaving.
- Algorithms. The complete system description also requires rules of operation, which are defined in this study in the form of algorithms that are uniform for all system participants. This makes the system easier to manage.
- Energy consumption. The solutions provided to the systems, including mobile devices, include an aspect of energy minimization.

The contribution of this work is to create complete system assumptions and ideas as well as a comprehensive description in terms of digital-data transmission theory. These elements are used to build an operating system for simulation and further research. To summarize, this study proposes novel ideas for a multi-data-source DPS that includes the use of DHT, and formulates an information theory based on the mathematics that describes the system. Algorithms, designed according to the proposed theory, included the minimization of energy consumption to make mobile systems more efficient. The solutions were implemented and tested, providing the experimentation results to be described in this paper.

LITERATURE OVERVIEW

Distributed processing systems are the subject of wide-ranging research in the literature. The communication layer is considered mostly as overlay network, hiding the packet and lower layers that are not essential, in this case. A survey of overlay network and related management issues was described in [1]. As the overlay networks are often used for distributed systems, some work can be found that describes overlay networks that have a special kind of abstract document [2]. In addition, overlay networks provide the separation of networking issues in the experimentation simulators. The only layer modeled can be the overlay; the lower layers do not have to be modeled in terms of implementation details. However, they have to be described correctly in terms of the parameters seen from the overlay. For this study, a universal communication simulator platform was built based on the experience and research results from our previous work in this area [3,4]. The DHT was chosen as the decentralization technique because since its introduction, the DHT approach has been widely used in many applications. It is a promising approach for decentralizing systems [5,6], and many authors have implement this approach to achieve the system decentralization. Authors of [7] implemented DHT, together with a Common Object Request Broker Architecture (CORBA) standard, in order to allow the overlay-network-based communication system to conduct event management. This approach can be compared to the communication platform using and Interconnection Structure (IS) that was developed for this study, used as a base to build the experimental system. However, the CORBA standard was not used in this study. Nodes in the system proposed in this study may contain data sources that are attached (they can represent sensors, external devices, or other type of unit providing digital data). This idea also has been found in structures widely known as wireless sensor networks [8], which usually contain massive sensor sets that are available for the clients. The scale of these systems affects the efficiency of the network as well as energy efficiency. Attempts have been made to provide a DHT-based approach to wireless sensor networks; for example, the Pastry algorithm was used to design the data sharing system for the P2P sensor structure by authors of [9]. The researchers used DHT Pastry to provide the current sensor data; however, their PAST also can access historical sensor values. The applications of distributed systems using DHT include vehicular ad hoc network [10], peer-to-peer data sharing networks [11], web caching [12], instant messaging, and many others.

SYSTEM DESCRIPTION

General Definitions

This section contains a comprehensive description of the system developed in this study, based on mathematical formulas. A distributed processing system contains V nodes: v,w V , 1, 2, , = L , which are connected using an interconnection structure

(IS) through which nodes are able to transmit data. Each node in the system has the same uniform structure, shown in Figure 1 and contains the following logical elements: DHT routing table, set of data sources, fz container, state indicator, network connection and two queues: messages in and messages out. Both queues are using FIFO mechanism and algorithms for dropping outdated elements. For the sake of simplicity in this paper 'processing' is interpreted as computing, although it can also mean processing the control functions, gathering real-time data, etc. There are Z computational tasks in the system: z=1,2….Z. These tasks are issued to the system by nodes. The node that enables a task for computation is called the task owner, and is denoted by $e_v=1$ (0 otherwise). Tasks contain massive amounts of digital data. The key idea of distributed processing is to process these kinds of tasks by using many computational units. Thus, each task is divided into blocks: $b=1,2,\cdots,B$, and binary variable $c_{zb}=1$ denotes that block b belongs to task z (0 otherwise). The computation of block b produces the result $r=1,2,\cdots,B$, and r belongs to task z when $c_{zr}=1$ (0 otherwise). The structure of a task is presented in Figure 2, and the structure of a block is shown in Figure 3. Many distributed processing systems are defined to divide tasks into uniform sized chunks. However, this kind of approach often does not match the real applications; thus, we propose to use variable-sized division. The size of each block b from task z is described by value of h_{zb}; also, h_{zr} is defined for result r. Each node is characterized by its processing power p_v, which represents the node's ability to quickly finish assigned computations.

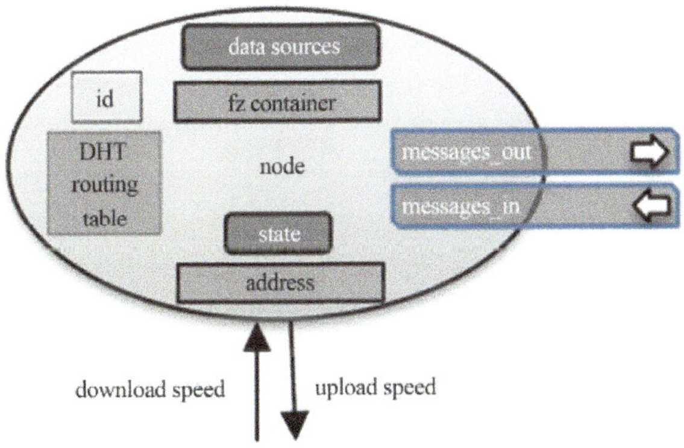

Figure 1. Node structure.

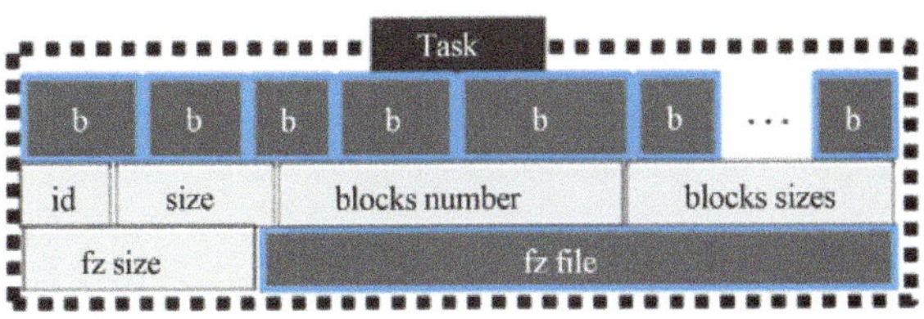

Figure 2: Task structure.

Figure 3: Blockstructure.

Besides the task binary data in the form of blocks, each task has an associated base file, f_z. This file contains all the definitions and common data used for blocks processing. File f_z is required to be present on the node that wants to process blocks from task z. The node acting as the task owner designates another node, called the task manager, which handles the f_z file.

This makes management of the DHT easier for all computing nodes, as described further in this section. A base file f_z of size h_{zf} is sent from the task owner to the task manager before computation starts for the blocks.

The system contains S data sources $s=1,2,\cdots,S$, which are physically present on the nodes. The presence of data sources on the nodes is denoted by $a_{vs}=1$ (0 otherwise). One node can have zero $(\Sigma_s a_{vs}=0)$, one, or many data sources. Each block b has its own requirements regarding data from data sources. Each requirement has to be satisfied before the start of block computation. The requirement for data source s made by block b belonging to task z is denoted by $q_{zbs}=1$ (0 otherwise). There are no rules about requiring data from sources: block may require zero source $(\Sigma_s q_{zbs}=0)$, one or many $(\Sigma_s q_{zbs}\geq 1)$.

In order to precisely describe the system, we divide the system's operating time span as the set of time slots t 1, 2, , T . This is the approach commonly used for modeling systems, and allows the assignment of any event to a precise moment in time:

- Block b belonging to task z is computed at node v during slot t: $x_{zbvt}=1$ (0 otherwise).
- The base-data file for task z is present on node v at time t: $f_{zvt}=1$ (0 otherwise).

- Block b belonging to task z is transmitted from node v to node w in slot t: y_{zbwvt} = (0 otherwise).
- The result r belonging to task z is transmitted from node v to node w in slot t: $y_{zrwvt} = 1$ (0 otherwise).
- The message m is transmitted from node v to node w in slot t: $y'_{mwvt} = 1$ (0 otherwise).
- The data file is transmitted from node v to node w in slot t: $y''_{fzwvt} = 1$ (0 otherwise).

Timing properties are used to define time-related properties of the system. Each node has an assigned upload speed u_v and download speed d_v, measured in kB/slot. These speeds characterize the network parameters of the link connecting the node to the network. As the nodes communicate with each other, the data transmission between two nodes is performed at the lower of the two speeds. The transmission time of block b belonging to task z from task owner w to node v is $\max\left(\left\lceil \frac{h_{zb}}{d_v} \right\rceil, \left\lceil \frac{h_{zb}}{u_w} \right\rceil\right)$.

Block size is given for each b, thus transmission time can be used to estimate the network delay. Given the size of block h_{zb} and the processing power p_v, the time of the computation for block b on node v can be determined: $\left\lceil \frac{h_{zb}}{p_v} \right\rceil$.

The DPS proposed in this study uses several messages:

- m1: request of a block: size: h_{m1}
- m2: request of a data source value:size: h_{m2}
- m3: data source value: size: h_{m3}
- m4: request of a file-base:size: h_{m4}

The time required to transmit message m from node w to node v can be formulated as $\max\left(\left\lceil \frac{h_{zb}}{p_v} \right\rceil, \left\lceil \frac{h_m}{u_w} \right\rceil\right)$ Messages are sent using data containers (Figure 4), which serve as the wrapper and are the basic unit of communication in IS.

Constraints Characteristics

The system's operation is limited by several constraints. Some of them provide the simple properties, and easily can be modified to include more complicated assumptions. We propose that one block can be computed on one node only. This assumes reliability such in a way that if the block was started for computation, then the node finished the processing before possible quit.

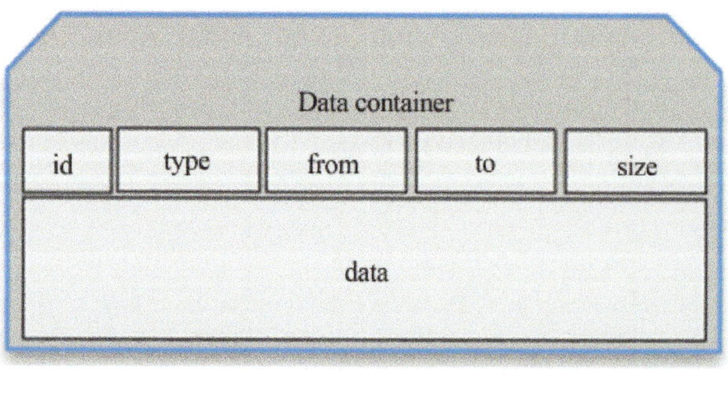

Figure 4: Data container.

This constraint can be formulated as

$$\sum_v \sum_t x_{zbvt} = \left\lceil \frac{h_{zb}}{p_v} \right\rceil \quad z = 1,2,\cdots,Z,$$

b =1,2, , ...B . Also, the node can process one block at the time: $\sum_z \sum_b \sum_v \sum_t x_{zbvt} \le 1$. There is no possibility that the node starts to process a block that is partially fetched. The block must be fully downloaded before its computation starts: $\sum_w y_{zbwvt} + x_{zbvt'} \le 1$, $z = 1,2,\cdots,Z$; $b = 1,2,\cdots,B$; $t,t' = 1,2,\cdots,T$; $t < t'$, $v = 1,2,\cdots,V$. As stated earlier, node v can compute the block b belonging to task z only if it possesses the base-file fz related to task z: $f_{zvt} - x_{zbvt} \ge 0$; $z = 1,2,\cdots,Z$; $v = 1,2,\cdots,V$; $b = 1,2,\cdots,B$; $t = 1,2,\cdots,T$. When the computation is finished, then the result is sent back to the task owner:

$$\sum_r \frac{\sum_t y_{zrwvt}}{\max\left(\left\lceil \frac{h_{zr}}{d_v} \right\rceil, \left\lceil \frac{h_{zr}}{u_w} \right\rceil\right)} = \sum_b \frac{\sum_t x_{zbwt}}{\left\lceil \frac{h_{zb}}{p_w} \right\rceil}$$

where $w,v = 1,2,\cdots,V$; $w \ne v$; $z = 1,2,\cdots,Z$

The above description mathematically defines the system proposed in this paper. This form clearly describes all the assumptions and properties. Formulas stated above were directly used in the implementation of the experimental system, its properties, structure, and algorithms.

Energy Emission

In this system the energy used for system operation is taken into consideration. The proposed algorithms shall not only provide the decentralized structure, but also minimize the energy used. The energy components are:

- Energy required to transmit (send and receive) 1 kB of data between nodes v and w: E_{1vw}.
- Energy required to completely route message m2 between nodes v and w: E_{2vw}.
- Energy required to transmit (send and receive) message m1, m3, or m4 from a data source or from node v to w: E_{3vw}.
- Energy required to compute the SHA1 on node v: E_{4v}.

The overall energy used by node v can be described in a following way:

$E_v = \sum_v ($

$$\sum_z \sum_n \frac{\sum_t y''_{fznvt}}{\max\left(\left\lceil \frac{h_{zf}}{d_v} \right\rceil, \left\lceil \frac{h_{zf}}{u_w} \right\rceil\right)} \left(E_{4v} + E_{2nv} + E_{1wv} h_{zf} + \right. \tag{1}$$

$$\sum_z \sum_b \frac{\sum_t x_{zbvt}}{\left\lceil \frac{h_{zb}}{p_v} \right\rceil} \left(E_{3vn} + E_{1nv} h_{zb} + \right. \tag{2}$$

$$\sum_s q_{zbs} * \left(E_{4v} + E_{2vn1} + E_{3n1v}\right)\Big)\Big) + \quad (3)$$

$$\sum_{n2} \sum_t y'_{m2n2vt} * E_{3vn2} + \quad (4)$$

$$\sum_{n2} \sum_t y'_{m2n2vt} * E_{1vn2} h_{zf} \Big) \quad (5)$$

where:

- w—the task manager node,
- n—the task owner,
- n1—the data source owner,
- n2—the requesting node.

The components state: (1) is the energy used for downloading fz base-file, including computing SHA1 function and routing the message in DHT; (2) is the energy used to fetch block b; (3) expresses the energy required to fetch data from all data sources that are required by block b; (4) energy required to send the data source value to requesting node; (5) energy emitted to send base file fz to requesting node. Nodes that are task issuers also must include the following:

$$\sum_z e_{zv} \Big($$

$$E_{4v} + \quad (6)$$

$$E_{1vw} h_{zf} + \quad (7)$$

$$\sum_b \sum_{n2} c_{zb} \frac{\sum_t y'_{m1n2vt}}{\max\left(\left\lceil \frac{h_{m1}}{d_v} \right\rceil, \left\lceil \frac{h_{m1}}{u_{n2}} \right\rceil\right)} * E_{3n2v} + \quad (8)$$

$$\sum_b \sum_{n2} c_{zb} \frac{\sum_t y_{zbvn2t}}{\max\left(\left\lceil \frac{h_{zb}}{d_{n2}} \right\rceil, \left\lceil \frac{h_{zb}}{u_v} \right\rceil\right)} * E_{1vn2} * h_{zb} + \quad (9)$$

$$\sum_r \sum_{n2} c_{zr} \frac{\sum_t y_{zrn2vt}}{\max\left(\left\lceil \frac{h_{zr}}{d_v} \right\rceil, \left\lceil \frac{h_{zr}}{u_{n2}} \right\rceil\right)} * E_{1vn2} * h_{zr} \Bigg) \quad (10)$$

The components meanings are: (6) the computation of SHA1 function of the task manager to handle fz file. (7) states the upload of base-file fz to task manager. (8) is the receiving of requests for blocks (messages of type m1). (9) denotes the energy used for sending all blocks from the task, and (10) describes the energy emitted to receive B results belonging to task z. The whole expression denotes the energy required to handle all tasks that are issued by node v. The values of particular energy consumption elements, used for experiments, were estimated using available datasheets and electronic simulation software. The definition of the system allows many other metrics to be easily added. In this study we focus on the energy emission, while others such as queuing issues, latency, network routing, and many other parameters are considered as a future work.

DHT Properties

The main goal of the system is to use the distributed hash table (DHT) to decentralize the whole organization. The following assumptions were formulated to define the DHT operation. SHA1 is the function used to generate hashes. The hash length is 40 bits, but this can be changed, if needed. The base-file fz is the DHT resource; it's hash is the key in DHT, and is generated based on the task name, DHT_k = sha1(task_name).

Data sources are the resources in DHT as well. DHT keys related to data sources are computed based on the data source's name, DHT_k = sha1(names). To identify the node in the DHT structure, we propose to use its physical address as the argument for the SHA1 function to compute the id in DHT, DHT_{id} = sha1($addr_v$). The node v associated with DHT_{id} is able to provide the following data to other nodes: a) the current value of the embedded data source and b) the base-files fz that are present on node v. To get the data from a data source, the requesting node has to compute the DHT key based on data source's name and further locate the data source by DHT algorithm. Following the DHT rules, the data source having the key equal to DHT_k will be located on the node of DHT_{id} = DHT_k. If there is no node with such DHT_{id}, the data is then placed on the node having the next higher DHT_{id} (the closest one in terms of DHT organization). The search of the DHT location is performed using chord.

Figure 5 shows the general organization scheme of IS. Pool is the logical unit containing all data containers being transmitted. IS uses DHT for localizing the resources in the network. DHT unit uses several internal functions, among which the most important are presented in Figure 5.

The general diagram of proposed system is shown on above Figure 6. System contains many nodes, some of them can decide to take the role of task issuer and issue computational task into the system. Task is divided into blocks of various sizes and includes fz file containing all necessary constants and definitions required for blocks processing. Blocks are sent to other nodes for processing, each block may require the values of one or more data sources for processing. Data sources and other assets are located using DHT.

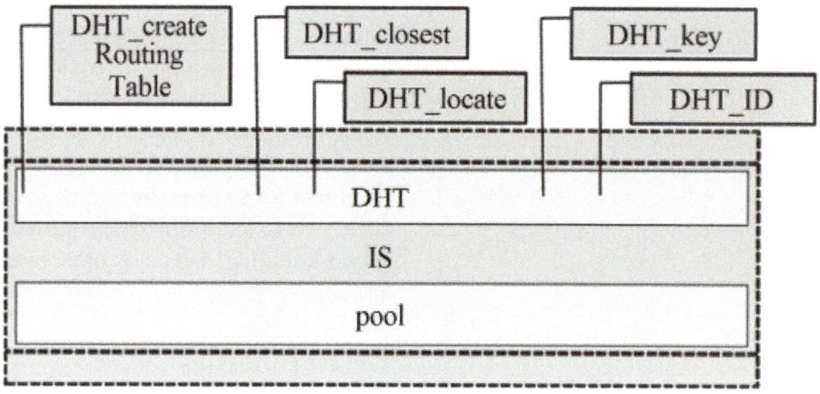

Figure 5: Structure of Distributed Hash Table (DHT).

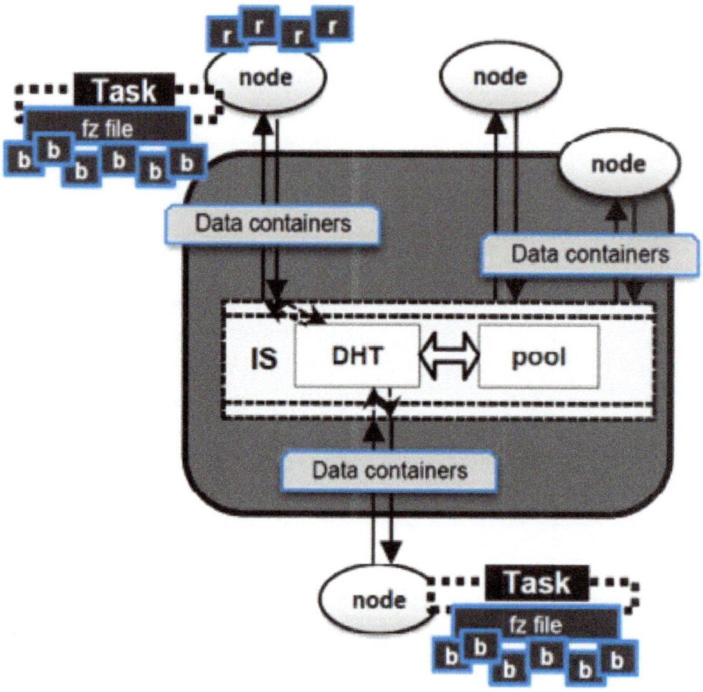

Figure 6: The overall schematic of the system.

Computation results are sent back to the task issuer, where they are combined into the final result. The interconnection structure IS, which provides communication, uses data containers to transmit all types of messages.

Proposed Algorithms

Along with the system definitions, constraints, energy aspects, and DHT-related properties, we propose the design of the universal operation algorithm, used for every node in our system. The universal for of the algorithm enables each node to act as task issuer, if needed. If a node operates as regular computing node, the task issuing part of the algorithm is not used.

EXPERIMENTATION RESULTS

The research was conducted using our experimentation communication platform, which allows defining various elements, such as message containers of many types, any network topology, the nodes' properties, their input/output queues, and communication rules. Experimentation communication platform and its extension for the purpose of this study were created in Ruby language. An additional DHT layer was added; and the related functions defined, such as sha1 computations, routing tables creation, routing of messages, and more. Further, energy consumption measurement factors were added. This resulted in a complete simulation system operating online, bringing its behavior much closer to those of real systems. The algorithms were coded such in a way that they are fully portable to physical nodes, such as PC machines connected over the Internet. The only element to be replaced, in that case, would be the IS layer with all the related and underlying layers. To ensure the proper operation of the whole system, the first experiment involved analyzing log files regarding the traffic in the IS and DHT layers.

To reach that goal, audit functions were implemented, among others, in a form of direct use of the parts of the mathematical model. This proved that a decentralized system structure was able to handle the distributed processing system. Each node contained on average 6.9 entries in DHT routing table, and the average number of hops during resource location was 3.2. The second experiment included the implementation of a centralized protocol, where the central server was used instead of a DHT structure, known as the Single Central Unit (SCU). Due to the lack of a DHT, there is no way of determining the locations of system resources, such as data sources or blocks; therefore, the nodes have to communicate through the server. The energy consumption when using the SCU approach was defined the same way as for the DHT, and mainly was based on the energy consumption per kilobyte, defined according to the network topology. The energy consumption for sending a certain amount of kilobytes between two nodes in the system was the same for both the DHT-based and serverbased approaches. In this way, it was possible to compare the energy emissions required by these two cases. The test data used for the comparison was generated according to predefined requirements: network parameters, processing-power parameters, network transmission-energy consumption, and computation-energy emission.

The requirements for parameters, including ranges from which final values were selected, were set to reflect real systems (e.g. uv and dv are reflecting network speeds available among Internet network). Number of nodes in the system was selected arbitrarily, network parameters were selected according to defined ranges, number of tasks and their sizes were set according to experimentation plan. Each system structure, containing all the parameters, together with tasks details states the experimentation load, so the experiment for each system + tasks definition can be repeated. The system studied in this paper includes the random delay which is present in distributed processing systems: message sent to destination node may be the subject of competition with a message coming from another node (exactly as in real networks). Due to FIFO nature of nodes' queues, the competition effect has the influence of system operation. To avoid uncertainty of the results, the experiment for each system-task (each point in the graphs) was repeated 50 times and resulting values were averaged. First, the energy emitted was measured according to the total number of blocks present in the system. The number of block includes blocks from all the tasks present in the system. The structure containing V = 50 nodes demonstrated that the DHT approach required less energy to perform the assigned tasks than SCU (Figure 7).

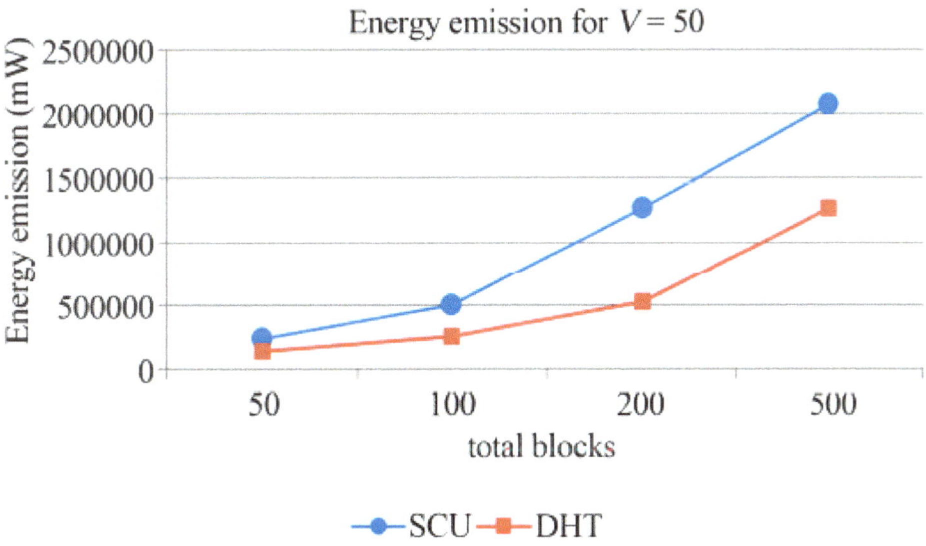

Figure 7: Energy emission for V = 50.

The difference increased slightly as the task size grew. However, in this case, the difference in energy stayed proportional to the increase in task size and stayed in the range 40% - 60%. The case presented in Figure 8 (V = 500) shows that the energy consumption was similar for SCU and DHT for tasks size B = 500, and the difference increased slightly with a bigger task size present in the system, staying around 30% - 40%, and increased to 60% for B = 2500. To compute a high number of blocks, the SCU approach exposed a significant increase as it started to suffer problems with single-unit congestion. The DHT kept the increase in the energy requirement proportional to the growth in task size. The next experiment investigated the complexity of the data sources structure on energy emission. The data sources provided relatively small amounts of data, which could be perceived as measurements; thus, the data seen in Figures 9 and 10 were averaged for each data point. The DHT structure demonstrated to be scalable and quite resistant to a growing number of nodes and the efficiency of DHT routing used (in the DHT, the average number of nodes taking part in a routing was small). The SCU showed the proportional relation between energy emission and the number of data sources present in the system as well as the complexity of data required from data sources in order to perform the block processing.

CONCLUSIONS

The stated goals of the design of a decentralized approach were fulfilled. The mathematical statements describing the system brought the advantage of a clear form of description. Additionally, statements were used directly in the algorithms, system design, and auditing functions. The mathematical model was easy to extend with new constraints and elements. The proposed algorithm was noted in the form of a pseudocode, which later was implemented directly in the experimental system. In order to build that system, the universal communications platform was extended with system-specific objects, properties, and functions. Further,

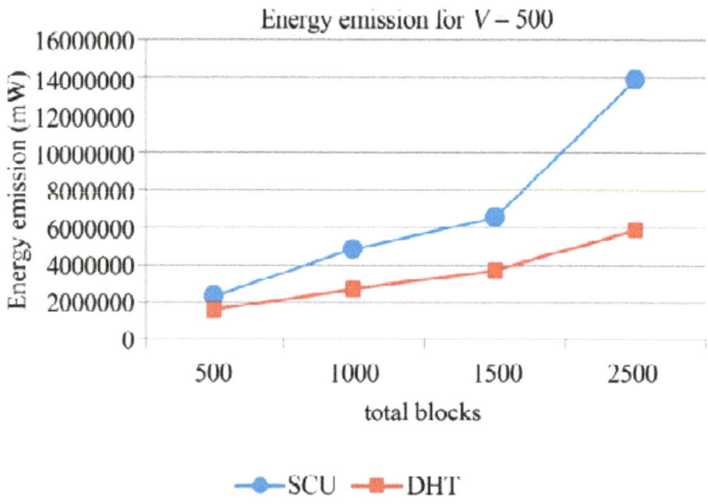

Figure 8: Energy emission for V = 500.

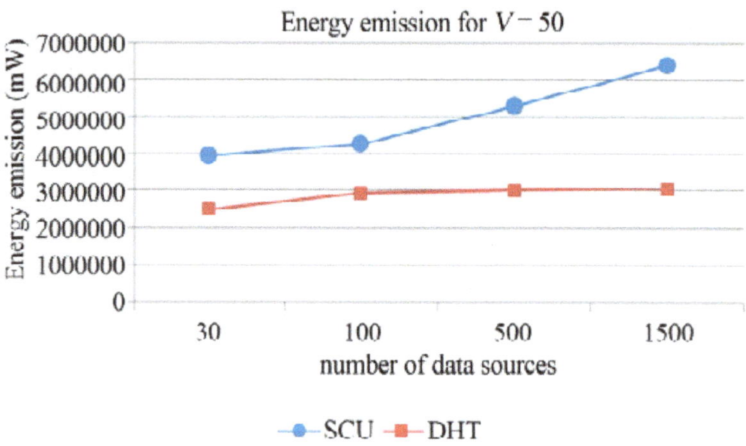

Figure 9: Energy emission for V = 50.

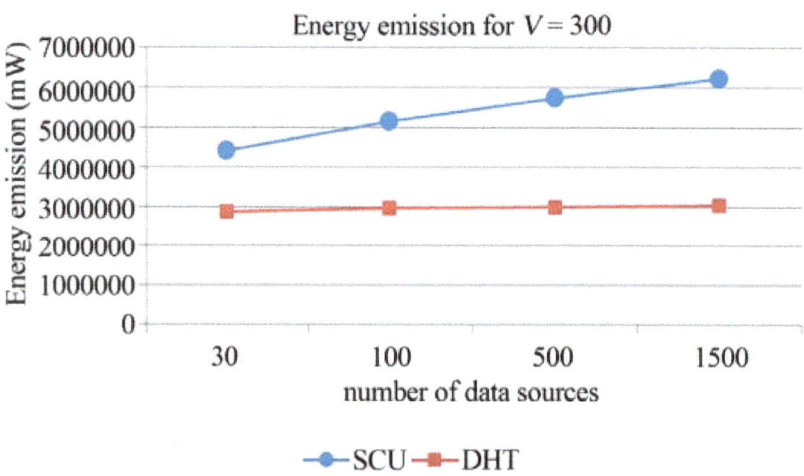

Figure 10: Energy emission for V = 300.

it was equipped with an additional communication layer, which provided DHT functionality. The research results proved that the proposed solutions in providing the decentralized architecture fulfilled their roles because the decentralized system was fully functional and efficient in its operation. The comparison between DHT and SCU approaches showed that the decentralized approach is able to reduce energy emissions and avoid communication congestions that are present in the SCU system. Future work includes extensive research of the DHT and other decentralized approaches and also the design of a universal decentralized communication system for distributed processing.

ACKNOWLEDGEMENTS

This work was supported in part by the Nevada EPSCoR program NSF award #EPS-IIA-1301726 and by the DOD-DTRA Grant/Award #: HDTRA1-12-1-0033.

REFERENCES

1. J. Ding, I. Balasingham and P. Bouvry, "Management of Overlay Networks: A Survey," Proceedings of 3rd International Conference on Mobile Ubiquitous Computing, Systems, Services and Technologies, Sliema, 11-16 October 2009, pp. 249-255. http://dx.doi.org/10.1109/UBICOMM.2009.49
2. D. Kasthurirathna and C. Keppetiyagama, "Architectural description based Overlay Networks," Proceedings of International Conference on Advances in ICT for Emerging Regions, Colombo, 1-2 September 2011, pp. 14-18.
3. G. Chmaj and K. Walkowiak, "A P2P Computing System for Overlay Networks," Future Generation Computer Systems, Vol. 29, No. 1, 2013, pp. 242-249. http://dx.doi.org/10.1016/j.future.2010.11.009
4. G. Chmaj and D. Zydek, "Software Development Approach for Discrete Simulators," Proceedings of 21st International Conference on Systems Engineering, Las Vegas, 16-18 August 2011, pp. 273-278.
5. K. P. N. Puttaswamy and B. Y. Zhao, "A Case for Unstructured Distributed Hash Tables," Proceedings of IEEE Global Internet Symposium, Anchorage, 11 May 2007, pp. 7-12. http://dx.doi.org/10.1109/GI.2007.4301423
6. Z. Zhang, "The Power of DHT as a Logical Space," Proceedings of 10th IEEE International Workshop on Future Trends of Distributed Computing Systems, Suzhou, 26-28 May 2004, pp. 325-331.
7. F. Umer and A. Qayyum, "Architecture for Decentralized, Distributed Event Communication Mechanism through Overlay Network," Proceedings of IEEE Symposium on Emerging Technologies, Islamabad, 17-18 Sepember 2005, pp. 252-257.
8. C. S. Raghavendra, K. M. Sivalingam and T. Znati (Editors), "Wireless Sensor Networks," Springer, 2004. http://dx.doi.org/10.1007/b117506
9. W. Song, S. Kim, S. Seok and D. Choi, "Pastry Based Sensor Data Sharing," Proceedings of 18th InternatonalConference on Computer Communications and Networks, San Francisco, 3-6 August 2009, pp. 1-6.
10. T. Delot, N. Mitton, S. Ilarri and T. Hien, "Decentralized Pull-Based Information Gathering in Vehicular Networks Using GeoVanet," Proceedings of 12th International Conference on Mobile Data Management, Lulea, 6-9 June 2011, pp. 174-183.
11. J. Timpanaro, T. Cholez, I. Chrisment and O. Festor, "When KAD Meets BitTorrent—Building a Stronger P2P Network," Proceedings of IEEE International Parallel & Distributed Processing Symposium, Shanghai, 2011, pp. 1635-1642.
12. E. Rosas, N. Hidalgo and M. Marin, "Two-Level Result Caching for Web Search Queries on Structured P2P Networks," Proceedings of IEEE 18th International Conference on Parallel and Distributed Systems, Singapore, 17-19 December 2012, pp. 221-228.

CHAPTER 18

WIRELESS DISTRIBUTED MONITORING TERMINAL USED FOR ON-LINE APPLICATION

Fenggui Wang, Lin Zhang, Zhongmin Wang, Yanbo Zhang

Institute of Automation, Shandong Academy of Sciences, Jinan, China

ABSTRACT

A wireless distributed monitoring terminal was designed with embedded Linux used on the basis of ARM board, and an application program was developed for data collection, processing and transmission. Data were collected from the surrounding environment and transmitted to a server via WLAN in the form of Extensible Markup Language (XML) stream, so the terminal had good flexibility to be compatible with different sensors, network devices and information systems from multiple manufacturers.

INTRODUCTION

On-line applications are becoming more and more widespread along with the popularity of the Internet of Things in various fields [1], such as environmental monitoring, public safety, telemedicine, etc [2,3]. In these applications, some terminals are necessary to execute data acquisition, processing and transmission. There may be different sensors, network devices and information systems from multiple manufacturers even if in one application, so it is important that every terminal has good flexibility to be compatible with them. ARM platform has been very popular in the area of mobile devices such as smart phones, personal players of audio and video, GPS systems and so forth, and can also compete with desktop computers based on i386 architecture microprocessors in some case [4]. ARM microcontrollers are convenient and efficient for designing and developing especially with embedded operating system used, so more and more terminals begin to adopt designs based on them nowadays. This paper deals with design of a wireless distributed monitoring terminal with embedded Linux used on the basis of ARM board, and development of an application program for data collection, processing and transmission. It collects data from the surrounding environment via RS485 or A/D convertor, carries out data analysis and processing, and transmits them to a server via Wireless Local Area Network (WLAN). The server stores these data to an oracle database and presents them through web pages. It is needed to be specially noted that these data are encapsulated into Extensible Markup Language (XML) stream by terminal before transmitting and then parsed to obtain the semantics by server after receiving [5], so as to enhance the flexibility of whole system.

Citation: Wang, F., Zhang, L., Wang, Z. and Zhang, Y. (2013), "Wireless Distributed Monitoring Terminal Used for On-Line Application". Communications and Network, vol. 5, 549-553. doi: 10.4236/cn.2013.53B2099.

HARDWARE DESIGN

The hardware of the wireless distributed monitoring terminal includes ARM9 board based on S3C2440A and Wi-Fi module to send and receive data wirelessly between it and the server. Also, it connects temperature/ humidity sensor and illumination sensor as example for monitoring changes of the surrounding environment. The structure diagram of the terminal is shown in Figure 1.

ARM9 Board

The board is based on S3C2440A microcontroller with 512 MB RAM and 512 MB flash memory. SAMSUNG's S3C2440A is designed to provide hand-held devices and general applications with low-power, and high-performance microcontroller solution in small die size. To reduce total system cost, the S3C2440A includes the following components: separate 16 KB Instruction and 16 KB Data Cache, MMU to handle virtual memory management, LCD Controller (STN & TFT), NAND Flash Boot Loader, System Manager (chip select logic and SDRAM Controller), 3-ch UART, 4-ch DMA, 4-ch Timers with PWM, I/O Ports, RTC, 8-ch 10-bit ADC and Touch Screen Interface, Camera interface, IIC-BUS Interface,

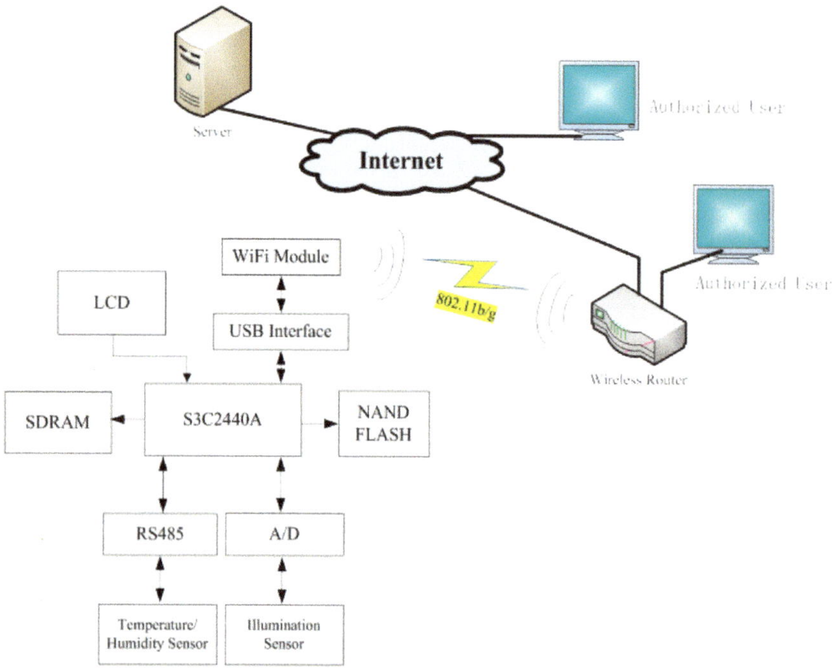

Figure 1: Structure diagram of wireless distributed monitoring terminal.

IIS-BUS Interface, USB Host, USB Device, SD Host & Multi-Media Card Interface, 2-ch SPI and PLL for clock generation [6]. The platform also offers a large number interface to support peripheral equipments, including USB host, USB device, LCD touch screen interface, RS232, RS485, 4 - 20 mA/0 - 5 V convertor and so on.

Wi-Fi Module

The Wi-Fi module adopted based on VIA Networking VT6656 is fully compliant with IEEE's security and 802.11 g standards [7]. Enabling data rates between wireless devices of up to 54 Mbps, it can deliver the bandwidth necessary for real-time streaming of high-definition digital multimedia content in home networks, and provide high-speed email, web and LAN access to multiple mobile users in corporate environments or public hotspots. Integrated WLAN into USB 2.0 with it, device also makes it more convenient to get on the net anywhere you are.

Sensors

The temperature/humidity sensor and illumination sensor are used to collect data from the surrounding environment in our system.

(1) Temperature/Humidity Sensor

This sensor adopts the most advanced digital sensor technology, overcoming disadvantages of the traditional analog temperature sensor, such as instability, much deviation from accurate data, vulnerability to interference, and requiring regular calibration. It processes the function of collecting information of temperature and humidity, with calculating data stably and accurately. Its operating voltage can be as low as 12 V, accuracy of temperature ±0.7°C, accuracy of humidity ±3% RH. Connected to the monitoring terminal via RS485, an industrial level communication network with long-distance transmission, high speed and high stability compared with RS232, the sensor transmits acquired temperature/humidity data using Modbus standard. It is an application layer messaging protocol that is positioned at level 7 of the OSI model and widely used in industrial environment.

(2) Illumination Sensor

This sensor has a wide light measurement range of 0 ~ 200,000 Lux, with high precision linear amplifier circuit and high sensitive photographic detectors. Its accuracy is less than ±7%, and operating voltage is 12 - 24 V. After data acquisition, the sensor transmits 4 - 20 mA current signal to the monitoring terminal, and then the 4 - 20 mA current signal is converted to 0 - 3.3 V voltage signal. Through an analog-digital converter, digital data are acquired and they can easily be processed and analyzed by S3C2440 to make them understood by human.

SOFTWARE DESIGN

The linux-2.6.28 distribution compiled for ARM9 platform is chosen as the operating system. The application program residing on the ARM platform is written in C language and compiled using the Linux GNU C compiler, which can be downloaded from the network free of charge.

Device Drivers

Device drivers take on a special role in Linux kernel. They are distinct "black boxes" that make a particular piece of hardware respond to a well-defined internal programming interface, and the details of how the device works are hidden completely by them [8]. User activities are performed by means of a set of standardized calls that are independent of the specific driver, mapping those calls to device-specific operations that act on real hardware is then the role of the device driver. This programming interface is such that drivers can be built separately from the rest of the kernel and "plugged in" at runtime when needed. This modularity makes Linux drivers easy to write, to the point that there are now hundreds of them available. Linux device driver belongs to the kernel part, and there are two ways of compiling and loading it into Linux kernel. One way is to directly compile device driver into the kernel, along with Linux starts when loading. Another way is to compile device drivers as dynamic loading and deleting modules, using the command of "insmod" to load and "rmmod" to delete. This way controls the size of the kernel, while the other way increases redundancy of the kernel, so it is adopted to compile USB wireless network card driver, exit key driver, A/D driver, etc.

Work Flow

The monitoring terminal firstly initializes, including starting Linux system, loading USB wireless network card driver, exit key driver and A/D driver and setting serial port, and sends archived data, which is stored in a local file when the network is unconnected. Then real time data is frequently acquired from sensors, analyzed by classification, stored into local file, and sent in the form of XML stream. When sent successfully, the data will be deleted from the local file immediately. Due to being stored into a local file first, data will not be lost even if the terminal is powered down suddenly. Next, the terminal will check whether the time point set beforehand has arrived. If the time point is up, it will send archived data stored in the local file, otherwise it still conducts as before. Also, if the terminal detects the exit key has been pressed, it will exit normally including releasing memory closing devices, unloading drivers, etc. The work flow of the terminal is shown in Figure 2.

TESTING

There is a wireless distributed monitoring terminal tested which collects data from the surrounding environment and transmits them to a server via WLAN. These data are stored to an oracle database and presented through web pages, as shown in Figures 3 and 4.

CONCLUSION

In this paper, an embedded Linux operation system combined with ARM9 platform is adopted to implement a wireless distributed monitoring terminal, and an application program is developed for data collection, processing and transmission. Data are sent in the form of XML stream, stored in oracle database and presented through web pages, so it's feasible to add any sensor to the terminal. Future possible works based on this terminal are adding more environment sensors and improving the XML streaming protocol.

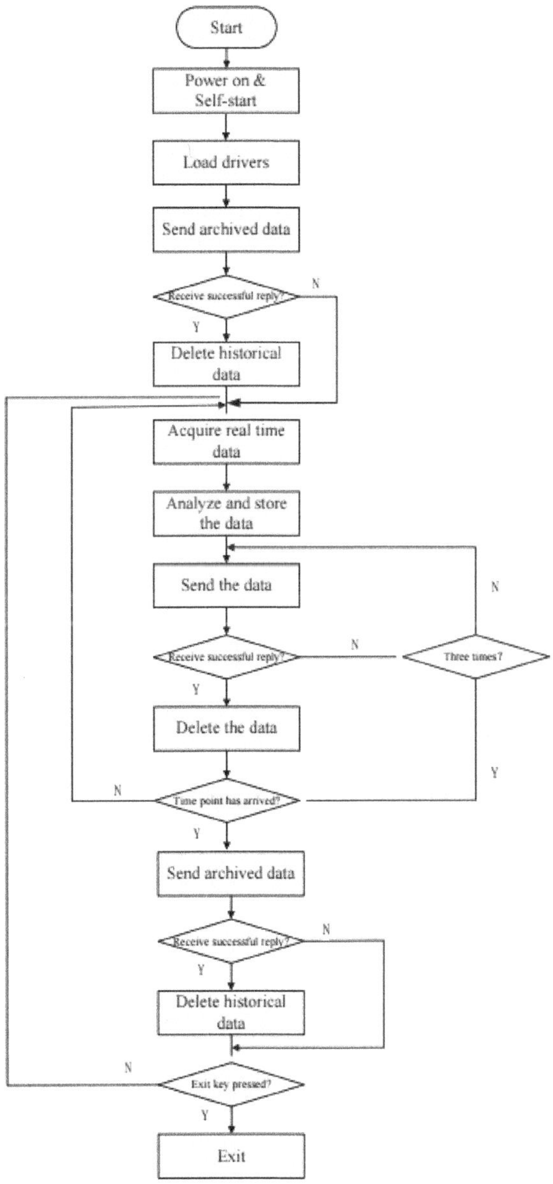

Figure 2: Flow chart of wireless distributed monitoring terminal.

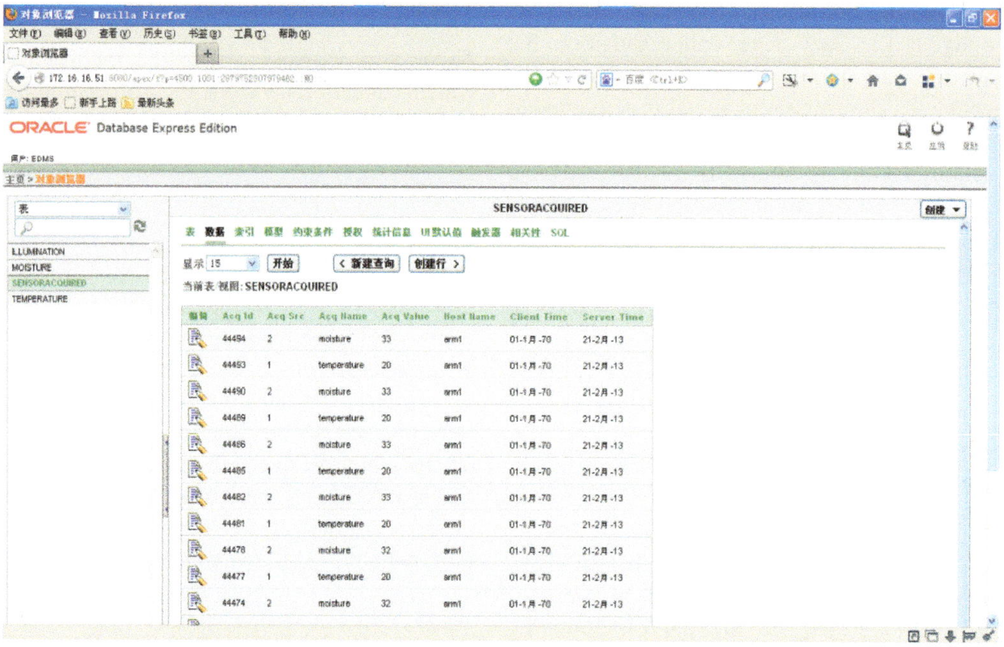

Figure 3: Data stored to oracle database.

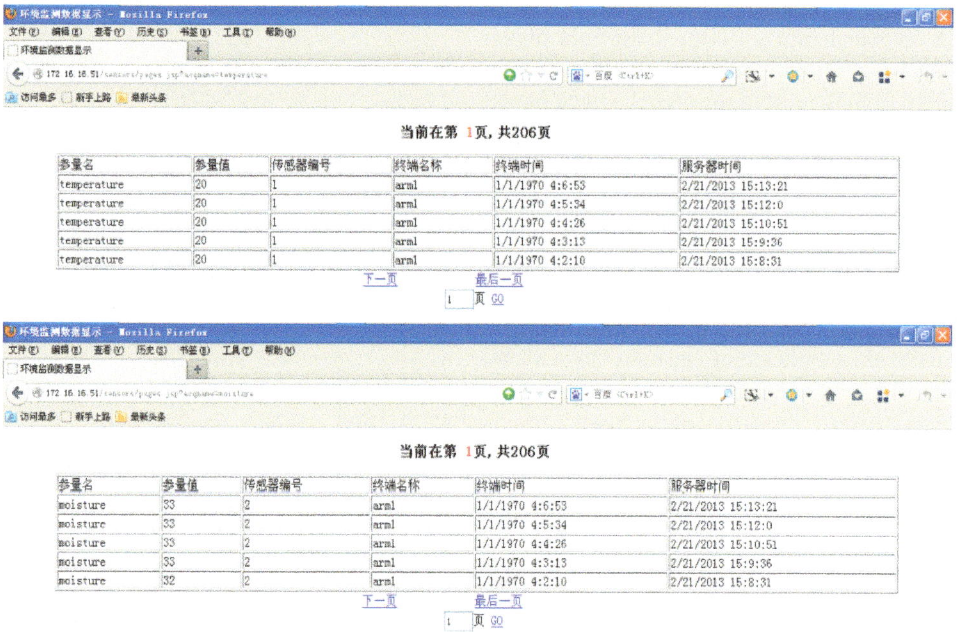

Figure 4: Data presented through web pages.

ACKNOWLEDGEMENTS

The paper is supported by Youth Science and Technology Star Program of Jinan City, China (Grant No. 20100105) and Youth Science Funds of Shandong Academy of Sciences, China (Grant No. 20100106). The authors would like to thank all collaborators, especially who are in the UWB & THz Innovation Team, Shandong Academy of Sciences, China.

REFERENCES

1. Wikipedia Foundation, "Internet of Things," 2013. http://en.wikipedia.org/wiki/Internet_of_Things
2. T. Qiao and L. Song, "The Design of Multi-Parameter Online Monitoring System of Water Quality Based on GPRS," IEEE 2010 International Conference on Multimedia Technology (ICMT), 2010, pp. 1-3.
3. W. Fu and X. Meng, "Remote Monitoring System Research and Implementation Based on Wireless Communication," 5th International Conference on Machine Vision (ICMV 12). International Society for Optics and Photonics, 2013.
4. Wikipedia Foundation, "ARM architecture," 2013. http://en.wikipedia.org/wiki/ARM_architecture.
5. F. Wang, H. Yang and D. Tian, "IM-based Communication Mechanism for an On-line Monitoring System," IEEE Proceedings of International Workshop on Intelligent Systems and Applications, 23-24 May 2009, Wuhan, 2009, pp. 145-148.

6. Samsung Electronics Co., Ltd., "S3C2440A 32-Bit RISC Microprocessor User's Manual (Revision 1.2)," 2004.
7. VIA Technologies, Inc., "VIA Solomon VT6656-802.11a/b/g Wireless LAN Controller with Integrated Baseband Processor-USB 2.0 Bus Interface," 2013. http://www.via.com.tw/en/products/networking/wireless/ vt6656.
8. J. Corbet, A. Rubini and G. Kroah-Hartman, "Linux Device Drivers," 3rd Edition, O'Reilly Media, 2007.

INDEX